PETERSON'S

CHOOSE A CHRISTIAN COLLEGE

A Guide to Academically Challenging Colleges Committed to a Christ-Centered Campus Life

Fourth Edition

Published in association with
the Christian College Coalition

Peterson's
Princeton, New Jersey

Library of Congress Cataloging-in-Publication Data

Choose a Christian college: a guide to academically
    challenging colleges committed to a Christ-centered
    campus life / Christian College Coalition.
        p.   cm.
    Includes index.
    ISBN 1-56079-434-8
    1. Christian colleges—United States—
Directories. I. Christian College Coalition (U.S.)
L901.C57   1992
378.73—dc20

                                    92-22622

Printed in the United States of America

10   9   8   7   6   5   4   3   2

Contents

MAP OF THE COLLEGES AND UNIVERSITIES (CANADA AND THE UNITED STATES)

Christian College Coalition Colleges and Universities

—————————— ᎒᎓ ——————————

Arizona
Grand Canyon University — 47

Arkansas
John Brown University — 52

California
Azusa Pacific University — 16
Biola University — 22
California Baptist College — 25
Fresno Pacific College — 41
The Master's College — 60
Pacific Christian College* — 76
Point Loma Nazarene College — 78
Simpson College — 82
Southern California College — 84
Westmont College — 99

Colorado
Colorado Christian University — 31

Florida
Palm Beach Atlantic College — 77
Warner Southern College — 97

Georgia
Covenant College — 33

Idaho
Northwest Nazarene College — 72

Illinois
Greenville College — 48
Judson College — 53
North Park College — 67
Olivet Nazarene University — 75
Trinity Christian College — 92
Trinity College — 93
Wheaton College — 100

Indiana
Anderson University — 13
Bethel College — 19
Goshen College — 45
Grace College — 46
Huntington College — 50
Indiana Wesleyan University — 51
Taylor University — 89
Taylor University,
    Fort Wayne Campus — 90

Iowa
Dordt College — 35
Northwestern College — 70

Kansas
Bethel College — 20
MidAmerica Nazarene College — 62
Sterling College — 87
Tabor College — 88

Kentucky
Asbury College — 14
Campbellsville College — 27

Massachusetts
Eastern Nazarene College — 38
Gordon College — 44

Michigan
Calvin College — 26
Cornerstone College — 32
Spring Arbor College — 86

Minnesota
Bethel College — 21
Northwestern College — 71

Mississippi
Belhaven College — 18
Mississippi College — 64

Missouri
Evangel College — 40

New York
Houghton College — 49
The King's College — 55
Nyack College — 73
Roberts Wesleyan College — 80

North Carolina
Campbell University — 28
Montreat-Anderson College — 65

Ohio
Bluffton College — 23
Cedarville College — 29
Malone College — 59
Mount Vernon Nazarene College — 66

Oklahoma
Bartlesville Wesleyan College — 17
Oklahoma Baptist University — 74
Southern Nazarene University — 85

Oregon
George Fox College — 43
Northwest Christian College — 68
Warner Pacific College — 96
Western Baptist College — 98

Pennsylvania
Eastern College — 36
Geneva College — 42
Messiah College — 61

South Carolina
Central Wesleyan College — 30
Erskine College — 39

South Dakota
Sioux Falls College — 83

Tennessee
Bryan College — 24
King College — 54
Lee College — 57
Milligan College — 63
Trevecca Nazarene College — 91
Union University — 95

Texas
Dallas Baptist University — 34
LeTourneau University — 58

Virginia
Eastern Mennonite University — 37

Washington
Northwest College — 69
Seattle Pacific University — 81
Whitworth College — 101

Canada
Atlantic Baptist College* — 15
The King's University College — 56
Redeemer College — 79
Trinity Western University — 94

Denotes provisional membership

How to
Use This Book

―――――― ❧ ――――――

It is likely you are reading this book because you are a student (or the parent of one) who is thinking seriously about going to college and wondering how to select a school that will best allow you to get everything you want out of your college years. If you believe that a college with an active Christian orientation might be what you're looking for, this book can help you by providing information on eighty-eight colleges and universities that combine academically challenging programs in the liberal arts and sciences with a Christ-centered campus life.

The Introduction: Why Choose a Christian College?

The introductory essay can help you determine whether a Christian college is the best choice for you. It provides a rich overview of what you can expect from a Christian liberal arts school compared to other colleges and universities.

The College Profiles

The heart of the book is detailed profiles of the eighty-eight member schools of the Christian College Coalition, containing data supplied by each of them. Each one provides information on things like enrollment, academic offerings, costs, athletic programs, admission procedures, and financial aid. Familiarizing yourself with the format of the profiles will help you review them and compare schools easily.

A special note from each school appears at the beginning of each profile. These notes include information about the school's mission, special programs and curricula emphases, and campus life.

Programs Sponsored by the Christian College Coalition

The Coalition makes available six student programs. These programs provide opportunities for off-campus study in Washington, D.C., Costa Rica, Hollywood, Egypt, Russia, and England. Consider these programs when choosing a college since they can not only round out your studies but also provide a rich setting for personal growth.

The Indexes

We've provided indexes at the back of the book to assist you in picking out the profiles you wish to review based on four criteria: academic majors, intercollegiate athletics, study-abroad opportunities, and

---

About the Christian College Coalition

The Christian College Coalition, a Washington, D.C.-based association of eighty-eight colleges and universities of the liberal arts and sciences, is North America's primary organization devoted specifically to serving and strengthening Christian higher education. Coalition institutions meet eight criteria for membership: an institutional commitment to the centrality of Jesus Christ to all campus life, integration of biblical faith with academics and student life, hiring practices that require a personal Christian commitment from each full-time faculty member and administrator, accreditation and primary orientation as a four-year liberal arts college, fund-raising activities consistent with the standards set by the Evangelical Council for Financial Accountability, a commitment to participating in Coalition programs, cooperation with and support of other Coalition colleges, and responsible financial operation. For more information, please contact the Christian College Coalition at 329 Eighth Street NE, Washington, D.C. 20002; 202-546-8713.

Profile Highlights
Lists facts about each school such as its total enrollment, tuition and fees, entrance difficulty, and denominational affiliation.

General Information
Gives an overall sense of the school by detailing the degrees awarded, the faculty, and library and computer resources.

KING COLLEGE
Bristol, Tennessee

SPECIAL NOTE FROM THE COLLEGE King College firmly believes that academic excellence can be fully integrated with Christian faith. More than 90% of King students are accepted into their first choice of graduate schools, and *U.S. News & World Report* has listed King College as one of America's best colleges for 4 consecutive years. King was also one of only 142 colleges in the nation to be rated "highly selective" by the Carnegie Foundation for the Advancement of Teaching. King College graduates are qualified in their chosen field of study, mature in their Christian faith, and committed to responsible service in the world.

Total Enrollment: 561 (all UG)
Women: 55%
Application Deadline: rolling
Entrance: moderately difficult
Tuition & Fees: $9364
Room & Board: $3350
SAT≥500: 35% V, 58% M **ACT≥21:** 87%
Denominational Affiliation: Presbyterian Church (U.S.A.)

GENERAL INFORMATION Independent-religious 4-year coed institution. Awards bachelor's degrees. Founded 1867. *Setting:* 135-acre suburban campus. *Faculty:* 64 (40 full-time, 65% with terminal degrees, 24 part-time); student-undergrad faculty ratio is 13:1. *Library Holdings:* 95,800 books, 550 microform titles, 645 periodicals, 7 on-line bibliographic services, 175 CD-ROMs, 1,960 records, tapes, and CDs. *Computers:* 46 terminals, PCs for student use in computer center, computer labs, library, student center, dorms, classroom buildings, multi-media network classroom lab. Students must have own computer. Access to campuswide network from computer center, computer labs, library, student center, dorms, student rooms. *Services:* e-mail, file transfer.

UNDERGRADUATE PROFILE 561 students from 28 states and territories, 6 other countries. 55% women, 8% part-time, 42% state residents, 75% live on campus, 20% transferred in, 80% have need-based financial aid, 50% have non-need-based financial aid, 5% international, 3% 25 or older, 0% Native American, 1% Hispanic, 1% African American, 1% Asian American. *Retention:* 68% of 1992 freshmen returned. *Graduation:* 38% graduate in 4 years.

FRESHMEN 142 total; 122 from public schools. 355 applied, 85% were accepted, 47% of whom enrolled. 34% from top 10% of their high school class, 65% from top quarter, 91% from top half. 4 valedictorians.

ACADEMIC PROGRAM Core, classical and scientific curriculum. Calendar: semesters. 280 courses offered in 1993–94; average class size 25 in required courses. English as a second language program offered during academic year and summer, advanced placement, self-designed majors, summer session for credit, part-time degree program (daytime), internships. Off-campus study at Virginia Intermont College. ROTC: Army (c). Unusual degree programs: 3-2 engineering with University of Maryland, Georgia Institute of Technology, University of Tennessee, medical technology with Holston Valley Hospital and Medical Center, Vanderbilt University.

CONTACT Director of Admissions, King College, 1350 King College Road, Bristol, TN 37620-2699; 615-652-4861 or toll-free 800-362-0014.

STUDY-ABROAD SITES France, Israel, Korea, Mexico, Morocco, the Netherlands, New Guinea, Spain.

MAJORS Accounting, art/fine arts, biblical studies, biology/biological sciences, business administration/commerce/management, business economics, chemistry, (pre)dentistry sequence, economics, education, elementary education, English, French, history, international business, (pre)law sequence, mathematics, medical technology, (pre)medicine sequence, music, physics, political science/government, psychology, religious studies, science, theater arts/drama, (pre)veterinary medicine sequence.

EXPENSES FOR 1994–95 Comprehensive fee of $12,714 includes full-time tuition ($8664), mandatory fees ($700), and college room and board ($3350). College room only: $1630.

FINANCIAL AID College-administered aid for undergraduates 1993–94: 287 need-based scholarships (average $4278), 321 non-need scholarships (average $2823), low-interest long-term loans from college funds (average $986), loans from external sources (average $3625), FSEOG, Federal Work-Study, 94 part-time jobs. Average total aid for freshmen: $7920, meeting 80% of need (aid provided to 100% of those qualified). *Application forms required:* institutional, FAFSA; required for some: FAF, IRS, financial aid transcript (for transfers). *Priority deadline:* 3/1. *Payment plan:* installment. *Waivers:* full or partial for employees or children of employees. *Notification:* continuous. *Average indebtedness of graduates:* $9000.

COLLEGE LIFE Orientation program (4 days, no cost, parents included). Drama-theater group, choral group, student-run newspaper. *Most popular organizations:* Student Government Association, Campus Life Committee, World Christian Fellowship. *Major annual events:* Fall Banquet and Fall Play, Dogwood/Alumni Weekend, Parents' Weekend. *Student services:* health clinic, personal-psychological counseling. *Safety:* late-night transport-escort service.

ATHLETICS Member NAIA. *Intercollegiate:* baseball M(s), basketball M(s)/W(s), golf M(s)/W, soccer M(s), softball W(s), tennis M(s)/W(s), volleyball W(s). *Intramural:* basketball, golf, soccer, swimming and diving, table tennis (Ping-Pong), tennis, volleyball, weight lifting. *Contact:* Mr. Joe Hakes, Athletic Director, 615-652-4849.

APPLYING/FRESHMEN *Options:* early entrance, midyear entrance. *Required:* essay, school transcript, SAT I or ACT. *Recommended:* 3 years of high school math and science, some high school foreign language, interview, TOEFL for international students. *Required for some:* recommendations, interview. Test scores used for admission. *Application deadline:* rolling.

APPLYING/TRANSFER *Required:* essay, college transcript, minimum 2.0 GPA. *Recommended:* standardized test scores, 3 years of high school math and science, some high school foreign language, interview. *Required for some:* interview. Entrance level: moderately difficult. *Application deadline:* rolling.

Financial Aid Shows how many students applied for aid and were judged to have need as well as the amount of the average aid package.

Athletics Details intercollegiate and intramural sports and notes if scholarships are available.

Applying/Freshmen Includes required tests and the application deadline.

---

graduate programs. In addition, to make it easy to pick out the schools that are in a particular geographical area, we've provided a geographical listing and map which appear at the front of the book immediately following the contents page.

Codes used in the Profiles:

Profile Highlights:
UG—undergraduate
N/R—not reported
N/Avail—not available
N/APP—not applicable
V—verbal SAT scores
M—math SAT scores

Freshman Admissions:
PSAT—Preliminary Scholastic Assessment Test
SAT I—Scholastic Assessment Test
ACT—American College Testing's ACT Assessment
TOEFL—Test of English as a Foreign Language
WPCT—Washington Pre-College Test

Financial Aid:
FSEOG—Federal Supplemental Educational Opportunity Grants, a federally funded needs-based award program administered by colleges
FAFSA/SAR—the federal government's Free Application for Federal Student Aid/Student Aid Report
FAF—Financial Aid Form of the College Scholarship Service
FFS—Family Financial Statement of the American College Testing Program
IRS—federal income tax form 1040

Athletics:
NCAA—National Collegiate Athletic Association
NAIA—National Association of Intercollegiate Athletics
NJCAA—National Junior College Athletic Association
NLCAA—National Little College Athletic Association

Individual Sports:
M—offered for men
F—offered for women
(s)—scholarships available
(c)—club sport

Why Choose a Christian College?

❧

Choosing a college is one of life's most important decisions. It not only represents a significant financial investment, but the choice influences so much of who we become in all areas of life—philosophy, values, intellectual and emotional preparedness for careers, long-term friendships, commitment to serving others, even the choice of marriage partners.

For those not sure what type of college they prefer, the array of choices is overwhelming. Even for students and families desiring a "Christian" college, the search can still be confusing. For example, some colleges are church-related only in the sense of being historically linked to a particular denomination. Some students, though deeply committed Christians, may feel the choice between a Christ-centered college and a secular one is not that important. Then there are all the choices among locations, academic offerings, available financial aid, and more.

This guide is a resource for exploring all these issues. We at the Christian College Coalition are absolutely convinced that a Christ-centered college is the very best decision for tens of thousands of students—more so today than ever before.

Choose a Christian College includes information to help you, such as indexes listing available majors, off-campus study opportunities, and athletic programs. Most importantly, this guide contains a full-page overview of each of eighty-eight Christ-centered colleges and universities in North America. All these institutions put the highest priority on integrating academic achievement with spiritual growth. They are unique and, we hope, will be of special interest to you.

This guide is our investment in helping you make a wise and informed college choice.

The Christian College Difference

There are approximately 3,500 colleges and universities in the United States, but only 600 or 700 maintain some tie to a specific church denomination or religious tradition. Of this subgroup, a smaller number are referred to as "Christ-centered." Eighty-eight of these colleges and universities are members of the Christian College Coalition, an association of regionally accredited four-year colleges and universities.

On the surface, most small colleges look a lot alike. They all promise a strong academic program, varied cocurricular offerings, a pleasant campus, and a friendly faculty. What sets Christ-centered colleges apart is the educational environment: the way in which faith, learning, and life come together.

The Christian faith is at the very heart of what a Christ-centered college or university is all about. These institutions seek to provide a Christian view of education, bringing to every discipline important questions of origins, meaning, and purpose. At Christian schools, combining faith and learning is ongoing. The Christian college environment helps students integrate faith and learning and prepares them to live out their faith in all areas of life.

Faculty members play a key role in making Chris-

Christian colleges and universities are places of learning where spiritual growth and academic achievement go hand in hand.

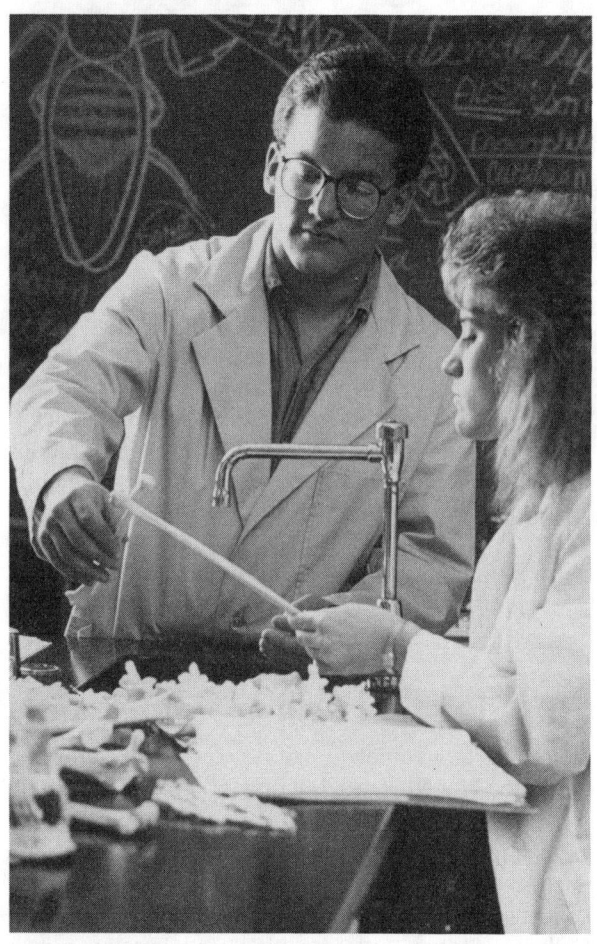

for good in America and abroad. Theirs is a voice for peace, justice, and the abundant life that comes from knowing Christ.

Alike But Different

The eighty-eight members of the Christian College Coalition differ in size, location, traditions, denominational ties, range of academic offerings, and life-style expectations. Christian colleges are located within a reasonable distance of almost any point in North America. About half are in major cities or urban areas, while the remainder call a small town home. Most Christian colleges are residential campuses, although the number of older students who commute to campuses is increasing.

The academic programs offered by Christian colleges also provide prospective students with considerable choice. Within the Coalition, a number of colleges continue to offer a traditional liberal arts curriculum, while others have expanded their course offerings to include professional programs of study. Several of the colleges emphasize technological programs of study, while others focus more on service areas such as nursing and social work. Many of the colleges allow students to shape their own interdisciplinary majors.

tian colleges and universities truly Christ-centered. Faculty members at Christian colleges are hired for their mature faith as well as their academic credentials. Classroom instruction is first-rate. Professors are not afraid to pose tough questions and challenge young scholars to think deeply about their faith. These professors are willing to reveal their own imperfections as humans and their uncertainties as Christians, thereby freeing students to ask honest questions or to take the courageous "leap of faith." For many students, faculty members become much more than teachers—they are role models, mentors, and lifelong friends.

In today's troubled times, the need is great for people who have experienced the Christian college difference. As God's ambassadors to a sinful and hurting world, graduates of Christian colleges are working

All Christian colleges take seriously the need to prepare men and women for lives of service to God, the world, and the Church.

Different But Alike

No matter what their uniqueness, all Christian colleges take seriously the need to prepare students for lives of service to God, the world, and the church. Across the membership of the Coalition, faculty and administrators share the following beliefs:

- That we live in a world that was created by God.
- That God is love.
- That Jesus Christ is the Son of God and the "author and finisher of our faith."
- That the key to abundant life is a relationship with Jesus Christ.
- That a high-quality education must deal with matters of the heart as well as of the mind.
- That a college education should provide a solid

foundation for living an active, meaningful, and contributing life in God's world and that a curriculum that is firmly grounded in the liberal arts is the surest basis for such a foundation.

- That faculty members should serve as both academic and spiritual mentors to their students.
- That cocurricular and resident-life activities are an important part of an educational experience.
- That in addition to a degree, sharpened intellectual skills, and current information, students should graduate with an enhanced sense of wholeness and the courage to ask questions.
- That no college experience, if it is to be whole and valuable, can ignore the problems of society or the major issues of the modern world.

An atmosphere of compassion, caring, teamwork, and trust characterizes campus life at Christian colleges.

commitment to Christ. Campus life is designed to encourage healthy friendships. Christian college campuses are not split into competitive Greek houses or divided by ethnic or religious categories. "Community" is more than just an idea, it is a reality on these campuses. And when students do encounter the day-to-day tensions present with any group of people living together, such problems are tempered by an atmosphere of compassion and caring, of teamwork and trust.

... and Beyond

Christian colleges are known for their commitment to service, which finds fulfillment in the outreach activities of the young people they enroll. Students at Christian colleges participate in volunteer efforts and Christian service projects in the United States and abroad. They tutor the young and read to the old. They march for hunger and speak out on social issues. They visit teenagers in jail and work with the terminally ill. They participate in political causes and lead Young Life groups. In short, these students

Life on a Christian College Campus . . .

As is the case at all small, residential colleges, campus life is an important part of the Christian college experience. However, the Christian emphasis of the colleges is clearly evident. Whether serving in student government or singing in the college choir, students are encouraged to use their talents and skills for the glory of God. Additionally, the Christian college campus is a place where students can "Just Say Yes" to a life-style that is free from alcohol and drug abuse.

When looking back at their undergraduate years, alumni of Christian colleges and universities speak of the lifelong friendships that continue to grow out of a shared

The college years are the most exciting of a young person's life. They are also the stepping stones to things to come.

witness to God's love with their time and with their actions, as well as their words.

A commitment to cultural diversity is evident on many Christian campuses, and students from various cultures and countries are encouraged to enroll. Additionally, many Christian colleges provide students with international study experiences around the world.

The Christian College Coalition sponsors several off-campus programs that are available to students from member institutions: the American Studies Program in Washington, D.C.; the Latin American Studies Program in San José, Costa Rica; the Los Angeles Film Studies Center; the Middle East Studies Program; the Russian Studies Program; and the Oxford Summer School Program in England. Other unique study opportunities are available through the Au Sable Institute of Environmental Studies in Michigan, the Oregon Extension Fall Semester, and various urban studies programs in Chicago and San Francisco. (Other foreign-study opportunities available through Christian College Coalition member institutions are provided in the Study Abroad Index on page 141.)

Life After College

That most graduates of Christian colleges have little trouble finding a first job or gaining admittance to graduate or professional schools is no accident. The colleges work hard at providing students with a broad array of resources and at helping alumni succeed in life after college.

Notable alumni who have graduated from a Christian college include evangelist Billy Graham; founder and president of Focus on the Family James Dobson; award-winning recording artist Sandi Patti; NFL running back Christian Okoye; U.S. senator Dan Coats; and sociologist, speaker, and author Tony Campolo. Other alumni are also making their mark on society as they serve in North America and abroad. Their collective faithfulness in dealing with life's minor and major issues stands as a testimony to the lifelong impact of a Christian college education.

Meeting the Cost of a Christian College Education

Any private college is a big investment. However, many thousands of families have found a Christian college education well worth the price. Parents and alumni alike agree that it is impossible to place a dollar value on the lifelong benefits of a Christ-centered undergraduate experience.

Most Christian colleges and universities provide generous aid packages to financially and/or academically qualified students. Indeed, at many Christian colleges about two thirds of all students receive some form of institutional aid. Financial aid officers are eager to work with families in structuring financial aid packages that fit individual situations. Students enrolled full-time at a Christian college may also be eligible for federal and state grants, scholarships, loans, and work-study opportunities.

Narrowing the Choice

We hope this guide helps you narrow your options to several Christian colleges from which you can request additional information. You will find their admissions offices to be friendly and anxious to be of service to you.

Whether you are just entering college or transferring from another institution, your choice is very important. We encourage you to conduct your search thoroughly, carefully, and prayerfully.

Dr. Robert C. Andringa
President
Christian College Coalition

College Profiles and Special Notes

This section contains detailed factual profiles of the member schools of the Christian College Coalition, covering such items as background facts, enrollment figures, number of faculty members, academic programs, majors, expenses, financial aid, campus life, athletics, admission procedures, and whom to contact for more information. In addition, there is a special note from each college describing the school's distinctive features.

The data in each of these profiles, collected from fall 1993 to spring 1994, come primarily from Peterson's Annual Survey of Undergraduate Institutions, which was sent to deans or admission officers at each institution.

ANDERSON UNIVERSITY

Anderson, Indiana

SPECIAL NOTE FROM THE UNIVERSITY Anderson University is a community of Christian higher education where high-quality learning and Christian service come alive. Believing that scholarship and scholars should serve a purpose, Anderson University is a mission-minded school that offers students a strong liberal arts foundation on which to build career credentials. Business, computer science, education, music, religious studies, social work, and sociology are among the most popular of the 60 majors and programs offered. The Tri-S program (study, serve, and share) is probably most representative of the spirit of the University. Through this program, more than 500 students volunteer each year for 50 different cross-cultural work projects throughout the world. Bill and Gloria Gaither and Sandi Patti are a few of the nearly 25,000 loyal alumni who make up the University's international alumni association and whose strength is not only in their numbers but also in their belief.

Total Enrollment: 2,256
UG Enrollment: 2,101 (58% W)
Application Deadline: 8/25
Entrance: moderately difficult
Tuition & Fees: $10,300
Room & Board: $3520
SAT≥500: 23% V, 38% M   **ACT≥21:** 53%
Denominational Affiliation: Church of God

GENERAL INFORMATION Independent-religious comprehensive coed institution. Awards associate, bachelor's, master's degrees. Founded 1917. *Setting:* 100-acre suburban campus with easy access to Indianapolis. *Faculty:* 201 (142 full-time, 61% with terminal degrees, 59 part-time); student-undergrad faculty ratio is 15:1. *Library Holdings:* 215,800 books, 184,890 microform titles, 928 periodicals, 12,000 records, tapes, and CDs. *Computers:* 125 terminals, PCs for student use in computer center, instructional materials center.

UNDERGRADUATE PROFILE 2,101 students from 42 states and territories, 11 other countries. 58% women, 13% part-time, 61% state residents, 57% live on campus, 7% transferred in, 40% have campus jobs, 1% international, 19% 25 or older, 1% Native American, 1% Hispanic, 5% African American, 1% Asian American. *Retention:* 73% of 1992 freshmen returned. *Graduation:* 35% graduate in 4 years.

FRESHMEN 466 total. 1,352 applied, 75% were accepted, 46% of whom enrolled. 19% from top 10% of their high school class, 40% from top quarter, 68% from top half.

ACADEMIC PROGRAM Core, liberal arts curriculum, honor code. Calendar: semesters. 687 courses offered in 1993–94; average class size 14 in required courses. Academic remediation for entering students, services for LD students, advanced placement, accelerated degree program, self-designed majors, summer session for credit, part-time degree program (daytime, evenings, summer), adult/continuing education programs, co-op programs and internships. Unusual degree programs: 3-2 engineering with Purdue University.

MAJORS Accounting, art education, art/fine arts, athletic training, biblical studies, biology/biological sciences, business administration/commerce/management, chemistry, communication, computer science, criminal justice, (pre)dentistry sequence, early childhood education, economics, education, elementary education, (pre)engineering sequence, English, family and consumer studies, finance/banking, French, German, graphic arts, health education, history, (pre)law sequence, liberal arts/general studies, marketing/retailing/merchandising, mathematics, medical technology, (pre)medicine sequence, ministries, music, music business, music education, nursing, pastoral studies, philosophy, physical education, physics, political science/government, psychology, religious studies, sacred music, science education, secretarial studies/office management, social work, sociology, Spanish, speech/rhetoric/public address/debate, studio art, theater arts/drama, (pre)veterinary medicine sequence.

EXPENSES FOR 1994–95 *Application fee:* $20. Comprehensive fee of $13,820 includes full-time tuition ($10,300) and college room and board ($3520). College room only: $1900. Part-time tuition: $420 per semester hour.

FINANCIAL AID *College-administered aid for undergraduates 1993–94:* 756 need-based scholarships (average $1470), 707 non-need scholarships (average $1530), low-interest long-term loans from external sources (average $3000), FSEOG, Federal Work-Study, 200 part-time jobs. *Application forms required:* institutional; accepted: FFS, FAF, FAFSA. *Priority deadline:* 3/1. *Payment plan:* installment. *Waivers:* full or partial for employees or children of employees and adult students. *Notification:* continuous.

COLLEGE LIFE Orientation program (3 days, no cost, parents included). Drama-theater group, choral group, student-run newspaper, radio station. *Social organizations:* 16 social clubs; 34% of eligible men and 46% of eligible women are members. *Most popular organizations:* social clubs, Adult and Continuing Education Students Association, Multicultural Student Union. *Major annual events:* Homecoming, Vision/Revision, Rush Week. *Student services:* health clinic, personal-psychological counseling. *Safety:* 24-hour emergency response devices and patrols, student patrols, late-night transport-escort service.

ATHLETICS Member NCAA. All Division III. *Intercollegiate:* baseball M, basketball M/W, cross-country running M/W, football M, golf M, soccer M/W, softball W, tennis M/W, track and field M/W, volleyball W. *Intramural:* basketball, softball, tennis, track and field, volleyball. *Contact:* Mr. Barrett Bates, Athletic Director, 317-641-4483.

APPLYING/FRESHMEN *Options:* early entrance, early decision, deferred entrance. *Required:* school transcript, 2 recommendations, SAT I or ACT, TOEFL for international students. *Recommended:* essay, 3 years of high school math and science, 1 year of high school foreign language. *Required for some:* campus interview. Test scores used for counseling/placement. *Application deadlines:* 8/25, 12/1 for early decision. *Notification:* continuous until 9/1, continuous until 1/15 for early decision.

APPLYING/TRANSFER *Required:* high school transcript, 2 recommendations, college transcript, minimum 2.0 GPA. *Required for some:* standardized test scores, campus interview. *Entrance level:* moderately difficult. *Application deadline:* 8/25.

CONTACT Director of Admissions, Anderson University, 1100 East Fifth Street, Anderson, IN 46012; 317-641-4080 or toll-free 800-428-6414.

ASBURY COLLEGE
Wilmore, Kentucky

SPECIAL NOTE FROM THE COLLEGE At Asbury College, students join a century-long tradition of personal, spiritual, and professional experience. Selected as one of the nation's "top fifty liberal arts schools" by the *National Review College Guide*, Asbury is a fully-accredited institution offering 54 majors. A leadership development program, along with many service opportunities, complement outstanding academics. The student community represents approximately 45 states and 20 foreign countries. Lexington's educational, commercial, and cultural resources are within a 20-minute commute of Wilmore. Founded in the Wesleyan holiness tradition, Asbury College is preparing Christian leadership for the 21st century.

Total Enrollment: 1,157 (all UG)

Women: 54%

Application Deadline: rolling

Entrance: moderately difficult

Tuition & Fees: $9113

Room & Board: $2764

SAT≥500: 39% V, 43% M   **ACT≥21:** 64%

Denominational Affiliation: interdenominational

GENERAL INFORMATION Independent-religious 4-year coed institution. Awards bachelor's degrees. Founded 1890. *Setting:* 500-acre small-town campus with easy access to Lexington. *Faculty:* 114 (84 full-time, 30 part-time); student-undergrad faculty ratio is 14:1. *Library Holdings:* 148,526 books, 692 microform titles, 582 periodicals, 7,170 records, tapes, and CDs. *Computers:* 40 terminals, PCs for student use in computer center.

UNDERGRADUATE PROFILE 1,157 students from 45 states and territories, 20 other countries. 54% women, 4% part-time, 22% state residents, 85% live on campus, 9% transferred in, 3% international, 10% 25 or older, 0% Native American, 1% Hispanic, 1% African American, 1% Asian American. *Retention:* 71% of 1992 freshmen returned.

FRESHMEN 313 total. 937 applied, 77% were accepted, 57% of whom enrolled. 21% from top 10% of their high school class, 42% from top quarter, 75% from top half. 4 National Merit Scholarship Finalists.

ACADEMIC PROGRAM Core, honor code. Calendar: semesters. Academic remediation for entering students, advanced placement, summer session for credit, internships. Off-campus study at members of the Christian College Consortium and the Christian College Coalition. Unusual degree programs: 3-2 engineering with University of Kentucky, nursing with Case Western Reserve University, University of Kentucky.

MAJORS Accounting, applied mathematics, art education, art/fine arts, biblical languages, biblical studies, biology/biological sciences, broadcasting, business administration/commerce/management, chemistry, computer science, education, elementary education, English, French, health science, history, journalism, mathematics, medical technology, (pre)medicine sequence, ministries, music, music education, nursing, philosophy, physical education, physical sciences, psychology, recreation and leisure services, religious education, science education, secondary education, social work, sociology, Spanish, speech/rhetoric/public address/debate.

EXPENSES FOR 1994–95 *Application fee:* $25. Comprehensive fee of $11,877 includes full-time tuition ($8988), mandatory fees ($125), and college room and board ($2764). Part-time tuition: $365 per semester hour.

FINANCIAL AID *College-administered aid for undergraduates 1993–94:* 824 need-based scholarships (average $2225), 220 non-need scholarships (average $1175), low-interest long-term loans from college funds (average $1050), loans from external sources (average $2975), FSEOG, Federal Work-Study, 120 part-time jobs. Average total aid for freshmen: $6916, meeting 80% of need. *Application forms required:* institutional, FAFSA; required for some: IRS, state. *Priority deadline:* 4/1. *Payment plans:* installment, deferred payment. *Waivers:* full or partial for employees or children of employees and senior citizens. *Notification:* 4/1.

COLLEGE LIFE Orientation program (4 days, $40, parents included). Drama-theater group, choral group, student-run newspaper, radio station. *Social organizations:* 20 open to all. *Student services:* health clinic, personal-psychological counseling, shuttle bus. *Safety:* 24-hour emergency response devices, controlled dormitory access, late night security personnel.

ATHLETICS Member NAIA. *Intercollegiate:* baseball M, basketball M/W, cross-country running M/W, soccer M, softball W, swimming M/W, tennis M/W, volleyball W. *Intramural:* basketball, football, soccer, softball, table tennis (Ping-Pong), tennis, volleyball. *Contact:* Mrs. Rita Pritchett, Athletic Director, 606-858-3511 Ext. 2163.

APPLYING/FRESHMEN *Options:* early entrance, deferred entrance, midyear entrance. *Required:* school transcript, 3 recommendations, 2.3 GPA, SAT I or ACT, TOEFL for international students. *Recommended:* 3 years of high school math and science, some high school foreign language. *Required for some:* essay, interview. Test scores used for admission and counseling/placement. *Application deadline:* rolling.

APPLYING/TRANSFER *Required:* high school transcript, 2 recommendations, college transcript, minimum 2.0 GPA. *Recommended:* standardized test scores, 3 years of high school math and science, some high school foreign language. *Required for some:* essay, interview. *Entrance level:* moderately difficult. *Application deadline:* rolling.

CONTACT Mr. Stan F. Wiggam, Dean of Admissions, Asbury College, 1 Macklem Drive, Wilmore, KY 40390; 606-858-3511 Ext. 2142.

ATLANTIC BAPTIST COLLEGE
Moncton, New Brunswick, Canada

Total Enrollment: 224 (all UG)
Women: 56%
Application Deadline: rolling
Entrance: minimally difficult
Tuition & Fees: $2725 (Can.)
Room & Board: $3665 (Can.)
Denominational Affiliation: Baptist

GENERAL INFORMATION Independent-religious 4-year coed institution. Awards associate, bachelor's degrees. Founded 1949. *Setting:* small-city campus. *Faculty:* 21 (10 full-time, 85% with terminal degrees, 11 part-time); student-undergrad faculty ratio is 17:1. *Library Holdings:* 35,000 books, 35 microform titles, 125 periodicals, 941 records, tapes, and CDs. *Computers:* 15 terminals, PCs for student use in computer labs.

UNDERGRADUATE PROFILE 224 students from 7 provinces and territories, 3 other countries. 56% women, 20% part-time, 50% live on campus, 12% transferred in, 48% have need-based financial aid, 52% have non-need-based financial aid, 16% have campus jobs, 2% international, 20% 25 or older, 1% Native American, 0% Hispanic, 1% black, 0% Asian. *Retention:* 55% of 1992 freshmen returned.

FRESHMEN 87 total. 123 applied, 96% were accepted, 74% of whom enrolled.

ACADEMIC PROGRAM Core, honor code. Calendar: semesters. 95 courses offered in 1993–94; average class size 50 in required courses. Tutorials, summer session for credit, part-time degree program (daytime, evenings).

MAJORS Biblical studies, English, history, liberal arts/general studies, religious studies, sociology.

EXPENSES FOR 1994–95 Comprehensive fee of $6390 includes full-time tuition ($2500), mandatory fees ($225), and college room and board ($3665). Part-time tuition: $260 per course. Part-time mandatory fees: $7 per semester. (All figures are in Canadian dollars.)

FINANCIAL AID *College-administered aid for undergraduates 1993–94:* 33 need-based scholarships (average $360), 35 non-need scholarships (average $850), 35 part-time jobs. *Application forms required:* FFS, institutional. *Priority deadline:* 8/1. *Payment plan:* installment. *Waivers:* full or partial for employees or children of employees and senior citizens. *Notification:* 9/8.

COLLEGE LIFE Orientation program (2 days, no cost). Drama-theater group, choral group, student-run newspaper. *Major annual events:* Christmas Banquet, Winter Carnival, Graduation. *Student services:* health clinic, personal-psychological counseling, shuttle bus. *Safety:* 24-hour emergency response devices.

ATHLETICS *Intercollegiate:* baseball M/W, basketball M/W, soccer M/W, softball M/W. *Intramural:* baseball, basketball, football, golf, ice hockey, softball, table tennis (Ping-Pong), volleyball.

APPLYING/FRESHMEN *Options:* deferred entrance, midyear entrance. *Required:* school transcript, minimum 2.0 GPA, 3 years of high school English, 2 years of high school math and science, 3 recommendations, TOEFL for international students. *Required for some:* interview. *Application deadline:* rolling.

APPLYING/TRANSFER *Required:* high school transcript, 3 years of high school English, 2 years of high school math and science, 3 recommendations, college transcript, minimum 2.0 GPA. *Required for some:* interview. *Entrance level:* minimally difficult. *Application deadline:* rolling.

CONTACT Admissions Officer, Atlantic Baptist College, 933 Salisbury Road, P.O. Box 6004, Moncton, NB E1C 9L7, Canada; 506-858-8970.

AZUSA PACIFIC UNIVERSITY
Azusa, California

SPECIAL NOTE FROM THE UNIVERSITY At APU, students participate in exceptional academic programs in 40 fields, dynamic leadership and music projects, innovative service opportunities, and on renowned athletic teams. They train alongside Olympic athletes; gain acceptance to America's most prestigious graduate schools (Harvard, Stanford, Georgetown); participate in Bridges, a San Francisco outreach to homeless people and AIDS patients, and Walk-About, an intense, 9-day wilderness excursion that hones leadership skills and deepens faith; and minister in Haiti, Guatemala, Laos, Mexico, Romania, and Russia. Whether in the classroom, in athletics, or on the mission field, Azusa Pacific students learn that serving others is the cornerstone of effective leadership.

Total Enrollment: 3,869
UG Enrollment: 2,126 (58% W)
Application Deadline: rolling
Entrance: moderately difficult
Tuition & Fees: $10,834
Room & Board: $3890
SAT≥500: 22% V, 43% M   **ACT≥21:** 63%
Denominational Affiliation: nondenominational

GENERAL INFORMATION Independent-religious comprehensive coed institution. Awards bachelor's, master's degrees. Founded 1899. *Setting:* 52-acre small-town campus with easy access to Los Angeles. *Faculty:* 337 (156 full-time, 48% with terminal degrees, 181 part-time); student-undergrad faculty ratio is 18:1. *Library Holdings:* 115,000 books, 950 periodicals, 2 on-line bibliographic services, 4 CD-ROMs, 5,000 records, tapes, and CDs. *Computers:* 56 terminals, PCs for student use in computer center. Student computer-purchase plan available.

UNDERGRADUATE PROFILE 2,126 students from 35 states and territories, 24 other countries. 58% women, 7% part-time, 79% state residents, 62% live on campus, 9% international, 16% 25 or older, 2% Native American, 10% Hispanic, 4% African American, 5% Asian American. *Retention:* 84% of 1992 freshmen returned.

FRESHMEN 482 total. 1,080 applied, 88% were accepted, 51% of whom enrolled. 25% from top 10% of their high school class, 52% from top quarter, 75% from top half.

ACADEMIC PROGRAM Core, honor code. Calendar: 4-4-1. Academic remediation for entering students, English as a second language program offered during academic year and summer, advanced placement, accelerated degree program, honors program, summer session for credit, part-time degree program (daytime, evenings), adult/continuing education programs, co-op programs and internships. ROTC: Army (c). Unusual degree programs: 3-2 engineering.

STUDY-ABROAD SITES Costa Rica, Ecuador, Japan, Taiwan.

MAJORS Accounting, applied art, art/fine arts, athletic training, biblical studies, biochemistry, biology/biological sciences, business administration/commerce/management, chemistry, communication, computer science, education, English, history, international studies, liberal arts/general studies, management information systems, marketing/retailing/merchandising, mathematics, ministries, music, nursing, philosophy, physical education, physics, political science/government, psychology, religious studies, social science, social work, sociology, theology.

EXPENSES FOR 1993–94 *Application fee:* $40. Comprehensive fee of $14,724 includes full-time tuition ($10,788), mandatory fees ($46), and college room and board ($3890). College room only: $1740 (minimum). Part-time tuition: $440 per unit.

FINANCIAL AID *College-administered aid for undergraduates 1993–94:* need-based scholarships, non-need scholarships (average $2358), low-interest long-term loans from external sources (average $2500), FSEOG, Federal Work-Study, part-time jobs. *Application forms required:* FAF, IRS, institutional, FAFSA; accepted: state. *Priority deadline:* 3/1. *Payment plan:* installment. *Waivers:* full or partial for employees or children of employees. *Average indebtedness of graduates:* $10,000.

COLLEGE LIFE Orientation program (4 days, no cost, parents included). Drama-theater group, choral group, student-run newspaper. *Social organizations:* 14 open to all. *Major annual events:* Mega Weekend-Homecoming/Dinner Rally, Mexicali Outreach, Night of Champions. *Student services:* health clinic, personal-psychological counseling, shuttle bus. *Safety:* 24-hour emergency response devices and patrols, student patrols, late-night transport-escort service.

ATHLETICS Member NAIA. *Intercollegiate:* baseball M(s), basketball M(s)/W(s), cross-country running M(s)/W(s), football M(s), soccer M(s)/W(s), softball W(s), tennis M(s), track and field M(s)/W(s), volleyball M/W(s). *Intramural:* basketball, football, skiing (downhill), soccer, volleyball. *Contact:* Dr. Terry Franson, Athletic Director, 818-812-3024.

APPLYING/FRESHMEN *Options:* deferred entrance, midyear entrance. *Required:* essay, school transcript, 2 recommendations, SAT I or ACT, SAT II: Writing Test, TOEFL for international students. *Required for some:* interview. Test scores used for admission. *Application deadline:* rolling. *Notification:* continuous.

APPLYING/TRANSFER *Required:* essay, 2 recommendations, college transcript, minimum 2.0 GPA. *Required for some:* standardized test scores, high school transcript, interview. *Entrance level:* moderately difficult. *Application deadline:* rolling. *Notification:* continuous.

CONTACT Ms. Deana Porterfield, Director of Undergraduate Admissions, Azusa Pacific University, 901 East Alosta Avenue, P.O. Box 7000, Azusa, CA 91702-7000; 818-812-3016.

BARTLESVILLE WESLEYAN COLLEGE
Bartlesville, Oklahoma

SPECIAL NOTE FROM THE COLLEGE Bartlesville Wesleyan College is a distinctive Christian college. The campus community strongly believes in providing a Christ-centered educational experience that will produce lifelong results. It is located in the south-central part of the United States, 45 miles north of suburban Tulsa. Bartlesville is a cosmopolitan city of 35,000 and is the world headquarters for Phillips Petroleum Company. Local cultural opportunities include a choral society, a civic ballet, a theater guild, a symphony orchestra, and an annual International OK Mozart festival. The focal point of the 27-acre campus is an elegant 60-year-old, 32-room, Spanish-style mansion overlooking a beautiful lake.

Total Enrollment: 508 (all UG)
Women: 60%
Application Deadline: rolling
Entrance: minimally difficult
Tuition & Fees: $6650
Room & Board: $3300
SAT≥500: N/R   **ACT≥21:** 46%
Denominational Affiliation: Wesleyan Church

GENERAL INFORMATION Independent-religious 4-year coed institution. Awards associate, bachelor's degrees. Founded 1909. *Setting:* 27-acre small-town campus with easy access to Tulsa. *Faculty:* 64 (34 full-time, 44% with terminal degrees, 30 part-time); student-undergrad faculty ratio is 14:1. *Library Holdings:* 124,722 books, 35,997 microform titles, 300 periodicals, 1,076 records, tapes, and CDs. *Computers:* 20 terminals, PCs for student use in computer center. Student computer-purchase plan available.

UNDERGRADUATE PROFILE 508 students from 26 states and territories, 9 other countries. 60% women, 34% part-time, 59% state residents, 42% live on campus, 16% transferred in, 29% have campus jobs, 5% international, 39% 25 or older, 5% Native American, 3% Hispanic, 4% African American, 1% Asian American. *Retention:* 81% of 1992 freshmen returned.

FRESHMEN 94 total. 258 applied, 43% were accepted, 85% of whom enrolled. 15% from top 10% of their high school class, 32% from top quarter, 72% from top half.

ACADEMIC PROGRAM Core, honor code. Calendar: semesters. Average class size 20 in required courses. Academic remediation for entering students, English as a second language program offered during academic year, advanced placement, self-designed majors, summer session for credit, part-time degree program (daytime, evenings), adult/continuing education programs, internships. Off-campus study at Tri-County Technical College.

MAJORS Accounting, behavioral sciences, biology/biological sciences, business administration/commerce/management, business education, chemistry, communication, computer information systems, education, elementary education, English, history, (pre)law

sequence, liberal arts/general studies, linguistics, mathematics, (pre)medicine sequence, ministries, natural sciences, nursing, physical education, political science/government, religious studies, science, science education, secondary education, secretarial studies/office management, social science, teaching English as a second language, theology, (pre)veterinary medicine sequence.

EXPENSES FOR 1994–95 *Application fee:* $25. Comprehensive fee of $9950 includes full-time tuition ($6450), mandatory fees ($200), and college room and board ($3300). Part-time tuition: $220 per credit hour. Part-time mandatory fees: $10 per credit hour.

FINANCIAL AID *College-administered aid for undergraduates 1993–94:* 20 need-based scholarships (average $750), 250 non-need scholarships (average $843), low-interest long-term loans from external sources (average $2625), FSEOG, Federal Work-Study, 30 part-time jobs. Average total aid for freshmen: $7039, meeting 90% of need (aid offered to 100% of those qualified). *Application forms required:* institutional, FAFSA. *Priority deadline:* 3/1. *Payment plans:* installment, deferred payment. *Waivers:* full or partial for employees or children of employees and senior citizens. *Notification:* continuous.

COLLEGE LIFE Orientation program (2 days, no cost, parents included). Choral group, student-run newspaper. *Most popular organizations:* Forensics Club, Young Republicans, Teachers Association, Theology Club. *Major annual events:* Intramural Olympics, Homecoming Festivities, seasonal banquets. *Student services:* health clinic, personal-psychological counseling. *Safety:* 24-hour patrols, controlled dormitory access.

ATHLETICS Member NAIA. *Intercollegiate:* basketball M(s)/W(s), soccer M(s)/W(s), volleyball W(s). *Intramural:* basketball, football, golf, racquetball, soccer, softball, swimming and diving, tennis, volleyball. *Contact:* Mr. Rocky Kent, Athletic Director, 918-333-3151.

APPLYING/FRESHMEN *Options:* early entrance, deferred entrance. *Required:* school transcript, SAT I or ACT. *Required for some:* TOEFL for international students. Test scores used for counseling/placement. *Application deadline:* rolling.

APPLYING/TRANSFER *Required:* high school transcript, college transcript, transfer information form, recommendation, minimum 2.0 GPA. *Entrance level:* minimally difficult. *Application deadline:* rolling.

CONTACT Mr. Jere Johnson, Enrollment Services Administrator, Bartlesville Wesleyan College, 2201 Silver Lake Road, Bartlesville, OK 74006; 918-335-6219 or toll-free 800-468-6292.

BELHAVEN COLLEGE
Jackson, Mississippi

SPECIAL NOTE FROM THE COLLEGE Founded in 1883, Belhaven College is located in a historic neighborhood of Jackson, Mississippi, the thriving center of cultural, educational, and political life in a state known for its Southern hospitality. Belhaven is a coeducational, liberal arts Christian college on a 42-acre campus, graced by traditional Southern architecture, serving students from throughout the United States and around the world. At the heart of the Belhaven College mission is its commitment to educate and prepare students to take their place as leaders and shapers of the future. Belhaven offers an academic program that unifies faith and reason, theory and application, learning and living, the rigor of scholarship, and the passion of Christian ministry.

Total Enrollment: 1,083 (all UG)

Women: 59%

Application Deadline: rolling

Entrance: moderately difficult

Tuition & Fees: $7620

Room & Board: $2900

SAT≥500: 40% V, 30% M   **ACT≥21:** 73%

Denominational Affiliation: Presbyterian

GENERAL INFORMATION Independent-religious 4-year coed institution. Awards bachelor's degrees. Founded 1883. *Setting:* 42-acre urban campus. *Faculty:* 80 (35 full-time, 80% with terminal degrees, 45 part-time); student-undergrad faculty ratio is 17:1. *Library Holdings:* 88,127 books, 4,898 microform titles, 451 periodicals, 2,295 records, tapes, and CDs. *Computers:* 29 terminals, PCs for student use in computer center, business building.

UNDERGRADUATE PROFILE 1,083 students from 19 states and territories, 19 other countries. 59% women, 32% part-time, 88% state residents, 30% live on campus, 23% transferred in, 3% international, 40% 25 or older, 0% Native American, 1% Hispanic, 15% African American, 1% Asian American.

FRESHMEN 121 total. 248 applied, 79% were accepted, 61% of whom enrolled. 25% from top 10% of their high school class, 54% from top quarter, 82% from top half. 4 valedictorians.

ACADEMIC PROGRAM Core, honor code. Calendar: semesters. 201 courses offered in 1993–94; average class size 25 in required courses. Academic remediation for entering students, English as a second language program offered during academic year, advanced placement, honors program, summer session for credit, part-time degree program (daytime, evenings, summer), internships. ROTC: Army (c). Unusual degree programs: 3-2 engineering with Mississippi State University.

MAJORS Accounting, art/fine arts, biblical studies, biology/biological sciences, business administration, chemistry, computer science, (pre)dentistry sequence, elementary education, (pre)engineering sciences sequence, English, history, humanities, (pre)law sequence, mathematics, (pre)medicine sequence, ministries, music, (pre)nursing sequence, philosophy, piano/organ, psychology, sacred music, science, voice.

EXPENSES FOR 1994–95 *Application fee:* $15. Comprehensive fee of $10,520 includes full-time tuition ($7490), mandatory fees ($130), and college room and board ($2900). Part-time tuition: $195 per semester hour.

FINANCIAL AID *College-administered aid for undergraduates 1993–94:* 180 need-based scholarships (average $1000), 600 non-need scholarships (average $3200), low-interest long-term loans from college funds (average $1000), loans from external sources (average $3200), FSEOG, Federal Work-Study. *Application forms required:* institutional, FAFSA; required for some: IRS; accepted: FFS, FAF. *Priority deadline:* 4/1. *Payment plan:* installment. *Waivers:* full or partial for employees or children of employees and senior citizens. *Average indebtedness of graduates:* $12,800.

COLLEGE LIFE Orientation program (2 days, no cost). Drama-theater group, choral group, student-run newspaper. *Social organizations:* 28 open to all; 2 local sororities; 1% of eligible women are members. *Most popular organizations:* Student Government Association, Reformed University Fellowship. *Major annual events:* Homecoming, Lake Day, Christmas Formal. *Student services:* health clinic, personal-psychological counseling. *Safety:* 24-hour patrols, late-night transport-escort service, controlled dormitory access, room security.

ATHLETICS Member NAIA. *Intercollegiate:* baseball M(s), basketball M(s)/W(s), cross-country running M(s)/W(s), golf M(s), soccer M(s)/W(c), softball W(c), tennis M(s)/W(s). *Intramural:* basketball, football, soccer, softball, volleyball. *Contact:* Mr. Hannibal Najjar, Athletic Director, 601-968-5956.

APPLYING/FRESHMEN *Options:* early entrance, deferred entrance, midyear entrance. *Required:* school transcript, minimum 2.0 GPA, recommendations, SAT I (minimum 820) or ACT (minimum 20), TOEFL for international students. *Recommended:* some high school foreign language. *Required for some:* essay, interview. Test scores used for admission and counseling/placement. *Application deadline:* rolling.

APPLYING/TRANSFER *Required:* recommendations, college transcript, minimum 2.0 GPA. *Recommended:* standardized test scores. *Required for some:* essay, high school transcript, interview. *Entrance level:* moderately difficult. *Application deadline:* rolling.

CONTACT Mrs. Karen Walling, Director of Enrollment Services, Belhaven College, 1500 Peachtree Street, Jackson, MS 39202-1789; 601-968-5940.

BETHEL COLLEGE
Mishawaka, Indiana

SPECIAL NOTE FROM THE COLLEGE Bethel College is located in northern Indiana on a beautiful 60-acre wooded campus. Bethel is the College of the Missionary Church, an evangelical denomination with roots in Methodist and Mennonite traditions. Since its founding in 1947, the hallmark of the College has been an emphasis on excellent teaching and warm student-faculty relationships. Bethel College has a challenging and participatory environment: students work hard in the classroom, on the athletic field, in performance, and in ministry opportunities. Bethel is a college with a deep Christian commitment. There is an open and joyful emphasis on the Christian life. Chapel meets 3 times a week and is the center of the campus culture. "With Christ at the helm" is more than a motto—it is the purpose and intent of living and studying together.

Total Enrollment: 1,158
UG Enrollment: 1,135 (60% W)
Application Deadline: rolling
Entrance: moderately difficult
Tuition & Fees: $8700
Room & Board: $2950
SAT≥500: 28% V, 43% M **ACT≥21:** 56%
Denominational Affiliation: Missionary Church

GENERAL INFORMATION Independent-religious comprehensive coed institution. Awards associate, bachelor's, master's degrees. Founded 1947. *Setting:* 60-acre suburban campus. *Undergraduate faculty:* 104 (53 full-time, 48% with terminal degrees, 51 part-time); student-undergrad faculty ratio is 19:1. *Library Holdings:* 73,686 books, 3,849 microform titles, 415 periodicals, 3,025 records, tapes, and CDs. *Computers:* 25 terminals, PCs for student use in computer center, library, dorms.

UNDERGRADUATE PROFILE 1,135 students from 23 states and territories, 7 other countries. 60% women, 35% part-time, 82% state residents, 33% live on campus, 35% have campus jobs, 1% international, 46% 25 or older, 1% Native American, 1% Hispanic, 13% African American, 1% Asian American. *Retention:* 70% of 1992 freshmen returned.

FRESHMEN 177 total. 492 applied, 84% were accepted, 43% of whom enrolled. 16% from top 10% of their high school class, 38% from top quarter, 68% from top half.

ACADEMIC PROGRAM Core, liberal arts curriculum. Calendar: semesters. 358 courses offered in 1993–94; average class size 20 in required courses. Academic remediation for entering students, English as a second language program, advanced placement, accelerated degree program, summer session for credit, part-time degree program (daytime, evenings, weekends), adult/continuing education programs, internships. Off-campus study at Northern Indiana Consortium for Education. Unusual degree programs: 3-2 engineering with University of Notre Dame.

STUDY-ABROAD SITES Ecuador, Jamaica.

MAJORS Accounting, aerospace engineering, art/fine arts, biblical languages, biblical studies, biology/biological sciences, business administration/commerce/management, business education, chemical engineering, chemistry, civil engineering, commercial art, communication, computer science, (pre)dentistry sequence, early childhood education, economics, education, electrical engineering, elementary education, engineering sciences, English, French, gerontology, health education, history, human resources, journalism, liberal arts/general studies, mathematics, mechanical engineering, (pre)medicine sequence, metallurgical engineering, ministries, music, music education, nursing, pastoral studies, philosophy, physical education, piano/organ, psychology, recreation and leisure services, religious studies, sacred music, science, science education, secondary education, secretarial studies/office management, social science, sociology, Spanish, theater arts/drama, voice.

EXPENSES FOR 1993–94 *Application fee:* $25. Comprehensive fee of $11,650 includes full-time tuition ($8500), mandatory fees ($200), and college room and board ($2950). College room only: $1250. Part-time tuition per semester hour ranges from $199 to $255. Part-time mandatory fees: $25 per semester. Tuition guaranteed not to increase for student's term of enrollment.

FINANCIAL AID *College-administered aid for undergraduates 1993–94:* need-based scholarships, 860 non-need scholarships (average $3312), low-interest long-term loans from college funds (average $1315), loans from external sources (average $2771), FSEOG, Federal Work-Study, 60 part-time jobs. *Application forms required:* institutional, FAFSA; required for some: IRS; accepted: FFS, FAF. *Priority deadline:* 3/1. *Payment plan:* installment. *Waivers:* full or partial for employees or children of employees and adult students.

COLLEGE LIFE Orientation program (5 days, $50, parents included). Drama-theater group, choral group, student-run newspaper, radio station. *Most popular organizations:* Spiritual Warfare Assault Team, Student Council, Center for Community Service, Mu Kappa. *Major annual events:* Homecoming, Christmas Banquet, Junior/Senior Banquet. *Student services:* health clinic, personal-psychological counseling. *Safety:* student patrols, controlled dormitory access, security on duty until 3 am, 7 days per week.

ATHLETICS Member NAIA. *Intercollegiate:* baseball M(s), basketball M(s)/W(s), cross-country running M(s)/W(s), golf M(s), soccer M(s), softball W(s), tennis M(s)/W(s), track and field M/W, volleyball W(s). *Intramural:* basketball, football, soccer, softball, table tennis (Ping-Pong), tennis, track and field, volleyball, weight lifting. *Contact:* Mr. Mike Lightfoot, Athletic Director, 219-257-3345.

APPLYING/FRESHMEN *Options:* early entrance, deferred entrance, midyear entrance. *Required:* school transcript, 1 recommendation, SAT I or ACT, TOEFL for international students. *Recommended:* minimum 2.0 GPA, 2 years of high school foreign language, interview. Test scores used for counseling/placement. *Application deadline:* rolling.

APPLYING/TRANSFER *Required:* high school transcript, 1 recommendation, college transcript, minimum 2.0 GPA. *Recommended:* standardized test scores, 2 years of high school foreign language, interview. *Entrance level:* moderately difficult. *Application deadline:* rolling.

CONTACT Mr. Steve Matteson, Dean of Admissions, Bethel College, 1001 West McKinley Avenue, Mishawaka, IN 46545; 800-422-4101 (toll-free).

BETHEL COLLEGE
North Newton, Kansas

> **SPECIAL NOTE FROM THE COLLEGE** Bethel College in Kansas offers academic excellence firmly rooted in a Christian heritage. Founded in 1887 by Mennonite immigrants, Bethel affirms a commitment to peace and service to others. While support of these ideals remains a cornerstone at the College, a prospective student does not need to be Mennonite to attend Bethel. In fact, approximately 50% of the Bethel student population has a religious orientation other than Mennonite. Within this context of spiritual belief, Bethel College offers a distinguished array of undergraduate liberal arts programming on its 60-acre, wooded campus. Noted for its high academic standards and achievements, Bethel ranks first among all Kansas colleges and universities in the percentage of graduates who earn doctoral degrees.

Total Enrollment: 638 (all UG)

Women: 59%

Application Deadline: 8/15

Entrance: moderately difficult

Tuition & Fees: $8740

Room & Board: $3580

SAT≥500: N/R **ACT≥21:** 61%

Denominational Affiliation: General Conference Mennonite Church

GENERAL INFORMATION Independent-religious 4-year coed institution. Awards bachelor's degrees. Founded 1887. *Setting:* 60-acre small-town campus. *Faculty:* 83 (54 full-time, 80% with terminal degrees, 29 part-time); student-undergrad faculty ratio is 13:1. *Library Holdings:* 125,000 books, 100 microform titles, 725 periodicals, 1,500 records, tapes, and CDs. *Computers:* 28 terminals, PCs for student use in computer center, computer labs.

UNDERGRADUATE PROFILE 638 students from 20 states and territories, 9 other countries. 59% women, 16% part-time, 68% state residents, 65% live on campus, 11% transferred in, 60% have need-based financial aid, 35% have non-need-based financial aid, 40% have campus jobs, 4% international, 22% 25 or older, 1% Native American, 2% Hispanic, 4% African American, 1% Asian American. *Retention:* 78% of 1992 freshmen returned. *Graduation:* 45% graduate in 4 years.

FRESHMEN 123 total. 202 applied, 91% were accepted, 67% of whom enrolled. 19% from top 10% of their high school class, 35% from top quarter, 64% from top half. 4 valedictorians.

ACADEMIC PROGRAM Core, liberal arts curriculum, honor code. Calendar: 4-1-4. 517 courses offered in 1993–94; average class size 25 in required courses. Academic remediation for entering students, advanced placement, contract degree programs, tutorials, summer session for credit, part-time degree program (daytime), internships. Off-campus study at 6 members of the Associated Colleges of Central Kansas. Unusual degree programs: 3-2 engineering with Washington University, BSN degree completion program.

STUDY-ABROAD SITES China, England, France, Germany, Japan, Mexico, Spain.

MAJORS Accounting, art education, art/fine arts, biblical studies, biology, business administration, chemistry, communication, (pre)dentistry sequence, early childhood education, economics, elementary education, English, environmental sciences, German, health education, history, human ecology, international studies, (pre)law sequence, mathematics, (pre)medicine sequence, music, music education, natural sciences, nursing, peace studies, physical education, physics, political science, psychology, religious studies, science, science education, social science, social work, sociology, special education, speech/rhetoric/public address/debate, theater arts/drama, theology.

EXPENSES FOR 1994–95 Comprehensive fee of $12,320 includes full-time tuition ($8540), mandatory fees ($200), and college room and board ($3580). Part-time tuition per credit hour ranges from $215 to $280.

FINANCIAL AID *College-administered aid for undergraduates 1993–94:* 380 need-based scholarships (average $2190), 223 non-need scholarships (average $1277), low-interest long-term loans from external sources (average $2600), FSEOG, Federal Work-Study, 139 part-time jobs. Average total aid for freshmen: $9129, meeting 85% of need (aid provided to 100% of those qualified). *Forms required for some financial aid applicants:* IRS; accepted: FFS, FAF, FAFSA. *Priority deadline:* 3/1. *Payment plans:* installment, deferred payment. *Waivers:* full or partial for employees or children of employees. *Notification:* continuous. Financial aid guaranteed for 4 years. *Average indebtedness of graduates:* $10,000.

COLLEGE LIFE Orientation program (3 days, no cost, parents included). Drama-theater group, choral group, student-run newspaper, radio station. *Social organizations:* 30 open to all, with 75% participating. *Most popular organizations:* Bethel College Service Corps (10% participate), The Collegian (7% participate), Student Alumni Association (4% participate). *Major annual events:* Fall Fest, Christmas Fest. *Student services:* health clinic, personal-psychological counseling.

ATHLETICS Member NAIA. *Intercollegiate:* basketball M(s)/W(s), football M(s), soccer M(s), tennis M(s)/W(s), track and field M(s)/W(s), volleyball W(s). *Intramural:* badminton, basketball, football, golf, table tennis (Ping-Pong), volleyball, weight lifting. *Contact:* Ms. Diane Flickner, Athletic Director, 316-283-2500.

APPLYING/FRESHMEN *Options:* early entrance, deferred entrance, midyear entrance. *Required:* school transcript, 2 recommendations, interview, SAT I or ACT, TOEFL for international students. *Recommended:* minimum 2.0 GPA, 3 years of high school math and science, some high school foreign language. Test scores used for admission. *Application deadline:* 8/15. *Notification:* continuous.

APPLYING/TRANSFER *Required:* high school transcript, 1 recommendation, interview, college transcript, minimum 2.0 GPA. *Recommended:* 3 years of high school math and science, some high school foreign language. *Required for some:* standardized test scores. *Entrance level:* moderately difficult. *Application deadline:* 8/15. *Notification:* continuous.

CONTACT Mr. J. Michael Lamb, Director of Admissions, Bethel College, 300 East 27th Street, North Newton, KS 67117; 316-283-2500 Ext. 230 or toll-free 800-522-1887.

BETHEL COLLEGE

St. Paul, Minnesota

> **SPECIAL NOTE FROM THE COLLEGE** A student's college years should be a time to ask tough questions, challenge one's intellect, and explore one's values and goals. Bethel creates a great environment for learning by offering diverse academic programs, expert faculty members, excellent facilities and location, and a wide variety of activities in which to get involved. Both in and out of the classroom, students have the time of their lives for learning, growing, shaping their futures, and becoming the person God wants each of them to be.

Total Enrollment: 2,101
UG Enrollment: 2,013 (59% W)
Application Deadline: rolling
Entrance: moderately difficult
Tuition & Fees: $11,700
Room & Board: $4220
SAT≥500: 46% V, 69% M   **ACT≥21:** 87%
Denominational Affiliation: Baptist General Conference

GENERAL INFORMATION Independent-religious comprehensive coed institution. Awards associate, bachelor's, master's degrees. Founded 1871. *Setting:* 231-acre suburban campus. *Undergraduate faculty:* 190 (111 full-time, 66% with terminal degrees, 79 part-time); student-undergrad faculty ratio is 15:1. *Library Holdings:* 129,000 books, 640 periodicals, 3,700 records, tapes, and CDs; on-line access to libraries at other institutions. *Computers:* PCs for student use in computer center, dorms. Student computer-purchase plan available. Access to campuswide network, Internet from computer center, dorms. *Service:* library catalog search and reservation.

UNDERGRADUATE PROFILE 2,013 students: 59% women, 6% part-time, 67% state residents, 67% live on campus, 10% transferred in, 1% international, 1% Native American, 1% Hispanic, 1% African American, 2% Asian American. *Retention:* 74% of 1992 freshmen returned. *Graduation:* 50% graduate in 4 years.

FRESHMEN 425 total. 919 applied, 82% were accepted, 56% of whom enrolled. 27% from top 10% of their high school class, 86% from top half.

ACADEMIC PROGRAM Core. Calendar: 4-1-4. Services for LD students, advanced placement, self-designed majors, summer session for credit, part-time degree program (daytime), adult/continuing education programs, internships. Off-campus study at members of the Christian College Consortium, Au Sable Trails Institute of Environmental Studies. ROTC: Army (c), Naval (c), Air Force (c). Unusual degree programs: 3-2 engineering with Washington University, Case Western Reserve University, University of Minnesota.

STUDY-ABROAD SITES England, Germany, Israel, Sweden.

MAJORS Accounting, adult and continuing education, art education, art/fine arts, art history, biblical studies, biology/biological sciences, business administration/commerce/management, chemistry, child care/child and family studies, communication, computer science, creative writing, (pre)dentistry sequence, early childhood education, economics, education, elementary education, (pre)engineering sequence, English, finance/banking, health education, history, international relations, international studies, (pre)law sequence, liberal arts/general studies, literature, management information systems, mathematics, (pre)medicine sequence, ministries, molecular biology, music, music education, nursing, philosophy, physical education, physics, political science/government, psychology, sacred music, science education, secondary education, social work, Spanish, speech/rhetoric/public address/debate, studio art, theater arts/drama, theology, (pre)veterinary medicine sequence.

EXPENSES FOR 1994–95 *Application fee:* $20. Comprehensive fee of $15,920 includes full-time tuition ($11,700) and college room and board ($4220). College room only: $2220. Part-time tuition: $420 per credit hour.

FINANCIAL AID *College-administered aid for undergraduates 1993–94:* need-based scholarships, non-need scholarships, short-term loans, low-interest long-term loans from external sources, FSEOG, Federal Work-Study, part-time jobs. *Application forms required:* IRS, institutional, FAFSA; required for some: state. *Priority deadline:* 4/15. *Payment plan:* installment. *Waivers:* full or partial for employees or children of employees and senior citizens.

COLLEGE LIFE Orientation program (5 days, no cost, parents included). Theater productions, music performance groups, Bible studies, chapel, student newspaper, radio station. *Student services:* health clinic, personal-psychological counseling, shuttle bus. *Safety:* 24-hour emergency response devices, student patrols, late-night transport-escort service, controlled dormitory access, room security.

ATHLETICS Member NCAA. All Division III. *Intercollegiate:* baseball M, basketball M/W, cross-country running M/W, football M, golf M, ice hockey M, soccer M/W, softball W, tennis M/W, track and field M/W, volleyball W. *Intramural:* basketball, football, golf, racquetball, table tennis (Ping-Pong), tennis, track and field, volleyball, weight lifting.

APPLYING/FRESHMEN *Options:* early entrance, deferred entrance, midyear entrance. *Required:* essay, school transcript, 2 recommendations, SAT I or ACT, TOEFL for international students, PSAT. *Recommended:* 3 years of high school math and science, interview. *Required for some:* interview. Test scores used for admission. *Application deadline:* rolling.

APPLYING/TRANSFER *Required:* essay, standardized test scores, 2 recommendations, college transcript, minimum 2.0 GPA. *Recommended:* interview. *Required for some:* high school transcript, interview. *Entrance level:* moderately difficult. *Application deadline:* rolling.

CONTACT John Lassen, Director of Admissions, Bethel College, 3900 Bethel Drive, St. Paul, MN 55112-6999; 612-638-6242 or toll-free 800-255-8706 Ext. 6242.

BIOLA UNIVERSITY
La Mirada, California

> **SPECIAL NOTE FROM THE UNIVERSITY** Biola University's suburban campus is just a short drive from the beach, the mountains, Disneyland, Hollywood, cultural events in Los Angeles, and many other Southern California attractions. Of the 88 members of the Christian College Coalition, which requires faculty members to be Christian, only 14 of them require that their students be Christian. Of those, Biola is one of 2 ranked by the Carnegie Commission as a Level II degree-granting institution, and it is the only one given *U.S. News & World Report's* highest ranking, that of a National University. Selected to the John Templeton Foundation Honor Roll for Character Building Colleges for 1993–94, Biola offers a solid biblical foundation, with 30 required units of Bible. Students may choose from among 123 programs and enjoy close contact with a highly qualified and caring staff.

Total Enrollment: 2,865

UG Enrollment: 2,001 (61% W)

Application Deadline: 6/1

Entrance: moderately difficult

Tuition & Fees: $11,954

Room & Board: $4800

SAT≥500: 29% V, 54% M **ACT≥21:** 65%

Denominational Affiliation: nondenominational

GENERAL INFORMATION Independent-religious coed institution. Awards bachelor's, master's, doctorate degrees. Founded 1908. *Setting:* 95-acre suburban campus with easy access to Los Angeles. *Undergraduate faculty:* 219 (126 full-time, 65% with terminal degrees, 93 part-time); student-undergrad faculty ratio is 17:1. *Library Holdings:* 257,000 books, 328,604 microform titles, 1,100 periodicals, 2 on-line bibliographic services, 9 CD-ROMs, 7,500 records, tapes, and CDs. *Computers:* 100 terminals, PCs for student use in computer center, computer labs. Student computer-purchase plan available. Access to campuswide network, BITNET, Internet from computer center, computer labs, dorms, student rooms. *Services:* e-mail, file transfer, mainframe access, database computer-search services.

UNDERGRADUATE PROFILE 2,001 students: 61% women, 6% part-time, 70% state residents, 65% live on campus, 30% transferred in, 80% have need-based financial aid, 70% have non-need-based financial aid, 32% have campus jobs, 7% international, 1% Native American, 7% Hispanic, 3% African American, 14% Asian American. *Retention:* 78% of 1992 freshmen returned. *Graduation:* 51% graduate in 4 years.

FRESHMEN 459 total. 1,118 applied, 80% were accepted, 51% of whom enrolled.

ACADEMIC PROGRAM Core, honor code. Calendar: 4-1-4. Average class size 25 in required courses. Academic remediation for entering students, English as a second language program offered during academic year, services for LD students, advanced placement, accelerated degree program, tutorials, summer session for credit, part-time degree program (daytime), adult/continuing education programs, co-op programs and internships. More than half of graduate courses open to undergraduate students. Off-campus study at Christian College Coalition, Au Sable Institute of Environmental Studies, University of Southern California, California State University–Long Beach, University of California–Los Angeles. ROTC: Army (c), Naval (c), Air Force (c). Unusual degree programs: 3-2 engineering with University of Southern California, biblical and theological studies, 5-year BS in nursing.

STUDY-ABROAD SITES Costa Rica, England, Israel, Japan, Korea, Russia.

MAJORS Accounting, adult and continuing education, anthropology, applied art, applied mathematics, art education, art/fine arts, art therapy, biblical studies, bilingual/bicultural education, biochemistry, biology/biological sciences, broadcasting, business administration/commerce/management, business economics, business education, chemistry, commercial art, communication, computer information systems, computer programming, computer science, economics, education, elementary education, English, European studies, film studies, Greek, history, humanities, information science, international studies, journalism, (pre)law sequence, liberal arts/general studies, literature, management information systems, marketing/retailing/merchandising, mathematics, (pre)medicine sequence, middle school education, ministries, modern languages, music, music education, nursing, painting/drawing, pastoral studies, philosophy, physical education, physical sciences, physics, piano/organ, psychology, public relations, radio and television studies, religious education, religious studies, science education, secondary education, social science, sociology, Spanish, speech pathology and audiology, speech therapy, studio art, teaching English as a second language, theater arts/drama, theology, voice.

EXPENSES FOR 1994–95 *Application fee:* $35. Comprehensive fee of $16,754 includes full-time tuition ($11,954) and college room and board ($4800). Part-time tuition: $499 per unit.

FINANCIAL AID *College-administered aid for undergraduates 1993–94:* 488 need-based scholarships (average $2800), 1,049 non-need scholarships (average $2945), low-interest long-term loans from college funds (average $1660), loans from external sources (average $2906), FSEOG, Federal Work-Study, 500 part-time jobs. Average total aid for freshmen: $9737 (aid provided to 100% of those qualified). *Application forms required:* FAF, FAFSA; required for some: state. *Priority deadline:* 3/2. *Payment plan:* installment. *Waivers:* full or partial for employees or children of employees.

COLLEGE LIFE Orientation program (5 days, no cost). Drama-theater group, choral group, student-run newspaper, radio station. *Social organizations:* 25 open to all. *Major annual events:* BAB Week (Betty Asks Bob), Celebrate the Son, Missions Conference. *Student services:* legal services, health clinic, personal-psychological counseling. *Safety:* 24-hour emergency response devices and patrols, late-night transport-escort service, controlled dormitory access, room security, access gates to roads through the middle of campus.

ATHLETICS Member NAIA. *Intercollegiate:* baseball M(s), basketball M(s)/W(s), cross-country running M(s)/W(s), soccer M(s)/W(s), softball W(s), tennis M(s)/W(s), track and field M(s)/W(s), volleyball W(s). *Intramural:* basketball, cross-country running, football, soccer, softball, tennis, track and field, volleyball. *Contact:* Physical Education Department, 310-903-4886.

APPLYING/FRESHMEN *Options:* early entrance, deferred entrance, midyear entrance. *Required:* essay, school transcript, 2 recommendations, interview, SAT I or ACT, TOEFL for international students. *Recommended:* minimum 2.8 GPA, 3 years of high school math and science, some high school foreign language. Test scores used for admission. *Application deadline:* 6/1.

APPLYING/TRANSFER *Required:* essay, high school transcript, 2 recommendations, interview, college transcript, minimum 2.0 GPA. *Recommended:* 3 years of high school math and science, some high school foreign language, minimum 3.0 GPA. *Required for some:* standardized test scores. *Entrance level:* moderately difficult. *Application deadline:* 6/1.

CONTACT Mr. Greg Vaughan, Director Enrollment Management, Biola University, 13800 Biola Avenue, La Mirada, CA 90639; 310-903-4752.

BLUFFTON COLLEGE
Bluffton, Ohio

> **SPECIAL NOTE FROM THE COLLEGE** Unique to Bluffton College is a seriously Mennonite peace church orientation with genuine openness to students of all racial, ethnic, and denominational backgrounds, including approximately 40 international students. Within this widely diverse and deeply caring Christian community, faculty and staff members and students seek to apply the insights of both the academic disciplines and the Bible to the problems of offender ministries, racial discrimination, oppression and poverty, and violence and war. Academic integrity, broad social concern, a caring community, spiritual nurturing, and a beautiful natural environment are all distinguishing characteristics of Bluffton.

Total Enrollment: 841 (all UG)

Women: 53%

Application Deadline: 8/15

Entrance: moderately difficult

Tuition & Fees: $9900

Room & Board: $3990

SAT≥500: N/R   **ACT≥21:** 65%

Denominational Affiliation: Mennonite

GENERAL INFORMATION Independent-religious 4-year coed institution. Awards bachelor's degrees. Founded 1899. *Setting:* 65-acre small-town campus with easy access to Toledo. *Faculty:* 81 (45 full-time, 69% with terminal degrees, 36 part-time); student-undergrad faculty ratio is 15:1. *Library Holdings:* 130,000 books, 65,000 microform titles, 580 periodicals, 650 records, tapes, and CDs. *Computers:* 52 terminals, PCs for student use in computer center, computer labs.

UNDERGRADUATE PROFILE 841 students from 14 states and territories, 18 other countries. 53% women, 10% part-time, 88% state residents, 15% transferred in, 72% have campus jobs, 4% international, 10% 25 or older, 1% Native American, 1% Hispanic, 3% African American, 1% Asian American. *Retention:* 72% of 1992 freshmen returned. *Graduation:* 47% graduate in 4 years.

FRESHMEN 209 total. 568 applied, 90% were accepted, 41% of whom enrolled. 20% from top 10% of their high school class, 50% from top quarter, 76% from top half.

ACADEMIC PROGRAM Core, interdisciplinary curriculum, honor code. Calendar: quarters. 445 courses offered in 1993–94; average class size 17 in required courses. Academic remediation for entering students, advanced placement, accelerated degree program, self-designed majors, Freshman Honors College, tutorials, honors program, summer session for credit, part-time degree program (daytime), adult/continuing education programs, internships. Off-campus study at Christian College Coalition.

STUDY-ABROAD SITES Costa Rica, Guatemala, Ireland, Mexico, Nicaragua, Poland, Russia.

MAJORS Accounting, art education, art/fine arts, biology/biological sciences, business administration/commerce/management, business economics, business education, chemistry, child care/child and family studies, child psychology/child development, commercial art, communication, computer science, criminal justice, dietetics, early childhood education, economics, education, elementary education, English, fashion design and technology, fashion merchandising, health education, history, home economics, home economics education, humanities, (pre)law sequence, liberal arts/general studies, mathematics, medical technology, (pre)medicine sequence, ministries, music, music education, nutrition, peace studies, philosophy, physical education, physical fitness/exercise science, physics, political science/government, psychology, recreation and leisure services, religious studies, retail management, secondary education, social science, social work, sociology, Spanish, special education, speech/rhetoric/public address/debate, sports administration, textiles and clothing.

ESTIMATED EXPENSES FOR 1994–95 *Application fee:* $20. Comprehensive fee of $13,890 includes full-time tuition ($9900) and college room and board ($3990). College room only: $1617. Part-time tuition: $220 per quarter hour.

FINANCIAL AID *College-administered aid for undergraduates 1993–94:* need-based scholarships, non-need scholarships, low-interest long-term loans from external sources (average $2760), FSEOG, Federal Work-Study, 547 part-time jobs. Average total aid for freshmen: $9943 (aid provided to 100% of those qualified). *Application forms required:* FAF, FAFSA; required for some: IRS, state. *Priority deadline:* 6/1. *Payment plan:* installment. *Waivers:* full or partial for employees or children of employees. Must reapply each year.

COLLEGE LIFE Orientation program (2 days, no cost, parents included). Drama-theater group, choral group, student-run newspaper, radio station. *Social organizations:* 30 open to all. *Most popular organizations:* Brothers and Sisters in Christ, Campus Government, Student Union Board, music groups/chorale. *Major annual events:* Homecoming, Christian Emphasis Week, May Day. *Student services:* health clinic, personal-psychological counseling. *Safety:* late-night transport-escort service.

ATHLETICS Member NCAA. All Division III. *Intercollegiate:* baseball M, basketball M/W, cross-country running M/W, football M, golf M, soccer M/W, softball W, tennis M/W, track and field M/W, volleyball W. *Intramural:* archery, badminton, basketball, bowling, football, golf, racquetball, soccer, table tennis (Ping-Pong), tennis, track and field, volleyball, weight lifting. *Contact:* Mr. Carlin B. Carpenter, Director of Athletics, 419-358-3226; Ms. Kim Fischer, Assistant Director of Athletics, 419-358-3226.

APPLYING/FRESHMEN *Options:* early entrance, deferred entrance, midyear entrance. *Required:* school transcript, 2 recommendations, rank in upper 50% of high school class or minimum 2.3 GPA, SAT I or ACT, TOEFL for international students. *Recommended:* 3 years of high school math and science, 3 years of high school foreign language, interview. *Required for some:* essay. Test scores used for admission. *Application deadline:* 8/15.

APPLYING/TRANSFER *Required:* high school transcript, 2 recommendations, college transcript, minimum 2.0 GPA. *Recommended:* 3 years of high school math and science, some high school foreign language, interview. *Required for some:* essay, standardized test scores. *Entrance level:* moderately difficult. *Application deadline:* rolling.

CONTACT Mr. Michael Hieronimus, Dean of Admissions, Bluffton College, 280 West College Avenue, Bluffton, OH 45817-1196; 419-358-3257 or toll-free 800-488-3257.

BRYAN COLLEGE
Dayton, Tennessee

BRYAN
COLLEGE

> **SPECIAL NOTE FROM THE COLLEGE** Bryan's motto, "Christ Above All," clarifies its priorities as a Christian liberal arts college. This is a lofty goal, but one that challenges the Bryan community to be exceptional and dynamic in faith and practice. The liberal arts curriculum exposes students to a broad scope of knowledge as well as key skills of communication, interpersonal relations, and critical thinking skills. A major thrust of a Bryan education is biblical world view. Students investigate various world view philosophies, then scrutinize them under the lens of Scripture. The scenic 120-acre campus is located 40 miles north of Chattanooga.

Total Enrollment: 417 (all UG)

Women: 52%

Application Deadline: rolling

Entrance: moderately difficult

Tuition & Fees: $7690

Room & Board: $3950

SAT≥500: 31% V, 41% M   **ACT≥21:** 74%

Denominational Affiliation: interdenominational

GENERAL INFORMATION Independent-religious 4-year coed institution. Awards associate, bachelor's degrees. Founded 1930. *Setting:* 120-acre small-town campus. *Faculty:* 41 (26 full-time, 15 part-time); student-undergrad faculty ratio is 14:1. *Library Holdings:* 69,088 books, 13,484 microform titles, 400 periodicals, 14 on-line bibliographic services, 12 CD-ROMs, 3,015 records, tapes, and CDs. *Computers:* 46 terminals, PCs for student use in computer center, library, dorms. Access to campuswide network from computer center, library, dorms; on-line documentation available. *Services:* e-mail, database computer-search services.

UNDERGRADUATE PROFILE 417 students from 33 states and territories, 10 other countries. 52% women, 1% part-time, 35% state residents, 88% live on campus, 9% transferred in, 3% international, 4% 25 or older, 0% Native American, 1% Hispanic, 2% African American, 1% Asian American. *Retention:* 67% of 1992 freshmen returned. *Graduation:* 43% graduate in 4 years.

FRESHMEN 99 total. 329 applied, 74% were accepted, 41% of whom enrolled.

ACADEMIC PROGRAM Core, liberal arts curriculum, honor code. Calendar: semesters. 301 courses offered in 1993–94; average class size 20 in required courses. Academic remediation for entering students, advanced placement, self-designed majors, tutorials, summer session for credit, part-time degree program (daytime, evenings), adult/continuing education programs, internships.

MAJORS Accounting, biblical studies, biology/biological sciences, business administration/commerce/management, communication, computer science, elementary education, English, history, liberal arts/general studies, mathematics, music, music business, music education, psychology, religious education, science education.

EXPENSES FOR 1993–94 *Application fee:* $20. Comprehensive fee of $11,640 includes full-time tuition ($7300), mandatory fees ($390), and college room and board ($3950). College room only: $1750. Part-time tuition: $310 per semester hour.

FINANCIAL AID *College-administered aid for undergraduates 1993–94:* 315 need-based scholarships (average $1150), 270 non-need scholarships (average $1700), short-term loans (average $500), low-interest long-term loans from external sources (average $3500), FSEOG, Federal Work-Study, 30 part-time jobs. Average total aid for freshmen: $8436, meeting 73% of need (aid provided to 100% of those qualified). *Application forms required:* institutional, FAFSA; required for some: IRS, state; accepted: FFS, FAF, FAFSA. *Priority deadline:* 5/1. *Payment plan:* installment. *Waivers:* full or partial for employees or children of employees and senior citizens. *Notification:* continuous. *Average indebtedness of graduates:* $7500.

COLLEGE LIFE Orientation program (2 days, no cost, parents included). Drama-theater group, choral group, student-run newspaper. *Social organizations:* 7 open to all, with 80% participating. *Most popular organizations:* Practical Christian Involvement, Student Senate, Student Union, Hilltop Players, Chorale. *Major annual events:* Homecoming, Christmas Banquet, Junior/Senior Banquet. *Student services:* personal-psychological counseling.

ATHLETICS Member NAIA. *Intercollegiate:* basketball M(s)/W(s), cross-country running M(s)/W(s), soccer M(s), volleyball W(s). *Intramural:* basketball, football, soccer, tennis, track and field, volleyball. *Contact:* Dr. Sandford Zensen, Director of Athletics, 615-775-7255.

APPLYING/FRESHMEN *Options:* early entrance, deferred entrance. *Required:* school transcript, 3 recommendations, SAT I or ACT, TOEFL for international students. *Required for some:* interview. Test scores used for counseling/placement. *Application deadline:* rolling.

APPLYING/TRANSFER *Required:* high school transcript, 3 recommendations, college transcript, minimum 2.0 GPA. *Required for some:* interview. *Entrance level:* moderately difficult. *Application deadline:* rolling.

CONTACT Mr. Thomas A. Shaw, Director of Admissions, Bryan College, Box 7000, Dayton, TN 37321; 615-775-2041 or toll-free 800-277-9522.

California Baptist College
Riverside, California

SPECIAL NOTE FROM THE COLLEGE California Baptist College is located in Southern California's Inland Empire, which is one of the most rapidly growing areas in the nation. Cal Baptist emphasizes a life of assisting others, whether in service-oriented careers such as counseling and teaching or in business, which is based on biblical principles. The College is diverse in its ethnicity, denominational affiliation, and the ages of its students, providing students with a global outlook in all areas of campus life. Cal Baptist, with offerings of 17 undergraduate majors and a master's degree in marriage, family, and child counseling, provides students with a diverse and challenging academic program and the opportunity for active participation in experiential learning and development. At California Baptist College, knowledge is enhanced through personal experience.

Total Enrollment: 870
UG Enrollment: 830 (49% W)
Application Deadline: rolling
Entrance: minimally difficult
Tuition & Fees: $8236
Room & Board: $4494
Denominational Affiliation: Southern Baptist

GENERAL INFORMATION Independent-religious comprehensive coed institution. Awards bachelor's, master's degrees. Founded 1950. *Setting:* 60-acre suburban campus with easy access to Los Angeles. *Undergraduate faculty:* 91 (47 full-time, 64% with terminal degrees, 44 part-time); student-undergrad faculty ratio is 12:1. *Library Holdings:* 70,000 books, 8,200 microform titles, 400 periodicals, 2,500 records, tapes, and CDs. *Computers:* 60 terminals, PCs for student use in computer center, library, business administration department.

UNDERGRADUATE PROFILE 830 students from 30 states and territories, 21 other countries. 49% women, 16% part-time, 69% state residents, 38% transferred in, 7% international, 1% Native American, 5% Hispanic, 7% African American, 2% Asian American. *Retention:* 64% of 1992 freshmen returned.

FRESHMEN 181 total.

ACADEMIC PROGRAM Core, honor code. Calendar: 4-1-4. Academic remediation for entering students, English as a second language program offered during academic year and summer, advanced placement, accelerated degree program, honors program, summer session for credit, part-time degree program (daytime, evenings), internships. ROTC: Air Force (c).

STUDY-ABROAD SITES China, Costa Rica, Russia.

MAJORS Art/fine arts, behavioral sciences, biology/biological sciences, business administration/commerce/management, communication, education, elementary education, English, history, liberal studies/general studies, music, physical education, physical sciences, political science/government, psychology, public administration, recreation and leisure services, religious studies, secondary education, social science, sociology, Spanish, theater arts/drama.

EXPENSES FOR 1994–95 *Application fee:* $30. Comprehensive fee of $12,730 includes full-time tuition ($7800), mandatory fees ($436), and college room and board ($4494). Part-time tuition: $300 per unit. Part-time mandatory fees per term range from $52 to $190.

FINANCIAL AID *College-administered aid for undergraduates 1993–94:* 540 need-based scholarships, 300 non-need scholarships (average $2405), low-interest long-term loans from external sources (average $2625), FSEOG, Federal Work-Study, 76 part-time jobs. Average total aid for freshmen: $7376, meeting 80% of need (aid provided to 100% of those qualified). *Application forms required:* FAF, IRS, institutional, FAFSA; required for some: state. *Priority deadline:* 4/1. *Payment plans:* installment, deferred payment. *Waivers:* full or partial for employees or children of employees. *Notification:* continuous.

COLLEGE LIFE Orientation program (1 week, $100, parents included). Drama-theater group, choral group, student-run newspaper and yearbook. *Student services:* health clinic, personal-psychological counseling. *Safety:* student patrols, late-night transport-escort service, controlled dormitory access.

ATHLETICS Member NAIA. *Intercollegiate:* baseball M(s), basketball M(s)/W(s), soccer M(s)/W(s), softball W(s), tennis M(s)/W(s), volleyball W(s). *Intramural:* baseball, basketball, football, golf, softball, volleyball. *Contact:* Mr. Jerry King, Athletic Director, 909-689-5771 Ext. 381.

APPLYING/FRESHMEN *Option:* deferred entrance. *Required:* essay, school transcript, 2 recommendations, SAT I or ACT, TOEFL for international students. *Recommended:* 3 years of high school math and science, some high school foreign language, SAT II: Subject Tests, SAT II: Writing Test. Test scores used for admission and counseling/placement. *Application deadline:* rolling.

APPLYING/TRANSFER *Required:* 2 recommendations, college transcript, minimum 2.0 GPA. *Required for some:* standardized test scores, high school transcript. *Application deadline:* rolling.

CONTACT Mr. Kent Dacus, Director of Admissions, California Baptist College, 8432 Magnolia Avenue, Riverside, CA 92504; 909-689-5771 or toll-free 800-782-3382.

CALVIN COLLEGE
Grand Rapids, Michigan

SPECIAL NOTE FROM THE COLLEGE Calvin College is one of the largest, oldest, and most respected of the Coalition schools. Calvin's modern 370-acre campus provides the setting for students and faculty members to explore a broad range of majors and programs. While awarding over half of its degrees in accredited professional programs, Calvin remains committed to a liberal arts approach to learning. Eager to become a partner with students in their Christian maturation, the College encourages students to make faithful and responsible decisions about how they will use their time and talents—without imposing an excessive list of rules and regulations.

Total Enrollment: 3,730

UG Enrollment: 3,537 (55% W)

Application Deadline: rolling

Entrance: moderately difficult

Tuition & Fees: $10,230

Room & Board: $3710

SAT≥500: 55% V, 73% M   **ACT≥21:** 83%

Denominational Affiliation: Christian Reformed Church

GENERAL INFORMATION Independent-religious comprehensive coed institution. Awards bachelor's, master's degrees. Founded 1876. *Setting:* 370-acre suburban campus. *Faculty:* 277 (220 full-time, 83% with terminal degrees, 57 part-time); student-undergrad faculty ratio is 16:1. *Library Holdings:* 635,000 books, 476,000 microform titles, 2,800 periodicals, 17,000 records, tapes, and CDs; on-line access to libraries at other institutions. *Computers:* 291 terminals, PCs for student use in computer center, computer labs, research center, library, student center, dorms. Student computer-purchase plan available. Access to campuswide network, BITNET, Internet from computer center, computer labs, library, dorms; on-line documentation available. *Services:* e-mail, file transfer, mainframe access, library catalog search and reservation.

UNDERGRADUATE PROFILE 3,537 students from 54 states and territories, 31 other countries. 55% women, 4% part-time, 53% state residents, 60% live on campus, 4% transferred in, 11% international, 5% 25 or older, 1% Native American, 1% Hispanic, 1% African American, 3% Asian American. *Retention:* 83% of 1992 freshmen returned. *Graduation:* 45% graduate in 4 years.

FRESHMEN 913 total. 1,784 applied, 85% were accepted, 60% of whom enrolled. 29% from top 10% of their high school class, 56% from top quarter, 84% from top half. 20 National Merit Scholarship Finalists, 20 National Merit Scholars.

ACADEMIC PROGRAM Core, Christ-centered liberal arts curriculum. Calendar: 4-1-4. 1,250 courses offered in 1993–94; average class size 24 in required courses. Academic remediation for entering students, English as a second language program offered during academic year, services for LD students, advanced placement, self-designed majors, tutorials, Honors Program, summer session for credit, part-time degree program (daytime), adult/continuing education programs, co-op programs and internships. Off-campus study at Central College, Trinity Christian College. Unusual degree programs: 3-2 communication disorders with Michigan State University, occupational therapy with Washington University.

STUDY-ABROAD SITES England, Germany, the Netherlands, Nigeria, Spain.

MAJORS Accounting, art education, art/fine arts, art history, biblical studies, bilingual/bicultural education, biochemistry, biology/biological sciences, business administration/commerce/management, business economics, chemistry, civil engineering, classics, communication, computer science, criminal justice, (pre)dentistry, early childhood education, economics, education, electrical engineering, elementary education, engineering, English, environmental sciences, European studies, film studies, French, geography, geology, German, Germanic languages and literature, Greek, history, humanities, interdisciplinary studies, Japanese, journalism, Latin, (pre)law, liberal arts/general studies, linguistics, literature, mathematics, mechanical engineering, medical technology, (pre)medicine, music, musical instrument technology, music education, music history, music therapy, natural sciences, nursing, occupational therapy, philosophy, physical education, physical sciences, physics, political science/government, psychology, recreation and leisure services, religious education, religious studies, rhetoric and communications, sacred music, science, science education, secondary education, social science, social work, sociology, Spanish, special education, speech pathology and audiology, sports medicine, studio art, telecommunications, theater arts/drama, theology, (pre)veterinary medicine, voice.

EXPENSES FOR 1994–95 *Application fee:* $25. Comprehensive fee of $13,940 includes full-time tuition ($10,230) and college room and board ($3710). Part-time tuition: $1330 per course.

FINANCIAL AID *College-administered aid for undergraduates 1993–94:* 2,600 need-based scholarships (average $2260), 3,900 non-need scholarships (average $935), short-term loans (average $100), low-interest long-term loans from college funds (average $2500), loans from external sources (average $3250), FSEOG, Federal Work-Study, 750 part-time jobs. Average total aid for freshmen: $8054, meeting 95% of need (aid provided to 100% of those qualified). *Application forms required:* institutional, FAFSA; required for some: IRS; accepted: FAF. *Priority deadline:* 2/15. *Payment plans:* tuition prepayment, installment. *Waivers:* full or partial for employees or children of employees. *Notification:* 3/31. *Average indebtedness of graduates:* $9500.

COLLEGE LIFE Orientation program (3 days, no cost, parents included). Drama-theater group, choral group, student-run newspaper, radio station. *Social organizations:* 32 open to all. *Major annual events:* Homecoming, Variety Night. *Student services:* health clinic, personal-psychological counseling. *Safety:* 24-hour patrols, late-night transport-escort service, crime prevention programs.

ATHLETICS Member NCAA. All Division III. *Intercollegiate:* baseball M, basketball M/W, cross-country running M/W, golf M/W, ice hockey M(c), lacrosse M(c), soccer M/W, softball W, swimming and diving M/W, tennis M/W, track and field M/W, volleyball M(c)/W. *Intramural:* badminton, basketball, cross-country running, football, golf, ice hockey, racquetball, soccer, softball, swimming and diving, table tennis (Ping-Pong), tennis, track and field, volleyball, water polo, weight lifting. *Contact:* Athletic Director, 616-957-6020 (men); 616-957-6223 (women).

APPLYING/FRESHMEN *Options:* early entrance, deferred entrance, midyear entrance. *Required:* school transcript, 1 recommendation, ACT, TOEFL for international students. *Recommended:* 3 years of high school math and science, 2 years of high school foreign language. Test scores used for admission and counseling/placement. *Application deadline:* rolling.

APPLYING/TRANSFER *Required:* standardized test scores, high school transcript, 1 recommendation, college transcript, minimum 2.0 GPA, minimum 2.5 GPA from community college. *Recommended:* 3 years of high school math and science. *Entrance level:* moderately difficult. *Application deadline:* rolling.

CONTACT Mr. Thomas E. McWhertor, Director of Admissions, Calvin College, 3201 Burton Street, SE, Grand Rapids, MI 49546; 616-957-6106 or toll-free 800-688-0122.

CAMPBELLSVILLE COLLEGE
Campbellsville, Kentucky

> **SPECIAL NOTE FROM THE COLLEGE** Campbellsville College is a private, comprehensive, 4-year coeducational college undergirded by a strong liberal arts component. Affiliated with the Kentucky Baptist Convention, Campbellsville is open to students of all denominations. The 50-acre campus is situated precisely in the center of Kentucky and is 1½ hours from Louisville and Lexington and just 2 hours from Nashville. Enrollment has soared more than 73% in just the last 6 years. Programs recently added include the Honors Program, Master of Arts in Education, Tiger Marching Band, women's volleyball, men's soccer, swimming, and much more. Summer international studies opportunities are also available.

Total Enrollment: 1,163
UG Enrollment: 1,119 (51% W)
Application Deadline: rolling
Entrance: moderately difficult
Tuition & Fees: $6060
Room & Board: $3070
Denominational Affiliation: Kentucky Baptist (SBC)

GENERAL INFORMATION Independent-religious comprehensive coed institution. Awards associate, bachelor's, master's degrees. Founded 1906. *Setting:* 50-acre small-town campus. *Faculty:* 73 (47 full-time, 69% with terminal degrees, 26 part-time); student-undergrad faculty ratio is 15:1. *Library Holdings:* 105,000 books, 500 microform titles, 465 periodicals, 4,000 records, tapes, and CDs. *Computers:* 90 terminals, PCs for student use in computer center, classrooms, library.

UNDERGRADUATE PROFILE 1,119 students from 22 states and territories, 13 other countries. 51% women, 19% part-time, 91% state residents, 8% transferred in, 1% international, 27% 25 or older, 1% Native American, 1% Hispanic, 8% African American, 1% Asian American. *Retention:* 64% of 1992 freshmen returned. *Graduation:* 46% graduate in 4 years.

FRESHMEN 289 total. 848 applied, 69% were accepted, 49% of whom enrolled. 28% from top 10% of their high school class, 54% from top quarter, 85% from top half. 20 class presidents, 12 valedictorians, 50 student government officers, 10 yearbook editors, 15 high school newspaper editors.

ACADEMIC PROGRAM Core. Calendar: semesters. Average class size 18 in required courses. Academic remediation for entering students, advanced placement, accelerated degree program, honors program, summer session for credit, part-time degree program (daytime, evenings), adult/continuing education programs, internships. Unusual degree programs: 3-2 engineering with University of Kentucky, nursing with Eastern Kentucky University.

STUDY-ABROAD SITES England, France, Israel.

MAJORS Accounting, art education, arts/fine arts, biblical studies, biology/biological sciences, business administration/commerce/management,business economics, business education, chemistry, church music, communications, computer information systems, criminal justice, data processing, (pre)dentistry sequence, econom-ics, elementary education, (pre)engineering sequence, English, health education, history, (pre)law sequence, mathematics, medical technology, (pre)medicine sequence, ministries, music, music education, (pre)nursing sequence, (pre)optometry sequence, pastoral studies, (pre)pharmacy sequence, physical education, (pre)physical therapy sequence, piano/organ, political science/government, psychology, recreation, religious education, religious studies, science education, secondary education, secretarial studies,/office management, social work, sociology, (pre)veterinary medicine sequence, voice.

EXPENSES FOR 1994–95 *Application fee:* $10. Comprehensive fee of $9130 includes full-time tuition ($6060) and college room and board ($3070). Part-time tuition: $238 per credit.

FINANCIAL AID *College-administered aid for undergraduates 1993–94:* 40 need-based scholarships (average $500), 300 non-need scholarships (average $1300), short-term loans (average $800), low-interest long-term loans from college funds (average $1000), loans from external sources (average $2500), FSEOG, Federal Work-Study, 20 part-time jobs. *Application forms required:* FAF, institutional; required for some: IRS; accepted: FAFSA. *Priority deadline:* 4/15. *Payment plans:* installment, deferred payment. *Waivers:* full or partial for employees or children of employees and senior citizens.

COLLEGE LIFE Drama-theater group, choral group, marching band, student-run newspaper, television station. *Student services:* health clinic, personal-psychological counseling.

ATHLETICS Member NAIA. *Intercollegiate:* baseball M(s), basketball M(s)/W(s), cross-country running M(s)/W(s), football M, golf M(s), soccer M(s), softball W(s), swimming M(s)/W(s), tennis M(s)/W(s), volleyball W. *Intramural:* basketball, football, soccer, table tennis (Ping-Pong), tennis, volleyball, weight lifting. *Contact:* Mr. Don Bishop, Athletic Director, 502-789-5257.

APPLYING/FRESHMEN *Options:* early entrance, deferred entrance. *Required:* school transcript, SAT I or ACT, TOEFL for international students. *Recommended:* essay, 3 years of high school math and science, recommendations, interview. Test scores used for admission. *Application deadline:* rolling. *Notification:* continuous.

APPLYING/TRANSFER *Required:* college transcript, SAT I or ACT, minimum 2.0 GPA. *Recommended:* essay, 3 years of high school math and science, recommendations, interview. *Required for some:* standardized test scores, high school transcript. *Entrance level:* moderately difficult. *Application deadline:* rolling. *Notification:* continuous.

CONTACT Mr. R. Trent Argo, Director of Admissions, Campbellsville College, 200 West College Street, Campbellsville, KY 42718-2799; 502-789-5220 or toll-free 800-264-6014.

CAMPBELL UNIVERSITY
Buies Creek, North Carolina

SPECIAL NOTE FROM THE UNIVERSITY Campbell University is a private liberal arts institution in southeastern North Carolina, born of a vision over 100 years ago—a vision that lives on today. Campbell's curriculum meets individual needs and interests and offers the range of majors that today's students expect from a high-quality institution, including preprofessional and professional studies. A comprehensive financial aid program helps families meet educational costs. The University has adapted to changing times and needs without losing sight of its heritage and mission to provide educational opportunities in a Christian environment.

Total Enrollment: 6,047

UG Enrollment: 5,017 (51% W)

Application Deadline: rolling

Entrance: moderately difficult

Tuition & Fees: $8559

Room & Board: $3080

SAT≥500: 26% V, 42% M   **ACT≥21:** N/R

Denominational Affiliation: Baptist

GENERAL INFORMATION Independent-religious coed institution. Awards associate, bachelor's, master's, first professional degrees. Founded 1887. *Setting:* 850-acre rural campus with easy access to Raleigh. *Faculty:* 302 (134 full-time, 77% with terminal degrees, 168 part-time); student-undergrad faculty ratio is 18:1. *Library Holdings:* 174,900 books, 950,000 microform titles, 995 periodicals, 4,300 records, tapes, and CDs. *Computers:* 60 terminals, PCs for student use in computer center, classrooms.

UNDERGRADUATE PROFILE 5,017 students from 50 states and territories, 37 other countries. 51% women, 10% part-time, 56% state residents, 14% transferred in, 85% have need-based financial aid, 8% international, 17% 25 or older, 1% Native American, 3% Hispanic, 7% African American, 5% Asian American. *Retention:* 87% of 1992 freshmen returned. *Graduation:* 48% graduate in 4 years.

FRESHMEN 610 total. 2,087 applied, 64% were accepted, 46% of whom enrolled. 13% from top 10% of their high school class, 23% from top quarter, 65% from top half.

ACADEMIC PROGRAM Core, honor code. Calendar: semesters. Academic remediation for entering students, advanced placement, accelerated degree program, honors program, summer session for credit, part-time degree program (daytime, evenings, summer), adult/continuing education programs, co-op programs and internships. A few graduate courses open to undergraduate students. Off-campus study at Central Carolina Community College. ROTC: Army. Unusual degree programs: 3-2 business administration, 3-3 law, 2-4 pharmacy.

STUDY-ABROAD SITES France, Mexico, Wales.

MAJORS Accounting, advertising, applied mathematics, art/fine arts, biblical studies, biology/biological sciences, biomedical technologies, broadcasting, business administration/commerce/management, business economics, chemistry, child care/child and family studies, commercial art, communication, computer information systems, computer science, data processing, (pre)dentistry sequence, early childhood education, earth science, economics, education, educational administration, elementary education, (pre)engineering sequence, English, fashion design and technology, fashion merchandising, finance/banking, food services management, French, graphic arts, health education, health science, history, home economics, home economics education, interior design, international business, international studies, journalism, (pre)law sequence, liberal arts/general studies, mathematics, medical technology, (pre)medicine sequence, middle school education, military science, music, music education, natural sciences, pastoral studies, philosophy, physical education, physical fitness/exercise science, physical therapy, physician's assistant studies, piano/organ, political science/government, psychology, public administration, public relations, radio and television studies, religious education, science education, secondary education, social science, social work, Spanish, sports administration, studio art, theater arts/drama, theology, (pre)veterinary medicine sequence, voice.

EXPENSES FOR 1994–95 *Application fee:* $15. Comprehensive fee of $11,639 includes full-time tuition ($8430), mandatory fees ($129), and college room and board ($3080). College room only: $1400. Part-time tuition: $140 per semester hour.

FINANCIAL AID *College-administered aid for undergraduates 1993–94:* 1,771 need-based scholarships (average $6226), 3,594 non-need scholarships (average $1600), low-interest long-term loans from external sources (average $2625), FSEOG, Federal Work-Study, 240 part-time jobs. Average total aid for freshmen: $8485, meeting 85% of need (aid provided to 98% of those qualified). *Application forms required:* institutional, FAFSA; required for some: IRS, state; accepted: FFS, FAF. *Priority deadline:* 3/15. *Payment plan:* installment. *Waivers:* full or partial for employees or children of employees.

COLLEGE LIFE Orientation program (2 days, $25, parents included). Drama-theater group, choral group, student-run newspaper, radio station. *Social organizations:* 40 open to all. *Most popular organizations:* Student Government Association, Baptist Student Union, Young Catholic Adults. *Major annual events:* Homecoming, Springfest, Parents' Day. *Student services:* health clinic, personal-psychological counseling. *Safety:* 24-hour emergency response devices and patrols, late-night transport-escort service.

ATHLETICS Member NCAA. All Division I. *Intercollegiate:* baseball M(s), basketball M(s)/W(s), cross-country running M(s)/W(s), golf M(s)/W(s), soccer M(s)/W(s), softball W(s), tennis M(s)/W(s), track and field M(s)/W(s), volleyball W(s), wrestling M(s). *Intramural:* basketball, football, golf, soccer, softball, swimming and diving, table tennis (Ping-Pong), tennis, track and field, volleyball, wrestling. *Contact:* Mr. Tom Collins, Athletic Director, 910-893-1327.

APPLYING/FRESHMEN *Options:* early entrance, deferred entrance, midyear entrance. *Required:* school transcript, 3 years of high school math and science, SAT I or ACT, TOEFL for international students. *Recommended:* some high school foreign language, recommendations, interview. Test scores used for admission and counseling/placement. *Application deadline:* rolling. *Notification:* continuous.

APPLYING/TRANSFER *Required:* high school transcript, college transcript, minimum 2.0 GPA, good standing at previous institution. *Recommended:* standardized test scores, 3 years of high school math, recommendations, interview. *Required for some:* minimum 3.0 GPA. *Application deadline:* rolling. *Notification:* continuous.

CONTACT Mr. Herbert Kerner, Dean of Admissions, Campbell University, Box 546, Buies Creek, NC 27506; 910-893-1200 Ext. 1320 or toll-free 800-334-4111.

CEDARVILLE COLLEGE
Cedarville, Ohio

SPECIAL NOTE FROM THE COLLEGE Cedarville College's mission is "to offer an education consistent with biblical truth." Commitment and achievement characterize this education. All students and faculty members testify to personal faith in Christ. A Bible minor complements every major. Relevant daily chapels encourage spiritual growth. Over 150 local and worldwide ministries provide avenues for outreach. Cedarville teams consistently finish among top universities in national academic competitions. National, regional, and local employers and graduate schools recruit students who pursue any of 75 academic programs. The College's campuswide computer network ranks among the nation's top 7. Reasonable costs and financial aid make Cedarville affordable.

Total Enrollment: 2,278 (all UG)
Women: 57%
Application Deadline: rolling
Entrance: moderately difficult
Tuition & Fees: $7470
Room & Board: $4410
SAT≥500: 43% V, 59% M   **ACT≥21:** 81%
Denominational Affiliation: Baptist

GENERAL INFORMATION Independent-religious 4-year coed institution. Awards associate, bachelor's degrees. Founded 1887. *Setting:* 105-acre rural campus with easy access to Columbus and Dayton. *Faculty:* 170 (130 full-time, 62% with terminal degrees, 40 part-time); student-undergrad faculty ratio is 17:1. *Library Holdings:* 122,220 books, 1,916 microform titles, 1,030 periodicals, 1 on-line bibliographic service, 15 CD-ROMs. *Computers:* 800 terminals, PCs for student use in computer center, library, dorms, academic buildings. Access to campuswide network, Internet from computer center, library, dorms, academic buildings. *Services:* e-mail, library catalog search and reservation.

UNDERGRADUATE PROFILE 2,278 students from 46 states and territories, 11 other countries. 57% women, 4% part-time, 38% state residents, 4% transferred in, 45% have need-based financial aid, 25% have campus jobs, 1% international, 4% 25 or older, 1% Native American, 1% Hispanic, 1% African American, 1% Asian American. *Retention:* 84% of 1992 freshmen returned. *Graduation:* 49% graduate in 4 years.

FRESHMEN 631 total; 349 from public schools. 1,307 applied, 83% were accepted, 58% of whom enrolled. 25% from top 10% of their high school class, 55% from top quarter, 86% from top half. 6 National Merit Scholarship Finalists, 56 valedictorians.

ACADEMIC PROGRAM Core, honor code. Calendar: quarters. Academic remediation for entering students, advanced placement, accelerated degree program, honors program, summer session for credit, part-time degree program (daytime), internships. ROTC: Army (c), Air Force (c).

STUDY-ABROAD SITE Spain.

MAJORS Accounting, American studies, athletic training, behavioral sciences, biblical studies, biology/biological sciences, broadcasting, business administration/commerce/management, business economics, business education, chemistry, communication, computer information systems, criminal justice, (pre)dentistry sequence, early childhood education, economics, education, electrical engineering, elementary education, engineering mechanics, English, environmental biology, finance/banking, health education, history, international business, international economics, international studies, (pre)law sequence, marketing/retailing/merchandising, mathematics, mechanical engineering, medical technology, (pre)medicine sequence, music, music education, nursing, pastoral studies, physi-cal education, physical fitness/exercise science, political science/government, psychology, public administration, radio and television studies, religious education, sacred music, science, science education, secondary education, secretarial studies/office management, social science, social work, sociology, Spanish, special education, speech/rhetoric/public address/debate, sports administration, technical writing, theater arts/drama, theology, (pre)veterinary medicine sequence, voice.

EXPENSES FOR 1994–95 *Application fee:* $20. Comprehensive fee of $11,880 includes full-time tuition ($7344), mandatory fees ($126), and college room and board ($4410). Part-time tuition: $153 per quarter hour.

FINANCIAL AID *College-administered aid for undergraduates 1993–94:* 594 need-based scholarships (average $983), 1,432 non-need scholarships (average $1043), short-term loans (average $1000), low-interest long-term loans from college funds (average $1200), loans from external sources (average $3170), FSEOG, Federal Work-Study, 499 part-time jobs. Average total aid for freshmen: $6550, meeting 64% of need (aid provided to 95% of those qualified). *Application forms required:* institutional, FAFSA; required for some: IRS. *Priority deadline:* 3/1. *Payment plan:* installment. *Waivers:* full or partial for employees or children of employees and senior citizens.

COLLEGE LIFE Orientation program (3 days, $72, parents included). Drama-theater group, choral group, student-run newspaper, radio station. *Most popular organizations:* Student Government Association, Alpha Chi, Pi Sigma Nu, Alpha Delta Omega, Delta Omega Epsilon. *Major annual events:* Homecoming, Junior/Senior Banquet, Cedar Day. *Student services:* health clinic, personal-psychological counseling. *Safety:* 24-hour emergency response devices and patrols, student patrols, late-night transport-escort service, room security.

ATHLETICS Member NAIA. *Intercollegiate:* baseball M(s), basketball M(s)/W(s), cross-country running M(s)/W(s), golf M(s), soccer M(s), softball W(s), tennis M(s)/W(s), track and field M(s)/W(s), volleyball W(s). *Intramural:* badminton, basketball, bowling, football, golf, racquetball, skiing (downhill), soccer, softball, table tennis (Ping-Pong), tennis, volleyball. *Contact:* Dr. Don Callan, Athletic Director, 513-766-7755.

APPLYING/FRESHMEN *Options:* early entrance, deferred entrance, midyear entrance. *Required:* essay, school transcript, minimum 2.9 GPA, 2 recommendations, SAT I or ACT, TOEFL for international students. *Recommended:* 3 years of high school math and science, 2 years of high school foreign language. *Required for some:* minimum 3.0 GPA, interview. Test scores used for counseling/placement. *Application deadline:* rolling. *Notification:* continuous.

APPLYING/TRANSFER *Required:* essay, high school transcript, 2 recommendations, college transcript, minimum 2.5 GPA. *Recommended:* 2 years of high school foreign language. *Required for some:* standardized test scores, interview. *Entrance level:* moderately difficult. *Application deadline:* rolling. *Notification:* continuous.

CONTACT Mr. Roscoe F. Smith, Associate Director of Admissions, Cedarville College, P.O. Box 601, Cedarville, OH 45314; 513-766-7700 or toll-free 800-CEDARVILLE.

CENTRAL WESLEYAN COLLEGE
Central, South Carolina

SPECIAL NOTE FROM THE COLLEGE Central Wesleyan College is committed to providing a top-quality education from a Christian perspective. The issues of faith are explored in each course of study and practiced in daily life. The faculty's personal dedication and skills enable it to serve students from a wide variety of backgrounds—ranging from those who might be underprepared to National Merit Finalists—by providing the right amount of support and the right amount of challenge. A cooperative program with nearby Clemson University allows Central Wesleyan's students to experience the atmosphere and fellowship of a Christian campus and the academic diversity of a large university. Graduates have distinguished themselves in their careers while maintaining active involvement in service to their communities and churches. An education at Central Wesleyan provides what's needed for a career and for a satisfying and balanced life. The main campus offers a traditional day class format for traditional-age students, while the Leadership Education for Adult Professionals (LEAP) program is offered in several locations throughout the state and is restricted to working adults who are at least 23 years old.

Total Enrollment: 1,372

UG Enrollment: 1,274 (53% W)

Application Deadline: 8/10

Entrance: minimally difficult

Tuition & Fees: $8500

Room & Board: $3080

SAT≥500: 15% V, 29% M   **ACT≥21:** 0%

Denominational Affiliation: The Wesleyan Church

GENERAL INFORMATION Independent-religious comprehensive coed institution. Awards associate, bachelor's, master's degrees. Founded 1906. *Setting:* 230-acre small-town campus. *Undergraduate faculty:* 173 (37 full-time, 62% with terminal degrees, 136 part-time); student-undergrad faculty ratio is 10:1. *Library Holdings:* 75,298 books, 345 microform titles, 390 periodicals, 2,537 records, tapes, and CDs. *Computers:* 50 terminals, PCs for student use in computer center, library, science, writing labs.

UNDERGRADUATE PROFILE 1,274 students (400 traditional) from 16 states and territories, 3 other countries. 53% women, 3% part-time, 80% state residents, 50% transferred in, 1% international, 70% 25 or older, 1% Native American, 1% Hispanic, 18% African American, 1% Asian American. *Retention:* 60% of 1992 freshmen returned. *Graduation:* 51% graduate in 4 years.

FRESHMEN 87 total. 153 applied, 75% were accepted, 76% of whom enrolled. 10% from top 10% of their high school class, 28% from top quarter, 57% from top half.

ACADEMIC PROGRAM Core, interdisciplinary curriculum. Calendar: semesters. 227 courses offered in 1993–94; average class size 25 in required courses. Academic remediation for entering students, services for LD students, advanced placement, accelerated degree program, tutorials, honors program, summer session for credit, part-time degree program (daytime, evenings, summer), internships. Off-campus study at Clemson University, Christian College Coalition, Tri County Technical College. ROTC: Army (c), Air Force (c).

STUDY-ABROAD SITE England.

MAJORS Accounting, biblical studies, biology/biological sciences, business administration/commerce/management, chemistry, criminal justice, early childhood education, education, elementary education, English, Greek, history, liberal arts/general studies, mathematics, medical technology, ministries, music, music education, nursing, pastoral studies, physical education, psychology, religious studies, sacred music, social science, special education, theology.

EXPENSES FOR 1994–95 Comprehensive fee of $11,580 includes full-time tuition ($8300), mandatory fees ($200), and college room and board ($3080). College room only: $1000. Part-time tuition: $280 per hour.

FINANCIAL AID *College-administered aid for undergraduates 1993–94:* need-based scholarships, 345 non-need scholarships (average $2400), low-interest long-term loans from external sources (average $2482), FSEOG, Federal Work-Study, 25 part-time jobs. Average total aid for freshmen: $9650, meeting 90% of need. *Application forms required:* institutional; required for some: IRS, state, FAFSA; accepted: FFS, FAF. *Priority deadline:* 4/15. *Payment plans:* tuition prepayment, installment. *Waivers:* full or partial for employees or children of employees and senior citizens.

COLLEGE LIFE Orientation program (2 days, no cost, parents included). Drama-theater group, choral group, student-run newspaper. *Social organizations:* 10 open to all. *Most popular organizations:* Rotaract, choral groups, Council for Exceptional Children, Science Club, BSU. *Major annual events:* Homecoming, Spiritual Emphasis Week, Missionary Conference. *Student services:* health clinic, career counseling, personal-psychological counseling.

ATHLETICS Member NAIA. *Intercollegiate:* baseball M, basketball M(s)/W(s), golf M(s), soccer M(s), softball W(s), volleyball W(s). *Intramural:* basketball, football, soccer, softball, table tennis (Ping-Pong), tennis, volleyball. *Contact:* Dr. Keith Connor, Athletic Director, 803-639-2453 Ext. 359.

APPLYING/FRESHMEN *Options:* early entrance, deferred entrance. *Required:* school transcript, recommendations, SAT I or ACT, TOEFL for international students. *Required for some:* interview. Test scores used for admission. *Application deadline:* 8/10. *Notification:* continuous.

APPLYING/TRANSFER *Required:* recommendations, college transcript. *Recommended:* minimum 2.0 GPA. *Required for some:* standardized test scores, high school transcript, interview. *Entrance level:* minimally difficult. *Application deadline:* 8/10. *Notification:* continuous.

CONTACT Mr. J. Charles Mealy, Dean of Enrollment Management, Central Wesleyan College, 1 Wesleyan Drive, Central, SC 29630-1020; 800-289-1CWC Ext. 327 (toll-free).

COLORADO CHRISTIAN UNIVERSITY
Lakewood, Colorado

SPECIAL NOTE FROM THE UNIVERSITY Colorado Christian University is located in suburban Denver, one of the most attractive, recreation-centered, major metropolitan regions in the nation. At the foot of the Rockies, the picturesque campus offers students solid academic preparation for opportunities requiring the spiritual, social, and technical skills to compete successfully in today's marketplaces. CCU has established a strong regional reputation for academic quality. Its teacher education, youth ministries, and computer sciences programs are widely recognized, and music and a theater ensemble company provide interested students with excellent opportunities for participation. An NCAA Division II school, CCU stresses achievement and excellence in its athletic programs. Housing is apartment-style living.

Total Enrollment: 2,511
UG Enrollment: 1,688 (59% W)
Application Deadline: rolling
Entrance: moderately difficult
Tuition & Fees: $7270
Room & Board: $3480
Denominational Affiliation: interdenominational

GENERAL INFORMATION Independent-religious comprehensive coed institution. Awards associate, bachelor's, master's degrees. Founded 1914. *Setting:* 28-acre suburban campus with easy access to Denver. *Undergraduate faculty:* 99 (46 full-time, 42% with terminal degrees, 53 part-time); student-undergrad faculty ratio is 21:1. *Library Holdings:* 42,500 books, 25 microform titles, 320 periodicals, 1 on-line bibliographic service, 1,530 records, tapes, and CDs; on-line access to libraries at other institutions. *Computers:* 50 terminals, PCs for student use in computer center, computer labs, library. Access to campuswide network from computer center, computer labs, library; general network orientation available. *Services:* file transfer, mainframe access, library catalog search and reservation.

UNDERGRADUATE PROFILE 1,688 students from 38 states and territories, 10 other countries. 59% women, 6% part-time, 68% state residents, 42% transferred in, 1% international, 58% 25 or older, 4% Hispanic, 5% African American, 2% Asian American. *Retention:* 53% of 1992 freshmen returned.

FRESHMEN 310 total. 79% of applicants were accepted, 53% of whom enrolled.

ACADEMIC PROGRAM Core, honor code. Calendar: semesters. 893 courses offered in 1993–94; average class size 25 in required courses. Academic remediation for entering students, English as a second language program offered during academic year and summer, advanced placement, accelerated degree program, self-designed majors, tutorials, honors program, summer session for credit, part-time degree program (daytime, evenings, weekends, summer), adult/continuing education programs, co-op programs and internships. A few graduate courses open to undergraduate students. Off-campus study at Colorado Institute of Art, Metropolitan State College, University of Colorado at Denver, Red Rocks Community College. ROTC: Army (c), Air Force (c).

MAJORS Accounting, adult and continuing education, biblical studies, biology/biological sciences, business administration/commerce/management, communication, computer information systems, elementary education, English, history, humanities, liberal arts/general studies, mathematics, ministries, music, music education, pastoral studies, political science/government, psychology, sacred music, secondary education, theater arts/drama, theology, voice.

EXPENSES FOR 1994–95 Comprehensive fee of $10,750 includes full-time tuition ($6720), mandatory fees ($550), and college room and board ($3480). Part-time tuition: $280 per semester hour.

FINANCIAL AID *College-administered aid for undergraduates 1993–94:* need-based scholarships, non-need scholarships, short-term loans, low-interest long-term loans from external sources, FSEOG, Federal Work-Study. *Application forms required:* institutional, FAFSA; required for some: IRS, state; accepted: FFS, FAF. *Priority deadline:* 3/15. *Payment plan:* installment. *Waivers:* full or partial for children of alumni and employees or children of employees.

COLLEGE LIFE Orientation program (2 days, no cost, parents included). Drama-theater group, choral group, student-run newspaper. *Major annual events:* Homecoming, O'Malley's Alley. *Student services:* legal services, health clinic, personal-psychological counseling. *Safety:* 24-hour emergency response devices and patrols, room security.

ATHLETICS Member NCAA. All Division II. *Intercollegiate:* basketball M(s)/W(s), golf M(s), soccer M(s)/W(s), tennis M(s)/W(s), volleyball W(s). *Contact:* Mr. Frank Evans, Athletic Director, 303-238-5386 Ext. 164.

APPLYING/FRESHMEN *Options:* deferred entrance, midyear entrance. *Required:* essay, school transcript, minimum 2.0 GPA, 2 recommendations, SAT I or ACT, TOEFL for international students. *Recommended:* 3 years of high school math and science, some high school foreign language, SAT II: Writing Test. *Required for some:* 3 recommendations, interview. Test scores used for admission. *Application deadline:* rolling.

APPLYING/TRANSFER *Required:* essay, 2 recommendations, college transcript, minimum 2.0 GPA. *Required for some:* standardized test scores, high school transcript, 3 recommendations, interview. *Entrance level:* moderately difficult. *Application deadline:* rolling.

CONTACT Ms. Mardie Hefferman, Admissions Office Manager, Colorado Christian University, 180 South Garrison Street, Lakewood, CO 80226; 303-238-5386 Ext. 125.

CORNERSTONE COLLEGE
Grand Rapids, Michigan

> **SPECIAL NOTE FROM THE COLLEGE** Cornerstone College, formerly Grand Rapids Baptist College, is unique for its internships. While most colleges have internship programs for some majors, Cornerstone College requires and arranges a practical internship for every student in all of its majors. The school's location in a large metropolitan area makes it possible for each student to have high-quality on-the-job experience before graduation. A major aim of the internship program is to allow students the opportunity to put their Christianity into practice in real-world circumstances. This unique feature provides the student with excellent preparation for life and for work after graduation.

Total Enrollment: 903
UG Enrollment: 715 (54% W)
Application Deadline: rolling
Entrance: minimally difficult
Tuition & Fees: $6852
Room & Board: $3888
SAT≥500: N/R **ACT≥21:** 60%
Denominational Affiliation: Baptist

GENERAL INFORMATION Independent-religious comprehensive coed institution. Awards associate, bachelor's, master's, doctorate degrees. Founded 1941. *Setting:* 132-acre suburban campus. *Undergraduate faculty:* 43 (40 full-time, 50% with terminal degrees, 3 part-time); student-undergrad faculty ratio is 17:1. *Library Holdings:* 93,111 books, 29 microform titles, 650 periodicals, 1 on-line bibliographic service, 3,200 records, tapes, and CDs. *Computers:* 34 terminals, PCs for student use in computer center. Access to campuswide network, Internet from computer center, computer labs, dorms. *Services:* e-mail, mainframe access, word processing.

UNDERGRADUATE PROFILE 715 students from 23 states and territories, 4 other countries. 54% women, 12% part-time, 79% state residents, 11% transferred in, 34% have campus jobs, 1% international, 12% 25 or older, 0% Native American, 1% Hispanic, 2% African American, 1% Asian American. *Retention:* 67% of 1992 freshmen returned.

FRESHMEN 171 total. 269 applied, 96% were accepted, 66% of whom enrolled. 18% from top 10% of their high school class, 38% from top quarter, 71% from top half.

ACADEMIC PROGRAM Core. Calendar: semesters. 292 courses offered in 1993–94. Academic remediation for entering students, advanced placement, honors program, summer session for credit, part-time degree program (daytime), adult/continuing education programs, internships. Off-campus study at Calvin College. ROTC: Army (c).

MAJORS Accounting, biblical languages, biblical studies, biology/biological sciences, broadcasting, business administration/commerce/management, business education, communication, computer information systems, education, elementary education, English, history, interdisciplinary studies, (pre)law sequence, marketing/retailing/merchandising, music, music education, pastoral studies, physical education, psychology, religious education, religious studies, science education, secondary education, social work, sociology, speech/rhetoric/public address/debate.

EXPENSES FOR 1994–95 *Application fee:* $25. Comprehensive fee of $10,740 includes full-time tuition ($6420), mandatory fees ($432), and college room and board ($3888). Part-time tuition: $246 per credit hour. Part-time mandatory fees per year (7 to 11 credit hours): $432.

FINANCIAL AID *College-administered aid for undergraduates 1993–94:* 180 need-based scholarships (average $1299), 340 non-need scholarships (average $890), low-interest long-term loans from college funds (average $1120), loans from external sources (average $2360), FSEOG, Federal Work-Study, 300 part-time jobs. *Application forms required:* FAF, IRS; required for some: state; accepted: FFS, FAFSA. *Priority deadline:* 3/1. *Payment plan:* installment. *Waivers:* full or partial for employees or children of employees.

COLLEGE LIFE Orientation program (3 days, no cost, parents included). Drama-theater group, choral group, student-run newspaper. *Most popular organizations:* Student Council, Student Education Association, Breakpoint. *Major annual events:* Homecoming, Winter Banquet, Spring Splash. *Student services:* health clinic, personal-psychological counseling.

ATHLETICS Member NAIA. *Intercollegiate:* baseball M(s), basketball M(s)/W(s), golf M(s), soccer M(s), softball W(s), tennis M(s), volleyball W(s). *Intramural:* basketball, football, soccer, volleyball. *Contact:* Mr. Kim Elders, Athletic Director, 616-949-5300.

APPLYING/FRESHMEN Preference given to applicants with clear Christian testimony. *Options:* early entrance, deferred entrance, midyear entrance. *Required:* essay, school transcript, 1 recommendation, SAT I or ACT, TOEFL for international students. *Recommended:* 3 years of high school math and science, 2 years of high school foreign language, interview. Test scores used for admission and counseling/placement. *Application deadline:* rolling.

APPLYING/TRANSFER *Required:* essay, standardized test scores, high school transcript, 1 recommendation, college transcript, minimum 2.0 GPA. *Recommended:* 3 years of high school math and science, 2 years of high school foreign language, interview. *Application deadline:* rolling.

CONTACT Mr. Rick Newberry, Director of Admissions, Cornerstone College, 1001 East Beltline Avenue, NE, Grand Rapids, MI 49505; 616-949-5300 Ext. 426 or toll-free 800-968-4722.

COVENANT COLLEGE
Lookout Mountain, Georgia

SPECIAL NOTE FROM THE COLLEGE Covenant's primary goal is to provide an environment of academic excellence that encourages students to develop a Christian world view. A Covenant education produces skills and values that equip students to serve effectively and live responsibly in a changing world. Covenant is more than a safe enclave for Christian students. It requires a distinctive experience that motivates and enables its young men and women to make an impact on the world for Christ. Covenant must not conform to the selfish dullness of the world, but must promote a rigorous discipline that, applied to academics, produces learning and, applied to spiritual life, produces wisdom.

Total Enrollment: 680
UG Enrollment: 639 (54% W)
Application Deadline: rolling
Entrance: moderately difficult
Tuition & Fees: $9960
Room & Board: $3800
SAT≥500: 48% V, 68% M **ACT≥21:** 89%
Denominational Affiliation: Presbyterian Church in America

GENERAL INFORMATION Independent-religious comprehensive coed institution. Awards associate, bachelor's, master's degrees (master's in education only). Founded 1955. *Setting:* 250-acre small-town campus with easy access to Atlanta and Nashville. *Undergraduate faculty:* 59 (40 full-time, 73% with terminal degrees, 19 part-time); student-undergrad faculty ratio is 14:1. *Library Holdings:* 70,460 books, 27,196 microform titles, 500 periodicals, 2 on-line bibliographic services, 7,625 records, tapes, and CDs. *Computers:* 54 terminals, PCs for student use in computer center, library, academic building. Student computer-purchase plan available.

UNDERGRADUATE PROFILE *1992–93:* 639 students from 40 states and territories, 14 other countries. 54% women, 5% part-time, 19% state residents, 81% live on campus, 7% transferred in, 82% have need-based financial aid, 18% have non-need-based financial aid, 43% have campus jobs, 4% international, 2% 25 or older, 1% Native American, 1% Hispanic, 3% African American, 1% Asian American. *Retention:* 74% of 1992 freshmen returned. *Graduation:* 28% graduate in 4 years.

FRESHMEN *1992–93:* 181 total. 407 applied, 78% were accepted, 57% of whom enrolled. 21% from top 10% of their high school class, 48% from top quarter, 80% from top half.

ACADEMIC PROGRAM Core, honor code. Calendar: semesters. 270 courses offered in 1993–94; average class size 27 in required courses. Academic remediation for entering students, advanced placement, accelerated degree program, tutorials, honors program, summer session for credit, part-time degree program (daytime, evenings), external degree programs, co-op programs. ROTC: Army. Unusual degree programs: 3-2 engineering with Georgia Institute of Technology.

MAJORS Biblical studies, biology/biological sciences, business administration/commerce/management, chemistry, computer science, elementary education, (pre)engineering sequence, English, health science, history, interdisciplinary studies, (pre)law sequence, (pre)medicine sequence, music, music education, natural sciences, nursing, piano/organ, psychology, sociology, stringed instruments, voice, wind and percussion instruments.

EXPENSES FOR 1994–95 *Application fee:* $20. Comprehensive fee of $13,766 includes full-time tuition ($9700), mandatory fees ($260), and college room and board ($3800). College room only: $1780. Part-time tuition: $404 per unit.

FINANCIAL AID *College-administered aid for undergraduates 1992–93:* 296 need-based scholarships (average $3146), 466 non-need scholarships (average $2724), low-interest long-term loans from college funds, loans from external sources (average $3811), FSEOG, 26 part-time jobs. Average total aid for freshmen: $8386, meeting 76% of need (aid provided to 100% of those qualified). *Application forms required:* IRS, institutional, FAFSA; required for some: Merit Scholarship Form. *Priority deadline:* 3/31. *Waivers:* full or partial for employees or children of employees and senior citizens. *Notification:* continuous. Must reapply each year. *Average indebtedness of graduates:* $6850.

COLLEGE LIFE Orientation program (4 days, $20). Drama-theater group, choral group, student-run newspaper. *Social organizations:* 44 open to all. *Major annual events:* Homecoming, madrigal dinners. *Student services:* health clinic, personal-psychological counseling. *Safety:* night security guards.

ATHLETICS Member NAIA. *Intercollegiate:* basketball M(s)/W(s), cross-country running M/W, soccer M(s), volleyball W. *Intramural:* basketball, football, soccer, tennis, volleyball. *Contact:* Dr. Brian Crossman, Intercollegiate Athletic Director, 706-820-1560 Ext. 1513.

APPLYING/FRESHMEN *Options:* early entrance, deferred entrance, midyear entrance. *Required:* essay, school transcript, 3 years of high school math, 2 recommendations, interview, minimum 2.5 GPA, SAT I or ACT, TOEFL for international students. *Recommended:* 2 years of high school foreign language, SAT II: Writing Test. Test scores used for admission. *Application deadline:* rolling.

APPLYING/TRANSFER *Required:* essay, high school transcript, 3 years of high school math, 2 recommendations, interview, college transcript, minimum 2.0 GPA. *Recommended:* standardized test scores, 2 years of high school foreign language. *Entrance level:* moderately difficult. *Application deadline:* rolling.

CONTACT Mr. Charlie Phillips, Vice President of Development and Admissions, Covenant College, Lookout Mountain, GA 30750; 706-820-1560 Ext. 145.

DALLAS BAPTIST UNIVERSITY
Dallas, Texas

SPECIAL NOTE FROM THE UNIVERSITY Servant-leadership is at the heart of the Dallas Baptist University educational experience. The academic commitment to the integration of faith and learning, coupled with an attitude of humility and service, provides the foundation for the development of Christian leadership that will extend into the 21st century. DBU's mission is to develop servant-leaders who will impact the world for Christ in their chosen profession. The University relies heavily on the *Intercessory Prayer Ministry* and the prayers of 1,000 senior adults who pray daily for the University to accomplish this mission.

Total Enrollment: 2,803
UG Enrollment: 2,390 (59% W)
Application Deadline: rolling
Entrance: moderately difficult
Tuition & Fees: $6880
Room & Board: $3180
SAT≥500: 30% V, 49% M   **ACT≥21:** N/R
Denominational Affiliation: Southern Baptist

GENERAL INFORMATION Independent-religious comprehensive coed institution. Awards associate, bachelor's, master's degrees. Founded 1965. *Setting:* 200-acre urban campus. *Faculty:* 179 (64 full-time, 50% with terminal degrees, 115 part-time); student-undergrad faculty ratio is 17:1. *Library Holdings:* 523,993 books, 314,602 microform titles, 496 periodicals, 2 CD-ROMs, 1,832 records, tapes, and CDs. *Computers:* 56 terminals, PCs for student use in computer center, library.

UNDERGRADUATE PROFILE 2,390 students from 28 states and territories, 49 other countries. 59% women, 65% part-time, 90% state residents, 17% live on campus, 6% international, 69% 25 or older, 1% Native American, 5% Hispanic, 17% African American, 6% Asian American.

FRESHMEN 155 total. 360 applied, 87% were accepted, 49% of whom enrolled. 5 valedictorians.

ACADEMIC PROGRAM Core, comprehensive liberal arts curriculum, honor code. Calendar: 4-1-4. Average class size 25 in required courses. English as a second language program offered during academic year and summer, advanced placement, summer session for credit, part-time degree program (daytime, evenings, weekends, summer), adult/continuing education programs, internships. Fewer than half of graduate courses open to undergraduate students. Off-campus study at Christian College Coalition. ROTC: Army (c), Air Force (c).

STUDY-ABROAD SITE England.

MAJORS Accounting, art/fine arts, biblical studies, biology/biological sciences, business administration/commerce/management, business economics, business education, computer management, computer science, criminal justice, (pre)dentistry sequence, early childhood education, economics, education, elementary education, English, finance/banking, history, interdisciplinary studies, (pre)law sequence, liberal arts/general studies, management information systems, marketing, mathematics, (pre)medicine sequence, ministries, music, music education, pastoral studies, philosophy, physical education, piano/organ, psychology, religious education, religious studies, sacred music, science education, secondary education, sociology, voice.

EXPENSES FOR 1994–95 *Application fee:* $25. Comprehensive fee of $10,060 includes full-time tuition ($6750), mandatory fees ($130), and college room and board ($3180). Part-time tuition: $225 per credit hour.

FINANCIAL AID *College-administered aid for undergraduates 1993–94:* need-based scholarships, non-need scholarships, low-interest long-term loans from college funds, loans from external sources, FSEOG, Federal Work-Study. *Application forms required:* FAF, IRS, institutional, FAFSA; accepted: FFS, state. *Priority deadline:* 5/15. *Payment plan:* installment. *Waivers:* full or partial for employees or children of employees. *Notification:* continuous.

COLLEGE LIFE Orientation program (4½ days, $10, parents included). Drama-theater group, choral group. *Social organizations:* 32 open to all. *Most popular organizations:* Student Activities Board, Baptist Student Union, Student Government. *Major annual events:* Homecoming, Freshman Orientation, Christmas Tree Lighting/Christmas Service. *Student services:* legal services, health clinic, personal-psychological counseling. *Safety:* 24-hour emergency response devices and patrols, controlled dormitory access.

ATHLETICS Member NAIA. *Intercollegiate:* baseball M(s), soccer M, volleyball W(s). *Intramural:* basketball, cross-country running, football, golf, table tennis (Ping-Pong), tennis, volleyball. *Contact:* Mr. Jim Harp, Director of Intercollegiate Athletics, 214-333-5324.

APPLYING/FRESHMEN *Options:* early entrance, deferred entrance, midyear entrance. *Required:* essay, school transcript, rank in upper 50% of high school class or minimum 3.0 GPA, SAT I or ACT, TOEFL for international students. *Recommended:* 3 years of high school math and science, some high school foreign language, recommendations, interview. Test scores used for admission. *Application deadline:* rolling. *Notification:* continuous.

APPLYING/TRANSFER *Required:* essay, college transcript, minimum 2.0 GPA. *Recommended:* recommendations, interview. *Required for some:* standardized test scores, high school transcript. *Entrance level:* minimally difficult. *Application deadline:* rolling. *Notification:* continuous.

CONTACT Dr. Bill Gilbert, Admissions Office, Dallas Baptist University, 3000 Mountain Creek Parkway, Dallas, TX 75211; 214-333-5360.

DORDT COLLEGE
Sioux Center, Iowa

> **SPECIAL NOTE FROM THE COLLEGE** Dordt College does not adhere to the traditional distinctions between liberal arts and professional training. The College instead focuses on transmitting "serviceable insight," a biblically based understanding of both the structure of creation and the nature and demands of a wide range of vocations and professions. This is why the College has majors such as agriculture, business, and computer science; why there are accredited programs in social work and engineering; why opportunities for internships and off-campus study abound; and why every course at Dordt will challenge students to think about the real-world applications of their learning.

Total Enrollment: 1,104 (all UG)

Women: 53%

Application Deadline: 9/1

Entrance: moderately difficult

Tuition & Fees: $9860

Room & Board: $2650

SAT: N/App **ACT≥21:** 81%

Denominational Affiliation: Christian Reformed

GENERAL INFORMATION Independent-religious 4-year coed institution. Awards associate, bachelor's degrees. Founded 1955. *Setting:* 45-acre small-town campus. *Faculty:* 90 (72 full-time, 63% with terminal degrees, 18 part-time); student-undergrad faculty ratio is 13:1. *Library Holdings:* 170,000 books, 14,819 microform titles, 550 periodicals, 3,616 records, tapes, and CDs; on-line access to libraries at other institutions. *Computers:* 120 terminals, PCs for student use in computer center, computer labs, library, student center, dorms. Access to campuswide network, BITNET, Internet from computer center, computer labs, library, student center, dorms; on-line documentation available. *Services:* e-mail, file transfer, library catalog search and reservation.

UNDERGRADUATE PROFILE 1,104 students from 33 states and territories, 8 other countries. 53% women, 5% part-time, 38% state residents, 78% live on campus, 3% transferred in, 15% international, 8% 25 or older, 0% Native American, 0% Hispanic, 0% African American, 1% Asian American. *Retention:* 90% of 1992 freshmen returned.

FRESHMEN 328 total. 604 applied, 93% were accepted, 58% of whom enrolled. 20% from top 10% of their high school class, 42% from top quarter, 73% from top half.

ACADEMIC PROGRAM Core, honor code. Calendar: semesters. 400 courses offered in 1993–94; average class size 20 in required courses. Academic remediation for entering students, English as a second language program offered during academic year, honors program, summer session for credit, internships. Off-campus study at Christian College Coalition, Chicago Metro Program, American Studies Program.

STUDY-ABROAD SITES Costa Rica, Egypt, Germany, Mexico, the Netherlands, Russia, Spain.

MAJORS Accounting, agricultural business, agricultural sciences, animal sciences, art/fine arts, biology/biological sciences, business administration/commerce/management, business education, chemistry, communication, computer science, (pre)dentistry sequence, education, elementary education, engineering, engineering science, English, environmental sciences, German, history, journalism, management information systems, mathematics, medical technology, (pre)medicine sequence, music, music education, natural sciences, philosophy, physical education, physical fitness/exercise science, physics, political science/government, psychology, secondary education, secretarial studies/office management, social science, social work, Spanish, teacher aide studies, theater arts/drama, theology, (pre)veterinary medicine sequence.

EXPENSES FOR 1994–95 *Application fee:* $10. Comprehensive fee of $12,510 includes full-time tuition ($9800), mandatory fees ($60), and college room and board ($2650). College room only: $1200. Part-time tuition: $385 per credit hour.

FINANCIAL AID *College-administered aid for undergraduates 1993–94:* 240 need-based scholarships (average $700), non-need scholarships (average $1300), low-interest long-term loans from college funds (average $900), loans from external sources (average $3200), FSEOG, Federal Work-Study, 800 part-time jobs. Average total aid for freshmen: $8755, meeting 92% of need (aid provided to 100% of those qualified). *Application forms required:* institutional; required for some: IRS; accepted: FFS, FAF, FAFSA. *Priority deadline:* 4/15. *Payment plan:* installment. *Waivers:* full or partial for children of alumni, employees or children of employees, and senior citizens. *Notification:* continuous. *Average indebtedness of graduates:* $9000.

COLLEGE LIFE Drama-theater group, choral and instrumental groups, student-run newspaper. *Student services:* health clinic, personal-psychological counseling, shuttle bus. *Safety:* 24-hour emergency response devices, student patrols, late-night transport-escort service, controlled dormitory access, room security.

ATHLETICS Member NAIA. *Intercollegiate:* basketball M/W, cross-country running M/W, golf M/W, ice hockey M, soccer M, softball W, tennis M/W, track and field M/W, volleyball W. *Intramural:* baseball, basketball, bowling, field hockey, gymnastics, ice hockey, racquetball, soccer, swimming and diving, table tennis (Ping-Pong), tennis, track and field, volleyball. *Contact:* Mr. Richard Vander Berg, Athletic Director, 712-722-6305.

APPLYING/FRESHMEN *Options:* early entrance, deferred entrance. *Required:* school transcript, minimum 2.0 GPA, SAT I or ACT, TOEFL for international students. *Recommended:* some high school foreign language. *Required for some:* interview. Test scores used for admission and counseling/placement. *Application deadline:* 9/1. *Notification:* continuous until 9/1.

APPLYING/TRANSFER *Required:* high school transcript, college transcript, minimum 2.0 GPA. *Required for some:* interview. *Application deadline:* 9/1. *Notification:* continuous until 9/1.

CONTACT Mr. Quentin Van Essen, Director of Admissions, Dordt College, 498 4th Avenue NE, Sioux Center, IA 51250; 712-722-6080 or toll-free 800-34-DORDT.

EASTERN COLLEGE
St. Davids, Pennsylvania

SPECIAL NOTE FROM THE COLLEGE Eastern College is known for its innovative academic programs, caring Christian community, commitment to social action, and exceptionally beautiful campus. Class sizes are kept small, and professors are both role models to their students and highly accomplished experts in their fields. In addition to integrating faith and learning, Eastern's creative academic programs encourage students to learn from many disciplines. The campus community is highly diverse, with a multiethnic student body that includes representatives from 18 countries. A strong campus ministries program and Eastern's proximity to the city of Philadelphia provide many opportunities for Christian service. The life of the Eastern College community is firmly centered in Jesus Christ.

Total Enrollment: 1,923
UG Enrollment: 1,492 (63% W)
Application Deadline: rolling
Entrance: moderately difficult
Tuition & Fees: $11,190
Room & Board: $4800
SAT≥500: 33% V, 44% M   **ACT≥21:** 80%
Denominational Affiliation: American Baptist

GENERAL INFORMATION Independent-religious comprehensive coed institution. Awards associate, bachelor's, master's degrees. Founded 1932. *Setting:* 100-acre small-town campus with easy access to Philadelphia. *Faculty:* 168 (62 full-time, 60% with terminal degrees, 106 part-time); student-undergrad faculty ratio is 15:1. *Library Holdings:* 111,416 books, 257,618 microform titles, 969 periodicals, 1 on-line bibliographic service, 12 CD-ROMs, 2,681 records, tapes, and CDs. *Computers:* 45 terminals, PCs for student use in computer center, library. Access to campuswide network from computer center.

UNDERGRADUATE PROFILE 1,492 students from 37 states and territories, 18 other countries. 63% women, 25% part-time, 69% state residents, 39% live on campus, 32% transferred in, 2% international, 52% 25 or older, 1% Native American, 2% Hispanic, 11% African American, 2% Asian American. *Retention:* 73% of 1992 freshmen returned.

FRESHMEN 250 total. 690 applied, 77% were accepted, 47% of whom enrolled. 16% from top 10% of their high school class, 41% from top quarter, 74% from top half.

ACADEMIC PROGRAM Core, biblical foundations curriculum. Calendar: semesters. 266 courses offered in 1993–94; average class size 30 in required courses. Academic remediation for entering students, English as a second language program offered during academic year, advanced placement, accelerated degree program, self-designed majors, tutorials, honors program, summer session for credit, part-time degree program (daytime, evenings, summer), adult/continuing education programs, internships. Fewer than half of graduate courses open to undergraduate students. Off-campus study at all American Baptist–related colleges, Cabrini College, Rosemont College, Ursinus College. ROTC: Army (c), Air Force (c).

MAJORS Art history, astronomy, biblical studies, biology/biological sciences, business administration/commerce/management, chemistry, communication, creative writing, elementary education, French, health education, health services administration, history, liberal arts/general studies, literature, mathematics, medical technology, ministries, music, nursing (RNs only), philosophy, physical education, political science/government, psychology, religious studies, secondary education, social work, sociology, Spanish, studio art.

EXPENSES FOR 1994–95 *Application fee:* $25. Comprehensive fee of $15,990 includes full-time tuition ($11,190) and college room and board ($4800). Part-time tuition: $270 per credit.

FINANCIAL AID *College-administered aid for undergraduates 1993–94:* need-based scholarships, non-need scholarships, low-interest long-term loans from college funds, loans from external sources, FSEOG, Federal Work-Study, part-time jobs. Average total aid for freshmen: $13,267, meeting 85% of need (aid provided to 100% of those qualified). *Application forms required:* IRS, institutional, FAFSA, financial aid transcript for transfers; required for some: state; accepted: FAF. *Application deadline:* continuous. *Payment plans:* installment, deferred payment. *Waivers:* full or partial for employees or children of employees. *Notification:* continuous.

COLLEGE LIFE Orientation program (2 days, no cost, parents included). Drama-theater group, choral group, marching band, student-run newspaper, radio station. *Social organizations:* 60 open to all. *Most popular organizations:* Black Student League, Society for the Advancement of Management, International Students Club. *Major annual events:* Homecoming, All Campus Christmas Party, Theme Weeks. *Student services:* health clinic, personal-psychological counseling. *Safety:* 24-hour patrols, late-night transport-escort service, controlled dormitory access, room security.

ATHLETICS *Intercollegiate:* baseball M, basketball M, cross-country running M/W, field hockey W, lacrosse W, soccer M/W, softball W, tennis M/W, volleyball M/W. *Intramural:* basketball, bowling, football, golf, table tennis (Ping-Pong), volleyball. *Contact:* Mr. Wayne Rasmussen, Director of Athletics, 610-341-1738.

APPLYING/FRESHMEN *Options:* early entrance, deferred entrance, midyear entrance. *Required:* essay, school transcript, minimum 2.0 GPA, 1 recommendation, SAT I or ACT, TOEFL for international students. *Recommended:* interview. Test scores used for admission. *Application deadline:* rolling. *Notification:* continuous.

APPLYING/TRANSFER *Required:* essay, high school transcript, 1 recommendation, college transcript, minimum 2.0 GPA. *Recommended:* interview. *Entrance level:* moderately difficult. *Application deadline:* rolling. *Notification:* continuous.

CONTACT Dr. Ronald L. Keller, Vice President for Enrollment Management, Eastern College, 10 Fairview Drive, St. Davids, PA 19087-3696; 610-341-5967.

EASTERN MENNONITE UNIVERSITY
Harrisonburg, Virginia

> **SPECIAL NOTE FROM THE UNIVERSITY** EMU students discover what it means to be a Christian and a world citizen. EMU's Global Village curriculum integrates the liberal arts and sciences with Christian values and personal contact with people of other cultures. Students spend a semester in the Middle East, Latin America, or Europe; a summer in China, Ireland, New Zealand, Appalachia, Mexico, South Africa, or Southeast Asia; or a year in Washington, DC, in a study-service program. Graduates are equipped with a distinctive intellectual framework and extraordinary, often life-transforming, experience in human relations. EMU alumni find that they are well prepared for advanced study and report that their careers and professional practice are profoundly enriched by a global perspective. Students come to see life as an opportunity for faithful Christian service and peacemaking in a needy world. All of this begins in a friendly campus community in the heart of the scenic and historic Shenandoah Valley of Virginia.

Total Enrollment: 1,102

UG Enrollment: 962 (59% W)

Application Deadline: 8/1

Entrance: moderately difficult

Tuition & Fees: $9650

Room & Board: $3800

SAT≥500: 42% V, 54% M   **ACT≥21:** 64%

Denominational Affiliation: Mennonite

GENERAL INFORMATION Independent-religious comprehensive coed institution. Awards associate, bachelor's, master's, first professional degrees. Founded 1917. *Setting:* 90-acre small-town campus. *Faculty:* 106 (79 full-time, 62% with terminal degrees, 27 part-time); student-undergrad faculty ratio is 16:1. *Library Holdings:* 135,070 books, 47,660 microform titles, 1,070 periodicals, 1 on-line bibliographic service, 4 CD-ROMs, 9,360 records, tapes, and CDs. *Computers:* 72 terminals, PCs for student use in computer center, library, dorms, science center.

UNDERGRADUATE PROFILE 962 students from 34 states and territories, 11 other countries. 59% women, 6% part-time, 32% state residents, 56% live on campus, 8% transferred in, 71% have need-based financial aid, 28% have non-need-based financial aid, 52% have campus jobs, 3% international, 3% 25 or older, 0% Native American, 2% Hispanic, 3% African American, 2% Asian American. *Retention:* 79% of 1992 freshmen returned. *Graduation:* 47% graduate in 4 years.

FRESHMEN 227 total. 486 applied, 91% were accepted, 52% of whom enrolled. 14% from top 10% of their high school class, 46% from top quarter, 80% from top half. 6 valedictorians.

ACADEMIC PROGRAM Core, Global Village curriculum. Calendar: semesters. 380 courses offered in 1993–94; average class size 40 in required courses. English as a second language program offered during academic year, self-designed majors, honors program, summer session for credit, part-time degree program (daytime), adult/continuing education programs, internships. Off-campus study at Christian College Coalition. Unusual degree programs: 3-2 engineering with Pennsylvania State University University Park Campus.

STUDY-ABROAD SITES China, Costa Rica, Egypt, El Salvador, England, France, Germany, Guatamala, Honduras, Ireland, Israel, Ivory Coast, Japan, Jordan, Russia.

MAJORS Accounting, art/fine arts, biblical studies, biochemistry, biology/biological sciences, business administration/commerce/management, chemistry, community services, computer information systems, computer programming, computer science, data processing, (pre)dentistry sequence, early childhood education, education, elementary education, (pre)engineering sequence, English, French, German, health education, history, international business, (pre)law sequence, liberal arts/general studies, mathematics, medical technology, (pre)medicine sequence, middle school education, ministries, music, music education, nursing, physical education, psychology, recreation therapy, religious studies, science education, secondary education, social work, sociology, Spanish, special education, teacher aide studies, theology, (pre)veterinary medicine sequence.

EXPENSES FOR 1994–95 *Application fee:* $15. Comprehensive fee of $13,450 includes full-time tuition ($9650) and college room and board ($3800). Part-time tuition: $380 per semester hour.

FINANCIAL AID *College-administered aid for undergraduates 1993–94:* 1,040 need-based scholarships (average $1530), 1,050 non-need scholarships (average $960), low-interest long-term loans from college funds (average $1000), loans from external sources (average $3400), FSEOG, Federal Work-Study, 90 part-time jobs. Average total aid for freshmen: $8040, meeting 100% of need (aid provided to 100% of those qualified). *Application forms required:* institutional, FAFSA; required for some: IRS, state; accepted: FFS, FAF. *Priority deadline:* 4/15. *Payment plan:* installment. *Waivers:* full or partial for employees or children of employees and senior citizens. *Average indebtedness of graduates:* $12,800.

COLLEGE LIFE Orientation program (3 days, parents included). Drama-theater group, choral group, student-run newspaper, radio station. *Social organizations:* 20 open to all. *Most popular organizations:* YPCA, Campus Activities Committee, Celebration Committee. *Major annual events:* Homecoming, Multicultural Week, Disability Awareness Week. *Student services:* health clinic, personal-psychological counseling. *Safety:* late-night transport-escort service, night watchman.

ATHLETICS Member NCAA. All Division III. *Intercollegiate:* baseball M, basketball M/W, cross-country running M/W, field hockey W, golf M(c), soccer M, softball W, tennis M/W(c), track and field M/W, volleyball M/W. *Intramural:* badminton, basketball, bowling, football, racquetball, soccer, softball, table tennis (Ping-Pong), tennis, track and field, volleyball, weight lifting. *Contact:* Mr. Lester R. Zook, Athletic Director, 703-432-4440.

APPLYING/FRESHMEN *Options:* early entrance, deferred entrance, midyear entrance. *Required:* essay, school transcript, 2 recommendations, statement of commitment, SAT I or ACT, TOEFL for international students. *Recommended:* 3 years of high school math and science, 2 years of high school foreign language, interview. Test scores used for admission. *Application deadline:* 8/1. *Notification:* continuous until 8/1.

APPLYING/TRANSFER *Required:* essay, high school transcript, 2 recommendations, college transcript, minimum 2.0 GPA, statement of commitment. *Recommended:* standardized test scores, 3 years of high school math and science, 2 years of high school foreign language, interview. *Entrance level:* moderately difficult. *Application deadline:* 8/1. *Notification:* continuous until 8/1.

CONTACT Mrs. Ellen B. Miller, Director of Admissions, Eastern Mennonite University, 1200 Park Road, Harrisonburg, VA 22801; 703-732-4118 or toll-free 800-368-2665 (out-of-state).

EASTERN NAZARENE COLLEGE
Quincy, Massachusetts

> **SPECIAL NOTE FROM THE COLLEGE** Eastern Nazarene College offers a strong commitment to a liberal arts education in a small-school Christian-oriented setting. ENC has been producing graduates in Quincy, Massachusetts, for over 70 years and has maintained a reputation for being a caring, yet academically demanding, school. Boston's libraries, universities, conservatories, museums, historic sights, and churches offer unsurpassed educational opportunities and abundant possibilities for employment and entertainment. ENC believes that the solid academic programs, supportive faculty, Christian values, and Boston area location provide students with unparalleled opportunities for personal growth. Moreover, Eastern Nazarene seeks to develop in each person a Christian world view and to encourage each person to become God's creative and redemptive agent in today's world.

Total Enrollment: 1,374

UG Enrollment: 1,249 (56% W)

Application Deadline: rolling

Entrance: moderately difficult

Tuition & Fees: $9360

Room & Board: $3500

SAT≥500: 26% V, 46% M   **ACT≥21:** N/R

Denominational Affiliation: Church of the Nazarene

GENERAL INFORMATION Independent-religious comprehensive coed institution. Awards associate, bachelor's, master's degrees. Founded 1918. *Setting:* 15-acre suburban campus with easy access to Boston. *Undergraduate faculty:* 66 (51 full-time, 55% with terminal degrees, 15 part-time); student-undergrad faculty ratio is 13:1. *Library Holdings:* 121,000 books, 240 microform titles, 545 periodicals, 530 records, tapes, and CDs. *Computers:* 70 terminals, PCs for student use in computer center, library.

UNDERGRADUATE PROFILE 1,249 students from 29 states and territories, 23 other countries. 56% women, 5% part-time, 42% state residents, 14% transferred in, 22% have campus jobs, 6% international, 10% 25 or older, 0% Native American, 1% Hispanic, 5% African American, 4% Asian American. *Retention:* 69% of 1992 freshmen returned.

FRESHMEN 200 total. 516 applied, 79% were accepted, 49% of whom enrolled. 17% from top 10% of their high school class, 41% from top quarter, 64% from top half.

ACADEMIC PROGRAM Core. Calendar: 4-1-4. 538 courses offered in 1993–94; average class size 33 in required courses. Academic remediation for entering students, English as a second language program offered during academic year, advanced placement, accelerated degree program, summer session for credit, part-time degree program (daytime, evenings, summer), adult/continuing education programs, internships. Off-campus study at Christian College Coalition, Boston University, Massachusetts College of Pharmacy and Allied Health Sciences. Unusual degree programs: 3-2 engineering with Boston University, pharmacy with Massachusetts College of Pharmacy.

STUDY-ABROAD SITES Belize, France, Germany, Great Britain, Spain, Switzerland.

MAJORS Aerospace engineering, athletic training, biblical studies, biology/biological sciences, biomedical engineering, business administration/commerce/management, chemistry, communication, computer engineering, computer information systems, computer science, (pre)dentistry sequence, early childhood education, education, electrical engineering, elementary education, engineering physics, English, French, history, (pre)law sequence, liberal arts/general studies, manufacturing engineering, mathematics, mechanical engineering, (pre)medicine sequence, ministries, music, music education, pastoral studies, physical education, physical therapy, physics, psychology, religious education, religious studies, science, social science, social work, sociology, Spanish, systems engineering, (pre)veterinary medicine sequence.

EXPENSES FOR 1994–95 *Application fee:* $20. Comprehensive fee of $12,860 includes full-time tuition ($8770), mandatory fees ($590), and college room and board ($3500).

FINANCIAL AID *College-administered aid for undergraduates 1993–94:* 100 need-based scholarships (average $1500), 300 non-need scholarships, short-term loans (average $400), low-interest long-term loans from external sources (average $3800), FSEOG, Federal Work-Study, 100 part-time jobs. Average total aid for freshmen: $8158, meeting 78% of need (aid provided to 100% of those qualified). *Application forms required:* FAF, IRS, state, institutional, FAFSA. *Priority deadline:* 3/1. *Waivers:* full or partial for employees or children of employees.

COLLEGE LIFE Orientation program (5 days, no cost, parents included). Drama-theater group, choral group, student-run newspaper, radio station. *Major annual events:* Festival of Life, Homecoming, Heritage Day/Alumni Day. *Student services:* health clinic, personal-psychological counseling. *Safety:* 24-hour emergency response devices and patrols, late-night transport-escort service, controlled dormitory access.

ATHLETICS Member NCAA. All Division III. *Intercollegiate:* baseball M, basketball M/W, cross-country running M/W, soccer M, softball W, tennis M/W, volleyball M(c)/W. *Intramural:* basketball, soccer, softball, volleyball.

APPLYING/FRESHMEN *Options:* early entrance, deferred entrance. *Required:* school transcript, 1 recommendation, SAT I or ACT, TOEFL for international students. *Recommended:* essay, 3 years of high school math and science, some high school foreign language, interview. Test scores used for counseling/placement. *Application deadline:* rolling. *Notification:* continuous.

APPLYING/TRANSFER *Required:* standardized test scores, high school transcript, 1 recommendation, college transcript, minimum 2.0 GPA. *Recommended:* interview. *Application deadline:* rolling. *Notification:* continuous.

CONTACT Mr. D. William Nichols, Director of Enrollment Management, Eastern Nazarene College, 23 East Elm Avenue, Quincy, MA 02170; 617-773-2373.

ERSKINE COLLEGE
Due West, South Carolina

SPECIAL NOTE FROM THE COLLEGE Dr. Paul Sharp, distinguished former president of 4 universities and colleges, said of Erskine College: "You have a remarkable academic village...Your whole College is a neighborhood." Stating that "the greatest asset of Erskine is its quality faculty," Dr. Sharp praised Erskine's "commitment to teaching and commitment to students." Commitment to students extends beyond the classroom to responsibility for self-government. Students respond to this responsibility by conducting a business that raises funds for computers, building their own alcohol- and drug-free student club, helping Erskine plan through representation on a "Futures Council," and maintaining Christian emphasis through a Student Christian Association.

Total Enrollment: 567 (all UG)

Women: 56%

Application Deadline: rolling

Entrance: moderately difficult

Tuition & Fees: $11,145

Room & Board: $3840

SAT≥500: 42% V, 62% M   **ACT≥21:** N/R

Denominational Affiliation: Associate Reformed Presbyterian Church

GENERAL INFORMATION Independent-religious 4-year coed institution. Administratively affiliated with Erskine Theological Seminary. Awards bachelor's degrees. Founded 1839. *Setting:* 85-acre rural campus. *Faculty:* 53 (40 full-time, 83% with terminal degrees, 13 part-time); student-undergrad faculty ratio is 13:1. *Library Holdings:* 215,000 books, 74,938 microform titles, 1,065 periodicals, 1,050 records, tapes, and CDs. *Computers:* 75 terminals, PCs for student use in computer center, computer labs, library. Student computer-purchase plan available. Access to campuswide network from computer center, computer labs, library; on-line documentation available. *Services:* file transfer, printer and software acquisition.

UNDERGRADUATE PROFILE 567 students from 19 states and territories, 7 other countries. 56% women, 6% part-time, 78% state residents, 86% live on campus, 6% transferred in, 79% have need-based financial aid, 11% have non-need-based financial aid, 50% have campus jobs, 1% international, 5% 25 or older, 1% Hispanic, 4% African American, 1% Asian American. *Retention:* 81% of 1992 freshmen returned. *Graduation:* 64% graduate in 4 years.

FRESHMEN 167 total. 659 applied, 85% were accepted, 30% of whom enrolled. 47% from top 10% of their high school class, 74% from top quarter, 93% from top half. 4 National Merit Scholarship Finalists, 1 National Merit Scholar, 12 class presidents, 6 valedictorians, 33 student government officers, 2 yearbook editors, 5 high school newspaper editors.

ACADEMIC PROGRAM Core, liberal arts curriculum, honor code. Calendar: 4-1-4. 650 courses offered in 1993–94; average class size 22 in required courses. Advanced placement, accelerated degree program, tutorials, summer session for credit, part-time degree program (daytime, summer), internships. Off-campus study at other colleges having a 4-1-4 calendar. Unusual degree programs: 3-2 engineering with Clemson University, allied health programs with Medical University of South Carolina.

STUDY-ABROAD SITES England, France, Scotland, Spain.

MAJORS Accounting, athletic training, behavioral sciences, biblical studies, biology/biological sciences, business administration/commerce/management, chemistry, early childhood education, elementary education, English, French, history, mathematics, music, music education, natural sciences, physical education, physics, piano/organ, psychology, religious education, sacred music, Spanish, special education, sports administration, voice.

EXPENSES FOR 1994–95 *Application fee:* $15. Comprehensive fee of $14,985 includes full-time tuition ($10,485), mandatory fees ($660), and college room and board ($3840). College room only: $1760. Part-time tuition: $255 per semester hour.

FINANCIAL AID *College-administered aid for undergraduates 1993–94:* 334 need-based scholarships (average $2317), 601 non-need scholarships (average $3001), short-term loans (average $45), low-interest long-term loans from college funds (average $1680), loans from external sources (average $3258), FSEOG, Federal Work-Study, 103 part-time jobs. Average total aid for freshmen: $9957, meeting 95% of need. *Application forms required:* IRS, state, institutional, FAFSA. *Priority deadline:* 4/1. *Payment plan:* installment. *Waivers:* partial for children of alumni and for employees, children of employees, and ARP students. *Notification:* continuous. Must reapply each year. *Average indebtedness of graduates:* $4325.

COLLEGE LIFE Orientation program (2 days, $15, parents included). Drama-theater group, choral group, student-run newspaper. *Social organizations:* 34 open to all; 3 local fraternities, 3 local sororities, 2 Little Sisters; 40% of eligible men and 40% of eligible women are members. *Most popular organizations:* literary societies (40% participate), religious organizations (35% participate), Student Government Organization (4% participate), publications (5% participate). *Major annual events:* Fall Fest, Spring Fling, Homecoming. *Student services:* health clinic, personal-psychological counseling. *Safety:* 24-hour patrols, controlled dormitory access.

ATHLETICS Member NCAA Division II. *Intercollegiate:* baseball M(s), basketball M(s)/W(s), cross-country running M(s)/W(s), equestrian sports W(c), golf M(s), soccer M(s)/W(s), softball W(s), tennis M(s)/W(s), volleyball W(s). *Intramural:* basketball, soccer, softball, tennis, volleyball. *Contact:* Mr. Bill Lesesne, Vice President of Student Services and Athletic Director, 803-379-8701.

APPLYING/FRESHMEN *Required:* school transcript, 1 recommendation, SAT I or ACT, TOEFL for international students. *Recommended:* 3 years of high school math and science, 2 years of high school foreign language, campus interview. *Required for some:* campus interview. Test scores used for admission. *Application deadline:* rolling. *Notification:* continuous.

APPLYING/TRANSFER *Required:* 1 recommendation, college transcript, minimum 2.0 GPA. *Recommended:* campus interview. *Required for some:* standardized test scores, high school transcript, campus interview. *Entrance level:* moderately difficult. *Application deadline:* rolling. *Notification:* continuous.

CONTACT Mrs. Dot Carter, Director of Admissions and Financial Aid, Erskine College, P.O. Box 176, Due West, SC 29639; 803-379-8838.

EVANGEL COLLEGE
Springfield, Missouri

SPECIAL NOTE FROM THE COLLEGE As the national college of arts and sciences of the Assemblies of God, Evangel comes from a full gospel, charismatic heritage. It is a residential college—80% of students live on campus in modern residence halls—and recruits from all 50 states and from several countries. Evangel offers 36 academic majors, from business to engineering to criminal justice to premed, and is located near 6 other colleges and a seminary. The Student Development Department provides planned programs that contribute to students' intellectual, social, vocational, physical, emotional, and spiritual development. Finally, Springfield is the gateway to the Ozark Mountains recreational haven and is close to numerous lakes, parks, the Silver Dollar City theme park, and the highly acclaimed music performance town of Branson, Missouri. Evangel believes recreation is a vital part of the total education process.

Total Enrollment: 1,503 (all UG)
Women: 55%
Application Deadline: 8/15
Entrance: moderately difficult
Tuition & Fees: $7002
Room & Board: $3150
SAT≥500: N/R **ACT≥21:** 58%
Denominational Affiliation: Assemblies of God

GENERAL INFORMATION Independent-religious 4-year coed institution. Awards associate, bachelor's degrees. Founded 1955. *Setting:* 80-acre urban campus. *Faculty:* 115 (84 full-time, 31 part-time); student-undergrad faculty ratio is 17:1. *Library Holdings:* 105,000 books, 23,000 microform titles, 610 periodicals, 2 on-line bibliographic services, 3,000 records, tapes, and CDs. *Computers:* 64 terminals, PCs for student use in computer center, library, labs.

UNDERGRADUATE PROFILE 1,503 students from 47 states and territories, 13 other countries. 55% women, 6% part-time, 36% state residents, 10% transferred in, 1% international, 1% 25 or older, 1% Native American, 1% Hispanic, 4% African American. *Retention:* 74% of 1992 freshmen returned. *Graduation:* 43% graduate in 4 years.

FRESHMEN 388 total. 445 applied, 96% were accepted, 91% of whom enrolled. 19% from top 10% of their high school class, 45% from top quarter, 77% from top half.

ACADEMIC PROGRAM Core, honor code. Calendar: semesters. 618 courses offered in 1993–94. Academic remediation for entering students, advanced placement, summer session for credit, part-time degree program (daytime, evenings, summer). ROTC: Army. Unusual degree programs: 3-2 engineering with Washington University.

MAJORS Accounting, art education, art/fine arts, behavioral sciences, biblical studies, biology/biological sciences, broadcasting, business administration/commerce/management, business education, chemistry, child care/child and family studies, communication, computer science, criminal justice, (pre)dentistry sequence, early childhood education, education, elementary education, English, history, journalism, laboratory technologies, (pre)law sequence, marketing/retailing/merchandising, mathematics, medical technology, (pre)medicine sequence, mental health/rehabilitation counseling, music, music education, physical education, political science/government, psychology, public administration, radio and television studies, recreation and leisure services, sacred music, science education, secondary education, secretarial studies/office management, social science, social work, sociology, Spanish, special education, speech/rhetoric/public address/debate, (pre)veterinary medicine sequence.

EXPENSES FOR 1994–95 *Application fee:* $25. Comprehensive fee of $10,152 includes full-time tuition ($6850), mandatory fees ($152), and college room and board ($3150). College room only: $1520. Part-time tuition: $266 per credit hour. Part-time mandatory fees: $66 per semester.

FINANCIAL AID *College-administered aid for undergraduates 1993–94:* 731 need-based scholarships (average $450), 831 non-need scholarships (average $1605), low-interest long-term loans from college funds (average $1637), loans from external sources (average $2770), FSEOG, Federal Work-Study, 129 part-time jobs. Average total aid for freshmen: $6103, meeting 83% of need (aid provided to 98% of those qualified). *Application forms required:* institutional, FAFSA; required for some: IRS; accepted: FFS. *Priority deadline:* 4/1. *Payment plan:* installment. *Waivers:* full or partial for employees or children of employees. *Average indebtedness of graduates:* $10,000.

COLLEGE LIFE Orientation program (3 days, $10, parents included). Drama-theater group, choral group, student-run newspaper, radio station. *Major annual events:* Homecoming, Harvest Fest, Spring Fling. *Student services:* health clinic, personal-psychological counseling. *Safety:* 24-hour emergency response devices and patrols, student patrols, late-night transport-escort service.

ATHLETICS Member NAIA. *Intercollegiate:* baseball M, basketball M(s)/W(s), cross-country running M(s)/W(s), football M(s), softball W(s), track and field M(s)/W(s), volleyball W(s). *Intramural:* baseball, basketball, football, soccer, softball, volleyball. *Contact:* Dr. David Stair, Athletic Director, 417-865-2811.

APPLYING/FRESHMEN *Options:* deferred entrance, midyear entrance. *Required:* school transcript, SAT I or ACT, TOEFL for international students. *Recommended:* minimum 2.0 GPA, 3 years of high school math and science, some high school foreign language. Test scores used for admission. *Application deadline:* 8/15. *Notification:* continuous.

APPLYING/TRANSFER *Required:* college transcript, minimum 2.0 GPA. *Required for some:* high school transcript. *Entrance level:* moderately difficult. *Application deadline:* 8/15. *Notification:* continuous.

CONTACT Mr. David I. Schoolfield, Executive Director of Enrollment, Evangel College, 1111 North Glenstone, Springfield, MO 65802; 800-EVANGEL (toll-free).

FRESNO PACIFIC COLLEGE
Fresno, California

> **SPECIAL NOTE FROM THE COLLEGE** Fresno Pacific has been regularly ranked as one of the 10 best regional liberal arts colleges in the West by *U.S. News & World Report*'s "America's Best Colleges." The tree-covered campus is located in the heart of the vast agricultural valley of central California, an hour's drive from the College's retreat center in the High Sierras and 2 hours from Pacific Ocean beaches. Pacific's academic program features a unique core sequence in Christian thinking as well as practical Christian service and professional internships. At Fresno Pacific, special emphasis is placed upon faculty-student mentoring, developing responsible personal freedom, and building strong Christian community. Prospective students should visit campus and meet faculty members and students. People make the difference at Fresno Pacific College.

Total Enrollment: 1,536

UG Enrollment: 759 (59% W)

Application Deadline: rolling

Entrance: moderately difficult

Tuition & Fees: $10,074

Room & Board: $3670

SAT≥500: 40% V, 65% M **ACT≥21:** N/R

Denominational Affiliation: Mennonite Brethren Church

GENERAL INFORMATION Independent-religious comprehensive coed institution. Awards associate, bachelor's, master's degrees. Founded 1944. *Setting:* 40-acre suburban campus. *Faculty:* 155 (56 full-time, 55% with terminal degrees, 99 part-time); student-undergrad faculty ratio is 15:1. *Library Holdings:* 138,000 books, 160,000 microform titles, 920 periodicals, 5,000 records, tapes, and CDs. *Computers:* 66 terminals, PCs for student use in computer center, library, student center.

UNDERGRADUATE PROFILE 759 students from 16 states and territories, 20 other countries. 59% women, 7% part-time, 85% state residents, 42% live on campus, 39% transferred in, 4% international, 32% 25 or older, 1% Native American, 14% Hispanic, 4% African American, 4% Asian American. *Retention:* 73% of 1992 freshmen returned.

FRESHMEN 146 total. 346 applied, 79% were accepted, 53% of whom enrolled. 50% from top 10% of their high school class, 82% from top quarter, 100% from top half.

ACADEMIC PROGRAM Core. Calendar: semesters. 541 courses offered in 1993–94; average class size 18 in required courses. Academic remediation for entering students, English as a second language program offered during academic year, advanced placement, self-designed majors, summer session for credit, part-time degree program (daytime, summer), adult/continuing education programs, internships. Fewer than half of graduate courses open to undergraduate students. Off-campus study at California State University, Fresno, Mennonite Brethren Biblical Seminary, San Joaquin College of Law.

STUDY-ABROAD SITES France, Germany, Israel, Mexico, Spain.

MAJORS Accounting, athletic training, biblical studies, bilingual/bicultural education, biology/biological sciences, business administration/commerce/management, business education, child psychology/child development, communication, computer science, education, elementary education, English, history, humanities, (pre)law sequence, liberal arts/general studies, literature, management information systems, mathematics, (pre)medicine sequence, ministries, music, music education, natural sciences, physical education, political science/government, psychology, religious studies, science education, secondary education, social science, social work, sociology, Spanish, sports administration.

EXPENSES FOR 1994–95 Comprehensive fee of $13,744 includes full-time tuition ($9900), mandatory fees ($174), and college room and board ($3670). College room only: $1500. Part-time tuition: $345 per unit. Part-time mandatory fees: $49 per semester.

FINANCIAL AID *College-administered aid for undergraduates 1993–94:* 586 need-based scholarships (average $1040), 1,012 non-need scholarships (average $1350), short-term loans (average $300), low-interest long-term loans from external sources (average $3115), FSEOG, Federal Work-Study, 250 part-time jobs. Average total aid for freshmen: $8966, meeting 81% of need (aid provided to 100% of those qualified). *Application forms required:* institutional, FAFSA; required for some: IRS; accepted: FFS, FAF. *Priority deadline:* 3/2. *Payment plan:* installment. *Waivers:* full or partial for employees or children of employees and senior citizens.

COLLEGE LIFE Orientation program (3 days, no cost, parents included). Drama-theater group, choral group, instrumental groups, student-run newspaper and yearbook. *Student services:* health clinic, personal-psychological counseling. *Safety:* 24-hour emergency response devices, late-night transport-escort service.

ATHLETICS Member NAIA. *Intercollegiate:* basketball M(s)/W(s), cross-country running M(s)/W(s), soccer M(s), track and field M(s)/W(s), volleyball W. *Intramural:* basketball, bowling, cross-country running, football, racquetball, skiing (cross-country), skiing (downhill), soccer, tennis, track and field, volleyball.

APPLYING/FRESHMEN *Options:* early entrance, deferred entrance. *Required:* essay, school transcript, 2 years of high school foreign language, 1 recommendation, SAT I or ACT. *Recommended:* TOEFL for international students. *Required for some:* interview. Test scores used for admission. *Application deadline:* rolling. *Notification:* continuous until 7/31.

APPLYING/TRANSFER *Required:* essay, high school transcript, 1 recommendation, college transcript, minimum 2.0 GPA. *Recommended:* minimum 3.0 GPA. *Required for some:* standardized test scores, interview. *Entrance level:* moderately difficult. *Application deadline:* rolling. *Notification:* continuous until 7/31.

CONTACT Mr. Cary Templeton, Director of Admissions, Fresno Pacific College, 1717 South Chestnut Avenue, Fresno, CA 93702; 209-453-2030 or toll-free 800-660-6089 (in-state).

GENEVA COLLEGE
Beaver Falls, Pennsylvania

SPECIAL NOTE FROM THE COLLEGE Founded in 1848, Geneva College is one of the oldest evangelical Christian colleges in the nation, the second oldest in the Christian College Coalition. It offers an education that articulates the implications of Christ's sovereignty over all his creation. Geneva was one of 14 model sites chosen for the Christian College Coalition Racial and Ethnic Diversity Project. Students of color are encouraged to explore educational opportunities at Geneva. Majors include engineering, speech pathology, and cardiovascular technology. Through a cooperative program, students can combine degrees in aviation, air traffic control, or aerospace management with a business degree. All students complete a core program, which integrates courses in history, music, art, literature, and culture with biblical Christianity. Cocurricular activities include intercollegiate programs in all major sports, theater, choir, an FM radio station, and marching and concert bands. Although Geneva seeks students with a biblical world and life view, all students are welcome.

Total Enrollment: 1,632

UG Enrollment: 1,564 (49% W)

Application Deadline: rolling

Entrance: moderately difficult

Tuition & Fees: $9516

Room & Board: $4300

SAT≥500: 32% V, 49% M   **ACT≥21:** N/R

Denominational Affiliation: Reformed Presbyterian Church of North America

GENERAL INFORMATION Independent-religious comprehensive coed institution. Awards associate, bachelor's, master's degrees. Founded 1848. *Setting:* 55-acre suburban campus with easy access to Pittsburgh. *Undergraduate faculty:* 102 (51 full-time, 66% with terminal degrees, 51 part-time); student-undergrad faculty ratio is 18:1. *Library Holdings:* 149,482 books, 72,346 microform titles, 737 periodicals, 1 on-line bibliographic service, 10,248 records, tapes, and CDs. *Computers:* 45 terminals, PCs for student use in computer center, computer labs. Student computer-purchase plan available.

UNDERGRADUATE PROFILE 1,564 students from 34 states and territories, 16 other countries. 49% women, 17% part-time, 79% state residents, 2% international, 0% Native American, 0% Hispanic, 14% African American, 1% Asian American. *Retention:* 77% of 1992 freshmen returned. *Graduation:* 54% graduate in 4 years.

FRESHMEN 237 total. 624 applied, 86% were accepted, 44% of whom enrolled. 20% from top 10% of their high school class, 78% from top half. 2 National Merit Scholarship Finalists, 4 valedictorians.

ACADEMIC PROGRAM Core, Christian liberal arts and sciences curriculum, honor code. Calendar: semesters. 800 courses offered in 1993–94; average class size 20 in required courses. Academic remediation for entering students, English as a second language program offered during summer, advanced placement, accelerated degree program, self-designed majors, tutorials, honors program, summer session for credit, part-time degree program (daytime, evenings), adult/continuing education programs, co-op programs and internships. Off-campus study at Pennsylvania State University Beaver Campus, Community College of Beaver County. Unusual degree programs: 3-2 nursing with University of Rochester.

STUDY-ABROAD SITES China, Costa Rica, England, Russia.

MAJORS Accounting, applied mathematics, aviation administration, biblical studies, biology/biological sciences, broadcasting, business administration/commerce/management, business education, chemical engineering, chemistry, civil engineering, communication, computer science, education, electrical engineering, elementary education, engineering (general), English, guidance and counseling, history, human resources, industrial engineering, journalism, Latin American studies, (pre)law sequence, mathematics, mechanical engineering, medical technology, (pre)medicine sequence, ministries, music, music business, music education, pastoral studies, philosophy, physics, political science/government, psychology, radio and television studies, science, secondary education, sociology, Spanish, speech pathology and audiology, speech/rhetoric/public address/debate.

EXPENSES FOR 1994–95 *Application fee:* $25. Comprehensive fee of $13,816 includes full-time tuition ($9476), mandatory fees ($40), and college room and board ($4300). Part-time tuition: $300 per credit.

FINANCIAL AID *College-administered aid for undergraduates 1993–94:* 1,233 need-based scholarships (average $2298), 421 non-need scholarships (average $576), short-term loans (average $100), low-interest long-term loans from external sources (average $2643), FSEOG, Federal Work-Study, 343 part-time jobs. Average total aid for freshmen: $6884, meeting 75% of need (aid provided to 98% of those qualified). *Application forms required:* institutional; required for some: IRS, state, FAFSA; accepted: FFS, FAF. *Priority deadline:* 4/15. *Payment plan:* installment. *Waivers:* full or partial for employees or children of employees.

COLLEGE LIFE Orientation program (2 days, $25, parents included). Drama-theater group, choral group, marching band, student-run newspaper, radio station. *Social organizations:* 17 open to all. *Most popular organizations:* marching band, Genevans A Capella Choir, ministry groups. *Major annual events:* Homecoming, Parents' Weekend, Alumni Weekend. *Student services:* health clinic, personal-psychological counseling. *Safety:* 24-hour emergency response devices, controlled dormitory access.

ATHLETICS Member NAIA. *Intercollegiate:* baseball M(s), basketball M(s)/W(s), cross-country running M(s)/W(s), football M(s), soccer M(s)/W(s), softball W(s), tennis M(s)/W(s), track and field M(s)/W(s), volleyball M(c)/W(s). *Intramural:* basketball, bowling, football, golf, ice hockey, racquetball, skiing (downhill), soccer, softball, volleyball. *Contact:* Mr. Jerry Slocum, Athletic Director, 412-847-6648.

APPLYING/FRESHMEN *Options:* early entrance, deferred entrance, midyear entrance. *Required:* essay, school transcript, 3 years of high school math and science, 2 years of high school foreign language, recommendations, SAT I or ACT, TOEFL for international students. *Recommended:* minimum 3.0 GPA. *Required for some:* interview. Test scores used for admission. *Application deadline:* rolling. *Notification:* continuous.

APPLYING/TRANSFER *Required:* essay, high school transcript, 3 years of high school math and science, 2 years of high school foreign language, college transcript, minimum 2.0 GPA. *Recommended:* minimum 3.0 GPA. *Required for some:* standardized test scores, recommendations, interview. *Entrance level:* moderately difficult. *Application deadline:* rolling. *Notification:* continuous.

CONTACT Dr. Bill Katip, Vice President for Enrollment Management, Geneva College, 3200 College Avenue, Beaver Falls, PA 15010; 412-847-6506 or toll-free 800-847-2428 (in-state), 800-847-8255 (out-of-state).

GEORGE FOX COLLEGE
Newberg, Oregon

Total Enrollment: 1,557
UG Enrollment: 1,326 (59% W)
Application Deadline: 6/1
Entrance: moderately difficult
Tuition & Fees: $12,650
Room & Board: $4130
Denominational Affiliation: Evangelical Friends

GENERAL INFORMATION Independent-religious comprehensive coed institution. Awards bachelor's, master's, doctorate degrees. Founded 1891. *Setting:* 73-acre small-town campus with easy access to Portland. *Faculty:* 133 (70 full-time, 55% with terminal degrees, 63 part-time); student-undergrad faculty ratio is 14:1. *Library Holdings:* 93,658 books, 1,852 microform titles, 870 periodicals, 1 on-line bibliographic service, 29 CD-ROMs, 2,033 records, tapes, and CDs. *Computers:* 1,200 terminals, PCs for student use in computer center, computer labs, library, student rooms. Computers provided to students. Access to campuswide network, Internet from computer center, computer labs, library. *Services:* e-mail, file transfer.

UNDERGRADUATE PROFILE 1,326 students from 22 states and territories, 12 other countries. 59% women, 4% part-time, 66% state residents, 75% live on campus, 15% transferred in, 5% international, 18% 25 or older, 1% Native American, 1% Hispanic, 1% African American, 2% Asian American. *Retention:* 66% of 1992 freshmen returned. *Graduation:* 43% graduate in 4 years.

FRESHMEN 350 total. 811 applied, 90% were accepted, 48% of whom enrolled. 19% from top 10% of their high school class, 42% from top quarter, 78% from top half. 6 National Merit Scholarship Finalists, 6 National Merit Scholars.

ACADEMIC PROGRAM Core. Calendar: semesters. 560 courses offered in 1993–94; average class size 25 in required courses. Academic remediation for entering students, English as a second language program offered during academic year, advanced placement, accelerated degree program, self-designed majors, honors program, summer session for credit, part-time degree program (daytime), adult/continuing education programs, internships. A few graduate courses open to undergraduate students. Off-campus study at members of the Christian College Consortium, Christian College Coalition. Unusual degree programs: 3-2 engineering with University of Portland, Washington University, Seattle Pacific University.

STUDY-ABROAD SITES Australia, Costa Rica, Egypt, France, Germany, Great Britain, Greece, Guatemala, Israel, Italy, Mexico, the Netherlands, Russia, Spain, Switzerland.

MAJORS Biblical studies, biology/biological sciences, business administration/commerce/management, business economics, chemistry, civil engineering, communication, computer engineer-

ing, computer information systems, computer science, (pre)dentistry sequence, economics, education, electrical engineering, elementary education, engineering (general), engineering and applied sciences, engineering sciences, English, fashion merchandising, history, home economics, home economics education, human resources, interdisciplinary studies, interior design, international studies, (pre)law sequence, liberal arts/general studies, literature, mathematics, (pre)medicine sequence, ministries, music, music education, physical education, psychology, religious studies, science, science education, secondary education, social work, sociology, Spanish, sports medicine, telecommunications, (pre)veterinary medicine sequence.

EXPENSES FOR 1994–95 *Application fee:* $30. Comprehensive fee of $16,780 includes full-time tuition ($12,500), mandatory fees ($150), and college room and board ($4130). Part-time mandatory fees: $40 per semester.

FINANCIAL AID *College-administered aid for undergraduates 1993–94:* 910 need-based scholarships (average $2306), 1,684 non-need scholarships (average $1141), low-interest long-term loans from external sources (average $3296), FSEOG, Federal Work-Study, 129 part-time jobs. Average total aid for freshmen: $13,581, meeting 70% of need (aid provided to 100% of those qualified). *Application forms required:* FAFSA. *Priority deadline:* 3/15. *Payment plans:* installment, deferred payment. *Waivers:* full or partial for minority students, employees or children of employees, and senior citizens. Must reapply each year.

COLLEGE LIFE Orientation program (3 days, no cost, parents included first day). Drama-theater group, choral group, forensics team, student-run newspaper, radio station. *Student services:* health clinic, personal-psychological counseling. *Safety:* 24-hour emergency response devices and patrols, student patrols, late-night transport-escort service, controlled dormitory access.

ATHLETICS Member NAIA. *Intercollegiate:* baseball M(s), basketball M(s)/W(s), cross-country running M(s)/W(s), soccer M(s)/W(s), softball W(s), tennis M/W, track and field M(s)/W(s), volleyball W(s). *Intramural:* badminton, basketball, football, racquetball, soccer, table tennis (Ping-Pong), tennis, volleyball, weight lifting. *Contact:* Mr. Craig Taylor, Athletic Director, 503-538-8383.

APPLYING/FRESHMEN *Options:* early entrance, deferred entrance, midyear entrance. *Required:* essay, school transcript, 2 recommendations, SAT I or ACT, TOEFL for international students. *Recommended:* 3 years of high school math and science, some high school foreign language. *Required for some:* interview. Test scores used for admission and counseling/placement. *Application deadline:* 6/1.

APPLYING/TRANSFER *Required:* essay, 2 recommendations, college transcript, minimum 2.3 GPA. *Recommended:* interview. *Required for some:* standardized test scores, high school transcript. *Entrance level:* moderately difficult. *Application deadline:* 6/1.

CONTACT Mr. Randy Comfort, Director of Admissions, George Fox College, Newberg, OR 97132; 503-538-8383 Ext. 2240.

GORDON COLLEGE
Wenham, Massachusetts

SPECIAL NOTE FROM THE COLLEGE Gordon College, on Boston's scenic North Shore, is New England's only nondenominational Christian college. It offers 29 majors, 17 national and international off-campus study options, and a Cooperative Education (Co-op) Program. Its 1,200 students, drawn from 36 states and 26 countries, are encouraged to participate in 22 ministry and service activities throughout the year. Gordon has won recognition for both its high quality and its reasonable cost. Edward Fiske lists it in his *Selective Guide*. Both Fiske and Barron's rate it as a "Best Buy," and *U.S. News & World Report* ranks it among the top national liberal arts colleges.

Total Enrollment: 1,228 (all UG)

Women: 63%

Application Deadline: rolling

Entrance: moderately difficult

Tuition & Fees: $13,300

Room & Board: $4230

SAT≥500: 41% V, 58% M **ACT≥21:** N/R

Denominational Affiliation: interdenominational

GENERAL INFORMATION Independent-religious 4-year coed institution. Awards bachelor's degrees. Founded 1889. *Setting:* 730-acre small-town campus with easy access to Boston. *Faculty:* 97 (73 full-time, 82% with terminal degrees, 24 part-time); student-undergrad faculty ratio is 16:1. *Library Holdings:* 232,585 books, 29,522 microform titles, 593 periodicals, 9,234 records, tapes, and CDs. *Computers:* 120 terminals, PCs for student use in computer center, library. Student computer-purchase plan available. Access to campuswide network from computer center. *Services:* e-mail, mainframe access, library catalog search and reservation.

UNDERGRADUATE PROFILE 1,228 students from 36 states and territories, 26 other countries. 63% women, 4% part-time, 32% state residents, 90% live on campus, 20% transferred in, 5% international, 1% Native American, 2% Hispanic, 2% African American, 4% Asian American. *Retention:* 81% of 1992 freshmen returned. *Graduation:* 58% graduate in 4 years.

FRESHMEN 282 total. 674 applied, 84% were accepted, 50% of whom enrolled. 27% from top 10% of their high school class, 58% from top quarter, 85% from top half.

ACADEMIC PROGRAM Core, liberal arts curriculum. Calendar: semesters. Average class size 35 in required courses. Academic remediation for entering students, advanced placement, self-designed majors, honors program, part-time degree program (daytime), co-op programs and internships. Off-campus study at members of the Christian College Consortium, Northeast Consortium of Colleges and Universities in Massachusetts. ROTC: Air Force (c). Unusual degree programs: 3-2 engineering with University of Massachusetts Lowell, nursing with Thomas Jefferson University.

STUDY-ABROAD SITES Costa Rica, Egypt, England, France, Germany, Israel, Kenya, Russia.

MAJORS Accounting, art, biblical studies, biology/biological sciences, business administration, chemistry, computer science, early childhood education, economics, elementary education, English, French, history, international affairs, mathematics, middle school education, modern languages, movement science, music, music education, philosophy, physics, political science/government, psychology, recreation and leisure services, secondary education, social work, sociology, Spanish, special education, youth ministries.

EXPENSES FOR 1994–95 *Application fee:* $40. Comprehensive fee of $17,530 includes full-time tuition ($12,750), mandatory fees ($550), and college room and board ($4230). College room only: $2710 (minimum).

FINANCIAL AID *College-administered aid for undergraduates 1993–94:* 953 need-based scholarships (average $5408), 482 non-need scholarships (average $3850), short-term loans (average $50), low-interest long-term loans from external sources (average $3550), FSEOG, Federal Work-Study, 500 part-time jobs. Average total aid for freshmen: $10,880, meeting 100% of need. *Application forms required:* FAF, state, institutional, FAFSA; required for some: IRS; accepted: FFS. *Priority deadline:* 3/15. *Payment plans:* tuition prepayment, installment. *Waivers:* full or partial for employees or children of employees. *Notification:* 4/1. Must reapply each year. *Average indebtedness of graduates:* $14,000.

COLLEGE LIFE Orientation program (4 days, no cost, parents included). Drama-theater group, choral group, student-run newspaper. *Social organizations:* 35 open to all. *Most popular organizations:* Student Government Association, Student Ministries, diverse music ensembles. *Major annual events:* Staley Lecture Series, Homecoming, Parent's Weekend. *Student services:* health clinic, personal-psychological counseling. *Safety:* 24-hour emergency response devices and patrols, late-night transport-escort service.

ATHLETICS Member NCAA. All Division III. *Intercollegiate:* baseball M, basketball M/W, cross-country running M/W, field hockey W, lacrosse M, soccer M/W, softball W, tennis M/W, volleyball W. *Intramural:* basketball, football, skiing (cross-country), skiing (downhill), soccer, volleyball. *Contact:* Dr. Walt Bowman, Director of Athletics, 508-927-2300 Ext. 4136.

APPLYING/FRESHMEN *Options:* early entrance, early decision, deferred entrance. *Required:* essay, school transcript, 1 recommendation, interview, SAT I or ACT, TOEFL for international students. *Recommended:* 3 years of high school math and science, 3 years of high school foreign language, SAT II: Subject Tests. Test scores used for admission. *Application deadlines:* rolling, 12/15 for early decision.

APPLYING/TRANSFER *Required:* essay, standardized test scores, 1 recommendation, interview, college transcript. *Recommended:* high school transcript, 3 years of high school math and science, 3 years of high school foreign language, minimum 2.0 GPA. *Entrance level:* moderately difficult. *Application deadline:* rolling.

CONTACT Mrs. Pamela B. Lazarakis, Director of Admissions, Gordon College, 255 Grapevine Road, Wenham, MA 01984; 508-927-2306 Ext. 4217 or toll-free 800-343-1379.

GOSHEN COLLEGE
Goshen, Indiana

Total Enrollment: 986 (all UG)

Women: 58%

Application Deadline: rolling

Entrance: moderately difficult

Tuition & Fees: $9420

Room & Board: $3730

SAT≥500: 48% V, 61% M   **ACT≥21:** N/R

Denominational Affiliation: Mennonite

GENERAL INFORMATION Independent-religious 4-year coed institution. Awards bachelor's degrees. Founded 1894. *Setting:* 135-acre small-town campus. *Faculty:* 125 (85 full-time, 62% with terminal degrees, 40 part-time). *Library Holdings:* 115,000 books, 100 microform titles, 860 periodicals, 2 on-line bibliographic services, 3 CD-ROMs, 1,500 records, tapes, and CDs. *Computers:* 80 terminals, PCs for student use in computer center, computer labs, dorms. Access to campuswide network, Internet from computer center, computer labs, dorms; on-line documentation available. *Services:* e-mail, file transfer, mainframe access.

UNDERGRADUATE PROFILE 986 students from 43 states and territories, 27 other countries. 58% women, 15% part-time, 49% state residents, 7% transferred in, 69% have need-based financial aid, 76% have non-need-based financial aid, 75% have campus jobs, 6% international, 19% 25 or older, 0% Native American, 4% Hispanic, 3% African American, 1% Asian American. *Retention:* 75% of 1992 freshmen returned. *Graduation:* 56% graduate in 4 years.

FRESHMEN 236 total. 550 applied, 84% were accepted, 51% of whom enrolled. 27% from top 10% of their high school class, 28% from top quarter, 76% from top half. 8 National Merit Scholarship Finalists, 8 National Merit Scholars.

ACADEMIC PROGRAM Core, Christian development curriculum, honor code. Calendar: semesters. 765 courses offered in 1993–94; average class size 25 in required courses. Academic remediation for entering students, English as a second language program offered during academic year, services for LD students, advanced placement, accelerated degree program, self-designed majors, summer session for credit, part-time degree program (daytime, evenings), adult/continuing education programs, co-op programs and internships. Off-campus study at Northern Indiana Consortium for Education. Unusual degree programs: 3-2 engineering with Case Western Reserve University, Washington University, Pennsylvania State University University Park Campus, University of Illinois.

STUDY-ABROAD SITES Costa Rica, Dominican Republic, Germany, Indonesia, Ivory Coast.

MAJORS Accounting, art education, art/fine arts, art therapy, biblical studies, bilingual/bicultural education, biology/biological sciences, broadcasting, business administration/commerce/management, business education, chemistry, child care/child and family studies, communication, computer information systems, computer science, (pre)dentistry sequence, dietetics, early childhood education, economics, education, elementary education, English, family services, German, Hispanic studies, history, journalism, (pre)law sequence, liberal arts/general studies, mathematics, (pre)medicine sequence, music, music education, natural sciences, nursing, nutrition, physical education, physical sciences, physics, political science/government, psychology, religious studies, science education, secondary education, social work, sociology, Spanish, teaching English as a second language, theater arts/drama, (pre)veterinary medicine sequence.

EXPENSES FOR 1994–95 *Application fee:* $15. Comprehensive fee of $13,150 includes full-time tuition ($9420) and college room and board ($3730). College room only: $1800. Part-time tuition per semester ranges from $215 to $4070.

FINANCIAL AID *College-administered aid for undergraduates 1993–94:* 888 need-based scholarships (average $1053), non-need scholarships (average $1180), low-interest long-term loans from college funds (average $4400), loans from external sources (average $2767), FSEOG, Federal Work-Study, 13 part-time jobs. Average total aid for freshmen: $9580, meeting 100% of need (aid provided to 100% of those qualified). *Application forms required:* institutional, FAFSA; required for some: IRS, state; accepted: FFS, FAF. *Priority deadline:* 3/1. *Waivers:* full or partial for employees or children of employees. *Notification:* continuous. Must reapply each year. *Average indebtedness of graduates:* $10,783.

COLLEGE LIFE Orientation program (3 days, no cost, parents included). Drama-theater group, choral group, student-run newspaper, radio station. *Social organizations:* 20 open to all, with 40% participating. *Most popular organizations:* Students for Shalom (5% participate), Environmental Concerns Group (5% participate), Nontraditional Student Network (5% participate), Goshen Student Women's Organization (5% participate). *Major annual events:* Carnival Fundraiser, Ethnic Fair, Fall Festival. *Student services:* health clinic, personal-psychological counseling, women's center. *Safety:* 24-hour emergency response devices, night security.

ATHLETICS Member NAIA. *Intercollegiate:* baseball M, basketball M/W, cross-country running M/W, golf M, soccer M/W, softball W, tennis M/W, track and field M/W, volleyball W. *Intramural:* badminton, basketball, cross-country running, skiing (cross-country), soccer, softball, table tennis (Ping-Pong), tennis, volleyball. *Contact:* Mrs. Linda Shetler, Assistant Professor of Physical Education, 219-535-7494.

APPLYING/FRESHMEN *Options:* early entrance, deferred entrance. *Required:* school transcript, 1 recommendation, SAT I or ACT, TOEFL for international students. *Recommended:* 3 years of high school math and science, some high school foreign language, interview. Test scores used for admission. *Application deadline:* rolling. *Notification:* continuous.

APPLYING/TRANSFER *Required:* high school transcript, 2 recommendations, college transcript, minimum 2.0 GPA. *Recommended:* 3 years of high school math and science, some high school foreign language, interview. *Entrance level:* moderately difficult. *Application deadline:* rolling. *Notification:* continuous.

CONTACT Ms. Marty Lehman, Director of Admissions, Goshen College, 1700 South Main Street, Goshen, IN 46526; 219-535-7535 or toll-free 800-348-7422; Electronic mail: Admissions@Goshen.edu.

GRACE COLLEGE
Winona Lake, Indiana

> **SPECIAL NOTE FROM THE COLLEGE** The mission at Grace College is to impact students' lives by strengthening their character, sharpening their competence, and preparing them for service. Every year, hundreds of Grace students volunteer their time in the local community. There are over 20 ministry opportunities to choose from at Grace including athletic outreach, inner-city missions, Halloween Funfest, and Youth for Christ. Grace students learn how they can have an effective ministry in any career, from youth pastor to business executive. Students who want to be a part of a community that makes ministry a priority should consider Grace.

Total Enrollment: 731 (all UG)

Women: 56%

Application Deadline: 8/1

Entrance: moderately difficult

Tuition & Fees: $8958

Room & Board: $3818

Denominational Affiliation: Fellowship of Grace Brethren Churches

GENERAL INFORMATION Independent-religious 4-year coed institution. Administratively affiliated with Grace Theological Seminary. Awards associate, bachelor's degrees. Founded 1948. *Setting:* 150-acre small-town campus. *Faculty:* 56 (30 full-time, 48% with terminal degrees, 26 part-time); student-undergrad faculty ratio is 17:1. *Library Holdings:* 143,000 books, 42,000 microform titles, 560 periodicals, 6,900 records, tapes, and CDs. *Computers:* 43 terminals, PCs for student use in computer center, library. Computers provided to students.

UNDERGRADUATE PROFILE 731 students from 32 states and territories, 15 other countries. 56% women, 15% part-time, 41% state residents, 68% live on campus, 8% transferred in, 80% have need-based financial aid, 9% have non-need-based financial aid, 24% have campus jobs, 2% international, 9% 25 or older, 1% Native American, 1% Hispanic, 1% African American, 1% Asian American. *Retention:* 78% of 1992 freshmen returned. *Graduation:* 39% graduate in 4 years.

FRESHMEN 190 total. 548 applied, 78% were accepted, 44% of whom enrolled. 20% from top 10% of their high school class, 39% from top quarter, 81% from top half.

ACADEMIC PROGRAM Core, honor code. Calendar: semesters. 449 courses offered in 1993–94; average class size 27 in required courses. Academic remediation for entering students, advanced placement, accelerated degree program, summer session for credit, part-time degree program (daytime), internships.

STUDY-ABROAD SITES France, Germany, Mexico, Russia, Spain.

MAJORS Accounting, art education, art/fine arts, behavioral sciences, biblical languages, biblical studies, biology/biological sciences, business administration/commerce/management, commercial art, communication, criminal justice, elementary education, English, French, German, graphic arts, Greek, (pre)law sequence, management information systems, mathematics, (pre)medicine sequence, ministries, music, music education, physical education, piano/organ, psychology, sacred music, science education, secretarial studies/office management, sociology, Spanish.

EXPENSES FOR 1994–95 *Application fee:* $20. Comprehensive fee of $12,776 includes full-time tuition ($8958) and college room and board ($3818). College room only: $1862. Part-time tuition per semester ranges from $167 to $3207. Part-time mandatory fees: $50 per year.

FINANCIAL AID *College-administered aid for undergraduates 1993–94:* need-based scholarships (average $1600), non-need scholarships (average $1600), low-interest long-term loans from college funds (average $1500), loans from external sources (average $2769), FSEOG, Federal Work-Study, part-time jobs. Average total aid for freshmen: $6619, meeting 100% of need (aid provided to 100% of those qualified). *Application forms required:* FAFSA; required for some: FAF; accepted: FFS, IRS. *Priority deadline:* 4/1. *Payment plan:* installment. *Waivers:* full or partial for employees or children of employees. *Notification:* continuous.

COLLEGE LIFE Orientation program (3 days, $190). Drama-theater group, choral group, student-run newspaper. *Social organizations:* 30 open to all, with 55% participating. *Most popular organizations:* Grace Ministries in Action (35% participate), Student Activities Board (7% participate), Student Senate (5% participate). *Major annual events:* Homecoming, Heart of the Holidays, Halloween Fun Fest. *Student services:* health clinic, personal-psychological counseling. *Safety:* student patrols.

ATHLETICS Member NAIA. *Intercollegiate:* baseball M(s), basketball M(s)/W(s), golf M(s), soccer M(s), softball W(s), tennis M(s)/W, track and field M/W, volleyball W(s). *Intramural:* basketball, football, volleyball. *Contact:* Mr. Phil Dick, Athletic Director, 219-372-5217.

APPLYING/FRESHMEN *Options:* early entrance, deferred entrance, midyear entrance. *Required:* school transcript, 2 recommendations, SAT I or ACT. *Recommended:* minimum 2.0 GPA, some high school foreign language. *Required for some:* 3 years of high school math and science, interview. Test scores used for admission. *Application deadline:* 8/1. *Notification:* continuous until 8/15.

APPLYING/TRANSFER *Required:* high school transcript, 2 recommendations, college transcript, minimum 2.0 GPA. *Recommended:* some high school foreign language. *Required for some:* 3 years of high school math and science, interview. *Entrance level:* moderately difficult. *Application deadline:* 8/1. *Notification:* continuous until 8/15.

CONTACT Mr. Ron Henry, Dean of Enrollment, Grace College, 200 Seminary Drive, Winona Lake, IN 46590; 219-372-5144 or toll-free 800-54-GRACE.

GRAND CANYON UNIVERSITY
Phoenix, Arizona

Total Enrollment: 1,963

UG Enrollment: 1,837 (63% W)

Application Deadline: 8/1

Entrance: moderately difficult

Tuition & Fees: $7738

Room & Board: $3100

SAT≥500: 27% V, 43% M **ACT≥21:** 49%

Denominational Affiliation: Southern Baptist

GENERAL INFORMATION Independent-religious comprehensive coed institution. Awards bachelor's, master's degrees. Founded 1949. *Setting:* 70-acre suburban campus. *Faculty:* 172 (78 full-time, 57% with terminal degrees, 94 part-time); student-undergrad faculty ratio is 16:1. *Library Holdings:* 134,452 books, 41,412 microform titles, 642 periodicals, 14 CD-ROMs, 4,113 records, tapes, and CDs. *Computers:* 60. terminals, PCs for student use in computer center, library, audiovisual lab.

UNDERGRADUATE PROFILE 1,837 students from 41 states and territories, 12 other countries. 63% women, 24% part-time, 87% state residents, 33% live on campus, 62% transferred in, 3% international, 35% 25 or older, 3% Native American, 6% Hispanic, 4% African American, 2% Asian American. *Retention:* 85% of 1992 freshmen returned.

FRESHMEN 172 total. 500 applied, 76% were accepted, 45% of whom enrolled. 20% from top 10% of their high school class, 40% from top quarter, 85% from top half.

ACADEMIC PROGRAM Core. Calendar: semesters. Academic remediation for entering students, English as a second language program offered during academic year, advanced placement, accelerated degree program, Freshman Honors College, honors program, summer session for credit, part-time degree program (daytime), internships. Fewer than half of graduate courses open to undergraduate students. Off-campus study at Christian College Coalition. ROTC: Army, Air Force (c). Unusual degree programs: 3-2 engineering with Arizona State University.

STUDY-ABROAD SITES Brazil, China, Hungary, Russia, Spain.

MAJORS Accounting, art education, art/fine arts, athletic training, biblical studies, biology/biological sciences, business administration/commerce/management, business economics, business education, chemistry, communication, computer science, criminal justice, (pre)dentistry sequence, economics, elementary education, English, environmental biology, finance/banking, graphic arts, history, human resources, international business, (pre)law sequence, liberal arts/general studies, literature, marketing/retailing/merchandising, mathematics, (pre)medicine sequence, ministries, music, music business, music education, nursing, physical education, physical fitness/exercise science, piano/organ, psychology, religious studies, sacred music, science education, secondary education, social science, sociology, special education, speech/rhetoric/public address/debate, studio art, theater arts/drama, theology, (pre)veterinary medicine sequence, voice, wind and percussion instruments.

EXPENSES FOR 1994–95 *Application fee:* $25. Comprehensive fee of $10,838 includes full-time tuition ($7328), mandatory fees ($410), and college room and board ($3100). Part-time tuition: $229 per semester hour.

FINANCIAL AID *College-administered aid for undergraduates 1993–94:* 1,189 need-based scholarships (average $1084), 533 non-need scholarships (average $2357), short-term loans (average $300), low-interest long-term loans from external sources (average $3130), FSEOG, Federal Work-Study, 64 part-time jobs. Average total aid for freshmen: $9112, meeting 94% of need (aid provided to 100% of those qualified). *Application forms required:* institutional, FAFSA; required for some: IRS; accepted: FFS, FAF, state. *Priority deadline:* 3/15. *Payment plan:* installment. *Waivers:* full or partial for employees or children of employees.

COLLEGE LIFE Orientation program (2 days, $25, parents included). Drama-theater group, choral group, student-run newspaper. *Student services:* health clinic, personal-psychological counseling.

ATHLETICS Member NCAA. All Division II except men's baseball (Division I). *Intercollegiate:* baseball M, basketball M(s)/W(s), cross-country running M(s)/W(s), golf M(s), soccer M(s), tennis W(s), volleyball W(s). *Intramural:* basketball, football, volleyball. *Contact:* Mr. Gil Stafford, Athletic Director, 602-589-2806.

APPLYING/FRESHMEN *Option:* early entrance. *Required:* essay, school transcript, 3 years of high school math, SAT I or ACT, TOEFL for international students. *Recommended:* minimum 3.0 GPA, 3 years of high school science, some high school foreign language. *Required for some:* 3 recommendations, campus interview. Test scores used for admission and counseling/placement. *Application deadline:* 8/1. *Notification:* continuous until 8/15.

APPLYING/TRANSFER *Required:* essay, college transcript, minimum 2.0 GPA. *Recommended:* standardized test scores, high school transcript, 3 years of high school math and science, some high school foreign language. *Required for some:* 3 recommendations, campus interview. *Entrance level:* moderately difficult. *Application deadline:* 8/1. *Notification:* continuous until 8/15.

CONTACT Director of Admissions and Enrollment Planning, Grand Canyon University, 3300 West Camelback Road, P.O. Box 11097, Phoenix, AZ 85017; 602-589-2855.

GREENVILLE COLLEGE
Greenville, Illinois

SPECIAL NOTE FROM THE COLLEGE Greenville College is located just 50 minutes east of downtown St. Louis, in beautiful central Illinois. Established in 1892, Greenville is fully accredited. Greenville has structured a thoroughly evangelical environment that supports and encourages growth of the whole person—spiritually, academically, and socially. Greenville graduates excel. For example, alumnus Bob Briner is president of ProServ Television; Chaz Corzine is vice president of Blanton/Herrell, Inc. (the talent management firm of Amy Grant and Michael W. Smith); Dr. Ernest Boyer, former US Commissioner of Education, is currently president of the Carnegie Foundation for the Advancement of Teaching; and hundreds of other graduates are teachers, doctors, businesspeople, missionaries, and laypeople in churches all over the world. Greenville College graduates are making a difference.

Total Enrollment: 830 (all UG)
Women: 52%
Application Deadline: rolling
Entrance: moderately difficult
Tuition & Fees: $10,426
Room & Board: $4334
SAT≥500: N/R   **ACT≥21:** 61%
Denominational Affiliation: Free Methodist

GENERAL INFORMATION Independent-religious 4-year coed institution. Awards bachelor's degrees. Founded 1892. *Setting:* 12-acre small-town campus with easy access to St. Louis. *Faculty:* 62 (56 full-time, 53% with terminal degrees, 6 part-time); student-undergrad faculty ratio is 14:1. *Library Holdings:* 119,621 books, 2,991 microform titles, 578 periodicals, 1 on-line bibliographic service, 3 CD-ROMs, 1,740 records, tapes, and CDs. *Computers:* 100 terminals, PCs for student use in computer center, library.

UNDERGRADUATE PROFILE 830 students from 42 states and territories, 11 other countries. 52% women, 7% part-time, 98% state residents, 8% transferred in, 8% 25 or older, 1% Native American, 3% Hispanic, 8% African American, 2% Asian American. *Retention:* 67% of 1992 freshmen returned. *Graduation:* 46% graduate in 4 years.

FRESHMEN 195 total. 594 applied, 64% were accepted, 51% of whom enrolled. 20% from top 10% of their high school class, 46% from top quarter, 76% from top half.

ACADEMIC PROGRAM Core, liberal arts curriculum, honor code. Calendar: 4-1-4. 500 courses offered in 1993–94. Academic remediation for entering students, English as a second language program offered during academic year, advanced placement, accelerated degree program, self-designed majors, honors program, summer session for credit, part-time degree program (daytime, evenings), co-op programs and internships. Off-campus study at 13 members of the Christian College Consortium. Unusual degree programs: 3-2 engineering with University of Illinois at Urbana-Champaign, nursing with Mennonite College of Nursing.

MAJORS Accounting, art education, art/fine arts, biblical studies, biology/biological sciences, business administration/commerce/management, business education, chemistry, communication, computer science, (pre)dentistry sequence, early childhood education, economics, education, elementary education, English, environmental biology, French, gerontology, history, (pre)law sequence, liberal arts/general studies, management information systems, marketing/retailing/merchandising, mathematics, medical technology, (pre)medicine sequence, ministries, modern languages, music, music education, pastoral studies, philosophy, physical education, physics, political science/government, psychology, recreation and leisure services, religious studies, sacred music, secondary education, social work, sociology, Spanish, special education, speech/rhetoric/public address/debate, theater arts/drama, theology, (pre)veterinary medicine sequence.

EXPENSES FOR 1994–95 *Application fee:* $10. Comprehensive fee of $14,760 includes full-time tuition ($10,306), mandatory fees ($120), and college room and board ($4334). Part-time tuition: $308 per credit hour.

FINANCIAL AID *College-administered aid for undergraduates 1993–94:* 624 need-based scholarships (average $3210), non-need scholarships (average $2425), low-interest long-term loans from college funds (average $1340), loans from external sources (average $3550), FSEOG, Federal Work-Study, 220 part-time jobs. Average total aid for freshmen: $9300, meeting 92% of need (aid provided to 100% of those qualified). *Application forms required:* IRS, FAFSA. *Priority deadline:* 6/1. *Payment plan:* installment. *Waivers:* full or partial for employees or children of employees and senior citizens.

COLLEGE LIFE Orientation program (5 days, no cost). Drama-theater group, choral group, student-run newspaper, radio station. *Social organizations:* 40 open to all, with 41% participating. *Most popular organizations:* John Wesley Club (3% participate), Rapport (4% participate), Club GC (25% participate), Education Students Professional Interest Council (4% participate), Elpinice Club. *Major annual events:* Homecoming, All College Picnic, All College Hike. *Student services:* personal-psychological counseling. *Safety:* 24-hour emergency response devices and patrols.

ATHLETICS Member NAIA. *Intercollegiate:* basketball M/W, cross-country running M/W, football M, golf M, soccer M/W(c), tennis M/W, track and field M/W, volleyball W. *Intramural:* badminton, basketball, football, table tennis (Ping-Pong), volleyball.

APPLYING/FRESHMEN *Options:* early entrance, deferred entrance. *Required:* school transcript, 2 recommendations, agreement to code of conduct, SAT I or ACT, TOEFL for international students. *Recommended:* 3 years of high school foreign language. *Required for some:* interview. Test scores used for counseling/placement. *Application deadline:* rolling. *Notification:* continuous.

APPLYING/TRANSFER *Required:* standardized test scores, 2 recommendations, college transcript, minimum 2.0 GPA, agreement to code of conduct. *Recommended:* high school transcript, 3 years of high school foreign language. *Required for some:* interview. *Entrance level:* moderately difficult. *Application deadline:* rolling. *Notification:* continuous.

CONTACT Kent Krober, Director of Admissions, Greenville College, 315 East College, Greenville, IL 62246; 618-664-1840 Ext. 218 or toll-free 800-248-2288 (in-state), 800-345-4440 (out-of-state).

HOUGHTON COLLEGE
Houghton, New York

HOUGHTON
A Christian College of Liberal Arts and Sciences

SPECIAL NOTE FROM THE COLLEGE For over 100 years Houghton College has provided an educational experience that integrates high academic quality with the Christian faith. The College is fully accredited and rated highly by national college publications. Physical facilities at Houghton include an equestrian farm, comprehensive art studios, downhill and cross-country ski trails, an initiative ropes course, and 4 major residence halls. Houghton offers 45 majors and programs on 2 campuses. The 1,300-acre Houghton campus in the beautiful countryside of western New York has 1,150 students. Programs in the sciences, education, music, and art are highly respected, and the religion department is rated among the best in the country. Over 100 international students and MKs (missionary's kids) come from over 20 countries to attend Houghton. Internships and study-abroad options are available.

Total Enrollment: 1,210 (all UG)
Women: 61%
Application Deadline: 8/1
Entrance: moderately difficult
Tuition & Fees: $10,300
Room & Board: $3550
SAT≥500: 51% V, 69% M **ACT≥21:** 78%
Denominational Affiliation: Wesleyan

GENERAL INFORMATION Independent-religious 4-year coed institution. Awards associate, bachelor's degrees. Founded 1883. *Setting:* 1,300-acre rural campus with easy access to Buffalo and Rochester. *Faculty:* 100 (64 full-time, 70% with terminal degrees, 36 part-time); student-undergrad faculty ratio is 14:1. *Library Holdings:* 216,857 books, 5,000 microform titles, 822 periodicals, 13,684 records, tapes, and CDs. *Computers:* 130 terminals, PCs for student use in computer center, computer labs, library, dorms, divisional offices.

UNDERGRADUATE PROFILE 1,210 students from 37 states and territories, 23 other countries. 61% women, 4% part-time, 62% state residents, 10% transferred in, 88% have need-based financial aid, 7% have non-need-based financial aid, 60% have campus jobs, 5% international, 6% 25 or older, 1% Native American, 1% Hispanic, 2% African American, 1% Asian American. *Retention:* 87% of 1992 freshmen returned. *Graduation:* 61% graduate in 4 years.

FRESHMEN 302 total; 236 from public schools. 949 applied, 83% were accepted, 38% of whom enrolled. 29% from top 10% of their high school class, 58% from top quarter, 92% from top half. 1 National Merit Scholarship Finalist, 17 valedictorians.

ACADEMIC PROGRAM Core, interdisciplinary curriculum, honor code. Calendar: semesters. 1,175 courses offered in 1993–94; average class size 25 in required courses. Academic remediation for entering students, English as a second language program offered during academic year and summer, services for LD students, advanced placement, tutorials, honors program, summer session for credit, part-time degree program (daytime), adult/continuing education programs, internships. Off-campus study at members of the Western New York Consortium and the Christian College Consortium. ROTC: Army (c). Unusual degree programs: 3-2 engineering with Clarkson University.

MAJORS Accounting, art education, art/fine arts, biblical studies, biology/biological sciences, business administration/commerce/ management, chemistry, communication, creative writing, (pre)dentistry sequence, early childhood education, education, elementary education, (pre)engineering sequence, English, French, history, humanities, international studies, (pre)law sequence, literature, mathematics, medical laboratory technology, medical technology, (pre)medicine sequence, ministries, music, music education, natural sciences, pastoral studies, philosophy, physical education, physical sciences, physics, piano/organ, political science/ government, psychology, recreation and leisure services, religious education, religious studies, sacred music, science, science education, secondary education, social science, sociology, Spanish, stringed instruments, (pre)veterinary medicine sequence, voice, wind and percussion instruments.

EXPENSES FOR 1994–95 Comprehensive fee of $13,850 includes full-time tuition ($9990), mandatory fees ($310), and college room and board ($3550). College room only: $1700. Part-time tuition per credit hour: $225 for the first 6 credit hours, $274 for the next 3 credit hours.

FINANCIAL AID *College-administered aid for undergraduates 1993–94:* need-based scholarships (average $2446), 550 non-need scholarships (average $1500), short-term loans (average $500), low-interest long-term loans from external sources (average $3000), FSEOG, Federal Work-Study, 170 part-time jobs. Average total aid for freshmen: $9531, meeting 85% of need (aid provided to 100% of those qualified). *Application forms required:* FAF, institutional, FAFSA; required for some: IRS, state; accepted: FFS. *Priority deadline:* 3/15. *Payment plan:* installment. *Waivers:* full or partial for minority students and employees or children of employees. *Notification:* 4/1. Must reapply each year. *Average indebtedness of graduates:* $13,000.

COLLEGE LIFE Orientation program (2 days, $35, parents included). Drama-theater group, choral group, student-run newspaper, radio station. *Social organizations:* 50 open to all, with 40% participating. *Most popular organizations:* Student Government, World Mission Fellowship. *Major annual events:* Homecoming, Winter Weekend, Christian Life Emphasis Week. *Student services:* health clinic, personal-psychological counseling, shuttle bus. *Safety:* 24-hour patrols, late-night transport-escort service, controlled dormitory access.

ATHLETICS Member NAIA. *Intercollegiate:* basketball M(s)/W(s), cross-country running M(s)/W(s), field hockey W(s), soccer M(s)/ W(s), track and field M(s)/W(s), volleyball W(s). *Intramural:* basketball, equestrian sports, football, racquetball, skiing (cross-country), skiing (downhill), soccer, swimming and diving, table tennis (Ping-Pong), tennis, volleyball, water polo, weight lifting. *Contact:* Mr. Harold Lord, Athletic Director, 716-567-9360.

APPLYING/FRESHMEN Preference given to Evangelical Christians. *Options:* early entrance, deferred entrance, midyear entrance. *Required:* essay, school transcript, 1 recommendation, pastoral recommendation, SAT I or ACT, TOEFL for international students. *Recommended:* 3 years of high school math, some high school foreign language, interview. Test scores used for admission. *Application deadline:* 8/1. *Notification:* continuous.

APPLYING/TRANSFER *Required:* essay, high school transcript, 1 recommendation, college transcript, minimum 2.5 GPA. *Recommended:* 3 years of high school math, some high school foreign language, interview. *Required for some:* standardized test scores. *Entrance level:* moderately difficult. *Application deadline:* 8/1. *Notification:* continuous.

CONTACT Mr. Timothy R. Fuller, Vice President for Alumni and Admissions, Houghton College, P.O. Box 128, Houghton, NY 14744; 716-567-9353 or toll-free 800-777-2556.

HUNTINGTON COLLEGE
Huntington, Indiana

SPECIAL NOTE FROM THE COLLEGE Huntington College is dedicated to impact the world with Christ-centered distinctives. One of these distinctives is the Huntington Plan, a guaranteed tuition program in which students pay a one-time fee equal to 10% of the current year's tuition to lock in tuition at that rate through graduation. Huntington is also home to the newly formed Link Institute for Faithful and Effective Youth Ministry.

Total Enrollment: 578
UG Enrollment: 540 (51% W)
Application Deadline: 8/15
Entrance: moderately difficult
Tuition & Fees: $10,200
Room & Board: $3920
SAT≥500: 20% V, 48% M   **ACT≥21:** 63%
Denominational Affiliation: Church of the United Brethren in Christ

GENERAL INFORMATION Independent-religious comprehensive coed institution. Awards associate, bachelor's, master's degrees. Founded 1897. *Setting:* 200-acre small-town campus. *Faculty:* 52 (42 full-time, 79% with terminal degrees, 10 part-time); student-undergrad faculty ratio is 12:1. *Library Holdings:* 73,049 books, 16,094 microform titles, 460 periodicals, 2 on-line bibliographic services, 1,594 records, tapes, and CDs. *Computers:* 75 terminals, PCs for student use in computer center, library, dorms. Student computer-purchase plan available.

UNDERGRADUATE PROFILE 540 students from 18 states and territories, 13 other countries. 51% women, 9% part-time, 65% state residents, 80% live on campus, 6% transferred in, 35% have campus jobs, 8% international, 13% 25 or older, 0% Native American, 0% Hispanic, 1% African American, 1% Asian American. *Retention:* 72% of 1992 freshmen returned. *Graduation:* 52% graduate in 4 years.

FRESHMEN 125 total. 450 applied, 96% were accepted, 29% of whom enrolled. 20% from top 10% of their high school class, 46% from top quarter, 83% from top half. 3 National Merit Scholarship Finalists.

ACADEMIC PROGRAM Core, honor code. Calendar: 4-1-4. Average class size 21 in required courses. Academic remediation for entering students, English as a second language program offered during academic year and summer, advanced placement, accelerated degree program, self-designed majors, tutorials, summer session for credit, part-time degree program (daytime, evenings), adult/continuing education programs, internships. Off-campus study at Saint Francis College (IN) in special education.

STUDY-ABROAD SITE Jamaica.

MAJORS Accounting, art/fine arts, biblical studies, biology/biological sciences, broadcasting, business administration/commerce/management, business economics, business education, chemistry, communication, computer science, (pre)dentistry sequence, econom-ics, education, elementary education, (pre)engineering sequence, English, graphic arts, history, (pre)law sequence, mathematics, medical technology, (pre)medicine sequence, missions ministries, music, music education, natural resource management, philosophy, physical education, physical fitness/exercise science, piano/organ, psychology, recreation and leisure services, religious studies, science, science education, secondary education, secretarial studies/office management, sociology, special education, theater arts/drama, theology, (pre)veterinary medicine sequence, voice, youth ministries.

EXPENSES FOR 1994–95 *Application fee:* $15. Comprehensive fee of $14,120 includes full-time tuition ($9950), mandatory fees ($250), and college room and board ($3920). Part-time tuition: $300 per semester hour.

FINANCIAL AID *College-administered aid for undergraduates 1993–94:* need-based scholarships (average $4000), non-need scholarships (average $2300), low-interest long-term loans from external sources (average $1500), FSEOG, Federal Work-Study, 150 part-time jobs. Average total aid for freshmen: $8848, meeting 91% of need (aid provided to 100% of those qualified). *Application forms required:* institutional, FAFSA; required for some: IRS; accepted: FFS, FAF. *Priority deadline:* 3/1.

COLLEGE LIFE Orientation program (3 days, no cost, parents included). Drama-theater group, choral group, student-run newspaper. *Social organizations:* 35 open to all, with 70% participating; 1 national fraternity, 1 national sorority; 7% of eligible men and 10% of eligible women are members. *Student services:* health clinic, personal-psychological counseling. *Safety:* 24-hour emergency response devices, late-night transport-escort service, room security, night patrols.

ATHLETICS Member NAIA. *Intercollegiate:* baseball M(s), basketball M(s)/W(s), cross-country running M(s)/W(s), golf M(s)/W(s), soccer M(s), softball W(s), tennis M(s)/W(s), track and field M(s)/W(s), volleyball W(s). *Intramural:* basketball, bowling, football, racquetball, soccer, tennis, volleyball, weight lifting. *Contact:* Mr. Tom King, Athletic Director, 219-356-6000 Ext. 2013.

APPLYING/FRESHMEN *Options:* early entrance, deferred entrance. *Required:* essay, school transcript, minimum 2.3 high school GPA, SAT I or ACT, TOEFL for international students. *Recommended:* 3 years of high school math and science, 1 year of high school foreign language, interview. Test scores used for counseling/placement. *Application deadline:* 8/15.

APPLYING/TRANSFER *Required:* essay, standardized test scores, high school transcript, college transcript, minimum 2.0 GPA. *Recommended:* 3 years of high school math and science, 1 year of high school foreign language, interview. *Entrance level:* moderately difficult. *Application deadline:* 8/15.

CONTACT Mr. Jeff Berggren, Dean of Enrollment Management, Huntington College, 2303 College Avenue, Huntington, IN 46750; 219-356-6000 Ext. 1016 or toll-free 800-642-6493.

INDIANA WESLEYAN UNIVERSITY
Marion, Indiana

SPECIAL NOTE FROM THE UNIVERSITY Uniqueness, a distinctly Christian approach, and dynamic growth characterize Indiana Wesleyan University. IWU's uniqueness is demonstrated by its academic programs, which include addictions counseling, athletic training, criminal justice, legal assistant/paralegal studies, medical laboratory technology, nursing, recreation management, and social work. Integration of biblical principles and faith in Christ occurs in classrooms, athletics, and extracurricular activities. Bible classes and chapel, along with accountability, discipleship, and Bible study groups, also enhance spiritual growth. New residence halls, a new art/communications classroom building, a new student center, new academic majors, and significant campus development have produced dynamic enrollment growth as the freshman class has increased from 218 students in 1987 to 366 students in 1993.

Total Enrollment: 4,182

UG Enrollment: 3,157 (66% W)

Application Deadline: rolling

Entrance: moderately difficult

Tuition & Fees: $9210

Room & Board: $3782

SAT≥500: 10% V, 26% M   **ACT≥21:** 44%

Denominational Affiliation: Wesleyan

GENERAL INFORMATION Independent-religious comprehensive coed institution. Awards associate, bachelor's, master's degrees. Founded 1920. *Setting:* 75-acre small-town campus with easy access to Indianapolis. *Undergraduate faculty:* 105 (67 full-time, 38 part-time); student-undergrad faculty ratio is 15:1. *Library Holdings:* 119,808 books, 7,592 microform titles, 750 periodicals, 18,604 records, tapes, and CDs. *Computers:* 50 terminals, PCs for student use in computer center, learning resource center, library, dorms, writing center.

UNDERGRADUATE PROFILE 3,157 students from 38 states and territories, 6 other countries. 66% women, 15% part-time, 80% state residents, 20% transferred in, 3% international, 62% 25 or older, 0% Native American, 1% Hispanic, 4% African American, 1% Asian American.

FRESHMEN 366 total. 1,100 applied, 74% were accepted, 44% of whom enrolled. 20% from top 10% of their high school class, 28% from top quarter, 75% from top half.

ACADEMIC PROGRAM Core. Calendar: 4-4-1. Academic remediation for entering students, services for LD students, advanced placement, accelerated degree program, self-designed majors, honors program, summer session for credit, part-time degree program (daytime, evenings), adult/continuing education programs, internships. Off-campus study at Taylor University.

MAJORS Accounting, art education, art/fine arts, biblical studies, biology/biological sciences, business administration/commerce/management, chemistry, communication, computer information systems, creative writing, criminal justice, (pre)dentistry sequence, economics, education, elementary education, (pre)engineering sequence, English, finance/banking, history, law enforcement/police sciences, (pre)law sequence, liberal arts/general studies, mathematics, medical laboratory technology, medical technology, (pre)medicine sequence, mental health/rehabilitation counseling, ministries, music, music business, music education, nursing, pastoral studies, philosophy, physical education, physical sciences, piano/organ, political science/government, psychology, recreational facilities management, recreation and leisure services, religious education, religious studies, sacred music, science, science education, secondary education, secretarial studies/office management, social science, social work, sociology, Spanish, studio art, theology, (pre)veterinary medicine sequence, voice, wind and percussion instruments.

EXPENSES FOR 1994–95 *Application fee:* $15. Comprehensive fee of $12,992 includes full-time tuition ($9210) and college room and board ($3782). College room only: $1558. Part-time tuition per term ranges from $197 to $3630.

FINANCIAL AID *College-administered aid for undergraduates 1993–94:* 686 need-based scholarships (average $1500), 1,100 non-need scholarships (average $900), low-interest long-term loans from college funds (average $1500), loans from external sources (average $2000), FSEOG, Federal Work-Study, 300 part-time jobs. Average total aid for freshmen: $8548, meeting 88% of need (aid provided to 99% of those qualified). *Application forms required:* FAF, institutional, FAFSA; required for some: IRS; accepted: FFS. *Priority deadline:* 4/1. *Payment plan:* installment. *Waivers:* full or partial for employees or children of employees.

COLLEGE LIFE Orientation program (4 days, no cost, parents included). Drama-theater group, choral group, student-run newspaper, radio station. *Student services:* health clinic, personal-psychological counseling.

ATHLETICS Member NAIA. *Intercollegiate:* baseball M(s), basketball M(s)/W(s), cross-country running M(s)/W(s), golf M(s), soccer M(s)/W(s), softball W(s), tennis M(s)/W(s), track and field M(s)/W(s), volleyball W(s). *Intramural:* badminton, basketball, bowling, football, golf, racquetball, soccer, table tennis (Ping-Pong), tennis, volleyball, weight lifting. *Contact:* Dr. Michael Fratzke, Director of Athletics, 317-674-2318.

APPLYING/FRESHMEN *Options:* early entrance, deferred entrance. *Required:* essay, school transcript, 1 recommendation, SAT I or ACT, TOEFL for international students. *Recommended:* interview. *Required for some:* interview. Test scores used for admission and counseling/placement. *Application deadline:* rolling. *Notification:* continuous.

APPLYING/TRANSFER *Required:* essay, high school transcript, 1 recommendation, college transcript, minimum 2.0 GPA. *Recommended:* standardized test scores, interview. *Required for some:* interview. *Entrance level:* moderately difficult. *Application deadline:* rolling. *Notification:* continuous.

CONTACT Mr. Herb Frye, Vice President for Enrollment Management, Indiana Wesleyan University, 4201 South Washington Street, Marion, IN 46953; 317-677-2138 or toll-free 800-332-6901.

John Brown University
Siloam Springs, Arkansas

> **SPECIAL NOTE FROM THE UNIVERSITY** The most distinctive feature of John Brown University is its career orientation. This orientation is reflected in some of JBU's unique programs: engineering, broadcasting, art and design, sports medicine, and construction management. It is also the cornerstone of traditional programs: business, teacher education, and science. At JBU, career orientation is found in more than its programs—it is an attitude. JBU wants its graduates to be successful Christian leaders no matter what their chosen fields are. JBU's second most distinctive feature is its intercultural perspective. With 130 international students and over 80 Third World culture missionary's kids, JBU offers a global approach to Christian higher education right in northwest Arkansas.

Total Enrollment: 1,060 (all UG)

Women: 53%

Application Deadline: 5/1

Entrance: moderately difficult

Tuition & Fees: $7086

Room & Board: $3672

SAT≥500: 43% V, 50% M   **ACT≥21:** 72%

Denominational Affiliation: nondenominational

GENERAL INFORMATION Independent-religious 4-year coed institution. Awards associate, bachelor's degrees. Founded 1919. *Setting:* 200-acre rural campus. *Faculty:* 95 (70 full-time, 70% with terminal degrees, 25 part-time); student-undergrad faculty ratio is 15:1. *Library Holdings:* 93,000 books, 125 microform titles, 620 periodicals, 2,400 records, tapes, and CDs. *Computers:* 130 terminals, PCs for student use in computer center, classrooms.

UNDERGRADUATE PROFILE 1,060 students from 43 states and territories, 36 other countries. 53% women, 9% part-time, 27% state residents, 70% live on campus, 15% transferred in, 75% have need-based financial aid, 10% have non-need-based financial aid, 40% have campus jobs, 12% international, 8% 25 or older, 1% Native American, 1% Hispanic, 2% African American, 1% Asian American. *Retention:* 78% of 1992 freshmen returned. *Graduation:* 51% graduate in 4 years.

FRESHMEN 266 total. 605 applied, 70% were accepted, 63% of whom enrolled. 24% from top 10% of their high school class, 53% from top quarter, 78% from top half. 2 National Merit Scholarship Finalists, 1 National Merit Scholar, 23 valedictorians.

ACADEMIC PROGRAM Core. Calendar: semesters. 300 courses offered in 1993–94; average class size 35 in required courses. Academic remediation for entering students, English as a second language program offered during academic year, advanced placement, honors program, internships. ROTC: Army (c).

MAJORS Accounting, art/fine arts, athletic training, biblical studies, biochemistry, biology/biological sciences, broadcasting, business administration/commerce/management, business education, chemistry, commercial art, communication, construction engineering, construction management, early childhood education, education, electrical engineering, elementary education, engineering (general), engineering management, engineering technology, English, graphic arts, health education, health services administration, history, interdisciplinary studies, international studies, journalism, (pre)law sequence, liberal arts/general studies, mathematics, mechanical engineering, medical technology, (pre)medicine sequence, middle school education, ministries, music, music education, pastoral studies, physical education, physical fitness/exercise science, piano/organ, psychology, public relations, radio and television studies, recreational facilities management, religious education, religious studies, secondary education, secretarial studies/office management, social science, special education, sports medicine, theology, voice.

EXPENSES FOR 1994–95 *Application fee:* $25. Comprehensive fee of $10,758 includes full-time tuition ($6938), mandatory fees ($148), and college room and board ($3672). Part-time tuition: $290 per semester hour.

FINANCIAL AID *College-administered aid for undergraduates 1993–94:* 650 need-based scholarships (average $730), 550 non-need scholarships (average $1475), low-interest long-term loans from college funds (average $2000), loans from external sources (average $2900), FSEOG, Federal Work-Study, 240 part-time jobs. Average total aid for freshmen: $7013, meeting 71% of need (aid provided to 100% of those qualified). *Application forms required:* IRS; required for some: FFS, state; accepted: FAF, FAFSA. *Priority deadline:* 4/1. *Payment plans:* tuition prepayment, installment. *Waivers:* full or partial for employees or children of employees and senior citizens. *Notification:* continuous.

COLLEGE LIFE Orientation program (3 days, $50, parents included). Drama-theater group, choral group, student-run newspaper, radio station. *Most popular organizations:* Student Government Association, Student Ministries Organization, Student Missionary Fellowship. *Major annual events:* Homecoming, Christmas Candlelight Service, Parents' Weekend. *Student services:* health clinic, personal-psychological counseling.

ATHLETICS Member NAIA. *Intercollegiate:* basketball M(s)/W(s), soccer M(s), swimming and diving M(s)/W(s), tennis M(s)/W(s), volleyball W(s). *Intramural:* basketball, football, racquetball, rugby, soccer, softball, tennis, volleyball. *Contact:* Dr. G. Robert Burns, Athletic Director, 501-524-7305.

APPLYING/FRESHMEN *Options:* early entrance, deferred entrance, midyear entrance. *Required:* school transcript, minimum 3.0 GPA, 3 years of high school math and science, 2 recommendations, SAT I or ACT, TOEFL for international students. *Recommended:* some high school foreign language. *Required for some:* essay, interview, 4 years of high school science for engineering majors. Test scores used for admission. *Application deadline:* 5/1.

APPLYING/TRANSFER *Required:* 2 recommendations, college transcript, minimum 2.0 GPA. *Required for some:* essay, standardized test scores, high school transcript, 3 years of high school math and science, interview. *Entrance level:* moderately difficult. *Application deadline:* 5/1.

CONTACT Mr. Don Crandall, Vice President of Enrollment Management, John Brown University, 2000 West University Street, Siloam Springs, AR 72761; 501-524-7150 or toll-free 800-634-6969.

JUDSON COLLEGE
Elgin, Illinois

Total Enrollment: 605 (all UG)

Women: 55%

Application Deadline: 8/15

Entrance: moderately difficult

Tuition & Fees: $9284

Room & Board: $4422

SAT≥500: N/R   **ACT≥21:** 54%

Denominational Affiliation: Baptist

GENERAL INFORMATION Independent-religious 4-year coed institution. Awards bachelor's degrees. Founded 1963. *Setting:* 80-acre suburban campus with easy access to Chicago. *Faculty:* 105 (29 full-time, 60% with terminal degrees, 76 part-time); student-undergrad faculty ratio is 15:1. *Library Holdings:* 75,767 books, 28,000 microform titles, 430 periodicals, 2 on-line bibliographic services, 6 CD-ROMs, 6,500 records, tapes, and CDs. *Computers:* 50 terminals, PCs for student use in computer center, library.

UNDERGRADUATE PROFILE 605 students from 21 states and territories, 9 other countries. 55% women, 17% part-time, 72% state residents, 57% live on campus, 13% transferred in, 80% have need-based financial aid, 50% have campus jobs, 2% international, 15% 25 or older, 5% Hispanic, 5% African American, 1% Asian American. *Retention:* 70% of 1992 freshmen returned.

FRESHMEN 133 total. 356 applied, 67% were accepted, 56% of whom enrolled. 13% from top 10% of their high school class, 29% from top quarter, 60% from top half.

ACADEMIC PROGRAM Core, liberal arts curriculum, honor code. Calendar: 4-1-4. 200 courses offered in 1993–94; average class size 15 in required courses. Academic remediation for entering students, advanced placement, accelerated degree program, honors program, part-time degree program (daytime, evenings), internships. Off-campus study at North Park College, Christian College Coalition Tuition Exchange. ROTC: Army (c).

MAJORS Accounting, anthropology, art/fine arts, biblical studies, biology/biological sciences, business administration/commerce/management, chemistry, communication, computer information systems, computer science, education, elementary education, English, history, (pre)law sequence, linguistics, literature, mathematics, (pre)medicine sequence, music, nursing, painting/drawing, philosophy, physical education, physical sciences, psychology, religious studies, science, social science, sociology, speech/rhetoric/public address/debate, theater arts/drama, voice.

EXPENSES FOR 1993–94 Comprehensive fee of $13,706 includes full-time tuition ($8884), mandatory fees ($400), and college room and board ($4422). Part-time tuition: $289 per semester hour.

FINANCIAL AID *College-administered aid for undergraduates 1993–94:* 437 need-based scholarships (average $1350), non-need scholarships (average $1297), low-interest long-term loans from external sources (average $2900), FSEOG, Federal Work-Study, 60 part-time jobs. Average total aid for freshmen: $9196, meeting 82% of need (aid provided to 100% of those qualified). *Application forms required:* institutional; required for some: IRS; accepted: FAFSA. *Priority deadline:* 5/1.

COLLEGE LIFE Orientation program (5 days, no cost, parents included). Drama-theater group, choral group, student-run radio station. *Most popular organizations:* Judson Choir, Nowhere Near Broadway. *Major annual events:* Founders' Day, Homecoming, Spiritual Emphasis Week. *Student services:* health clinic, personal-psychological counseling. *Safety:* 24-hour patrols, controlled dormitory access, room security.

ATHLETICS Member NAIA. *Intercollegiate:* baseball M(s), basketball M(s)/W(s), cross-country running M(s)/W(s), soccer M(s)/W(s), softball W(s), tennis M(s)/W(s), volleyball W(s). *Intramural:* badminton, basketball, football, racquetball, soccer, softball, tennis, volleyball. *Contact:* Mr. Steve Burke, Athletic Director, 708-695-2500 Ext. 3801.

APPLYING/FRESHMEN *Options:* deferred entrance, midyear entrance. *Required:* essay, school transcript, minimum 2.0 GPA, SAT I or ACT, TOEFL for international students. *Recommended:* 3 years of high school math and science. *Required for some:* 1 recommendation, campus interview. Test scores used for admission. *Application deadline:* 8/15. *Notification:* continuous.

APPLYING/TRANSFER *Required:* essay, college transcript, minimum 2.0 GPA. *Recommended:* 3 years of high school math and science. *Required for some:* standardized test scores, high school transcript, 1 recommendation, campus interview. *Entrance level:* moderately difficult. *Application deadline:* 8/15. *Notification:* continuous.

CONTACT Mr. Matthew Osborne, Director of Enrollment Services, Judson College, 1151 North State Street, Elgin, IL 60123; 800-TRY-JDSN (toll-free).

KING COLLEGE
Bristol, Tennessee

> **SPECIAL NOTE FROM THE COLLEGE** King College firmly believes that academic excellence can be fully integrated with Christian faith. More than 90% of King students are accepted into their first choice of graduate schools, and *U.S. News & World Report* has listed King College as one of America's best colleges for 4 consecutive years. King was also one of only 142 colleges in the nation to be rated "highly selective" by the Carnegie Foundation for the Advancement of Teaching. King College graduates are qualified in their chosen field of study, mature in their Christian faith, and committed to responsible service in the world.

Total Enrollment: 561 (all UG)

Women: 55%

Application Deadline: rolling

Entrance: moderately difficult

Tuition & Fees: $9364

Room & Board: $3350

SAT≥500: 35% V, 58% M   **ACT≥21:** 87%

Denominational Affiliation: Presbyterian Church (U.S.A.)

GENERAL INFORMATION Independent-religious 4-year coed institution. Awards bachelor's degrees. Founded 1867. *Setting:* 135-acre suburban campus. *Faculty:* 64 (40 full-time, 65% with terminal degrees, 24 part-time); student-undergrad faculty ratio is 13:1. *Library Holdings:* 95,800 books, 550 microform titles, 645 periodicals, 7 on-line bibliographic services, 175 CD-ROMs, 1,960 records, tapes, and CDs. *Computers:* 46 terminals, PCs for student use in computer center, computer labs, library, student center, dorms, classroom buildings, multi-media network classroom lab. Students must have own computer. Access to campuswide network from computer center, computer labs, library, student center, dorms, student rooms. *Services:* e-mail, file transfer.

UNDERGRADUATE PROFILE 561 students from 28 states and territories, 6 other countries. 55% women, 8% part-time, 42% state residents, 75% live on campus, 20% transferred in, 80% have need-based financial aid, 50% have non-need-based financial aid, 5% international, 3% 25 or older, 0% Native American, 1% Hispanic, 1% African American, 1% Asian American. *Retention:* 68% of 1992 freshmen returned. *Graduation:* 38% graduate in 4 years.

FRESHMEN 142 total; 122 from public schools. 355 applied, 85% were accepted, 47% of whom enrolled. 34% from top 10% of their high school class, 65% from top quarter, 91% from top half. 4 valedictorians.

ACADEMIC PROGRAM Core, classical and scientific curriculum. Calendar: semesters. 280 courses offered in 1993–94; average class size 25 in required courses. English as a second language program offered during academic year and summer, advanced placement, self-designed majors, summer session for credit, part-time degree program (daytime), internships. Off-campus study at Virginia Intermont College. ROTC: Army (c). Unusual degree programs: 3-2 engineering with University of Maryland, Georgia Institute of Technology, University of Tennessee, medical technology with Holston Valley Hospital and Medical Center, Vanderbilt University.

STUDY-ABROAD SITES France, Israel, Korea, Mexico, Morocco, the Netherlands, New Guinea, Spain.

MAJORS Accounting, art/fine arts, biblical studies, biology/biological sciences, business administration/commerce/management, business economics, chemistry, (pre)dentistry sequence, economics, education, elementary education, English, French, history, international business, (pre)law sequence, mathematics, medical technology, (pre)medicine sequence, music, physics, political science/government, psychology, religious studies, science, theater arts/drama, (pre)veterinary medicine sequence.

EXPENSES FOR 1994–95 Comprehensive fee of $12,714 includes full-time tuition ($8664), mandatory fees ($700), and college room and board ($3350). College room only: $1630.

FINANCIAL AID *College-administered aid for undergraduates 1993–94:* 287 need-based scholarships (average $4278), 321 non-need scholarships (average $2823), low-interest long-term loans from college funds (average $986), loans from external sources (average $3625), FSEOG, Federal Work-Study, 94 part-time jobs. Average total aid for freshmen: $7920, meeting 80% of need (aid provided to 100% of those qualified). *Application forms required:* institutional, FAFSA; required for some: FAF, IRS, financial aid transcript (for transfers). *Priority deadline:* 3/1. *Payment plan:* installment. *Waivers:* full or partial for employees or children of employees. *Notification:* continuous. *Average indebtedness of graduates:* $9000.

COLLEGE LIFE Orientation program (4 days, no cost, parents included). Drama-theater group, choral group, student-run newspaper. *Most popular organizations:* Student Government Association, Campus Life Committee, World Christian Fellowship. *Major annual events:* Fall Banquet and Fall Play, Dogwood/Alumni Weekend, Parents' Weekend. *Student services:* health clinic, personal-psychological counseling. *Safety:* late-night transport-escort service.

ATHLETICS Member NAIA. *Intercollegiate:* baseball M(s), basketball M(s)/W(s), golf M(s)/W, soccer M(s), softball W(s), tennis M(s)/W(s), volleyball W(s). *Intramural:* basketball, golf, soccer, swimming and diving, table tennis (Ping-Pong), tennis, volleyball, weight lifting. *Contact:* Mr. Joe Hakes, Athletic Director, 615-652-4849.

APPLYING/FRESHMEN *Options:* early entrance, midyear entrance. *Required:* essay, school transcript, SAT I or ACT. *Recommended:* 3 years of high school math and science, some high school foreign language, interview, TOEFL for international students. *Required for some:* recommendations, interview. Test scores used for admission. *Application deadline:* rolling.

APPLYING/TRANSFER *Required:* essay, college transcript, minimum 2.0 GPA. *Recommended:* standardized test scores, 3 years of high school math and science, some high school foreign language, interview. *Required for some:* interview. *Entrance level:* moderately difficult. *Application deadline:* rolling.

CONTACT Director of Admissions, King College, 1350 King College Road, Bristol, TN 37620-2699; 615-652-4861 or toll-free 800-362-0014.

THE KING'S COLLEGE
Briarcliff Manor, New York

Total Enrollment: 230 (all UG)
Women: 60%
Application Deadline: rolling
Entrance: moderately difficult
Tuition & Fees: $8938
Room & Board: $3920
SAT≥500: 25% V, 33% M   **ACT≥21:** N/R
Denominational Affiliation: nondenominational

GENERAL INFORMATION Independent-religious 4-year coed institution. Awards associate, bachelor's degrees. Founded 1938. *Setting:* 80-acre suburban campus with easy access to New York City. *Faculty:* 49 (26 full-time, 46% with terminal degrees, 23 part-time); student-undergrad faculty ratio is 9:1. *Library Holdings:* 87,030 books, 11,067 microform titles, 3,307 periodicals, 1,500 records, tapes, and CDs. *Computers:* 25 terminals, PCs for student use in computer center, library. Access to campuswide network from computer center, computer labs, learning resource center, library.

UNDERGRADUATE PROFILE 230 students from 25 states and territories, 10 other countries. 60% women, 8% part-time, 45% state residents, 60% live on campus, 24% transferred in, 40% have campus jobs, 4% international, 5% 25 or older, 1% Native American, 5% Hispanic, 6% African American, 6% Asian American.

FRESHMEN 72 total; 41 from public schools. 356 applied, 65% were accepted, 31% of whom enrolled. 16% from top 10% of their high school class, 24% from top quarter, 40% from top half. 2 valedictorians.

ACADEMIC PROGRAM Core, interdisciplinary curriculum. Calendar: semesters. 145 courses offered in 1993–94; average class size 20 in required courses. Academic remediation for entering students, English as a second language program offered during academic year and summer, advanced placement, accelerated degree program, tutorials, summer session for credit, part-time degree program (daytime), internships. Off-campus study at Pace University, New York State Visiting Student Program, members of the Christian College Coalition. Unusual degree programs: nursing with Pace University, 4-1 MBA in public accounting with Pace University.

STUDY-ABROAD SITES England, France, Mexico, Russia, Spain.

MAJORS Accounting, biblical studies, biology/biological sciences, business administration/commerce/management, chemistry, computer science, early childhood education, education, elementary education, English, French, history, liberal arts/general studies, mathematics, medical technology, modern languages, music, music education, nursing, physical education, psychology, religious education, religious studies, secondary education, sociology, Spanish.

EXPENSES FOR 1994–95 *Application fee:* $20. Comprehensive fee of $13,108 includes full-time tuition ($8938), mandatory fees ($250), and college room and board ($3920). College room only: $1928. Part-time tuition: $275 per semester hour.

FINANCIAL AID *College-administered aid for undergraduates 1993–94:* 118 need-based scholarships (average $1160), 137 non-need scholarships (average $2628), low-interest long-term loans from external sources (average $2550), FSEOG, Federal Work-Study, part-time jobs. Average total aid for freshmen: $12,061, meeting 93% of need (aid provided to 100% of those qualified). *Application forms required:* FAF, IRS, institutional, FAFSA; required for some: state; accepted: FFS. *Priority deadline:* 4/5. *Payment plan:* installment. *Waivers:* full or partial for employees or children of employees. *Average indebtedness of graduates:* $13,000.

COLLEGE LIFE Orientation program (3 days, parents included). Drama-theater group, choral group, student-run newspaper. *Social organizations:* 6 open to all. *Most popular organizations:* outreach programs, Student Government, Drama Club. *Major annual events:* King's Tourney, Homecoming. *Student services:* health clinic, personal-psychological counseling. *Safety:* 24-hour emergency response devices, student patrols, late-night transport-escort service.

ATHLETICS Member NAIA. *Intercollegiate:* basketball M(s)/W(s), cross-country running M(s)/W(s), soccer M(s)/W(s), softball W(s). *Intramural:* basketball, football, weight lifting. *Contact:* Ms. Lynn Sabia, Athletic Director, 914-944-5554.

APPLYING/FRESHMEN *Options:* early entrance, deferred entrance, midyear entrance. *Required:* school transcript, 2 recommendations, SAT I or ACT, TOEFL for international students. *Recommended:* essay, 3 years of high school math and science, some high school foreign language. *Required for some:* campus interview. Test scores used for admission. *Application deadline:* rolling.

APPLYING/TRANSFER *Required:* 2 recommendations, college transcript, minimum 2.0 GPA. *Recommended:* essay, 3 years of high school math and science, some high school foreign language. *Required for some:* standardized test scores, high school transcript, campus interview. *Entrance level:* moderate. *Application deadline:* rolling.

CONTACT Cheryl Burdick, Director of Admissions, The King's College, 150 Lodge Road, Briarcliff Manor, NY 10510; 800-344-4926.

THE KING'S UNIVERSITY COLLEGE
Edmonton, Alberta, Canada

> **SPECIAL NOTE FROM THE COLLEGE** The King's University College is an independent, Christian liberal arts college located in an urban setting in one of western Canada's major cities. Christian students learn how to be "in the world, but not of the world" through an education that integrates the Christian faith with life and learning, with an emphasis on the unique task of the Christian in a secular society. The College is close to the University of Alberta, one of Canada's largest, allowing for significant interaction with that institution. At the same time, the College's small size and highly qualified faculty contribute to a caring and intellectually stimulating environment for learning and personal growth. Continued development of degree programs and an attractive new campus combine to project exciting years of growth for the College and its students.

Total Enrollment: 420 (all UG)
Women: 56%
Application Deadline: rolling
Entrance: moderately difficult
Tuition & Fees: $4125
Room & Board: $4025
Denominational Affiliation: nondenominational

GENERAL INFORMATION Independent-religious 3-year coed institution. Awards bachelor's degrees. Founded 1979. *Setting:* 20-acre urban campus. *Faculty:* 65 (28 full-time, 100% with terminal degrees, 37 part-time); student-undergrad faculty ratio is 12:1. *Library Holdings:* 51,000 books, 280 periodicals, 1,800 records, tapes, and CDs. *Computers:* 30 terminals, PCs for student use in computer labs.

UNDERGRADUATE PROFILE 420 students from 7 provinces and territories, 10 other countries. 56% women, 12% part-time, 86% province residents, 14% live on campus, 4% have campus jobs, 4% international, 21% 25 or older, 1% Native American, 2% black, 4% Asian. *Retention:* 54% of 1992 freshmen returned.

FRESHMEN 224 total. 437 applied, 70% were accepted, 74% of whom enrolled.

ACADEMIC PROGRAM Core, honor code. Calendar: standard year. 200 courses offered in 1993–94; average class size 21 in required courses. Academic remediation for entering students, tutorials, part-time degree program (daytime), adult/continuing education programs, internships.

MAJORS Biology/biological sciences, chemistry, English, history, music, philosophy, psychology, social science.

EXPENSES FOR 1994–95 *Application fee:* $35. Comprehensive fee of $8150 includes full-time tuition ($3900), mandatory fees ($225), and college room and board ($4025). Part-time tuition: $390 per course. Part-time mandatory fees: $112.50 per term.

FINANCIAL AID *College-administered aid for undergraduates 1993–94:* 17 need-based scholarships (average $520), 39 non-need scholarships (average $347), low-interest long-term loans from external sources, 18 part-time jobs. *Application forms required:* institutional. *Application deadline:* 3/31. *Waivers:* partial for employees.

COLLEGE LIFE Orientation program. Drama-theater group, choral group, student-run newspaper. *Social organizations:* 8 open to all. *Student services:* personal-psychological counseling. *Safety:* 24-hour emergency response devices, student patrols, controlled dormitory access, room security.

ATHLETICS *Intercollegiate:* basketball M/W, volleyball M/W. *Contact:* Dr. Bob Day, Athletic Director, 403-465-3500.

APPLYING/FRESHMEN *Option:* midyear entrance. *Required:* school transcript, 1 recommendation, TOEFL for international students. *Required for some:* interview. Test scores used for admission. *Application deadline:* rolling. *Notification:* continuous until 8/15.

APPLYING/TRANSFER *Required:* high school transcript, 1 recommendation, college transcript, minimum 2.0 GPA. *Required for some:* campus interview. *Entrance level:* minimally difficult. *Application deadline:* rolling. *Notification:* continuous until 8/15.

CONTACT Mr. Fred Woudstra, Director of Liaison, The King's University College, 9125 50th Street, Edmonton, AB T6B 2H3, Canada; 403-465-3500 or toll-free 800-661-TKUC; fax: 403-465-3534.

LEE COLLEGE
Cleveland, Tennessee

SPECIAL NOTE FROM THE COLLEGE The dynamic growth of Lee College—to more than 2,000 students today from 960 just 10 years ago—marks it as an institution "on the move." Lee's beautiful campus in East Tennessee has doubled in size during that same period with the addition of a 500-seat theater/recital hall, a student recreation/fitness complex, 3 new dorms, and 2 classroom buildings. Lee offers its own study programs in England, Ukraine, China, and Germany. Lee is well known for the vitality of its student life. Over one third of its students play intramural sports, and 400 of them perform in travelling musical groups. It has ranked at the top of all Coalition colleges in tuition affordability for 4 straight years.

Total Enrollment: 2,011 (all UG)
Women: 51%
Application Deadline: rolling
Entrance: minimally difficult
Tuition & Fees: $4882
Room & Board: $3320
SAT≥500: 22% V, 33% M   **ACT≥21:** 47%
Denominational Affiliation: Church of God

GENERAL INFORMATION Independent-religious 4-year coed institution. Awards bachelor's degrees. Founded 1918. *Setting:* 45-acre small-town campus. *Faculty:* 163 (76 full-time, 50% with terminal degrees, 87 part-time); student-undergrad faculty ratio is 18:1. *Library Holdings:* 128,744 books, 27,142 microform titles, 805 periodicals, 3 on-line bibliographic services, 3 CD-ROMs, 6,619 records, tapes, and CDs; on-line access to libraries at Cleveland Public Library. *Computers:* 38 terminals, PCs for student use in computer center. Access to campuswide network from computer center, dorms; on-line documentation available. *Services:* on-line class registration, e-mail, file transfer, mainframe access, database computer-search services, library catalog search and reservation.

UNDERGRADUATE PROFILE 2,011 students from 43 states and territories, 22 other countries. 51% women, 5% part-time, 75% state residents, 65% live on campus, 10% transferred in, 11% have campus jobs, 6% international, 16% 25 or older, 1% Native American, 3% Hispanic, 2% African American, 1% Asian American. *Retention:* 72% of 1992 freshmen returned.

FRESHMEN 453 total. 651 applied, 76% were accepted, 91% of whom enrolled. 30% from top 10% of their high school class, 48% from top quarter, 66% from top half.

ACADEMIC PROGRAM Core, honor code. Calendar: semesters. Average class size 35 in required courses. Academic remediation for entering students, English as a second language program offered during academic year, services for LD students, advanced placement, honors program, summer session for credit, part-time degree program (daytime), external degree programs, adult/continuing education programs, co-op programs and internships. Off-campus study.

STUDY-ABROAD SITES China, England, Germany, Ukraine.

MAJORS Accounting, biblical studies, biology/biological sciences, business administration/commerce/management, business education, chemistry, communication, computer information systems, education, elementary education, English, health education, history, human development, international studies, mathematics, medical technology, modern languages, music, music education, natural sciences, pastoral studies, physical education, piano/organ, psychology, religious education, respiratory therapy, science, secondary education, secretarial studies/office management, social science, sociology, theology, voice.

EXPENSES FOR 1993–94 *Application fee:* $25. Comprehensive fee of $8202 includes full-time tuition ($4788), mandatory fees ($94), and college room and board ($3320). College room only: $1660. Part-time tuition: $200 per semester hour.

FINANCIAL AID *College-administered aid for undergraduates 1993–94:* 675 need-based scholarships (average $500), non-need scholarships, short-term loans (average $150), low-interest long-term loans from external sources (average $2800), FSEOG, Federal Work-Study, part-time jobs. Average total aid for freshmen: $5476, meeting 65% of need (aid provided to 95% of those qualified). *Application forms required:* institutional; required for some: IRS; accepted: FAFSA. *Priority deadline:* 4/15. *Payment plan:* installment. *Waivers:* full or partial for employees or children of employees and senior citizens. Must reapply each year.

COLLEGE LIFE Orientation program (2 days, no cost, parents included). Drama-theater group, choral group, student-run newspaper. *Social organizations:* 55 open to all, with 33% participating; 4 local fraternities, 3 local sororities; 20% of eligible men and 20% of eligible women are members. *Most popular organizations:* Campus Choir, Lee Singers, Phi Beta Lambda, Student National Education Association, Alpha Gamma Chi. *Major annual events:* Lee Day, Homecoming, Summer Honors. *Student services:* health clinic, personal-psychological counseling. *Safety:* 24-hour emergency response devices and patrols, late-night transport-escort service, room security.

ATHLETICS Member NAIA. *Intercollegiate:* basketball M(s)/W(s), golf M(s), soccer M(s), softball M/W(s), tennis M(s)/W(s), volleyball W(s). *Intramural:* basketball, football, racquetball, soccer, softball, table tennis (Ping-Pong), tennis, volleyball. *Contact:* Dr. Henry Smith, Interim Athletic Director, 615-472-2111.

APPLYING/FRESHMEN *Options:* early entrance, deferred entrance, midyear entrance. *Required:* school transcript, SAT I or ACT, TOEFL for international students. *Recommended:* immunization record. *Required for some:* 1 recommendation. Test scores used for admission and counseling/placement. *Application deadline:* rolling. *Notification:* continuous.

APPLYING/TRANSFER *Required:* college transcript, minimum 2.0 GPA, immunization record. *Entrance level:* minimally difficult. *Application deadline:* rolling. *Notification:* continuous.

CONTACT Mr. Gary Ray, Director of Admissions, Lee College, 1120 North Ocoee Street, Cleveland, TN 37311; 615-478-7316 or toll-free 800-LEE-9930.

LETOURNEAU UNIVERSITY
Longview, Texas

> **SPECIAL NOTE FROM THE UNIVERSITY** Set apart by a special "spirit of ingenuity," LeTourneau University continues to expand on the excellence and inventive zeal of its heritage. Always striving to excel, LeTourneau was the first evangelical Christian college to receive professional accreditation by the Accreditation Board for Engineering and Technology (ABET). The University provides solid programs in more than 40 majors, with special emphasis on aviation, business, engineering, and technology. Set in the beautiful pine woods and lakes of East Texas, the spacious contemporary campus is home to innovative students from virtually every state and 25 nations. At LeTourneau, "Faith brings us together, ingenuity sets us apart."

Total Enrollment: 1,745

UG Enrollment: 1,617 (30% W)

Application Deadline: 8/15

Entrance: moderately difficult

Tuition & Fees: $8970

Room & Board: $4240

SAT≥500: 49% V, 68% M   **ACT≥21:** 74%

Denominational Affiliation: nondenominational

GENERAL INFORMATION Independent-religious comprehensive coed institution. Awards associate, bachelor's, master's degrees. (Undergraduate enrollment figures include students in the LeTourneau Education for Adult Professionals program. There are 976 students in residence at Longview.) Founded 1946. *Setting:* 162-acre suburban campus. *Faculty:* 214 (51 full-time, 67% with terminal degrees, 163 part-time); student-undergrad faculty ratio is 15:1. *Library Holdings:* 98,641 books, 38,520 microform titles, 435 periodicals, 2,670 records, tapes, and CDs. *Computers:* 170 terminals, PCs for student use in computer center, computer labs, library.

UNDERGRADUATE PROFILE 1,617 students from 46 states and territories, 25 other countries. 30% women, 10% part-time, 67% state residents, 7% transferred in, 77% have need-based financial aid, 14% have non-need-based financial aid, 36% have campus jobs, 4% international, 13% 25 or older, 1% Native American, 1% Hispanic, 4% African American, 1% Asian American. *Retention:* 64% of 1992 freshmen returned. *Graduation:* 22% graduate in 4 years.

FRESHMEN 278 total. 700 applied, 82% were accepted, 66% of whom enrolled. 45% from top 10% of their high school class, 75% from top quarter, 95% from top half.

ACADEMIC PROGRAM Core. Calendar: semesters. 335 courses offered in 1993–94; average class size 16 in required courses. Academic remediation for entering students, advanced placement, summer session for credit, part-time degree program (daytime, evenings), adult/continuing education programs, co-op programs and internships. Off-campus study at Christian College Coalition.

MAJORS Accounting, aircraft maintenance, automotive technologies, aviation technology, biblical studies, biology/biological sciences, business administration/commerce/management, chemistry, computer engineering, computer science, computer technologies, (pre)dentistry sequence, drafting and design, electrical engineering, electrical engineering technology, engineering (general), engineering design, engineering technology, English, flight training, history, industrial administration, (pre)law sequence, marketing/ retailing/merchandising, mathematics, mechanical design technology, mechanical engineering, mechanical engineering technology, (pre)medicine sequence, ministries, natural sciences, physical education, psychology, religious studies, sports administration, (pre)veterinary medicine sequence, welding engineering, welding technology.

EXPENSES FOR 1994–95 *Application fee:* $20. Comprehensive fee of $13,210 includes full-time tuition ($8840), mandatory fees ($130), and college room and board ($4240). Part-time tuition per semester ranges from $120 to $4035.

FINANCIAL AID *College-administered aid for undergraduates 1993–94:* 632 need-based scholarships (average $1070), 336 non-need scholarships (average $1066), low-interest long-term loans from college funds (average $1350), loans from external sources (average $2530), FSEOG, Federal Work-Study, 190 part-time jobs. Average total aid for freshmen: $7438, meeting 80% of need (aid provided to 100% of those qualified). *Application forms required:* FAF, FAFSA; required for some: IRS; accepted: FFS. *Priority deadline:* 2/15. *Payment plan:* installment. *Notification:* continuous. Must reapply each year. *Average indebtedness of graduates:* $16,000.

COLLEGE LIFE Orientation program (1 week, parents included). Drama-theater group, choral group, student-run newspaper. *Social organizations:* 27 open to all; 5 local fraternities; 13% of eligible men are members. *Most popular organizations:* Automotive Society, Themelios, Student Foundation. *Major annual events:* Hootenanny, Go Kart Races, Homecoming. *Student services:* health clinic, personal-psychological counseling. *Safety:* 24-hour emergency response devices and patrols, late-night transport-escort service, controlled dormitory access, room security.

ATHLETICS Member NAIA. *Intercollegiate:* baseball M(s), basketball M(s)/W(s), cross-country running M/W, soccer M(s), track and field M/W, volleyball W(s). *Intramural:* badminton, basketball, bowling, cross-country running, field hockey, football, golf, racquetball, soccer, softball, swimming and diving, table tennis (Ping-Pong), tennis, track and field, volleyball, weight lifting, wrestling. *Contact:* Dr. Richard Beach, Director of Athletics, 903-753-0231.

APPLYING/FRESHMEN *Options:* early entrance, deferred entrance, midyear entrance. *Required:* essay, school transcript, minimum 2.0 GPA, 2 recommendations, SAT I or ACT, TOEFL for international students. *Recommended:* 3 years of high school science. *Required for some:* 3 years of high school math, campus interview. Test scores used for admission and counseling/placement. *Application deadline:* 8/15. *Notification:* continuous.

APPLYING/TRANSFER *Required:* essay, 2 recommendations, college transcript, minimum 2.0 GPA. *Required for some:* standardized test scores, high school transcript. *Entrance level:* moderately difficult. *Application deadline:* 8/15. *Notification:* continuous.

CONTACT Mr. Howard Wilson, Director of Admissions, LeTourneau University, P.O. Box 7001, Longview, TX 75607; 903-753-0231 Ext. 240 or toll-free 800-759-8811.

MALONE COLLEGE
Canton, Ohio

> **SPECIAL NOTE FROM THE COLLEGE** Malone College, located in Canton, Ohio, and only minutes from the Professional Football Hall of Fame, offers all students the opportunity to put their faith and careers into motion by combining classroom work with hands-on experience through internships and cooperative work experience. Academic excellence enables students to fully prepare for their future. In addition, students can participate in a variety of campus activities, ranging from mission trips to all-nighters! If it's athletic life students desire, Malone's nationally ranked teams charge head-to-head with the nation's best.

Total Enrollment: 1,929

UG Enrollment: 1,820 (59% W)

Application Deadline: 7/1

Entrance: moderately difficult

Tuition & Fees: $9993

Room & Board: $3700

SAT≥500: 25% V, 39% M   **ACT≥21:** 53%

Denominational Affiliation: Evangelical Friends Church–Eastern Region

GENERAL INFORMATION Independent-religious comprehensive coed institution. Awards associate, bachelor's, master's degrees. Founded 1892. *Setting:* 78-acre suburban campus with easy access to Cleveland. *Faculty:* 141 (71 full-time, 46% with terminal degrees, 70 part-time); student-undergrad faculty ratio is 13:1. *Library Holdings:* 127,372 books, 337,227 microform titles, 1,094 periodicals, 12 CD-ROMs, 5,861 records, tapes, and CDs. *Computers:* 50 terminals, PCs for student use in computer center, computer labs, library, writing lab.

UNDERGRADUATE PROFILE 1,820 students from 18 states and territories, 9 other countries. 59% women, 12% part-time, 95% state residents, 48% live on campus, 6% transferred in, 73% have need-based financial aid, 71% have non-need-based financial aid, 26% have campus jobs, 1% international, 26% 25 or older, 1% Native American, 1% Hispanic, 5% African American, 1% Asian American. *Retention:* 69% of 1992 freshmen returned. *Graduation:* 29% graduate in 4 years.

FRESHMEN 434 total; 389 from public schools. 874 applied, 87% were accepted, 57% of whom enrolled. 21% from top 10% of their high school class, 46% from top quarter, 78% from top half. 12 valedictorians.

ACADEMIC PROGRAM Core, arts, sciences and professional curriculum, honor code. Calendar: semesters. 329 courses offered in 1993–94; average class size 22 in required courses. Services for LD students, advanced placement, accelerated degree program, self-designed majors, tutorials, summer session for credit, part-time degree program (daytime), adult/continuing education programs, co-op programs and internships. Fewer than half of graduate courses open to undergraduate students. Off-campus study at members of the Christian College Consortium.

STUDY-ABROAD SITES Costa Rica, Guatemala, Hong Kong, Kenya, Russia.

MAJORS Accounting, art education, art/fine arts, biblical studies, biology/biological sciences, broadcasting, business administration/commerce/management, business education, chemistry, communication, computer science, (pre)dentistry sequence, early childhood education, education, elementary education, (pre)engineering sequence, English, health education, history, journalism, (pre)law sequence, liberal arts/general studies, mathematics, medical technology, (pre)medicine sequence, ministries, music, music education, nursing, physical education, psychology, radio and television studies, radiological sciences, religious education, sacred music, science, science education, secondary education, social science, social work, Spanish, special education, sports medicine, studio art, theater arts/drama, theology, (pre)veterinary medicine sequence.

EXPENSES FOR 1994–95 *Application fee:* $20. Comprehensive fee of $13,693 includes full-time tuition ($9858), mandatory fees ($135), and college room and board ($3700). Part-time tuition: $238 per credit hour. Part-time mandatory fees: $30 per semester.

FINANCIAL AID *College-administered aid for undergraduates 1993–94:* 1,350 need-based scholarships (average $1434), 1,180 non-need scholarships, low-interest long-term loans from college funds (average $1939), loans from external sources (average $3025), FSEOG, Federal Work-Study, 123 part-time jobs. Average total aid for freshmen: $8112, meeting 79% of need (aid provided to 100% of those qualified). *Application forms required:* institutional, FAFSA; *required for some:* IRS; *accepted:* FAF. *Priority deadline:* 3/31. *Payment plans:* installment, deferred payment. *Waivers:* full or partial for employees or children of employees and senior citizens. Must reapply each year. *Average indebtedness of graduates:* $12,000.

COLLEGE LIFE Orientation program (4 days, $10, parents included). Drama-theater group, choral group, student-run newspaper, radio station. *Social organizations:* 28 open to all, with 30% participating. *Most popular organizations:* Student Activities Committee, Thursdays, Student Senate, Spiritual Life, World Awareness and Social Issues. *Major annual events:* Homecoming, Christmas Celebration, Martin Luther King, Jr. Day Celebration. *Student services:* health clinic, personal-psychological counseling, shuttle bus. *Safety:* 24-hour emergency response devices and patrols, late-night transport-escort service.

ATHLETICS Member NAIA and NCAA. *Intercollegiate:* baseball M(s), basketball M(s)/W(s), cross-country running M(s)/W(s), football M(s), golf M(s), soccer M(s), softball W(s), tennis M(s)/W(s), track and field M(s)/W(s), volleyball W(s). *Intramural:* basketball, bowling, cross-country running, football, racquetball, skiing (cross-country), softball, table tennis (Ping-Pong), tennis, volleyball, weight lifting. *Contact:* Mr. Hal Smith, Director of Intercollegiate Athletics, 216-471-8296.

APPLYING/FRESHMEN *Options:* early entrance, deferred entrance, midyear entrance. *Required:* essay, school transcript, SAT I or ACT, TOEFL for international students. *Recommended:* 3 years of high school math and science, some high school foreign language. *Required for some:* 2 recommendations, interview. Test scores used for counseling/placement. *Application deadline:* 7/1. *Notification:* continuous until 6/30.

APPLYING/TRANSFER *Required:* essay, high school transcript, 1 recommendation, college transcript, minimum 2.0 GPA. *Recommended:* 3 years of high school math and science, some high school foreign language. *Required for some:* standardized test scores, interview. *Entrance level:* moderately difficult. *Application deadline:* 7/1. *Notification:* continuous until 6/30.

CONTACT Mr. Leland J. Sommers, Dean of Admissions, Malone College, 515 25th Street, NW, Canton, OH 44709; 216-471-8100 or toll-free 800-521-1146.

THE MASTER'S COLLEGE
Santa Clarita, California

> **SPECIAL NOTE FROM THE COLLEGE** The Master's College, on its 98-acre campus, enjoys the solitude and safety of the Santa Clarita Valley. Within an hour's drive of campus are beaches, mountains, and the cultural advantages of Los Angeles. College faculty and staff members are committed to equipping students for excellence in the Master's service. Baccalaureate programs include a Bachelor of Arts in 35 emphases and a Bachelor of Science in 12 emphases. Also offered are a rapidly growing Professional Studies Program for working adults and a 1-year diploma program in Bible for individuals desiring a better understanding of Scripture. Powerful chapels and ever-expanding local and worldwide ministry opportunities help students develop academically, spiritually, and socially.

Total Enrollment: 797

UG Enrollment: 748 (53% W)

Application Deadline: rolling

Entrance: moderately difficult

Tuition & Fees: $9140

Room & Board: $4194

SAT≥500: 32% V, 41% M   **ACT≥21:** N/R

Denominational Affiliation: nondenominational

GENERAL INFORMATION Independent-religious comprehensive coed institution. Awards bachelor's, master's degrees. Founded 1927. *Setting:* 98-acre suburban campus with easy access to Los Angeles. *Undergraduate faculty:* 79 (45 full-time, 49% with terminal degrees, 34 part-time); student-undergrad faculty ratio is 18:1. *Library Holdings:* 150,000 books, 1,500 microform titles, 892 periodicals, 8 CD-ROMs, 3,000 records, tapes, and CDs. *Computers:* 20 terminals, PCs for student use in computer center, library, business center.

UNDERGRADUATE PROFILE 748 students from 36 states and territories, 19 other countries. 53% women, 9% part-time, 96% state residents, 63% live on campus, 15% transferred in, 70% have need-based financial aid, 4% international, 10% 25 or older, 1% Native American, 4% Hispanic, 2% African American, 4% Asian American. *Retention:* 50% of 1992 freshmen returned. *Graduation:* 42% graduate in 4 years.

FRESHMEN 160 total. 337 applied, 88% were accepted, 54% of whom enrolled. 27% from top 10% of their high school class, 53% from top quarter, 80% from top half. 2 National Merit Scholarship Finalists, 2 National Merit Scholars.

ACADEMIC PROGRAM Core, biblically-based curriculum, honor code. Calendar: semesters. 320 courses offered in 1993–94; average class size 22 in required courses. Academic remediation for entering students, services for LD students, advanced placement, accelerated degree program, summer session for credit, part-time degree program (daytime). Off-campus study at College of the Canyons.

MAJORS Accounting, biblical languages, biblical studies, biology/biological sciences, business administration/commerce/management, communication, education, elementary education, English, finance/banking, history, home economics, liberal arts/general studies, mathematics, ministries, music, music education, natural sciences, physical education, political science/government, public relations, radio and television studies, secondary education, special education, speech/rhetoric/public address/debate, theology.

EXPENSES FOR 1994–95 *Application fee:* $25. Comprehensive fee of $13,334 includes full-time tuition ($9084), mandatory fees ($56), and college room and board ($4194). Part-time tuition: $296 per unit.

FINANCIAL AID *College-administered aid for undergraduates 1993–94:* 415 need-based scholarships (average $1716), 396 non-need scholarships (average $2502), low-interest long-term loans from external sources (average $3021), FSEOG, Federal Work-Study, part-time jobs. *Application forms required:* FAF, IRS, state, institutional; required for some: FAFSA; accepted: FFS. *Application deadline:* continuous to 8/1. *Payment plan:* installment. *Waivers:* full or partial for employees or children of employees.

COLLEGE LIFE Orientation program (5 days, no cost, parents included). Drama-theater group, choral group, student-run radio station. *Major annual events:* Missions Conference, College View Weekend, Homecoming. *Student services:* health clinic, personal-psychological counseling. *Safety:* 24-hour patrols, room security.

ATHLETICS Member NAIA. *Intercollegiate:* baseball M(s), basketball M(s)/W(s), cross-country running M(s)/W(s), soccer M(s)/W(s), volleyball W(s). *Intramural:* basketball, football, softball, volleyball. *Contact:* Mr. Bill Oates, Athletic Director, 805-259-3540 Ext. 222.

APPLYING/FRESHMEN *Option:* deferred entrance. *Required:* essay, school transcript, 3 years of high school math, 2 years of high school foreign language, 2 recommendations, SAT I or ACT, TOEFL for international students. *Recommended:* interview, SAT II: Subject Tests, SAT II: Writing Test. Test scores used for admission. *Application deadline:* rolling. *Notification:* continuous until 9/7.

APPLYING/TRANSFER *Required:* essay, 2 recommendations, college transcript, minimum 2.0 GPA. *Recommended:* interview. *Required for some:* standardized test scores, high school transcript. *Entrance level:* moderately difficult. *Application deadline:* rolling. *Notification:* continuous until 9/7.

CONTACT Director of Admissions, The Master's College, 21726 Placerita Canyon Road, Santa Clarita, CA 91321; 805-259-3540 Ext. 347 or toll-free 800-568-6248; fax: 805-288-1037.

MESSIAH COLLEGE
Grantham, Pennsylvania

SPECIAL NOTE FROM THE COLLEGE Messiah College is a 4-year, residential Christian college of the arts and sciences. The size of the enrollment (about 2,300) provides numerous advantages, including personal contact between students and faculty members. Located in Grantham, Pennsylvania, 10 miles south of Harrisburg, Messiah's 310-acre campus is easily accessible by interstate highways, Harrisburg International Airport, and train and bus lines. Messiah offers more than 40 majors, including traditional liberal arts curricula and professional and preprofessional programs in business, computer science, education, engineering, medicine, and nursing. Cooperative education, internships, and international service opportunities are also available at Messiah. Most of Messiah's excellent facilities have been constructed within the past 15 years, enabling the College to offer a high-quality education in an ever-changing world.

Total Enrollment: 2,311 (all UG)
Women: 59%
Application Deadline: rolling
Entrance: moderately difficult
Tuition & Fees: $9804
Room & Board: $4860
SAT≥500: 49% V, 71% M   **ACT≥21:** 75%
Denominational Affiliation: Brethren in Christ Church

GENERAL INFORMATION Independent-religious 4-year coed institution. Awards bachelor's degrees. Founded 1909. *Setting:* 310-acre small-town campus. *Faculty:* 196 (146 full-time, 68% with terminal degrees, 50 part-time); student-undergrad faculty ratio is 18:1. *Library Holdings:* 180,000 books, 5,000 microform titles, 1,000 periodicals, 5,500 records, tapes, and CDs. *Computers:* 250 terminals, PCs for student use in computer center, computer labs, research center, classrooms, learning resource center, library, dorms. Access to campuswide network, Internet from computer center, computer labs, research center, classrooms, learning resource center, library, dorms, student rooms; general network orientation available. *Services:* e-mail, mainframe access, database computer-search services, library catalog search and reservation.

UNDERGRADUATE PROFILE 2,311 students from 56 states and territories, 27 other countries. 59% women, 2% part-time, 49% state residents, 93% live on campus, 5% transferred in, 45% have campus jobs, 1% international, 3% 25 or older, 0% Native American, 3% Hispanic, 3% African American, 3% Asian American. *Retention:* 86% of 1992 freshmen returned. *Graduation:* 58% graduate in 4 years.

FRESHMEN 607 total. 1,742 applied, 79% were accepted, 44% of whom enrolled. 33% from top 10% of their high school class, 68% from top quarter, 98% from top half. 6 National Merit Scholarship Finalists.

ACADEMIC PROGRAM Core, honor code. Calendar: 4-1-4. 1,170 courses offered in 1993–94; average class size 25 in required courses. Advanced placement, accelerated degree program, self-designed majors, honors program, summer session for credit, part-time degree program (daytime, evenings), adult/continuing education programs, internships. Off-campus study at 13 members of the Christian College Consortium.

STUDY-ABROAD SITES China, Colombia, England, France, Germany, Greece, Israel, Japan, Kenya, Spain.

MAJORS Accounting, art/fine arts, art history, behavioral sciences, biblical studies, business administration/commerce/management, chemistry, civil engineering technology, clinical psychology, communication, computer information systems, computer science, dietetics, early childhood education, education, elementary educa-tion, English, experimental psychology, family services, French, geography, German, history, home economics, humanities, human resources, journalism, (pre)law sequence, liberal arts/general studies, marketing/retailing/merchandising, mathematics, medical technology, (pre)medicine sequence, modern languages, music, music education, natural sciences, nursing, pastoral studies, physical education, physics, psychology, radio and television studies, recreation and leisure services, religious education, religious studies, secondary education, social science, social work, sociology, Spanish, speech/rhetoric/public address/debate, sports medicine, stringed instruments, theology, (pre)veterinary medicine sequence, voice.

EXPENSES FOR 1993–94 *Application fee:* $20. Comprehensive fee of $14,664 includes full-time tuition ($9720), mandatory fees ($84), and college room and board ($4860). College room only: $2400. Part-time tuition: $400 per credit.

FINANCIAL AID *College-administered aid for undergraduates 1993–94:* 1,050 need-based scholarships (average $3000), 1,250 non-need scholarships (average $1275), low-interest long-term loans from external sources (average $2750), FSEOG, Federal Work-Study, 400 part-time jobs. Average total aid for freshmen: $9953, meeting 84% of need (aid provided to 100% of those qualified). *Application forms required:* FAFSA; required for some: state; accepted: FAF. *Priority deadline:* 4/1. *Payment plan:* installment. *Waivers:* full or partial for employees or children of employees and senior citizens. *Notification:* continuous. Must reapply each year.

COLLEGE LIFE Orientation program (2 days, $25). Drama-theater group, choral group, student-run newspaper, radio station. *Social organizations:* 58 open to all, with 75% participating. *Most popular organizations:* Student Government, Outreach Board (service) (12% participate), Education Association (5% participate), music ensembles (5% participate). *Major annual events:* Family Weekend, Homecoming, Christmas Tradition Banquet. *Student services:* personal-psychological counseling. *Safety:* 24-hour emergency response devices and patrols, late-night transport-escort service.

ATHLETICS Member NCAA. All Division III. *Intercollegiate:* baseball M, basketball M/W, cross-country running M/W, field hockey W, golf M, soccer M/W, softball W, tennis M/W, track and field M/W, volleyball W, wrestling M. *Intramural:* baseball, basketball, cross-country running, field hockey, football, golf, gymnastics, soccer, softball, tennis, track and field, volleyball, wrestling. *Contact:* Dr. Layton Shoemaker, Athletic Director, 717-766-2511.

APPLYING/FRESHMEN *Options:* early entrance, deferred entrance. *Required:* essay, school transcript, 2 recommendations, SAT I or ACT. *Recommended:* 3 years of high school math and science. *Required for some:* some high school foreign language. Test scores used for admission. *Application deadline:* rolling. *Notification:* continuous.

APPLYING/TRANSFER *Required:* essay, 2 recommendations, college transcript, minimum 2.5 GPA. *Entrance level:* moderately difficult. *Application deadline:* rolling. *Notification:* continuous.

CONTACT Mr. Ron E. Long, Vice President for Admissions, Financial Aid, and Communications, Messiah College, Grantham, PA 17027; 717-766-2511 Ext. 6000 or toll-free 800-382-1349 (in-state), 800-233-4220 (out-of-state).

MidAmerica Nazarene College
Olathe, Kansas

> **SPECIAL NOTE FROM THE COLLEGE** MidAmerica Nazarene College is a private holiness college in the Wesleyan tradition. Sponsored by the Church of the Nazarene, it is a coeducational, career-oriented, liberal arts college offering 5 degree options: Associate of Arts, Bachelor of Arts, Bachelor of Science in Nursing, Master of Education, and Master of Business Administration. Among the most popular new programs is the management and human relations degree-completion program. The 105-acre campus is 19 miles southwest of Kansas City. The College has as its purpose the Christian education of individuals in a liberal arts context for personal development, service to God and humanity, and career preparation.

Total Enrollment: 1,434

UG Enrollment: 1,297 (54% W)

Application Deadline: rolling

Entrance: noncompetitive

Tuition & Fees: $7312

Room & Board: $3720

Denominational Affiliation: Church of the Nazarene

GENERAL INFORMATION Independent-religious comprehensive coed institution. Awards associate, bachelor's, master's degrees (master's in education and business administration). Founded 1966. *Setting:* 105-acre suburban campus with easy access to Kansas City. *Undergraduate faculty:* 113 (58 full-time, 44% with terminal degrees, 55 part-time); student-undergrad faculty ratio is 20:1. *Library Holdings:* 77,392 books, 103,285 microform titles, 380 periodicals, 208,668 CD-ROMs, 2,396 records, tapes, and CDs. *Computers:* 33 terminals, PCs for student use in library.

UNDERGRADUATE PROFILE 1,297 students from 40 states and territories, 10 other countries. 54% women, 15% part-time, 62% state residents, 45% live on campus, 44% transferred in, 3% international, 29% 25 or older, 1% Native American, 1% Hispanic, 4% African American, 1% Asian American. *Retention:* 70% of 1992 freshmen returned.

FRESHMEN 225 total. 331 applied, 100% were accepted, 68% of whom enrolled.

ACADEMIC PROGRAM Core, honor code. Calendar: semesters. Academic remediation for entering students, English as a second language program offered during academic year, services for LD students, advanced placement, accelerated degree program, summer session for credit, part-time degree program (daytime, evenings), adult/continuing education programs. ROTC: Army (c), Naval (c), Air Force (c).

MAJORS Accounting, agricultural business, athletic training, biology/biological sciences, business administration/commerce/management, business education, chemistry, communication, computer science, early childhood education, elementary educa-

tion, English, health education, history, human resources, international business, liberal arts/general studies, mathematics, ministries, modern languages, music, music education, nursing, physical education, physics, psychology, public relations, religious education, religious studies, sacred music, secondary education, Spanish.

EXPENSES FOR 1994–95 *Application fee:* $15. Comprehensive fee of $11,032 includes full-time tuition ($6840), mandatory fees ($472), and college room and board ($3720). Part-time tuition: $228 per semester hour.

FINANCIAL AID *College-administered aid for undergraduates 1993–94:* 94 need-based scholarships (average $872), 575 non-need scholarships (average $2166), low-interest long-term loans from external sources (average $5301), FSEOG, Federal Work-Study, part-time jobs. Average total aid for freshmen: $8719, meeting 80% of need (aid provided to 100% of those qualified). *Application forms required:* institutional, FAFSA; required for some: IRS and verification worksheet, state. *Priority deadline:* 3/1. *Payment plan:* installment. *Waivers:* full or partial for employees or children of employees and senior citizens. *Notification:* 5/1.

COLLEGE LIFE Orientation program (4 days, $25, parents included). Drama-theater group, choral group, student-run newspaper. *Most popular organizations:* Associated Student Government, Circle K, ministry groups. *Major annual event:* Homecoming. *Student services:* health clinic, personal-psychological counseling. *Safety:* 24-hour emergency response devices, student patrols, late-night transport-escort service, controlled dormitory access, room security.

ATHLETICS Member NAIA. *Intercollegiate:* baseball M(s), basketball M(s)/W(s), cross-country running M(s)/W(s), football M(s), softball W(s), track and field M(s)/W(s), volleyball W(s). *Intramural:* baseball, basketball, football, track and field, volleyball. *Contact:* Mr. Harold Olsen, Athletic Director, 913-782-3750 Ext. 260.

APPLYING/FRESHMEN Open admission. *Options:* early entrance, deferred entrance. *Required:* school transcript, 2 recommendations, ACT, TOEFL for international students. Test scores used for counseling/placement. *Application deadline:* rolling. *Notification:* continuous.

APPLYING/TRANSFER *Required:* college transcript. *Required for some:* standardized test scores. *Entrance level:* noncompetitive. *Application deadline:* rolling. *Notification:* continuous.

CONTACT Dr. Bob Drummond, Vice President for Student Development, MidAmerica Nazarene College, 2030 East College Way, Olathe, KS 66062-1899; 913-791-3380.

MILLIGAN COLLEGE
Milligan College, Tennessee

Total Enrollment: 776
UG Enrollment: 737 (55% W)
Application Deadline: rolling
Entrance: moderately difficult
Tuition & Fees: $8200
Room & Board: $3300
SAT≥500: 32% V, 55% M   **ACT≥21:** 72%
Denominational Affiliation: Christian Church/ Church of Christ

GENERAL INFORMATION Independent-religious comprehensive coed institution. Awards associate, bachelor's, master's degrees. Founded 1866. *Setting:* 145-acre suburban campus. *Faculty:* 76 (52 full-time, 70% with terminal degrees, 24 part-time); student-undergrad faculty ratio is 14:1. *Library Holdings:* 90,525 books, 23,541 microform titles, 595 periodicals, 1 on-line bibliographic service, 2,641 records, tapes, and CDs. *Computers:* 48 terminals, PCs for student use in computer center, computer labs, classrooms, library. Access to campuswide network from computer center, computer labs, library. *Services:* e-mail, database computer-search services.

UNDERGRADUATE PROFILE 737 students from 38 states and territories, 8 other countries. 55% women, 9% part-time, 29% state residents, 63% live on campus, 12% transferred in, 1% international, 20% 25 or older, 1% Native American, 1% Hispanic, 1% African American, 1% Asian American. *Retention:* 62% of 1992 freshmen returned. *Graduation:* 40% graduate in 4 years.

FRESHMEN 189 total. Of the students who applied, 75% were accepted, 41% of whom enrolled.

ACADEMIC PROGRAM Core, liberal arts education in Christian setting, honor code. Calendar: semesters. 400 courses offered in 1993–94; average class size 25 in required courses. Academic remediation for entering students, advanced placement, accelerated degree program, tutorials, summer session for credit, part-time degree program (daytime), adult/continuing education programs, co-op programs and internships. Fewer than half of graduate courses open to undergraduate students. Off-campus study at East Tennessee State University. ROTC: Army (c). Unusual degree programs: 3-2 engineering with Georgia Institute of Technology, medical technology with Western Carolina University.

MAJORS Accounting, adult and continuing education, advertising, art/fine arts, biblical studies, biology/biological sciences, broadcasting, business administration/commerce/management, business economics, chemistry, communication, computer science, (pre)dentistry sequence, early childhood education, education, elementary education, engineering (general), English, funeral service, health education, history, humanities, human services, liberal arts/general studies, mathematics, (pre)medicine sequence, ministries, music, music education, nursing, paralegal studies, pastoral studies, physical education, piano/organ, psychology, radio and television studies, religious education, religious studies, sacred music, science, science education, secretarial studies/office management, social work, sociology, special education, theater arts/drama, (pre)veterinary medicine sequence.

EXPENSES FOR 1994–95 *Application fee:* $25. Comprehensive fee of $11,500 includes full-time tuition ($8000), mandatory fees ($200), and college room and board ($3300). College room only: $1500. Part-time tuition per semester ranges from $779 to $3690. Part-time mandatory fees: $50 per semester.

FINANCIAL AID *College-administered aid for undergraduates 1993–94:* need-based scholarships (average $750), non-need scholarships (average $2000), low-interest long-term loans from external sources (average $2625), FSEOG, Federal Work-Study, 450 part-time jobs. *Application forms required:* IRS, institutional; required for some: state; accepted: FFS, FAF, FAFSA. *Priority deadline:* 3/15. *Payment plan:* installment. *Waivers:* full or partial for employees or children of employees. *Average indebtedness of graduates:* $12,000.

COLLEGE LIFE Orientation program (1 week, no cost, parents included). Drama-theater group, choral group, student-run newspaper. *Social organizations:* 25 open to all, with 50% participating. *Most popular organizations:* Delta Kappa, Buffalo Ramblers, Big Brother/Big Sister. *Major annual events:* Wonderful Wednesday, Jr/Sr Banquet, Valentine's Banquet. *Student services:* health clinic, personal-psychological counseling. *Safety:* 24-hour patrols, late-night transport-escort service, room security.

ATHLETICS Member NAIA. *Intercollegiate:* baseball M, basketball M(s)/W(s), golf M(s), soccer M(s), softball W, tennis M(s)/W(s), volleyball W(s). *Intramural:* basketball, field hockey, football, soccer, softball, table tennis (Ping-Pong), tennis, volleyball. *Contact:* Mr. Duard Walker, Athletic Director, 615-461-8738.

APPLYING/FRESHMEN *Options:* early entrance, deferred entrance, midyear entrance. *Required:* essay, school transcript, minimum 2.0 GPA, 2 recommendations, SAT I or ACT, TOEFL for international students. *Recommended:* minimum 3.0 GPA, 3 years of high school math and science, 2 years of high school foreign language. *Required for some:* interview. Test scores used for admission. *Application deadline:* rolling. *Notification:* continuous.

APPLYING/TRANSFER *Required:* essay, high school transcript, 2 recommendations, college transcript, minimum 2.0 GPA. *Recommended:* 3 years of high school math, 2 years of high school foreign language. *Required for some:* interview. *Entrance level:* moderately difficult. *Application deadline:* rolling. *Notification:* continuous.

CONTACT Mr. Mike Johnson, Director of Admissions, Milligan College, Milligan College, TN 37682; 615-461-8736.

MISSISSIPPI COLLEGE
Clinton, Mississippi

MC · VERITAS ET VIRTUS · 1826

SPECIAL NOTE FROM THE COLLEGE Mississippi College is a private, 4-year college supported by the Mississippi Baptist Convention. Founded in 1826, it is Mississippi's oldest institution of higher learning. The student body consists of approximately 4,000 students. There is a Graduate School that offers 14 degrees and a fully accredited School of Law in downtown Jackson. It is listed among the elite in the country in *U.S. News & World Report* and is recognized by the Templeton Foundation as one of the nation's top character-building institutions. Steeped in Baptist heritage since 1850, the goal of the College is to see the Christian faith permeate the entire education process.

Total Enrollment: 3,781
UG Enrollment: 2,425 (61% W)
Application Deadline: rolling
Entrance: moderately difficult
Tuition & Fees: $5888
Room & Board: $2830
Denominational Affiliation: Southern Baptist

GENERAL INFORMATION Independent-religious comprehensive coed institution. Awards bachelor's, master's, first professional degrees. Founded 1826. *Setting:* 320-acre small-town campus. *Undergraduate faculty:* 234 (149 full-time, 85 part-time); student-undergrad faculty ratio is 18:1. *Library Holdings:* 230,000 books, 14,000 microform titles, 768 periodicals, 10,576 records, tapes, and CDs. *Computers:* 67 terminals, PCs for student use in computer center. Access to campuswide network.

UNDERGRADUATE PROFILE 2,425 students from 40 states and territories, 6 other countries. 61% women, 24% part-time, 87% state residents, 25% transferred in, 1% international, 44% 25 or older, 1% Native American, 1% Hispanic, 15% African American, 1% Asian American. *Retention:* 75% of 1992 freshmen returned.

FRESHMEN 303 total. 594 applied, 65% were accepted, 64% of whom enrolled. 25% from top 10% of their high school class, 66% from top quarter, 89% from top half. 13 National Merit Scholarship Finalists, 13 National Merit Scholars.

ACADEMIC PROGRAM Core. Calendar: semesters. Academic remediation for entering students, English as a second language program offered during academic year, advanced placement, accelerated degree program, honors program, summer session for credit, part-time degree program (daytime, evenings, summer), adult/continuing education programs, co-op programs and internships. ROTC: Army (c). Unusual degree programs: 3-2 engineering with Auburn University, University of Mississippi.

STUDY-ABROAD SITES England, Germany.

MAJORS Accounting, applied art, art education, art/fine arts, biblical studies, biology/biological sciences, business administration, chemistry, communication, computer science, criminal justice, (pre)dentistry sequence, economics, education, elementary education, English, history, home economics, home economics education, interior design, journalism, law enforcement/police sciences, (pre)law sequence, mathematics, medical technology, (pre)medicine sequence, modern languages, music, music education, nursing, paralegal studies, physics, piano/organ, political science/government, psychology, religious education, religious studies, science education, social science, social work, sociology, Spanish, special education.

EXPENSES FOR 1994–95 Comprehensive fee of $8718 includes full-time tuition ($5580), mandatory fees ($308), and college room and board ($2830). College room only: $1260. Part-time tuition: $186 per credit hour.

FINANCIAL AID *College-administered aid for undergraduates 1993–94:* need-based scholarships, 550 non-need scholarships (average $1000), short-term loans (average $100), low-interest long-term loans from college funds (average $1500), loans from external sources (average $2500), FSEOG, Federal Work-Study, 250 part-time jobs. *Application forms required:* FAF, institutional. *Priority deadline:* 4/1. *Payment plans:* installment, deferred payment. *Waivers:* full or partial for employees or children of employees.

COLLEGE LIFE Orientation program. Drama-theater group, choral group, marching band, student-run newspaper, 2 commercially licensed radio stations. *Social organizations:* 3 men's service clubs, 4 social clubs; 17% of eligible men and 33% of eligible women are members. *Student services:* health clinic, personal-psychological counseling. *Safety:* 24-hour patrols, late-night transport-escort service.

ATHLETICS Member NCAA Division II. *Intercollegiate:* basketball M(s)/W(s), cross-country running M(s), football M(s), golf M(s), tennis M(s)/W(s), track and field M(s), volleyball W(s). *Intramural:* basketball, cross-country running, football, golf, soccer, tennis, track and field, volleyball.

APPLYING/FRESHMEN *Option:* early entrance. *Required:* school transcript, SAT I or ACT, TOEFL for international students. Test scores used for admission. *Application deadline:* rolling. *Notification:* continuous.

APPLYING/TRANSFER *Required:* college transcript, minimum 2.0 GPA. *Entrance level:* moderately difficult. *Application deadline:* rolling. *Notification:* continuous.

CONTACT The Office of Admissions, Mississippi College, Clinton, MS 39058; 601-925-3240 or toll-free 800-738-1236.

MONTREAT-ANDERSON COLLEGE
Montreat, North Carolina

> **SPECIAL NOTE FROM THE COLLEGE** This small but vibrant campus provides a close-knit and personal atmosphere along with a qualified faculty committed to teaching excellence. Surrounded by the Blue Ridge Mountains, wooded hiking trails, mountain streams, and a mountain lake, M-AC takes advantage of this inspiring location by offering one of the most challenging and unique outdoor recreation programs in the country. M-AC offers students a meditative mountain setting; small, challenging classes; friendly, enthusiastic students; and a variety of degree programs plus the warmth, security, and values that only a Christ-centered school can provide.

Total Enrollment: 316 (all UG)

Women: 47%

Application Deadline: 8/20

Entrance: minimally difficult

Tuition & Fees: $8438

Room & Board: $3372

SAT≥500: 15% V, 21% M   **ACT≥21:** N/R

Denominational Affiliation: Presbyterian

GENERAL INFORMATION Independent-religious 4-year coed institution. Awards associate, bachelor's degrees. Founded 1916. *Setting:* 100-acre small-town campus. *Faculty:* 35 (24 full-time, 61% with terminal degrees, 11 part-time); student-undergrad faculty ratio is 11:1. *Library Holdings:* 62,945 books, 515 microform titles, 425 periodicals, 1,620 records, tapes, and CDs. *Computers:* 30 terminals, PCs for student use in computer center, library, student center.

UNDERGRADUATE PROFILE 316 students from 16 states and territories, 4 other countries. 47% women, 5% part-time, 62% state residents, 85% live on campus, 14% transferred in, 4% international, 7% 25 or older, 1% Native American, 1% Hispanic, 5% African American, 1% Asian American. *Retention:* 60% of 1992 freshmen returned.

FRESHMEN 103 total. 263 applied, 85% were accepted, 46% of whom enrolled.

ACADEMIC PROGRAM Core, Christian liberal arts curriculum. Calendar: semesters. Average class size 20 in required courses. Advanced placement, honors program, part-time degree program (daytime), internships. Off-campus study.

MAJORS American studies, Bible and religion, business administration (accounting, economics, general business, marketing), English (literature, communications, secondary education), environmental studies, history (education), human services and cultural studies, liberal arts, mathematics, outdoor recreation.

EXPENSES FOR 1994–95 *Application fee:* $15. Comprehensive fee of $11,810 includes full-time tuition ($8438) and college room and board ($3372). Part-time tuition: $200 per semester hour.

FINANCIAL AID *College-administered aid for undergraduates 1993–94:* 257 need-based scholarships (average $7933), 44 non-need scholarships, Federal Pell Grants FSEOG, subsidized and unsubsidized Federal Stafford Loans, Federal Work-Study, M-AC Work Study. Average total aid for freshmen: $8368 (aid provided to 100% of those qualified). *Application forms required:* FAFSA, institutional; required for some: IRS. *Priority deadline:* 3/15. *Payment plan:* Academic Management Services. *Notification:* continuous.

COLLEGE LIFE Orientation program (3 days, no cost). Drama-theater group, choral group, student-run newspaper. *Most popular organizations:* Student Government, Adventure Club, Interact (Christian Fellowship). *Major annual events:* Homecoming, Winter Dance, Spring Dance. *Student services:* health clinic, personal-psychological counseling. *Safety:* 24-hour patrols, room security.

ATHLETICS Member NAIA. *Intercollegiate:* baseball M(s), basketball M(s)/W(s), soccer M(s), volleyball W(s). *Intramural:* basketball, golf, skiing (cross-country), skiing (downhill), table tennis (Ping-Pong), tennis, volleyball. *Contact:* Mr. Steve McNamara, Athletic Director, 704-669-8011, Ext. 3401.

APPLYING/FRESHMEN *Options:* early entrance, early action, deferred entrance. *Required:* essay, school transcript, minimum 2.25 GPA, SAT I or ACT, TOEFL for international students. *Recommended:* 3 years of high school math and science, some high school foreign language, 1 recommendation. *Required for some:* interview. Test scores used for admission. *Application deadlines:* 8/20, 9/1 for early action. *Notification:* continuous, continuous for early action.

APPLYING/TRANSFER *Required:* essay, standardized test scores, high school transcript, college transcript. *Recommended:* 3 years of high school math and science, some high school foreign language, 1 recommendation, minimum 2.0 GPA. *Required for some:* interview. *Entrance level:* minimally difficult. *Application deadline:* 8/20. *Notification:* continuous.

CONTACT Mr. David Walters, Director of Admissions, Montreat-Anderson College, P.O. Box 1267, Montreat, NC 28757; 704-669-8011 Ext. 3102 or toll-free 800-MAC-N-YOU.

MOUNT VERNON NAZARENE COLLEGE
Mount Vernon, Ohio

SPECIAL NOTE FROM THE COLLEGE Mount Vernon Nazarene College exists to "train servant leaders for the 21st Century." A closer look at MVNC reveals not only a Christ-centered education but a service-oriented outlook on life. Students invest themselves in a variety of missions and ministry projects during the school year, during the January term, and during the summer in places across the state, around the nation, and throughout the world. MVNC's rural setting, apartment-style living, and comprehensive campus-ministries program headed by the College's full-time chaplain/campus pastor promote a sense of family. A 4-1-4 calendar allows off-campus classes midyear. An extensive high-quality academic program and abundant extracurricular activities in a peaceful country setting make MVNC a wonderful place to live and grow.

Total Enrollment: 1,223
UG Enrollment: 1,208 (55% W)
Application Deadline: 8/15
Entrance: moderately difficult
Tuition & Fees: $7732
Room & Board: $3384
SAT: N/App   **ACT≥21:** 56%
Denominational Affiliation: Nazarene

GENERAL INFORMATION Independent-religious comprehensive coed institution. Awards associate, bachelor's, master's degrees. Founded 1964. *Setting:* 210-acre small-town campus with easy access to Columbus. *Undergraduate faculty:* 69 (51 full-time, 56% with terminal degrees, 18 part-time); student-undergrad faculty ratio is 18:1. *Library Holdings:* 85,124 books, 3,294 microform titles, 526 periodicals. *Computers:* 100 terminals, PCs for student use in computer center, computer labs, business, education labs.

UNDERGRADUATE PROFILE 1,208 students from 31 states and territories, 6 other countries. 55% women, 7% part-time, 81% state residents, 68% live on campus, 7% transferred in, 63% have need-based financial aid, 26% have non-need-based financial aid, 25% have campus jobs, 1% international, 7% 25 or older, 1% Hispanic, 1% African American, 1% Asian American. *Retention:* 76% of 1992 freshmen returned.

FRESHMEN 334 total. 510 applied, 95% were accepted, 69% of whom enrolled. 6 valedictorians.

ACADEMIC PROGRAM Core, distribution curriculum, honor code. Calendar: 4-1-4. 652 courses offered in 1993–94; average class size 23 in required courses. Academic remediation for entering students, advanced placement, tutorials, summer session for credit, part-time degree program (daytime, evenings, summer), adult/continuing education programs, internships. Off-campus study at Kenyon College, Capital University.

MAJORS Accounting, applied art, art education, art/fine arts, biblical studies, biochemistry, biology/biological sciences, broadcasting, business administration/commerce/management, business education, chemistry, communication, computer science, computer technologies, criminal justice, data processing, (pre)dentistry sequence, early childhood education, education, elementary education, (pre)engineering sequence, English, health science, history, home economics, home economics education, human services, (pre)law sequence, liberal arts/general studies, literature, marketing/retailing/merchandising, mathematics, medical technology, (pre)medicine sequence, modern languages, music, music education, natural resource management, nursing, philosophy, physical education, piano/organ, psychology, religious education, religious studies, sacred music, science, science education, secondary education, secretarial studies/office management, social science, social work, sociology, Spanish, special education, sports administration, sports medicine, theater arts/drama, theology, (pre)veterinary medicine sequence, voice, wind and percussion instruments.

EXPENSES FOR 1994–95 *Application fee:* $20. Comprehensive fee of $11,116 includes full-time tuition ($7732) and college room and board ($3384). Part-time tuition: $264 per credit hour. Part-time mandatory fees: $12 per term.

FINANCIAL AID *College-administered aid for undergraduates 1993–94:* need-based scholarships (average $774), non-need scholarships (average $844), low-interest long-term loans from external sources (average $2620), FSEOG, Federal Work-Study, part-time jobs. Average total aid for freshmen: $7702, meeting 75% of need (aid provided to 100% of those qualified). *Application forms required:* institutional, FAFSA; required for some: IRS, state. *Priority deadline:* 4/15. *Waivers:* full or partial for employees or children of employees.

COLLEGE LIFE Orientation program (2 days, $25, parents included). Drama-theater group, choral group, student-run newspaper, radio station. *Social organizations:* 27 open to all. *Most popular organizations:* Living Witness, Student Government, Drama Club, Mandate. *Major annual events:* Homecoming, concerts, special services/speakers. *Student services:* health clinic, personal-psychological counseling. *Safety:* 24-hour emergency response devices and patrols, room security.

ATHLETICS Member NAIA. *Intercollegiate:* baseball M(s), basketball M(s)/W(s), golf M(s), soccer M(s), softball W(s), volleyball W(s). *Intramural:* basketball, bowling, golf, skiing (downhill), soccer, softball, table tennis (Ping-Pong), tennis, volleyball. *Contact:* Mr. Scott Flemming, Athletic Director, 614-397-1244.

APPLYING/FRESHMEN *Options:* early entrance, deferred entrance, midyear entrance. *Required:* essay, school transcript, minimum 2.0 GPA, 2 recommendations, ACT, TOEFL for international students. *Recommended:* 3 years of high school math and science, 2 years of high school foreign language, interview. Test scores used for counseling/placement. *Application deadline:* 8/15.

APPLYING/TRANSFER *Required:* essay, high school transcript, 2 recommendations, college transcript, minimum 2.0 GPA. *Recommended:* 3 years of high school math and science, 2 years of high school foreign language, interview. *Required for some:* standardized test scores. *Entrance level:* moderately difficult. *Application deadline:* 8/15.

CONTACT Rev. Bruce Oldham, Director, Admissions and Student Recruitment, Mount Vernon Nazarene College, 800 Martinsburg Road, Mount Vernon, OH 43050; 614-397-1244 Ext. 4500 or toll-free 800-782-2435.

NORTH PARK COLLEGE
Chicago, Illinois

> **SPECIAL NOTE FROM THE COLLEGE** Of the 136 regional liberal arts colleges in the Midwest, North Park has been ranked 11th, 10th (twice), 8th, and 6th in the last 5 *U.S. News & World Report* best colleges ratings. Located in a park-like setting on Chicago's far north side (20 minutes by public transportation from O'Hare International Airport), North Park draws students from across America (40 states) and around the world (25 countries). Building on its world-class city setting, North Park offers several hundred convenient internships, 20 urban ministry opportunities (involving 45% of the student body annually), and on-campus African-American, Korean, Latino/a, and Scandinavian cultural study centers.

Total Enrollment: 1,417

UG Enrollment: 1,034 (57% W)

Application Deadline: rolling

Entrance: moderately difficult

Tuition & Fees: $12,580

Room & Board: $4410

SAT≥500: 41% V, 58% M   **ACT≥21:** 54%

Denominational Affiliation: Evangelical Covenant Church

GENERAL INFORMATION Independent-religious comprehensive coed institution. Awards bachelor's, master's degrees. Founded 1891. *Setting:* 30-acre urban campus. *Undergraduate faculty:* 80 (78% of full-time faculty have terminal degrees); student-undergrad faculty ratio is 14:1. *Library Holdings:* 217,024 books, 1,571 microform titles, 982 periodicals, 1 on-line bibliographic service, 7 CD-ROMs, 5,005 records, tapes, and CDs. *Computers:* 55 terminals, PCs for student use in computer center, computer labs, classrooms, library. Access to campuswide network, Internet from computer center, computer labs, classrooms, library; on-line documentation and general network orientation available. *Services:* e-mail, file transfer, mainframe access.

UNDERGRADUATE PROFILE 1,034 students from 40 states and territories, 25 other countries. 57% women, 15% part-time, 58% state residents, 30% transferred in, 12% international, 16% 25 or older, 2% Hispanic, 5% African American, 19% Asian American. *Retention:* 84% of 1992 freshmen returned. *Graduation:* 55% graduate in 4 years.

FRESHMEN 176 total. 465 applied, 78% were accepted, 49% of whom enrolled. 11% from top 10% of their high school class, 30% from top quarter, 56% from top half. 5 National Merit Scholarship Finalists, 5 National Merit Scholars.

ACADEMIC PROGRAM Core, interdisciplinary, thematic curriculum. Calendar: semesters. 565 courses offered in 1993–94; average class size 16 in required courses. Academic remediation for entering students, English as a second language program offered during academic year and summer, advanced placement, accelerated degree program, self-designed majors, tutorials, honors program, summer session for credit, part-time degree program (daytime, evenings, weekends), internships. Off-campus study at Christian College Coalition. Unusual degree programs: 3-2 engineering with University of Illinois at Champaign-Urbana, Case Western Reserve University, Washington University, University of Minnesota, prephysical therapy, preoccupational therapy.

STUDY-ABROAD SITES Costa Rica, Egypt, England, France, Germany, Japan, Korea, Mexico, Norway, Russia, South Africa, Sweden.

MAJORS Accounting, anthropology, art education, art/fine arts, biblical studies, biology/biological sciences, business administration/commerce/management, chemistry, communication, (pre)dentistry sequence, early childhood education, economics, education, elementary education, English, finance/banking, French, German, history, international business, international studies, (pre)law sequence, literature, marketing, mathematics, medical technology, (pre)medicine sequence, modern languages, music, music education, nursing, philosophy, physical education, physical fitness/exercise science, physics, political science/government, psychology, religious studies, Scandinavian languages/studies, secondary education, social science, sociology, Spanish, sports medicine, studio art, theater arts/drama, theology, (pre)veterinary medicine sequence, voice, youth ministries.

EXPENSES FOR 1994–95 *Application fee:* $20. Comprehensive fee of $16,990 includes full-time tuition ($12,580) and college room and board ($4410). Part-time tuition: $450 per semester hour.

FINANCIAL AID *College-administered aid for undergraduates 1993–94:* 615 need-based scholarships (average $3975), 125 non-need scholarships (average $2375), low-interest long-term loans from external sources (average $2850), FSEOG, Federal Work-Study, 123 part-time jobs. Average total aid for freshmen: $10,256, meeting 92% of need (aid provided to 100% of those qualified). *Application forms required:* FAF, IRS, institutional; required for some: state, FAFSA. *Priority deadline:* 8/15. *Payment plan:* installment. *Waivers:* full or partial for employees or children of employees and adult students. Must reapply each year.

COLLEGE LIFE Orientation program. Drama-theater group, chapel (optional), choral group, student-run newspaper. *Social organizations:* 10 open to all. *Most popular organizations:* Student Association, Urban Outreach (45% participate), College Life (20% participate), college music (20% participate), International Student Association, Gospel choir, debate team. *Major annual events:* Homecoming, Spring Event, New Student Orientation. *Student services:* health clinic, personal-psychological counseling, career counseling and job placement services. *Safety:* 24-hour patrols, late-night transport-escort service.

ATHLETICS Member NCAA. All Division III. *Intercollegiate:* baseball M, basketball M/W, cross-country running M/W, football M, soccer M/W, softball W, tennis M/W, track and field M/W, volleyball M/W. *Intramural:* basketball, football, volleyball. *Contact:* Mr. Jerry Chaplin, Director of Athletics, 312-583-2700 Ext. 4370.

APPLYING/FRESHMEN *Options:* early entrance, midyear entrance. *Required:* essay, school transcript, recommendations, SAT I or ACT, TOEFL for international students. *Recommended:* minimum 3.0 GPA, 3 years of high school math and science, some high school foreign language. *Required for some:* interview. Test scores used for admission and counseling/placement. *Application deadline:* rolling. *Notification:* continuous.

APPLYING/TRANSFER *Required:* essay, recommendations, college transcript, minimum 2.0 GPA. *Recommended:* 3 years of high school math and science, some high school foreign language. *Required for some:* standardized test scores, high school transcript, interview. *Entrance level:* moderately difficult. *Application deadline:* rolling. *Notification:* continuous.

CONTACT Mr. John Schafer, Dean of Admissions, North Park College, 3225 West Foster Avenue, Chicago, IL 60625; 312-244-6200 Ext. 4500 or toll-free 800-888-NPC8.

NORTHWEST CHRISTIAN COLLEGE
Eugene, Oregon

> **SPECIAL NOTE FROM THE COLLEGE** A deep sense of pride and excitement fills the campus as Northwest Christian College celebrates its 100th year. Several characteristics have come to be identified with NCC, such as a superb teaching faculty, a personal faith-affirming campus, and an option for "cooperative" majors with neighboring University of Oregon. NCC is ever changing as well. The curriculum has added new internship and study-abroad opportunities. Courses have been designed to teach communication and leadership skills. Majors have been extended to career areas like business administration, communications, and counseling. Even the long-standing program in ministry has branched into specialties for youth, music, and missions. NCC is ideally situated to help students deepen their faith, develop their strengths, and establish their professional potential.

Total Enrollment: 351
UG Enrollment: 300 (48% W)
Application Deadline: rolling
Entrance: minimally difficult
Tuition & Fees: $8725
Room & Board: $3870
SAT≥500: 26% V, 53% M   **ACT≥21:** N/R
Denominational Affiliation: interdenominational

GENERAL INFORMATION Independent-religious comprehensive coed institution. Awards associate, bachelor's, master's degrees. Founded 1895. *Setting:* 10-acre small-city campus. *Faculty:* 19 (13 full-time, 72% with terminal degrees, 7 part-time); student-undergrad faculty ratio is 15:1. *Library Holdings:* 57,024 books, 608 microform titles, 260 periodicals, 15 CD-ROMs, 1,650 records, tapes, and CDs. *Computers:* 10 terminals, PCs for student use in library. Student computer-purchase plan available.

UNDERGRADUATE PROFILE 300 students from 12 states and territories, 6 other countries. 48% women, 25% part-time, 61% state residents, 37% live on campus, 40% transferred in, 7% international, 19% 25 or older, 1% Hispanic, 1% African American, 2% Asian American. *Retention:* 64% of 1992 freshmen returned.

FRESHMEN 78 total. 197 applied, 71% were accepted, 56% of whom enrolled.

ACADEMIC PROGRAM Core, honor code. Calendar: quarters. 118 courses offered in 1993–94. Academic remediation for entering students, English as a second language program offered during summer, advanced placement, tutorials, adult/continuing education programs, co-op programs and internships. Off-campus study at University of Oregon, Lane Community College. ROTC: Army (c).

MAJORS Adult and continuing education, biblical studies, business administration/commerce/management, communication, interdisciplinary studies, liberal arts/general studies, ministries, missions, pastoral studies, psychology, religious studies, sacred music, theology.

EXPENSES FOR 1994–95 *Application fee:* $25. Comprehensive fee of $12,595 includes full-time tuition ($8550), mandatory fees ($175), and college room and board ($3870). Part-time tuition: $190 per quarter hour. Tuition guaranteed not to increase for student's term of enrollment.

FINANCIAL AID *College-administered aid for undergraduates 1993–94:* 243 need-based scholarships (average $1298), 76 non-need scholarships (average $827), low-interest long-term loans from external sources (average $2993), FSEOG, Federal Work-Study, 87 part-time jobs. *Application forms required:* FAFSA, institutional; required for some: IRS. *Priority deadline:* 3/1. *Payment plans:* installment, deferred payment. *Waivers:* full or partial for employees or children of employees.

COLLEGE LIFE Orientation program (7 days, $40, parents included). Choral groups, student-run newspaper. *Most popular organizations:* ACTS, Spirit Club. *Major annual events:* Ropes Confidence Course Retreat, musicals, Spring Formal, Parents' Weekend. *Student services:* health clinic, personal-psychological counseling. *Safety:* Campus patrols, late-night escort service.

ATHLETICS *Intercollegiate:* basketball M, cross-country running W. *Intramural:* basketball, football, racquetball, softball, volleyball. *Contact:* Mr. David Lipp, Athletic Director, 503-343-1641.

APPLYING/FRESHMEN *Option:* deferred entrance. *Required:* school transcript, 2 recommendations, SAT I or ACT, TOEFL for international students. *Recommended:* interview. Test scores used for admission and scholarship decisions. *Application deadline:* rolling. *Notification:* continuous.

APPLYING/TRANSFER *Required:* 2 recommendations, college transcript. *Recommended:* interview, minimum 2.0 GPA. *Required for some:* standardized test scores, high school transcript. *Entrance level:* minimally difficult. *Application deadline:* rolling. *Notification:* continuous.

CONTACT Dr. Randy Jones, Director of Admissions, Northwest Christian College, 828 East 11th Avenue, Eugene, OR 97401; 503-343-1641.

NORTHWEST COLLEGE
Kirkland, Washington

> **SPECIAL NOTE FROM THE COLLEGE** The Northwest—lakes...trees...mountains. Situated on 60 beautiful acres, the campus overlooks Lake Washington, just 10 miles east of Seattle. Northwest College's athletic programs include basketball, volleyball, soccer, cross-country, and club-level baseball. Almost 800 students at Northwest choose from nearly 50 academic programs, including teacher education, biblical literature, behavioral science, church ministries, business management and administration, religion and philosophy, and teaching English as a second language. Since 1934, Northwest has provided a high-quality education to prepare students for service and leadership. Student Ministries provide a range of opportunities in music and drama as well as opportunities to serve children, the homeless, and prison and inner-city populations. Check it out—Northwest College, intensely academic, distinctly Christian!

Total Enrollment: 757 (all UG)

Women: 52%

Application Deadline: 8/1

Entrance: moderately difficult

Tuition & Fees: $7210

Room & Board: $3480

Denominational Affiliation: Assemblies of God

GENERAL INFORMATION Independent-religious 4-year coed institution. Awards associate, bachelor's degrees. Founded 1934. *Setting:* 60-acre suburban campus with easy access to Seattle. *Faculty:* 61 (33 full-time, 50% with terminal degrees, 28 part-time). *Library Holdings:* 92,000 books, 610 periodicals, 2,000 CD-ROMs, 2,000 records, tapes, and CDs. *Computers:* 18 terminals, PCs for student use in computer center, library.

UNDERGRADUATE PROFILE 757 students from 20 states and territories, 8 other countries. 52% women, 7% part-time, 71% state residents, 18% transferred in, 66% have need-based financial aid, 33% have non-need-based financial aid, 15% have campus jobs, 3% international, 20% 25 or older, 2% Native American, 3% Hispanic, 1% African American, 4% Asian American. *Retention:* 65% of 1992 freshmen returned.

FRESHMEN 167 total. 201 applied, 99% were accepted, 84% of whom enrolled.

ACADEMIC PROGRAM Core, honor code. Calendar: semesters. 310 courses offered in 1993–94; average class size 25 in required courses. Academic remediation for entering students, advanced placement, accelerated degree program, self-designed majors, summer session for credit, part-time degree program (daytime), adult/continuing education programs, internships.

MAJORS Behavioral sciences, biblical studies, business administration/commerce/management, choral music, elementary education, English, health science, history/social studies, interdisciplinary studies, liberal arts/general studies, middle school education, ministries, pastoral studies, philosophy, piano/organ, psychology, religious education, religious studies, sacred music, secondary education, TESOL, theology, voice.

EXPENSES FOR 1994–95 *Application fee:* $20. Comprehensive fee of $10,690 includes full-time tuition ($6550), mandatory fees ($660), and college room and board ($3480). Part-time tuition: $250 per credit hour. Part-time mandatory fees: $21 per credit hour.

FINANCIAL AID *College-administered aid for undergraduates 1993–94:* 231 need-based scholarships (average $577), 556 non-need scholarships, short-term loans, low-interest long-term loans from external sources (average $3221), FSEOG, Federal Work-Study, 100 part-time jobs. Average total aid for freshmen: $6726, meeting 78% of need (aid provided to 100% of those qualified). *Application forms required:* institutional, FAFSA; required for some: IRS. *Priority deadline:* 3/1. *Payment plans:* tuition prepayment, installment, deferred payment. *Waivers:* full or partial for employees or children of employees and senior citizens. *Notification:* 4/15.

COLLEGE LIFE Orientation program (4 days, no cost, parents included). Drama-theater group, choral group, student-run radio station. *Social organizations:* 10 open to all, with 60% participating. *Most popular organizations:* Pep Club (7% participate), Psychology Club (5% participate), Association of Business Students (4% participate), Drama Club (3% participate), Student Ministries (62% participate). *Major annual events:* Harvest Time Social, Homecoming, All-School Banquet. *Student services:* health clinic, personal-psychological counseling. *Safety:* 24-hour emergency response devices and patrols, controlled dormitory access.

ATHLETICS *Intercollegiate:* basketball M/W, cross-country running M/W, soccer M, volleyball W. *Intramural:* basketball, football, table tennis (Ping-Pong), tennis, volleyball. *Contact:* Mr. Steven R. Emerson, Athletic Director, 206-822-8266 Ext. 5233.

APPLYING/FRESHMEN *Options:* early entrance, early action, deferred entrance, midyear entrance. *Required:* essay, school transcript, minimum 2.3 GPA, 2 recommendations, SAT I or ACT, TOEFL for international students. *Recommended:* some high school foreign language. *Required for some:* interview. Test scores used for counseling/placement. *Application deadlines:* 8/1 for fall, 12/15 for spring, 11/15 for early action. *Notification:* continuous, continuous until 12/1 for early action.

APPLYING/TRANSFER *Required:* essay, high school transcript, 2 recommendations, college transcript, minimum 2.3 GPA. *Recommended:* some high school foreign language. *Required for some:* standardized test scores, interview. *Entrance level:* moderately difficult. *Application deadline:* 8/1 for fall, 12/15 for spring. *Notification:* continuous.

CONTACT Dr. Calvin L. White, Director of Enrollment Services, Northwest College, P.O. Box 579, Kirkland, WA 98083; 800-6NWEST1 (toll-free).

NORTHWESTERN COLLEGE
Orange City, Iowa

> **SPECIAL NOTE FROM THE COLLEGE** Northwestern College offers students and faculty members an academic journey that reflects on what it means to be a reformed, evangelical Christian in today's society. The academic program nurtures the development of a biblical perspective. Student development programs provide opportunities for holistic growth and Christian service. Eighty percent of Northwestern's academic facilities have been built or renovated since 1986, along with an award-winning chapel, intercollegiate athletic center, and cafeteria. A fiber-optic computer network connects nearly every campus building, linking 180 workstations and allowing students to explore the resources of Ramaker Library without leaving their residence hall.

Total Enrollment: 1,110

UG Enrollment: 1,092 (56% W)

Application Deadline: rolling

Entrance: moderately difficult

Tuition & Fees: $9900

Room & Board: $3075

SAT≥500: N/R   **ACT≥21:** 78%

Denominational Affiliation: Reformed Church in America

GENERAL INFORMATION Independent-religious comprehensive coed institution. Awards associate, bachelor's, master's degrees. Founded 1882. *Setting:* 40-acre rural campus. *Undergraduate faculty:* 91 (60 full-time, 70% with terminal degrees, 31 part-time); student-undergrad faculty ratio is 16:1. *Library Holdings:* 104,500 books, 500 periodicals, 300 records, tapes, and CDs. *Computers:* 180 terminals, PCs for student use in computer center, classrooms, learning resource center, library, dorms, Demco Business Center, Kresge Education Center. Access to campuswide network, Internet from computer center, classrooms, learning resource center, library, dorms, Demco Business Center, Kresge Education Center. *Services:* e-mail, mainframe access.

UNDERGRADUATE PROFILE 1,092 students from 32 states and territories, 14 other countries. 56% women, 5% part-time, 70% state residents, 80% live on campus, 5% transferred in, 75% have need-based financial aid, 20% have non-need-based financial aid, 40% have campus jobs, 5% international, 1% 25 or older, 1% Native American, 0% Hispanic, 2% African American. *Retention:* 85% of 1992 freshmen returned. *Graduation:* 41% graduate in 4 years.

FRESHMEN 366 total. 840 applied, 93% were accepted, 47% of whom enrolled. 27% from top 10% of their high school class, 60% from top quarter, 87% from top half.

ACADEMIC PROGRAM Core, Western civilization and interdisciplinary curriculum, honor code. Calendar: semesters. 445 courses offered in 1993–94; average class size 30 in required courses. Academic remediation for entering students, English as a second language program offered during academic year and summer, advanced placement, accelerated degree program, self-designed majors, honors program, summer session for credit, co-op programs and internships. Fewer than half of graduate courses open to undergraduate students. Off-campus study at 5 members of the Mid-America States Universities Association. Unusual degree programs: 3-2 engineering with Washington University, nursing with Trinity Christian College, physical therapy with University of Iowa.

STUDY-ABROAD SITES Costa Rica, Egypt, France, Mexico, the Netherlands, Russia, Spain.

MAJORS Accounting, art, biology/biological sciences, business administration/commerce/management, business education, chemistry, Christian education, communication, computer science, (pre)dentistry sequence, economics, elementary education, English, environmental science, French, health science, history, humanities, (pre)law sequence, mathematics, medical technology, (pre)medicine sequence, music, music education, philosophy, physical education, political science/government, psychology, recreation and leisure services, religious studies, secretarial studies/office management, social work, sociology, Spanish, theater arts/drama, theater/speech, (pre)veterinary medicine sequence.

EXPENSES FOR 1994–95 *Application fee:* $20. Comprehensive fee of $12,975 includes full-time tuition ($9900) and college room and board ($3075). College room only: $1275. Part-time tuition per semester ranges from $160 to $3500.

FINANCIAL AID *College-administered aid for undergraduates 1993–94:* 850 need-based scholarships (average $1910), 400 non-need scholarships (average $2750), low-interest long-term loans from college funds (average $1300), loans from external sources (average $3000), FSEOG, Federal Work-Study, 235 part-time jobs. Average total aid for freshmen: $8811, meeting 95% of need (aid provided to 100% of those qualified). *Application forms required:* institutional; required for some: IRS, FAFSA, FFS Institutional Verification Form; accepted: FFS, FAF. *Priority deadline:* 4/1. *Payment plan:* installment. *Waivers:* full or partial for employees or children of employees. *Notification:* continuous. Must reapply each year. *Average indebtedness of graduates:* $12,250.

COLLEGE LIFE Orientation program (3 days, no cost, parents included). Drama-theater group, choral group, student-run newspaper, radio station. *Social organizations:* 30 open to all, with 60% participating. *Most popular organizations:* Phi Beta Lambda, Student Ministries Board, Student Iowa State Education Association. *Major annual events:* Homecoming, Springfest, Parents' Day. *Student services:* health clinic, personal-psychological counseling. *Safety:* 24-hour emergency response devices, controlled dormitory access.

ATHLETICS Member NAIA. *Intercollegiate:* baseball M(s), basketball M(s)/W(s), cross-country running M(s)/W(s), football M(s), golf M(s)/W(s), soccer M(s)/W(s), softball W(s), tennis M(s)/W(s), track and field M(s)/W(s), volleyball W(s), wrestling M(s). *Intramural:* badminton, basketball, bowling, cross-country running, football, golf, racquetball, soccer, softball, table tennis (Ping-Pong), tennis, volleyball. *Contact:* Mr. Todd Barry, Director of Athletics, 712-737-7281.

APPLYING/FRESHMEN *Options:* deferred entrance, midyear entrance. *Required:* school transcript, 1 recommendation, SAT I or ACT, TOEFL for international students. *Recommended:* 3 years of high school math and science, interview. Test scores used for admission and counseling/placement. *Application deadline:* rolling. *Notification:* continuous until 8/30.

APPLYING/TRANSFER *Required:* 1 recommendation, college transcript, minimum 2.0 GPA. *Recommended:* interview. *Application deadline:* rolling. *Notification:* continuous until 8/30.

CONTACT Mr. Ronald K. De Jong, Director of Admissions, Northwestern College, 101 College Lane, Orange City, IA 51041-1996; 712-737-7130 or toll-free 800-747-4757.

NORTHWESTERN COLLEGE
St. Paul, Minnesota

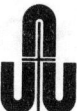

Total Enrollment: 1,244 (all UG)
Women: 58%
Application Deadline: 8/15
Entrance: moderately difficult
Tuition & Fees: $10,659
Room & Board: $2895
SAT≥500: N/R   **ACT≥21:** 61%
Denominational Affiliation: nondenominational

GENERAL INFORMATION Independent-religious 4-year coed institution. Awards associate, bachelor's degrees. Founded 1902. *Setting:* 95-acre suburban campus. *Faculty:* 110 (57 full-time, 48% with terminal degrees, 53 part-time); student-undergrad faculty ratio is 16:1. *Library Holdings:* 82,000 books, 244 microform titles, 570 periodicals, 1 on-line bibliographic service, 3 CD-ROMs, 4,029 records, tapes, and CDs. *Computers:* 58 terminals, PCs for student use in computer center, computer labs, classrooms. Access to campuswide network from computer labs, learning resource center, library; general network orientation available. *Service:* e-mail.

UNDERGRADUATE PROFILE 1,244 students from 36 states and territories, 13 other countries. 58% women, 5% part-time, 66% state residents, 10% transferred in, 2% international, 10% 25 or older, 0% Native American, 0% Hispanic, 1% African American, 1% Asian American. *Retention:* 70% of 1992 freshmen returned.

FRESHMEN 341 total. 539 applied, 98% were accepted, 65% of whom enrolled. 25% from top 10% of their high school class, 52% from top quarter, 77% from top half. 5 National Merit Scholarship Finalists.

ACADEMIC PROGRAM Core, honor code. Calendar: quarters. Average class size 16 in required courses. Academic remediation for entering students, English as a second language program, advanced placement, summer session for credit, part-time degree program (daytime), adult/continuing education programs, internships. Off-campus study at Christian College Coalition. ROTC: Air Force (c). Unusual degree programs: 3-2 engineering with University of Minnesota, Twin Cities Campus.

STUDY-ABROAD SITES Costa Rica, Egypt, France, Honduras, Ireland, Israel, Japan.

MAJORS Accounting, adult and continuing education, agricultural business, art education, art/fine arts, biblical studies, broadcasting, business administration/commerce/management, communication, computer information systems, education, elementary education, (pre)engineering sequence, English, finance/banking, graphic arts, human resources, international business, journalism, legal secretarial studies, liberal arts/general studies, literature, marketing/retailing/merchandising, mathematics, ministries, music, music education, pastoral studies, physical education, psychology, religious education, science, secondary education, secretarial studies/office management, social science, theater arts/drama, theology.

EXPENSES FOR 1993–94 Comprehensive fee of $13,554 includes full-time tuition ($10,659) and college room and board ($2895). College room only: $1800. Part-time tuition: $275 per credit.

FINANCIAL AID *College-administered aid for undergraduates 1993–94:* 629 need-based scholarships (average $1449), 723 non-need scholarships (average $857), low-interest long-term loans from external sources (average $2450), FSEOG, Federal Work-Study, 172 part-time jobs. Average total aid for freshmen: $9209, meeting 82% of need (aid provided to 100% of those qualified). *Application forms required:* IRS, FAFSA; required for some: institutional; accepted: FFS, FAF. *Priority deadline:* 3/1. *Waivers:* full or partial for employees or children of employees and senior citizens.

COLLEGE LIFE Orientation program (3 days, no cost, parents included). Drama-theater group, choral group, student-run newspaper, radio station. *Social organizations:* 1 open to all. *Most popular organizations:* yearbook, Cadance (magazine), Fellowship of Christian Athletes, NWSA (government), speech/forensics. *Major annual events:* Fall Musical, Christmas at Northwestern, Graduation. *Student services:* health clinic, personal-psychological counseling, shuttle bus. *Safety:* 24-hour patrols, student patrols, late-night transport-escort service.

ATHLETICS *Intercollegiate:* baseball M(s), basketball M(s)/W(s), cross-country running M(s)/W(s), football M(s), golf M(s), soccer M(s), softball W(s), tennis M(s), track and field M(s)/W(s), volleyball W(s). *Intramural:* badminton, basketball, bowling, football, ice hockey, racquetball, sailing, skiing (cross-country), softball, table tennis (Ping-Pong), tennis, volleyball. *Contact:* Mr. Joe Smith, Athletic Director, 612-631-5238.

APPLYING/FRESHMEN *Options:* early entrance, deferred entrance. *Required:* essay, school transcript, 2 recommendations, lifestyle agreement, statement of Christian faith, SAT I or ACT, TOEFL for international students, PSAT. *Recommended:* 3 years of high school math and science, 2 years of high school foreign language. *Required for some:* campus interview. Test scores used for counseling/placement. *Application deadline:* 8/15. *Notification:* continuous until 9/1.

APPLYING/TRANSFER *Required:* essay, 2 recommendations, college transcript, lifestyle agreement, statement of Christian faith. *Recommended:* high school transcript, 2 years of high school foreign language, minimum 2.0 GPA. *Required for some:* standardized test scores, campus interview. *Entrance level:* moderately difficult. *Application deadline:* 8/15. *Notification:* continuous until 9/1.

CONTACT Mr. Ralph D. Anderson, Dean of Admissions, Northwestern College, 3003 North Snelling Avenue, St. Paul, MN 55113; 612-631-5111 or toll-free 800-827-6827.

NORTHWEST NAZARENE COLLEGE
Nampa, Idaho

SPECIAL NOTE FROM THE COLLEGE Northwest Nazarene College is proud of the fact that it has been selected to be among the top 10 liberal arts colleges in the western United States for 2 years in a row by *U.S. News and World Report*. Northwest Nazarene is a unique blend of academic excellence and a strong spiritual commitment. As expressed by Rick Heib, a NASA astronaut and 1977 graduate: "The solid academic preparation is important and the personal involvement of the faculty with students is something crucial to scholastic development....I think of NNC experiences, ranging from music, athletics, and student body activities to community involvement, all in the overall framework of putting others ahead of oneself."

Total Enrollment: 1,288
UG Enrollment: 1,212 (52% W)
Application Deadline: 9/19
Entrance: moderately difficult
Tuition & Fees: $10,179
Room & Board: $2820
SAT≥500: N/R   **ACT≥21:** 78%
Denominational Affiliation: Church of the Nazarene

GENERAL INFORMATION Independent-religious comprehensive coed institution. Awards associate, bachelor's, master's degrees. Founded 1913. *Setting:* 65-acre small-town campus. *Undergraduate faculty:* 121 (75 full-time, 59% with terminal degrees, 46 part-time); student-undergrad faculty ratio is 15:1. *Library Holdings:* 127,200 books, 47,319 microform titles, 736 periodicals, 2,721 records, tapes, and CDs; on-line access to libraries at other institutions. *Computers:* 150 terminals, PCs for student use in computer center, computer labs, library. Student computer-purchase plan available. Access to campuswide network, Internet from computer center, computer labs, library. *Services:* e-mail, file transfer.

UNDERGRADUATE PROFILE 1,212 students from 32 states and territories, 12 other countries. 52% women, 7% part-time, 38% state residents, 27% transferred in, 1% international, 13% 25 or older, 1% Native American, 2% Hispanic, 1% African American, 1% Asian American. *Retention:* 73% of 1992 freshmen returned.

FRESHMEN 323 total; 259 from public schools. 576 applied, 83% were accepted, 68% of whom enrolled. 29% from top 10% of their high school class, 52% from top quarter, 84% from top half. 2 National Merit Scholarship Finalists, 10 class presidents, 30 debating team members, 27 valedictorians, 8 yearbook editors, 10 high school newspaper editors.

ACADEMIC PROGRAM Core, liberal arts core curriculum. Calendar: quarters. Academic remediation for entering students, advanced placement, accelerated degree program, self-designed majors, Freshman Honors College, tutorials, honors program, summer session for credit, part-time degree program (daytime, summer), co-op programs and internships. Fewer than half of graduate courses open to undergraduate students. Off-campus study at Albertson College. ROTC: Army. Unusual degree programs: 3-2 engineering with University of Idaho.

MAJORS Accounting, applied art, art education, art/fine arts, biblical studies, biology/biological sciences, broadcasting, business administration/commerce/management, business education, chemical engineering technology, chemistry, computer information systems, computer programming, computer science, data processing, (pre)dentistry sequence, dietetics, drama therapy, education, elementary education, engineering physics, (pre)engineering sequence, English, family and consumer studies, family services, fashion merchandising, graphic arts, health education, health science, his-

tory, home economics, home economics education, human services, interdisciplinary studies, interior design, international studies, (pre)law sequence, liberal arts/general studies, mathematics, medical technology, (pre)medicine sequence, ministries, music, music education, painting/drawing, pastoral studies, philosophy, physical education, physics, political science/government, psychology, recreation and leisure services, religious education, religious studies, sacred music, science, science education, secondary education, secretarial studies/office management, social science, social work, sociology, special education, speech pathology and audiology, speech/rhetoric/public address/debate, studio art, theology, (pre)veterinary medicine sequence.

EXPENSES FOR 1994–95 *Application fee:* $10. Comprehensive fee of $12,999 includes full-time tuition ($9840), mandatory fees ($339), and college room and board ($2820). Part-time tuition: $283 per credit.

FINANCIAL AID *College-administered aid for undergraduates 1993–94:* need-based scholarships (average $1698), non-need scholarships (average $4396), low-interest long-term loans from college funds (average $1000), loans from external sources (average $3636), FSEOG, Federal Work-Study, 363 part-time jobs. Average total aid for freshmen: $8081, meeting 79% of need (aid provided to 100% of those qualified). *Application forms required:* institutional, FAFSA; required for some: IRS; accepted: FFS, FAF. *Priority deadline:* 3/1. *Payment plan:* installment. *Waivers:* full or partial for minority students, employees or children of employees, adult students, and senior citizens.

COLLEGE LIFE Orientation program (2 days, no cost, parents included). Drama-theater group, choral group, student-run newspaper. *Most popular organizations:* Student Government, Are You Serving Him (RUSH), ministry clubs. *Major annual events:* Malibu-A Spring Festival, RUSH Days, Intramural Snowball Game. *Student services:* health clinic, personal-psychological counseling.

ATHLETICS Member NAIA. *Intercollegiate:* basketball M(s)/W(s), soccer M(s), track and field M(s)/W(s), volleyball W(s). *Intramural:* archery, badminton, basketball, cross-country running, gymnastics, racquetball, skiing (cross-country), skiing (downhill), soccer, swimming and diving, table tennis (Ping-Pong), track and field, volleyball, weight lifting. *Contact:* Mr. Eric Foreth, Director of Athletics, 208-467-8348.

APPLYING/FRESHMEN *Options:* early entrance, deferred entrance, midyear entrance. *Required:* school transcript, minimum 2.0 GPA, recommendations, TOEFL for international students. *Recommended:* 3 years of high school math and science, some high school foreign language, SAT I or ACT, WPCT. *Required for some:* interview. Test scores used for counseling/placement. *Application deadline:* 9/19. *Notification:* continuous.

APPLYING/TRANSFER *Required:* recommendations, college transcript, minimum 2.0 GPA. *Recommended:* 3 years of high school math and science, some high school foreign language. *Required for some:* standardized test scores, high school transcript, interview. *Entrance level:* moderately difficult. *Application deadline:* 9/19. *Notification:* continuous.

CONTACT Mr. Terrence A. Blom, Director of Enrollment Management, Northwest Nazarene College, Nampa, ID 83686; 800-NNC-4-YOU (toll-free).

NYACK COLLEGE
Nyack, New York

Total Enrollment: 980
UG Enrollment: 577 (57% W)
Application Deadline: 9/11
Entrance: moderately difficult
Tuition & Fees: $8400
Room & Board: $3810
SAT≥500: 24% V, 33% M   **ACT≥21:** 20%
Denominational Affiliation: The Christian and Missionary Alliance

GENERAL INFORMATION Independent-religious comprehensive coed institution. Awards associate, bachelor's, master's degrees. Founded 1882. *Setting:* 64-acre small-town campus with easy access to New York City. *Faculty:* 112 (77 full-time, 35 part-time). *Library Holdings:* 77,000 books, 420 microform titles, 614 periodicals. *Computers:* 60 terminals, PCs for student use in computer center, library.

UNDERGRADUATE PROFILE 577 students from 31 states and territories, 3 other countries. 57% women, 6% part-time, 63% state residents, 48% transferred in, 1% international, 0% Native American, 16% Hispanic, 10% African American, 16% Asian American. *Retention:* 71% of 1992 freshmen returned.

FRESHMEN 112 total. 504 applied, 66% were accepted, 33% of whom enrolled. 11% from top 10% of their high school class, 19% from top quarter, 45% from top half.

ACADEMIC PROGRAM Core, honor code. Calendar: semesters. Academic remediation for entering students, English as a second language program offered during academic year, advanced placement, summer session for credit, part-time degree program (daytime), adult/continuing education programs, internships. Off-campus study at Rockland Community College, Calvin College, St. Thomas Aquinas College.

MAJORS Adult and continuing education, biblical studies, business administration/commerce/management, communication, early childhood education, education, elementary education, English, history, interdisciplinary studies, liberal arts/general studies, ministries, music, music education, nursing, pastoral studies, philosophy, piano/organ, psychology, religious education, religious studies, sacred music, secondary education, social science, voice.

EXPENSES FOR 1993–94 *Application fee:* $15. Comprehensive fee of $12,210 includes full-time tuition ($7950), mandatory fees ($450), and college room and board ($3810). College room only: $1680. Part-time tuition: $330 per credit hour. Part-time mandatory fees per semester range from $35 to $58.

FINANCIAL AID *College-administered aid for undergraduates 1993–94:* need-based scholarships, non-need scholarships (average $530), low-interest long-term loans from external sources (average $1200), FSEOG, Federal Work-Study, 200 part-time jobs. *Application forms required:* FAF, IRS, institutional, FAFSA; required for some: state; accepted: FFS. *Priority deadline:* 5/15. *Payment plan:* installment. *Waivers:* full or partial for employees or children of employees.

COLLEGE LIFE Orientation program (3 days, no cost, parents included). Drama-theater group, choral group, student-run newspaper, radio station. *Most popular organizations:* Brooklyn Gospel Team, Drama Club, Student Government Association. *Major annual events:* Homecoming, Sadie Hawkins Day, Spiritual Emphasis Week. *Student services:* health clinic, personal-psychological counseling. *Safety:* 24-hour emergency response devices, student patrols, patrols by trained security personnel.

ATHLETICS Member NAIA. *Intercollegiate:* baseball M, basketball M(s)/W(s), soccer M(s)/W, softball W, volleyball M/W(s). *Intramural:* basketball, football, soccer, softball, tennis, volleyball. *Contact:* Mr. Dan Bailey, Athletic Director, 914-358-1710 Ext. 180.

APPLYING/FRESHMEN *Options:* early entrance, deferred entrance. *Required:* essay, school transcript, 3 recommendations, TOEFL for international students. *Recommended:* 3 years of high school math and science, some high school foreign language. *Required for some:* interview, SAT I or ACT. Test scores used for admission. *Application deadline:* 9/11. *Notification:* continuous.

APPLYING/TRANSFER *Required:* essay, 3 recommendations, college transcript, minimum 2.0 GPA. *Recommended:* some high school foreign language. *Required for some:* standardized test scores, high school transcript, interview. *Entrance level:* moderately difficult. *Application deadline:* 9/11. *Notification:* continuous.

CONTACT Mr. Miguel Sanchez, Director of Admissions, Nyack College, Nyack, NY 10960; 914-358-1710 Ext. 350 or toll-free 800-33-NYACK.

OKLAHOMA BAPTIST UNIVERSITY
Shawnee, Oklahoma

> **SPECIAL NOTE FROM THE UNIVERSITY** Unique athletic programs and an emphasis on learning through doing are hallmarks of Oklahoma Baptist University. Growing from the vision of Baptists of the Oklahoma Territory, OBU is a leader in ministry training, business, teacher education, nursing, premedicine, music, and many other fields. OBU's innovative Unified Studies program provides a carefully constructed common core that integrates what students learn in various academic disciplines, providing a well-rounded liberal arts foundation for living in a rapidly changing world. Students excel in national exams and competitions and in their commitment to international service. OBU is a leader among Southern Baptist institutions in the number of mission volunteers. Nationally competitive in athletics, OBU has compiled 8 top-5 finishes in the 1990s.

Total Enrollment: 2,432
UG Enrollment: 2,412 (53% W)
Application Deadline: 8/1
Entrance: moderately difficult
Tuition & Fees: $5436
Room & Board: $3050
SAT≥500: N/R **ACT≥21:** 72%
Denominational Affiliation: Southern Baptist

GENERAL INFORMATION Independent-religious comprehensive coed institution. Awards bachelor's, master's degrees. Founded 1910. *Setting:* 125-acre small-town campus with easy access to Oklahoma City. *Undergraduate faculty:* 157 (107 full-time, 63% with terminal degrees, 50 part-time); student-undergrad faculty ratio is 14:1. *Library Holdings:* 200,000 books, 300,000 microform titles, 600 periodicals, 7,200 records, tapes, and CDs. *Computers:* 150 terminals, PCs for student use and access to campuswide network in computer center, computer labs, library. *Services:* e-mail, library catalog search and reservation.

UNDERGRADUATE PROFILE 2,412 students from 44 states and territories, 28 other countries. 53% women, 29% part-time, 73% state residents, 61% live on campus, 30% transferred in, 1% international, 15% 25 or older, 6% Native American, 1% Hispanic, 4% African American, 1% Asian American. *Retention:* 79% of 1992 freshmen returned.

FRESHMEN 484 total. 717 applied, 95% were accepted, 71% of whom enrolled. 31% from top 10% of their high school class, 52% from top quarter, 76% from top half. 5 National Merit Scholarship Finalists, 23 valedictorians.

ACADEMIC PROGRAM Core, liberal arts and Western Civilization curriculum, honor code. Calendar: 4-1-4. Average class size 30 in required courses. Academic remediation for entering students, advanced placement, self-designed majors, Freshman Honors College, honors program, summer session for credit, part-time degree program (daytime), co-op programs and internships. Off-campus study at St. Gregory's College. Unusual degree programs: 3-2 engineering with Oklahoma State University.

STUDY-ABROAD SITES China, Japan.

MAJORS Accounting, American studies, applied art, art education, art/fine arts, biblical studies, biology/biological sciences, broadcasting, business administration/commerce/management, business education, chemistry, child care/child and family studies, child psychology/child development, communication, computer information systems, computer management, computer science, corrections, criminal justice, (pre)dentistry sequence, economics, education, elementary education, English, finance/banking, French, German, health services administration, history, humanities, information science, interdisciplinary studies, journalism, (pre)law sequence, management information systems, marketing/retailing/merchandising, marriage and family counseling, mathematics, medical laboratory technology, (pre)medicine sequence, ministries,

modern languages, music, music education, natural sciences, nursing, pastoral studies, philosophy, physical education, physical fitness/exercise science, physical sciences, physics, piano/organ, political science/government, psychology, public affairs and policy studies, public relations, radio and television studies, recreation and leisure services, religious education, religious studies, sacred music, science, science education, secondary education, secretarial studies/office management, social science, social work, sociology, Spanish, special education, speech/rhetoric/public address/debate, sports medicine, stringed instruments, telecommunications, theater arts/drama, theology, (pre)veterinary medicine sequence, voice.

EXPENSES FOR 1993–94 *Application fee:* $25. Comprehensive fee of $8486 includes full-time tuition ($4930), mandatory fees ($506), and college room and board ($3050). College room only: $1300. Part-time tuition: $165 per credit hour. Part-time mandatory fees: $122.50 per term.

FINANCIAL AID *College-administered aid for undergraduates 1993–94:* need-based scholarships, non-need scholarships, short-term loans (average $100), low-interest long-term loans from college funds (average $1000), loans from external sources (average $2500), FSEOG, Federal Work-Study, 400 part-time jobs. Average total aid for freshmen: $4850, meeting 84% of need (aid provided to 100% of those qualified). *Application forms required:* IRS, institutional, FAFSA; required for some: state. *Priority deadline:* 3/1. *Payment plan:* installment. *Waivers:* full or partial for minority students, children of alumni, employees or children of employees, and senior citizens.

COLLEGE LIFE Orientation program (3 days, no cost, parents included). Drama-theater group, choral group, student-run newspaper. *Social organizations:* 50 open to all; 5 local fraternities, 5 local sororities; 18% of eligible men and 16% of eligible women are members. *Major annual events:* Stampede of Stars, Spring Affair, Christmas Hanging of the Green. *Student services:* health clinic, personal-psychological counseling. *Safety:* 24-hour emergency response devices and patrols, late-night transport-escort service.

ATHLETICS Member NAIA. *Intercollegiate:* baseball M(s), basketball M(s)/W(s), cross-country running M(s)/W(s), tennis M(s), track and field M(s)/W(s). *Intramural:* basketball, bowling, football, racquetball, soccer, softball, swimming and diving, table tennis (Ping-Pong), tennis, volleyball. *Contact:* Athletic Director, 405-878-2132.

APPLYING/FRESHMEN *Option:* deferred entrance. *Required:* school transcript, minimum 2.0 GPA, medical history, SAT I or ACT, TOEFL for international students. *Recommended:* 3 years of high school math and science, some high school foreign language. *Required for some:* recommendations, interview. Test scores used for admission and counseling/placement. *Application deadline:* 8/1. *Notification:* continuous until 9/1.

APPLYING/TRANSFER *Required:* standardized test scores, high school transcript, college transcript, minimum 2.0 GPA, medical history. *Recommended:* 3 years of high school math and science, some high school foreign language. *Required for some:* recommendations, interview. *Entrance level:* moderately difficult. *Application deadline:* 8/1. *Notification:* continuous until 9/1.

CONTACT Mr. Jody Johnson, Dean of Admissions, Oklahoma Baptist University, 500 West University, Shawnee, OK 74801; 405-878-2033 or toll-free 800-654-3285.

OLIVET NAZARENE UNIVERSITY
Kankakee, Illinois

> **SPECIAL NOTE FROM THE UNIVERSITY** Olivet Nazarene University offers students a liberal arts education based on Christian values. Located 60 miles south of Chicago's Loop, the 160-acre campus offers the tranquility of a small community as well as access to the culture and recreation of a world-class city. There are 29 major buildings including a 3,000-seat convocation/athletic center, a 35,000-watt FM radio station, and a planetarium. Five years after graduation, 85% of Olivet's alumni report employment in an area related to their college major. Two choirs, a concert band, a symphony orchestra, and other ensembles involve 400 students. The intramural sports program involves over 500 students. Ten spiritual life organizations provide opportunities for service and ministry both on and off campus. Olivet specializes in campus visits and welcomes prospective students.

Total Enrollment: 2,194

UG Enrollment: 1,558 (55% W)

Application Deadline: 8/1

Entrance: minimally difficult

Tuition & Fees: $7836

Room & Board: $4140

Denominational Affiliation: Church of the Nazarene

GENERAL INFORMATION Independent-religious comprehensive coed institution. Awards associate, bachelor's, master's degrees. Founded 1907. *Setting:* 160-acre suburban campus with easy access to Chicago. *Undergraduate faculty:* 120 (90 full-time, 52% with terminal degrees, 30 part-time); student-undergrad faculty ratio is 18:1. *Library Holdings:* 153,000 books, 42,000 microform titles, 900 periodicals, 6,000 records, tapes, and CDs. *Computers:* 350 terminals, PCs for student use in computer center, library, various departments.

UNDERGRADUATE PROFILE 1,558 students from 40 states and territories, 19 other countries. 55% women, 8% part-time, 44% state residents, 20% transferred in, 4% international, 10% 25 or older, 0% Native American, 1% Hispanic, 4% African American, 1% Asian American. *Retention:* 70% of 1992 freshmen returned.

FRESHMEN 606 total. 1,132 applied, 98% were accepted, 55% of whom enrolled. 20% from top 10% of their high school class, 40% from top quarter, 71% from top half.

ACADEMIC PROGRAM Core. Calendar: semesters. Academic remediation for entering students, English as a second language program offered during academic year, advanced placement, accelerated degree program, self-designed majors, summer session for credit, part-time degree program (daytime), adult/continuing education programs, co-op programs and internships. Off-campus study at Christian College Coalition. ROTC: Army (c).

STUDY-ABROAD SITES England, France, Spain.

MAJORS Accounting, adult and continuing education, anthropology, art education, art/fine arts, athletic training, biblical studies, biochemistry, biology/biological sciences, biophysics, broadcasting, business administration/commerce/management, business economics, chemistry, child care/child and family studies, child psychology/child development, communication, computer information systems, computer science, criminal justice, (pre)dentistry sequence, dietetics, early childhood education, earth science, economics, education, elementary education, engineering (general), engineering physics, engineering sciences, English, environmental sciences, family services, fashion merchandising, film studies, finance/banking, food sciences, food services management, geochemistry, geology, geophysics, graphic arts, history, home economics, home economics education, human resources, interdisciplinary studies, journalism, (pre)law sequence, liberal arts/general studies, literature, marketing/retailing/merchandising, mathematics, medical technology, (pre)medicine sequence, modern languages, music, music education, natural sciences, nursing, pastoral studies, philosophy, physical education, physical sciences, physical therapy, piano/organ, psychology, radio and television studies, religious education, religious studies, Romance languages, sacred music, science, science education, secondary education, secretarial studies/office management, social science, speech/rhetoric/public address/debate, stringed instruments, teacher aide studies, textiles and clothing, theology, (pre)veterinary medicine sequence, voice, wind and percussion instruments.

EXPENSES FOR 1993–94 Comprehensive fee of $11,976 includes full-time tuition ($7700), mandatory fees ($136), and college room and board ($4140). College room only: $1960. Part-time tuition: $320 per semester hour.

FINANCIAL AID *College-administered aid for undergraduates 1993–94:* need-based scholarships, non-need scholarships (average $591), low-interest long-term loans from external sources (average $1000), FSEOG, Federal Work-Study, 400 part-time jobs. Average total aid for freshmen: $8094, meeting 100% of need (aid provided to 100% of those qualified). *Application forms required:* FAF, institutional, FAFSA; required for some: IRS, state; accepted: FFS. *Priority deadline:* 8/1. *Payment plan:* installment. *Waivers:* full or partial for employees or children of employees.

COLLEGE LIFE Orientation program (2 days, no cost, parents included). Drama-theater group, choral group, student-run newspaper, radio station. *Student services:* health clinic, personal-psychological counseling. *Safety:* 24-hour patrols, late-night transport-escort service.

ATHLETICS Member NAIA. *Intercollegiate:* baseball M(s), basketball M(s)/W(s), cross-country running M(s)/W(s), football M(s), golf M, soccer M, softball W(s), tennis M/W, volleyball M/W. *Intramural:* basketball, cross-country running, football, golf, soccer, softball, table tennis (Ping-Pong), tennis, track and field, volleyball. *Contact:* Mr. Larry Watson, Director of Athletics, 815-939-5123.

APPLYING/FRESHMEN *Options:* early entrance, deferred entrance. *Required:* school transcript, 2 recommendations, ACT, TOEFL for international students. *Recommended:* 3 years of high school science, interview. *Required for some:* 3 years of high school math, some high school foreign language. Test scores used for counseling/placement. *Application deadline:* 8/1. *Notification:* continuous.

APPLYING/TRANSFER *Required:* 3 recommendations, college transcript, minimum 2.0 GPA. *Recommended:* interview. *Required for some:* high school transcript. *Entrance level:* minimally difficult. *Application deadline:* 8/1. *Notification:* continuous.

CONTACT Rev. John Mongerson, Director of Admissions, Olivet Nazarene University, P.O. Box 592, Kankakee, IL 60901; 815-939-5203.

PACIFIC CHRISTIAN COLLEGE
Fullerton, California

SPECIAL NOTE FROM THE COLLEGE Pacific Christian College prepares students to be servant leaders in the church and in society. The Southern California location makes possible cross-cultural experiences with persons from around the world while also offering a variety of internship and recreational opportunities for students. A formal relationship with Cal State University, which is adjacent to campus, allows students to study at both institutions. Students can be involved in service opportunities that include the local school system and missions projects in Mexico. At Pacific Christian College, students prepare for life and career in a spiritual atmosphere with a caring faculty and staff.

Total Enrollment: 765
UG Enrollment: 592 (52% W)
Application Deadline: 7/1
Entrance: minimally difficult
Tuition & Fees: $7310
Room & Board: $3115
Denominational Affiliation: Christian Church/ Church of Christ

GENERAL INFORMATION Independent-religious comprehensive coed institution. Awards associate, bachelor's, master's degrees. Founded 1928. *Setting:* 11-acre suburban campus with easy access to Los Angeles. *Faculty:* 63 (25 full-time, 60% with terminal degrees, 38 part-time); student-undergrad faculty ratio is 16:1. *Library Holdings:* 61,225 books, 15 microform titles, 428 periodicals, 1 on-line bibliographic service, 3,950 records, tapes, and CDs. *Computers:* 13 terminals, PCs for student use in computer labs, library.

UNDERGRADUATE PROFILE 592 students from 27 states and territories, 19 other countries. 52% women, 13% part-time, 53% state residents, 42% live on campus, 10% transferred in, 50% have need-based financial aid, 82% have non-need-based financial aid, 22% have campus jobs, 11% international, 35% 25 or older, 1% Native American, 6% Hispanic, 5% African American, 8% Asian American. *Retention:* 66% of 1992 freshmen returned.

FRESHMEN 93 total. 167 applied, 85% were accepted, 65% of whom enrolled.

ACADEMIC PROGRAM Core, writing-oriented curriculum, honor code. Calendar: 4-1-4. 168 courses offered in 1993–94; average class size 25 in required courses. Academic remediation for entering students, English as a second language program offered during academic year, advanced placement, accelerated degree program, self-designed majors, summer session for credit, part-time degree program (daytime), adult/continuing education programs, internships. A few graduate courses open to undergraduate students. Off-campus study at California State University, Fullerton.

MAJORS Art/fine arts, biblical studies, business administration/ commerce/management, child psychology/child development, children's ministry, communication, early childhood education, elementary education, English, liberal arts/general studies, ministries, music, pastoral studies, physical education, psychology, religious education, secondary education, social science, social work, theology, youth ministry.

EXPENSES FOR 1994–95 *Application fee:* $30. Comprehensive fee of $10,425 includes full-time tuition ($7100), mandatory fees ($210), and college room and board ($3115). College room only: $1485. Part-time tuition: $260 per unit. Part-time mandatory fees: $210 per year.

FINANCIAL AID *College-administered aid for undergraduates 1993–94:* 230 need-based scholarships (average $1606), 383 non-need scholarships (average $1794), low-interest long-term loans from college funds, loans from external sources (average $3184), FSEOG, Federal Work-Study. Average total aid for freshmen: $8599, meeting 96% of need (aid provided to 100% of those qualified). *Application forms required:* institutional, FAFSA; required for some: IRS, state. *Priority deadline:* 3/2. *Payment plan:* installment. *Waivers:* full or partial for employees or children of employees and senior citizens. *Average indebtedness of graduates:* $10,485.

COLLEGE LIFE Orientation program (3 days, $75, parents included). Drama-theater group, choral group, student-run newspaper. *Social organizations:* 5 social clubs; 50% of eligible men and 50% of eligible women are members. *Major annual events:* Spring Banquet, Sadie Hawkins Day. *Student services:* career counseling, health clinic, personal-psychological counseling. *Safety:* 24-hour emergency response devices, student patrols, late-night transport-escort service, controlled dormitory access.

ATHLETICS *Intercollegiate:* basketball M/W, soccer M, softball W, volleyball M/W. *Intramural:* bowling, football, golf, skiing (downhill), soccer, softball, table tennis (Ping-Pong), tennis, volleyball, weight lifting. *Contact:* Mr. Lee Ericson, Athletic Director, 714-879-3901 Ext. 288.

APPLYING/FRESHMEN *Options:* early entrance, deferred entrance, midyear entrance. *Required:* essay, school transcript, 2 recommendations, minimum 2.5 GPA, TOEFL for international students. *Required for some:* interview, SAT I or ACT. Test scores used for counseling/placement. *Application deadline:* 7/1. *Notification:* continuous until 7/1.

APPLYING/TRANSFER *Required:* essay, 2 recommendations, college transcript, minimum 2.5 GPA. *Required for some:* standardized test scores, high school transcript, interview. *Entrance level:* minimally difficult. *Application deadline:* 7/1. *Notification:* continuous until 7/1.

CONTACT Ms. Diane LeJeune, Director of Admissions, Pacific Christian College, 2500 East Nutwood Avenue, Fullerton, CA 92631; 714-879-3901 or toll-free 800-762-1294; fax: 714-526-0231.

PALM BEACH ATLANTIC COLLEGE
West Palm Beach, Florida

SPECIAL NOTE FROM THE COLLEGE Palm Beach Atlantic College encourages students to put their Christian beliefs into action. Workship ("work" and "worship") requires each full-time student to contribute 45 hours annually to community service. Students choose from a wide range of nonprofit agencies and work individually or in groups on projects such as cleaning up streets and beaches or helping children, the elderly, or others in need. Student missions efforts may be as near as Backyard Bible Clubs in inner-city West Palm Beach or as far as China. Several on-campus groups allow students to minister to each other and to the community.

Total Enrollment: 1,867
UG Enrollment: 1,766 (55% W)
Application Deadline: rolling
Entrance: moderately difficult
Tuition & Fees: $8400
Room & Board: $3500
Denominational Affiliation: Southern Baptist

GENERAL INFORMATION Independent-religious comprehensive coed institution. Awards bachelor's, master's degrees. Founded 1968. *Setting:* 25-acre urban campus with easy access to Miami. *Faculty:* 110 (68 full-time, 73% with terminal degrees, 42 part-time); student-undergrad faculty ratio is 17:1. *Library Holdings:* 62,017 books, 551 microform titles, 856 periodicals, 4 on-line bibliographic services, 16 CD-ROMs, 2,495 records, tapes, and CDs. *Computers:* 75 terminals, PCs for student use in computer center, library, learning center. Access to campuswide network, BITNET, Internet from computer center, dorms. *Services:* e-mail, library catalog search and reservation.

UNDERGRADUATE PROFILE 1,766 students from 35 states and territories, 23 other countries. 55% women, 19% part-time, 63% state residents, 48% live on campus, 14% transferred in, 5% international, 26% 25 or older, 1% Native American, 5% Hispanic, 5% African American, 1% Asian American. *Retention:* 59% of 1992 freshmen returned. *Graduation:* 19% graduate in 4 years.

FRESHMEN 353 total. 688 applied, 91% were accepted, 56% of whom enrolled. 15% from top 10% of their high school class, 37% from top quarter, 71% from top half.

ACADEMIC PROGRAM Core. Calendar: semesters. 701 courses offered in 1993–94; average class size 18 in required courses. Academic remediation for entering students, English as a second language program offered during academic year, advanced placement, Freshman Honors College, tutorials, honors program, summer session for credit, part-time degree program (daytime, evenings), adult/continuing education programs, internships.

STUDY-ABROAD SITE England.

MAJORS Accounting, art education, art/fine arts, biology/biological sciences, business administration/commerce/management, communication, computer information systems, (pre)dentistry sequence, early childhood education, economics, education, elementary education, English, finance/banking, history, international business, (pre)law sequence, marketing/retailing/merchandising, mathematics, (pre)medicine sequence, music, music education, physical education, political science/government, psychology, religious studies, science, secondary education.

EXPENSES FOR 1994–95 *Application fee:* $25. Comprehensive fee of $11,900 includes full-time tuition ($7900), mandatory fees ($500), and college room and board ($3500 minimum). Part-time tuition: $220 per credit hour.

FINANCIAL AID *College-administered aid for undergraduates 1993–94:* need-based scholarships, non-need scholarships, low-interest long-term loans from external sources, FSEOG, Federal Work-Study. Average total aid for freshmen: $9551, meeting 80% of need (aid provided to 100% of those qualified). Forms required for some financial aid applicants: IRS, institutional; accepted: FFS, FAF, FAFSA. *Priority deadline:* 5/1. *Waivers:* full or partial for employees or children of employees and senior citizens.

COLLEGE LIFE Orientation program (3 days, $50, parents included). Drama-theater groups, choral groups, student-run newspaper. *Most popular organizations:* Campus Activities Board, Student Government Association, Phi Beta Lambda, Science Club, Impact. *Major annual events:* Homecoming, Welcome Week, Spring Happening. *Student services:* health clinic, personal-psychological counseling. *Safety:* room security.

ATHLETICS Member NAIA. *Intercollegiate:* baseball M(s), basketball M(s), cross-country W(s), golf M(s)/W(s), soccer M(s)/W(s), tennis W(s), volleyball W(s). *Intramural:* basketball, bowling, football, golf, racquetball, softball, table tennis (Ping-Pong), tennis, volleyball. *Contact:* Mr. Brent Wellman, Athletic Director, 407-650-7625.

APPLYING/FRESHMEN *Options:* early entrance, deferred entrance, midyear entrance. *Required:* essay, school transcript, minimum 2.5 GPA, 2 recommendations, SAT I or ACT, TOEFL for international students. *Recommended:* minimum 3.0 GPA, 3 years of high school math and science, some high school foreign language, interview. Test scores used for counseling/placement. *Application deadline:* rolling. *Notification:* continuous.

APPLYING/TRANSFER *Required:* essay, 2 recommendations, college transcript, minimum 2.0 GPA. *Recommended:* standardized test scores, 3 years of high school math and science, some high school foreign language, interview, minimum 3.0 GPA. *Required for some:* high school transcript. *Entrance level:* moderately difficult. *Application deadline:* rolling. *Notification:* continuous.

CONTACT Mr. Buck James, Dean of Admissions, Palm Beach Atlantic College, 901 S. Flagler Drive, P.O. Box 24708, West Palm Beach, FL 33416-4708; 407-835-4309 or toll-free 800-238-3998.

POINT LOMA NAZARENE COLLEGE
San Diego, California

> **SPECIAL NOTE FROM THE COLLEGE** Point Loma Nazarene College is a distinctively Christian college that has provided a high-quality education for almost 100 years. Located on the crest of historic Point Loma, collegians enjoy a clear view westward overlooking the Pacific Ocean and eastward across downtown San Diego, where many cultural and employment opportunities are available. Point Loma offers a wide variety of academic programs, continually modified to meet changing needs. The 18 academic departments offer 44 majors plus many subspecialties, credentials, and certificates. The nearly 2,500 students come from 34 states and 25 countries. At Point Loma Nazarene, students strive for 3 holistic goals: spiritual formation, academic excellence, and personal development.

Total Enrollment: 2,484
UG Enrollment: 2,106 (61% W)
Application Deadline: rolling
Entrance: moderately difficult
Tuition & Fees: $10,310
Room & Board: $4190
SAT≥500: 23% V, 41% M   **ACT≥21:** 48%
Denominational Affiliation: Nazarene

GENERAL INFORMATION Independent-religious comprehensive coed institution. Awards bachelor's, master's degrees. Founded 1902. *Setting:* 88-acre suburban campus. *Faculty:* 143 (121 full-time, 72% with terminal degrees, 22 part-time); student-undergrad faculty ratio is 15:1. *Library Holdings:* 155,904 books, 36,934 microform titles, 656 periodicals, 2,499 records, tapes, and CDs; on-line access to libraries at University of San Diego, San Diego State University. *Computers:* 75 terminals, PCs for student use in computer center, computer labs. Access to campuswide network, Internet. *Service:* library catalog search and reservation.

UNDERGRADUATE PROFILE 2,106 students from 34 states and territories, 25 other countries. 61% women, 10% part-time, 87% state residents, 63% live on campus, 13% transferred in, 3% international, 12% 25 or older, 1% Native American, 7% Hispanic, 3% African American, 4% Asian American. *Retention:* 69% of 1992 freshmen returned. *Graduation:* 30% graduate in 4 years.

FRESHMEN 426 total. 809 applied, 85% were accepted, 62% of whom enrolled. 20% from top 10% of their high school class, 43% from top quarter, 69% from top half.

ACADEMIC PROGRAM Core. Calendar: semesters. 566 courses offered in 1993–94; average class size 30 in required courses. Academic remediation for entering students, English as a second language program offered during academic year and summer, advanced placement, accelerated degree program, tutorials, honors program, summer session for credit, part-time degree program, internships. Fewer than half of graduate courses open to undergraduate students. Off-campus study at American University, Christian College Coalition. ROTC: Army (c), Naval (c), Air Force (c).

MAJORS Accounting, art education, art/fine arts, athletic training, biblical studies, biochemistry, biology/biological sciences, business administration/commerce/management, business education, chemistry, child psychology/child development, communication, computer science, (pre)dentistry sequence, dietetics, economics, engineering physics, family services, graphic arts, history, home economics, home economics education, human resources, journalism, (pre)law sequence, liberal arts/general studies, literature,

management information systems, mathematics, (pre)medicine sequence, music, music business, music education, nursing, pastoral studies, philosophy, physical education, physics, political science/government, psychology, religious education, religious studies, sacred music, secretarial studies/office management, sociology, Spanish, theater arts/drama, theology, (pre)veterinary medicine sequence.

EXPENSES FOR 1994–95 *Application fee:* $20. Comprehensive fee of $14,500 includes full-time tuition ($10,176), mandatory fees ($134), and college room and board ($4190). Part-time tuition: $318 per unit.

FINANCIAL AID *College-administered aid for undergraduates 1993–94:* need-based scholarships, non-need scholarships, low-interest long-term loans from external sources (average $2000), FSEOG, Federal Work-Study, 100 part-time jobs. *Application forms required:* FAF, state, institutional, FAFSA. *Priority deadline:* 4/10. *Payment plan:* installment. *Waivers:* full or partial for employees or children of employees and senior citizens. *Notification:* continuous.

COLLEGE LIFE Orientation program (2 days, $15, parents included). Drama-theater group, choral group, student-run newspaper. *Social organizations:* 1 national sorority, 3 local fraternities, 2 local sororities; 8% of eligible men and 5% of eligible women are members. *Major annual events:* Homecoming, Christmas Messiah Concert. *Student services:* health clinic, personal-psychological counseling, shuttle bus. *Safety:* 24-hour patrols, late-night transport-escort service.

ATHLETICS Member NAIA. *Intercollegiate:* baseball M(s), basketball M(s)/W(s), cross-country running M(s)/W(s), golf M(s), soccer M(s), softball W, tennis M(s)/W(s), track and field M(s)/W(s), volleyball W(s). *Intramural:* badminton, baseball, basketball, bowling, cross-country running, football, golf, racquetball, sailing, soccer, softball, swimming and diving, table tennis (Ping-Pong), tennis, track and field, volleyball, water polo, weight lifting. *Contact:* Dr. Carroll Land, Director of Athletics, 619-221-2266.

APPLYING/FRESHMEN *Options:* early entrance, deferred entrance, midyear entrance. *Required:* school transcript, 2 years of high school foreign language, 2 recommendations, SAT I or ACT, TOEFL for international students. *Recommended:* minimum 2.5 GPA, 3 years of high school math and science. *Required for some:* campus interview. Test scores used for counseling/placement. *Application deadline:* rolling. *Notification:* continuous.

APPLYING/TRANSFER *Required:* 2 years of high school foreign language, 2 recommendations, college transcript, minimum 2.0 GPA. *Recommended:* 3 years of high school math and science. *Required for some:* high school transcript, campus interview. *Entrance level:* moderately difficult. *Application deadline:* rolling. *Notification:* continuous.

CONTACT Mr. Bill Young, Executive Director for Enrollment Services, Point Loma Nazarene College, 3900 Lomaland Drive, San Diego, CA 92106; 619-221-2225.

REDEEMER COLLEGE
Ancaster, Ontario, Canada

SPECIAL NOTE FROM THE COLLEGE Redeemer College is a place that's big enough to offer a full range of majors and minors yet small enough for students to get to know their classmates and professors. It's a university-college where the dorms are fully equipped 4-bedroom town houses and the facilities are modern. The College has the tradition of excellence of the British university system combined with the strengths of a Christian liberal arts program. An innovative financial aid program makes tuition surprisingly affordable. The current exchange rate for the Canadian dollar provides American applicants with an educational bargain.

Total Enrollment: 474 (all UG)

Women: 60%

Application Deadline: rolling

Entrance: moderately difficult

Tuition & Fees: $6360 (Can.)

Room & Board: $4020 (Can.)

Denominational Affiliation: interdenominational

GENERAL INFORMATION Independent-religious 4-year coed institution. Awards bachelor's degrees. Founded 1980. *Setting:* 78-acre small-town campus with easy access to Toronto. *Faculty:* 49 (32 full-time, 94% with terminal degrees, 17 part-time); student-undergrad faculty ratio is 14:1. *Library Holdings:* 90,000 books, 275 periodicals, 1 on-line bibliographic service, 8 CD-ROMs, 1,000 records, tapes, and CDs. *Computers:* 20 terminals, PCs for student use in computer center, dorms.

UNDERGRADUATE PROFILE 474 students from 6 provinces and territories, 3 other countries. 60% women, 7% part-time, 95% province residents, 80% live on campus, 3% transferred in, 57% have need-based financial aid, 30% have non-need-based financial aid, 34% have campus jobs, 2% international, 6% 25 or older, 1% Hispanic, 1% black, 1% Asian. *Retention:* 75% of 1992 freshmen returned.

FRESHMEN 173 total. 232 applied, 95% were accepted, 79% of whom enrolled.

ACADEMIC PROGRAM Core, liberal arts curriculum, honor code. Calendar: semesters. 220 courses offered in 1993–94; average class size 22 in required courses. Academic remediation for entering students, services for LD students, honors program, summer session for credit, part-time degree program (daytime, evenings), internships. Off-campus study.

STUDY-ABROAD SITES France, the Netherlands.

MAJORS Accounting, art/fine arts, behavioral sciences, biblical studies, biology/biological sciences, botany/plant sciences, business administration/commerce/management, clinical psychology, (pre)dentistry sequence, education, elementary education, English, experimental psychology, French, history, humanities, (pre)law sequence, liberal arts/general studies, literature, mathematics, (pre)medicine sequence, modern languages, music, natural sciences, philosophy, physical education, political science/government, psychology, religious studies, Romance languages, science, secondary education, sociology, theater arts/drama, theology, (pre)veterinary medicine sequence.

EXPENSES FOR 1994–95 *Application fee:* $30. Comprehensive fee of $10,658 includes full-time tuition and mandatory fees ($6360) and college room and board ($4020). Part-time tuition: $675 per course. All expense figures are in Canadian dollars.

FINANCIAL AID *College-administered aid for undergraduates 1993–94:* 142 non-need scholarships (average $1012), low-interest long-term loans from external sources, 163 part-time jobs. *Application forms required:* government; required for some: institutional; accepted: FFS, FAF. *Application deadline:* continuous to 1/15. *Payment plans:* installment, deferred payment. *Waivers:* full or partial for employees or children of employees and senior citizens. Must reapply each year. *Average indebtedness of graduates:* $18,000.

COLLEGE LIFE Orientation program (2 days, $10, parents included). Drama-theater group, choral group, student-run newspaper. *Social organizations:* 25 open to all, with 100% participating. *Most popular organizations:* Fellowship Hour (21% participate), Coffee House (16% participate), cell groups (10% participate), Choir (8% participate). *Major annual events:* Choir Concert, Mainstage Productions, Mid Night Breakfast. *Student services:* personal-psychological counseling. *Safety:* 24-hour emergency response devices, student patrols, late-night transport-escort service, room security.

ATHLETICS *Intercollegiate:* badminton M/W, basketball M/W, cross-country running M/W, ice hockey M/W, soccer M/W, volleyball M/W. *Intramural:* archery, badminton, basketball, bowling, ice hockey, racquetball, skiing (cross-country), skiing (downhill), soccer, squash, swimming and diving, volleyball. *Contact:* Mr. Allan Brown, Athletic Director, 905-648-2131 Ext. 221.

APPLYING/FRESHMEN Preference given to Christians. *Options:* deferred entrance, midyear entrance. *Required:* school transcript, 2 recommendations, pastoral reference, TOEFL for international students. *Recommended:* 4 years of high school math and science, 4 years of high school foreign language. *Required for some:* essay, interview, SAT I or ACT. Test scores used for admission. *Application deadlines:* rolling, rolling for nonresidents.

APPLYING/TRANSFER *Required:* high school transcript, 2 recommendations, college transcript, minimum 2.0 GPA, pastoral reference. *Recommended:* 4 years of high school math and science, 4 years of high school foreign language. *Required for some:* essay, standardized test scores, interview, minimum 3.0 GPA. *Entrance level:* moderately difficult. *Application deadline:* rolling.

CONTACT Mr. Mark Van Beveren, Admissions Director, Redeemer College, 777 Highway 53 East, Ancaster, ON L9K 1J4, Canada; 905-648-2131 or toll-free 800-263-6467 (in Canada).

ROBERTS WESLEYAN COLLEGE
Rochester, New York

SPECIAL NOTE FROM THE COLLEGE Roberts Wesleyan College provides the ideal setting for a contemporary liberal arts education in the Christian tradition. The modern, parklike campus, which is located just 10 miles from the center of Rochester, provides students with the advantages of a rural setting within a vibrant metropolitan area. Rochester offers numerous cultural, recreational, internship, and career opportunities for students and graduates. The College's broadly based curriculum of 40 majors and preprofessional programs include 4 with national professional accreditation: art, music, nursing, and social work. Roberts is honoring its 128-year commitment to address society's ever-changing needs through high-quality, accredited educational programs in a climate where students are encouraged in their faith as well as in their intellectual and professional development. Roberts also offers a Master of Education degree program.

Total Enrollment: 1,115

UG Enrollment: 1,039 (61% W)

Application Deadline: rolling

Entrance: moderately difficult

Tuition & Fees: $9952

Room & Board: $3366

SAT≥500: 24% V, 41% M **ACT≥21:** 53%

Denominational Affiliation: Free Methodist Church of North America

GENERAL INFORMATION Independent-religious comprehensive coed institution. Awards associate, bachelor's, master's degrees. Founded 1866. *Setting:* 75-acre suburban campus. *Faculty:* 110 (51 full-time, 48% with terminal degrees, 59 part-time); student-undergrad faculty ratio is 15:1. *Library Holdings:* 99,869 books, 678 periodicals, 1 on-line bibliographic service, 2,242 records, tapes, and CDs. *Computers:* 47 terminals, PCs for student use in computer center, computer labs, learning resource center, library.

UNDERGRADUATE PROFILE 1,039 students from 24 states and territories, 14 other countries. 61% women, 10% part-time, 93% state residents, 67% live on campus, 18% transferred in, 82% have need-based financial aid, 50% have campus jobs, 6% international, 22% 25 or older, 1% Native American, 2% Hispanic, 6% African American, 1% Asian American. *Retention:* 73% of 1992 freshmen returned.

FRESHMEN 212 total. 459 applied, 92% were accepted, 50% of whom enrolled. 22% from top 10% of their high school class, 49% from top quarter, 73% from top half. 9 valedictorians.

ACADEMIC PROGRAM Core, honor code. Calendar: semesters. Academic remediation for entering students, English as a second language program offered during summer, advanced placement, Freshman Honors College, tutorials, honors program, summer session for credit, external degree programs, adult/continuing education programs, co-op programs and internships. Off-campus study at Rochester Area Colleges. ROTC: Army (c), Air Force (c). Unusual degree programs: 3-2 engineering with Clarkson University, Rensselaer Polytechnic Institute, Rochester Institute of Technology.

STUDY-ABROAD SITES Dominican Republic, England, France, Russia.

MAJORS Accounting, art education, art/fine arts, biology/biological sciences, business administration/commerce/management, chemistry, communication, computer science, criminal justice, (pre)dentistry sequence, education, elementary education, English, gerontology, graphic arts, history, humanities, human resources, mathematics, medical technology, ministries, music, music education, natural sciences, nursing, physical sciences, physics, piano/organ, psychology, religious studies, science, secondary education, social science, social work, sociology, studio art, voice.

EXPENSES FOR 1993–94 *Application fee:* $25. Comprehensive fee of $13,318 includes full-time tuition ($9722), mandatory fees ($230), and college room and board ($3366). College room only: $2210. Part-time tuition per semester hour ranges from $182 to $405.

FINANCIAL AID *College-administered aid for undergraduates 1993–94:* 589 need-based scholarships (average $1330), 811 non-need scholarships (average $1560), low-interest long-term loans from college funds (average $1000), loans from external sources (average $3600), FSEOG, Federal Work-Study, 200 part-time jobs. *Application forms required:* FAF, FAFSA; required for some: IRS, state; accepted: FFS. *Priority deadline:* 6/15. *Payment plan:* installment. *Waivers:* full or partial for employees or children of employees. *Average indebtedness of graduates:* $13,860.

COLLEGE LIFE Orientation program (3 days, no cost, parents included). Drama-theater group, choral group, student-run newspaper. *Student services:* health clinic, personal-psychological counseling. *Safety:* 24-hour emergency response devices and patrols, late-night transport-escort service, controlled dormitory access.

ATHLETICS *Intercollegiate:* basketball M(s)/W(s), cross-country running M(s)/W(s), soccer M(s)/W(s), track and field M(s)/W(s). *Intramural:* basketball, racquetball, soccer, table tennis (Ping-Pong), tennis, volleyball. *Contact:* Mr. Michael Faro, Athletic Director, 716-594-6130.

APPLYING/FRESHMEN *Options:* early entrance, deferred entrance. *Required:* essay, school transcript, 1 recommendation, SAT I or ACT, TOEFL for international students. *Recommended:* 3 years of high school math and science, 3 years of high school foreign language, campus interview. Test scores used for counseling/placement. *Application deadline:* rolling.

APPLYING/TRANSFER *Required:* essay, high school transcript, 1 recommendation, college transcript, minimum 2.0 GPA. *Recommended:* standardized test scores, 3 years of high school math and science, 3 years of high school foreign language, campus interview. *Entrance level:* moderately difficult. *Application deadline:* rolling.

CONTACT Miss Linda Kurtz, Director of Admissions, Roberts Wesleyan College, 2301 Westside Drive, Rochester, NY 14624; 716-594-9471 Ext. 410 or toll-free 800-777-4792.

SEATTLE PACIFIC UNIVERSITY
Seattle, Washington

Seattle Pacific University

> **SPECIAL NOTE FROM THE UNIVERSITY** Seattle Pacific University is a comprehensive university of liberal arts (arts and sciences) and professional programs (i.e., business, electrical engineering, nursing), with the premier teacher-education program in the state of Washington. Regional accreditation is provided by the Northwest Association of Schools and Colleges, with national accreditation in dietetics, engineering, nursing, and teacher education. National accreditation is in process for the School of Business and Economics. Seattle Pacific's urban setting is ideal for internship, service-learning, and ministry opportunities. SPU provides students with numerous formal avenues for leadership development. SPU's location on the Pacific Rim provides a gateway to international study and learning experiences. In 1994–95, students may access SPU's new library by computer from dorm rooms as well as the nation through Internet.

Total Enrollment: 3,437

UG Enrollment: 2,400 (64% W)

Application Deadline: 9/1

Entrance: moderately difficult

Tuition & Fees: $12,669

Room & Board: $4875

SAT≥500: 51% V, 56% M   **ACT≥21:** N/R

Denominational Affiliation: Free Methodist

GENERAL INFORMATION Independent-religious comprehensive coed institution. Awards bachelor's, master's, doctorate degrees. Founded 1891. *Setting:* 35-acre urban campus. *Faculty:* 203 (150 full-time, 85% with terminal degrees, 53 part-time); student-undergrad faculty ratio is 12:1. *Library Holdings:* 170,000 books, 380,000 microform titles, 1,500 periodicals, 2 on-line bibliographic services, 3,800 records, tapes, and CDs. *Computers:* 140 terminals, PCs for student use in 5 labs, media center. Student computer-purchase plan available. Access to campuswide network, Internet from student rooms, 5 labs, media center; on-line documentation and general network orientation available. *Services:* e-mail, mainframe access, library catalog search and reservation.

UNDERGRADUATE PROFILE 2,400 students from 38 states and territories, 45 other countries. 64% women, 16% part-time, 60% state residents, 47% live on campus, 40% transferred in, 25% have campus jobs, 5% international, 20% 25 or older, 1% Native American, 2% Hispanic, 2% African American, 4% Asian American. *Retention:* 72% of 1992 freshmen returned. *Graduation:* 24% graduate in 4 years.

FRESHMEN 407 total. 1,183 applied, 86% were accepted, 40% of whom enrolled. 3 National Merit Scholarship Finalists, 3 National Merit Scholars.

ACADEMIC PROGRAM Core, Christian foundations and general education curriculum, honor code. Calendar: quarters. 800 courses offered in 1993–94; average class size 26 in required courses. Academic remediation for entering students, English as a second language program offered during academic year and summer, services for LD students, advanced placement, self-designed majors, honors program, summer session for credit, part-time degree program (daytime, evenings), external degree programs, adult/continuing education programs, co-op programs and internships. Off-campus study at 13 members of the Christian College Consortium. ROTC: Army (c), Naval (c), Air Force (c).

STUDY-ABROAD SITES Costa Rica, Kenya, Korea, Russia, Spain, Taiwan.

MAJORS Accounting, art/fine arts, biblical studies, biology/biological sciences, business administration/commerce/management, chemistry, communication, computer science, dietetics, economics, education, electrical engineering, elementary education, engineering and applied sciences, English, European studies, family and consumer studies, food sciences, history, interdisciplinary studies, liberal arts/general studies, mathematics, middle school education, music, music education, nursing, nutrition, philosophy, physical education, physical fitness/exercise science, physics, political science/government, psychology, reading education, recreation and leisure services, religious education, religious studies, science, secondary education, social science, sociology, special education, textiles and clothing, theater arts/drama, theology.

EXPENSES FOR 1994–95 *Application fee:* $35. Comprehensive fee of $17,544 includes full-time tuition ($12,669) and college room and board ($4875). Part-time tuition per credit ranges from $202 to $353.

FINANCIAL AID *College-administered aid for undergraduates 1993–94:* 1,194 need-based scholarships (average $5363), 1,325 non-need scholarships (average $1818), short-term loans (average $200), low-interest long-term loans from external sources (average $3975), FSEOG, Federal Work-Study, 353 part-time jobs. Average total aid for freshmen: $12,185, meeting 95% of need (aid provided to 100% of those qualified). *Application forms required:* FAFSA; required for some: IRS. *Priority deadline:* 3/1. *Payment plan:* installment. *Waivers:* full or partial for employees or children of employees and senior citizens. *Average indebtedness of graduates:* $15,000.

COLLEGE LIFE Orientation program (3 days, no cost, parents included). Drama-theater group, choral group, student-run newspaper. *Social organizations:* 50 open to all. *Most popular organizations:* Centurions, Falconettes, Forensics, Amnesty International, University Players. *Major annual events:* Homecoming, Spring Picnic, Ivy Cutting. *Student services:* health clinic, personal-psychological counseling. *Safety:* 24-hour emergency response devices and patrols, late-night transport-escort service, closed circuit TV monitors.

ATHLETICS Member NCAA. All Division II. *Intercollegiate:* basketball M(s)/W(s), crew M/W, cross-country running M(s)/W(s), gymnastics W(s), soccer M(s), track and field M(s)/W(s), volleyball W(s). *Intramural:* badminton, basketball, bowling, cross-country running, football, golf, skiing (cross-country), skiing (downhill), soccer, softball, swimming and diving, table tennis (Ping-Pong), tennis, track and field, volleyball, weight lifting, wrestling. *Contact:* Mr. Keith R. Phillips, Director of Athletics, 206-281-2085.

APPLYING/FRESHMEN *Options:* early entrance, early decision, deferred entrance. *Required:* essay, school transcript, minimum 2.5 GPA, some high school foreign language, 1 recommendation, SAT I or ACT, TOEFL for international students. *Recommended:* 3 years of high school math and science, interview. Test scores used for counseling/placement. *Application deadlines:* 9/1, 12/1 for early decision. *Notification:* continuous, 2/15 for early decision.

APPLYING/TRANSFER *Required:* essay, high school transcript, some high school foreign language, 1 recommendation, college transcript, minimum 2.5 GPA. *Recommended:* 3 years of high school math and science, interview. *Required for some:* standardized test scores. *Entrance level:* moderately difficult. *Application deadline:* 9/1. *Notification:* continuous.

CONTACT Office of Admissions, Seattle Pacific University, 3307 Third Avenue West, Seattle, WA 98119; 206-281-2021 or toll-free 800-366-3344.

SIMPSON COLLEGE
Redding, California

Total Enrollment: 670
UG Enrollment: 518 (60% W)
Application Deadline: rolling
Entrance: minimally difficult
Tuition & Fees: $7060
Room & Board: $3690
Denominational Affiliation: The Christian and Missionary Alliance

GENERAL INFORMATION Independent-religious comprehensive coed institution. Awards associate, bachelor's, master's degrees. Founded 1921. *Setting:* 60-acre suburban campus. *Undergraduate faculty:* 29 (20 full-time, 9 part-time); student-undergrad faculty ratio is 18:1. *Library Holdings:* 55,169 books, 31 microform titles, 332 periodicals, 2 on-line bibliographic services, 1,848 records, tapes, and CDs. *Computers:* 14 terminals, PCs for student use in computer center.

UNDERGRADUATE PROFILE 518 students from 13 states and territories, 5 other countries. 60% women, 2% part-time, 87% state residents, 65% transferred in, 2% international, 2% Native American, 2% Hispanic, 1% African American, 8% Asian American. *Retention:* 67% of 1992 freshmen returned.

FRESHMEN 81 total. 199 applied, 75% were accepted, 54% of whom enrolled.

ACADEMIC PROGRAM Core, honor code. Calendar: semesters. 165 courses offered in 1993–94; average class size 20 in required courses. Academic remediation for entering students, English as a second language program offered during academic year, advanced placement, self-designed majors, summer session for credit, part-time degree program (daytime), adult/continuing education programs, internships. Fewer than half of graduate courses open to undergraduate students. Off-campus study at Christian College Coalition.

MAJORS Accounting, biblical studies, business administration/management, education, elementary education, English, history, human resources, liberal arts/general studies, ministries, music, music education, pastoral studies, psychology, religious education, sacred music, secondary education, social science.

EXPENSES FOR 1994–95 *Application fee:* $20. Comprehensive fee of $10,750 includes full-time tuition ($6600), mandatory fees ($460), and college room and board ($3690). Part-time tuition: $330 per credit.

FINANCIAL AID *College-administered aid for undergraduates 1993–94:* 101 need-based scholarships (average $1428), 144 non-need scholarships (average $1182), low-interest long-term loans from college funds (average $1143), loans from external sources (average $2709), FSEOG, Federal Work-Study, 35 part-time jobs. Average total aid for freshmen: $7246, meeting 70% of need (aid provided to 99% of those qualified). *Application forms required:* institutional, FAFSA; required for some: IRS, state. *Priority deadline:* 3/2. *Payment plan:* installment. *Waivers:* full or partial for employees or children of employees. Must reapply each year.

COLLEGE LIFE Orientation program (3 days, no cost, parents included). Drama-theater group, choral group, student-run newspaper. *Social organizations:* 4 open to all, with 25% participating; men's and women's associations; 100% of eligible men and 100% of eligible women are members. *Most popular organizations:* Student Senate (7% participate), Missions Committee (4% participate), Psychology Club (4% participate), Drama Club (10% participate). *Major annual events:* Missions Week, Christmas Banquet, Homecoming. *Student services:* personal-psychological counseling. *Safety:* student patrols, room security.

ATHLETICS *Intercollegiate:* basketball M/W, soccer M, softball W, volleyball M/W. *Intramural:* badminton, basketball, football, golf, soccer, softball, table tennis (Ping-Pong), tennis, volleyball. *Contact:* Mr. Vern Howard, Athletic Director, 916-224-5600 Ext. 2157.

APPLYING/FRESHMEN *Options:* early entrance, deferred entrance. *Required:* school transcript, minimum 2.0 GPA, 2 recommendations, SAT I or ACT, TOEFL for international students. *Recommended:* 3 years of high school English, math, and science; some high school foreign language. Test scores used for admission. *Application deadline:* rolling. *Notification:* continuous.

APPLYING/TRANSFER *Required:* 2 recommendations, college transcript, minimum 2.0 GPA. *Recommended:* 3 years of high school math and science, some high school foreign language, minimum 3.0 GPA. *Required for some:* standardized test scores, high school transcript. *Entrance level:* minimally difficult. *Application deadline:* rolling. *Notification:* continuous.

CONTACT Office of Admissions, Simpson College, 2211 College View Drive, Redding, CA 96003-8606; 916-224-5606 or toll-free 800-598-2493; fax: 916-224-5627.

SIOUX FALLS COLLEGE
Sioux Falls, South Dakota

SPECIAL NOTE FROM THE COLLEGE Sioux Falls College is a 4-year Christian liberal arts college affiliated with the American Baptist Churches. In an environment that both challenges and supports, students are encouraged to develop knowledge and wisdom for discerning truth and meeting human needs, to build a value system in keeping with Christ's teachings, to achieve emotional maturity, to pursue physical fitness, and to gain interpersonal skills. Students develop close, caring relationships with professors in and out of the classroom. Beyond the classroom, there are numerous cocurricular activities important to a college education. Sioux Falls is large enough to provide many opportunities for involvement and small enough to encourage participation.

Total Enrollment: 951

UG Enrollment: 885 (60% W)

Application Deadline: rolling

Entrance: moderately difficult

Tuition & Fees: $8990

Room & Board: $3190

Denominational Affiliation: American Baptist

GENERAL INFORMATION Independent-religious comprehensive coed institution. Awards associate, bachelor's, master's degrees. Founded 1883. *Setting:* 22-acre suburban campus. *Faculty:* 70 (38 full-time, 65% with terminal degrees, 32 part-time); student-undergrad faculty ratio is 16:1. *Library Holdings:* 75,000 books, 450 periodicals, 4,600 records, tapes, and CDs. *Computers:* 42 terminals, PCs for student use in computer center, computer labs, library. Access to campuswide network, Internet from computer center, computer labs, library. *Services:* e-mail, word processing.

UNDERGRADUATE PROFILE 885 students from 19 states and territories, 8 other countries. 60% women, 23% part-time, 72% state residents, 43% live on campus, 8% transferred in, 80% have need-based financial aid, 1% international, 46% 25 or older, 1% Native American, 1% African American, 1% Asian American. *Retention:* 53% of 1992 freshmen returned.

FRESHMEN 178 total. 437 applied, 92% were accepted, 45% of whom enrolled. 11% from top 10% of their high school class, 39% from top quarter, 90% from top half.

ACADEMIC PROGRAM Core. Calendar: 4-1-4. 150 courses offered in 1993–94; average class size 40 in required courses. Academic remediation for entering students, advanced placement, accelerated degree program, self-designed majors, honors program, summer session for credit, part-time degree program (daytime, evenings), adult/continuing education programs, co-op programs and internships. All graduate courses open to undergraduate students. Off-campus study at Colleges of Mid-America, Augustana College (SD), North American Baptist Seminary, Christian College Coalition. Unusual degree programs: 3-2 engineering with South Dakota State University, religious studies with North American Baptist Seminary.

STUDY-ABROAD SITE Japan.

MAJORS Accounting, applied art, applied mathematics, art education, behavioral sciences, biology/biological sciences, business administration/commerce/management, chemistry, child psychology/child development, commercial art, communication, computer information systems, computer science, (pre)dentistry sequence, early childhood education, economics, education, elementary education, (pre)engineering sequence, English, health education, history, humanities, interdisciplinary studies, (pre)law sequence, liberal arts/general studies, management information systems, marketing/retailing/merchandising, mathematics, medical technology, (pre)medicine sequence, middle school education, music, music business, music education, pastoral studies, philosophy, physical education, physical fitness/exercise science, piano/organ, political science/government, psychology, public relations, radio and television studies, radiological technology, religious studies, science education, secondary education, secretarial studies/office management, social science, social work, sociology, speech/rhetoric/public address/debate, theater arts/drama, (pre)veterinary medicine sequence, voice, wind and percussion instruments.

EXPENSES FOR 1994–95 *Application fee:* $20. Comprehensive fee of $12,180 includes full-time tuition ($8990) and college room and board ($3190).

FINANCIAL AID *College-administered aid for undergraduates 1993–94:* 70 need-based scholarships (average $400), 300 non-need scholarships (average $1500), low-interest long-term loans from external sources (average $3925), FSEOG, Federal Work-Study. Average total aid for freshmen: $6884, meeting 90% of need (aid provided to 100% of those qualified). *Application forms required:* FFS, institutional, FAFSA; required for some: IRS, state; accepted: FAF. *Priority deadline:* 4/1. *Payment plan:* installment. *Waivers:* full or partial for employees or children of employees and senior citizens. *Average indebtedness of graduates:* $12,600.

COLLEGE LIFE Orientation program (3 days, no cost, parents included). Drama-theater group, choral group, student-run newspaper, radio station. *Social organizations:* 12 open to all. *Most popular organizations:* Fellowship of Christian Athletes, Campus Ministry Outreach. *Major annual events:* Homecoming, madrigals, Fully Alive. *Student services:* health clinic, personal-psychological counseling, women's center. *Safety:* late-night transport-escort service, controlled dormitory access.

ATHLETICS Member NAIA. *Intercollegiate:* baseball M(c), basketball M(s)/W(s), cross-country running M(s)/W(s), football M(s), tennis M(s)/W(s), track and field M(s)/W(s), volleyball W(s). *Intramural:* basketball, football, racquetball, table tennis (Ping-Pong), tennis, volleyball. *Contact:* Mr. Ken Kortemeyer, Athletic Director, 605-331-6656.

APPLYING/FRESHMEN *Options:* early entrance, deferred entrance, midyear entrance. *Required:* school transcript, ACT, TOEFL for international students. *Recommended:* essay, 3 years of high school math and science, 1 year of high school foreign language, SAT I. *Required for some:* 2 recommendations, interview. Test scores used for admission. *Application deadline:* rolling.

APPLYING/TRANSFER *Required:* high school transcript, college transcript, minimum 2.0 GPA. *Recommended:* essay, standardized test scores, 3 years of high school math and science, 1 year of high school foreign language. *Required for some:* 2 recommendations, interview. *Application deadline:* rolling.

CONTACT Admissions Office, Sioux Falls College, 1501 South Prairie Avenue, Sioux Falls, SD 57105; 605-331-6600 or toll-free 800-888-1047.

SOUTHERN CALIFORNIA COLLEGE
Costa Mesa, California

SPECIAL NOTE FROM THE COLLEGE Southern California College is located 5 miles from the Pacific Ocean in Costa Mesa, California. Founded in 1920 and affiliated with the Assemblies of God, SCC is the largest Christian college in the charismatic tradition west of the Rocky Mountains. SCC offers 29 academic majors and opportunities for off-campus study in archaeology during the summer in Israel or in missions and language at the College's study center in San José, Costa Rica. The campus is ideally located in Orange County, where business and recreational activities provide students with countless jobs, internships, and recreational opportunities.

Total Enrollment: 965
UG Enrollment: 900 (55% W)
Application Deadline: rolling
Entrance: moderately difficult
Tuition & Fees: $9520
Room & Board: $4124
SAT≥500: 25% V, 40% M,   **ACT≥21:** 64%
Denominational Affiliation: Assemblies of God

GENERAL INFORMATION Independent-religious comprehensive coed institution. Awards bachelor's, master's degrees. Founded 1920. *Setting:* 38-acre suburban campus with easy access to Los Angeles. *Undergraduate faculty:* 51 (45 full-time, 67% with terminal degrees, 6 part-time); student-undergrad faculty ratio is 16:1. *Library Holdings:* 115,000 books, 8,300 microform titles, 810 periodicals, 3,600 records, tapes, and CDs. *Computers:* 50 terminals, PCs for student use in computer center, computer labs, library, dorms.

UNDERGRADUATE PROFILE 900 students from 38 states and territories, 14 other countries. 55% women, 13% part-time, 75% state residents, 52% live on campus, 31% transferred in, 2% international, 10% 25 or older, 1% Native American, 12% Hispanic, 3% African American, 6% Asian American. *Retention:* 71% of 1992 freshmen returned.

FRESHMEN 191 total. 502 applied, 88% were accepted, 43% of whom enrolled. 23% from top 10% of their high school class, 53% from top quarter, 78% from top half.

ACADEMIC PROGRAM Core, honor code. Calendar: semesters. 500 courses offered in 1993–94; average class size 16 in required courses. Academic remediation for entering students, advanced placement, accelerated degree program, summer session for credit, part-time degree program (daytime, evenings), adult/continuing education programs, internships. Fewer than half of graduate courses open to undergraduate students. Off-campus study at Christian College Coalition. ROTC: Army (c), Naval (c), Air Force (c).

STUDY-ABROAD SITES Costa Rica, Israel.

MAJORS Accounting, anthropology, biblical studies, biology/biological sciences, broadcasting, business administration/commerce/management, chemistry, communication, education, elementary education, English, finance/banking, history, humanities, journalism, (pre)law sequence, marketing/retailing/merchandising, mathematics, (pre)medicine sequence, ministries, music, music education, pastoral studies, physical education, political science/government, psychology, radio and television studies, religious education, religious studies, science, secondary education, social science, sociology, speech/rhetoric/public address/debate, theater arts/drama, (pre)veterinary medicine sequence.

EXPENSES FOR 1994–95 *Application fee:* $30. Comprehensive fee of $13,644 includes full-time tuition ($9220), mandatory fees ($300), and college room and board ($4124). Part-time tuition: $378 per credit.

FINANCIAL AID *College-administered aid for undergraduates 1993–94:* 412 need-based scholarships (average $1351), 736 non-need scholarships (average $2471), short-term loans (average $200), low-interest long-term loans from external sources (average $3407), FSEOG, Federal Work-Study, 206 part-time jobs. Average total aid for freshmen: $7394, meeting 80% of need (aid provided to 100% of those qualified). *Application forms required:* state, institutional, FAFSA; required for some: IRS. *Priority deadline:* 3/2. *Payment plan:* installment. *Waivers:* full or partial for employees or children of employees. Must reapply each year. *Average indebtedness of graduates:* $10,000.

COLLEGE LIFE Orientation program (4 days, $40). Drama-theater group, choral group, student-run newspaper, Associated Student Body (ASB) government. *Student services:* personal-psychological counseling. *Safety:* 24-hour emergency response devices and patrols, late-night transport-escort service.

ATHLETICS Member NAIA. *Intercollegiate:* baseball M(s), basketball M(s)/W(s), cross-country running M(s)/W(s), soccer M(s)/W(s), softball W(s), tennis M, track and field M(s)/W(s), volleyball W(s). *Intramural:* badminton, basketball, football, golf, racquetball, table tennis (Ping-Pong), tennis, volleyball, weight lifting. *Contact:* Mr. Ron Prettyman, Athletic Director, 714-556-3610 Ext. 279.

APPLYING/FRESHMEN Preference given to Christians. *Option:* deferred entrance. *Required:* essay, school transcript, 1 recommendation, SAT I or ACT, TOEFL for international students. *Recommended:* 3 years of high school math and science. *Required for some:* campus interview. Test scores used for counseling/placement. *Application deadline:* rolling. *Notification:* continuous until 8/31.

APPLYING/TRANSFER *Required:* essay, 1 recommendation, college transcript, minimum 2.0 GPA. *Required for some:* standardized test scores, high school transcript, campus interview. *Entrance level:* moderately difficult. *Application deadline:* rolling. *Notification:* continuous until 8/31.

CONTACT Mr. Rick Hardy, Assistant Dean for Enrollment Management, Southern California College, 55 Fair Drive, Costa Mesa, CA 92626; 714-556-3610 Ext. 223 or toll-free 800-722-6279.

SOUTHERN NAZARENE UNIVERSITY
Bethany, Oklahoma

> **SPECIAL NOTE FROM THE UNIVERSITY** Southern Nazarene University, founded in 1899, is dedicated to preparing responsible Christian persons. Students from 38 states and 24 countries come to SNU to receive excellent professional and academic preparation in the context of a warm, Christian community. SNU offers fully accredited programs in more than 60 major fields of study, with a national reputation for its programs in the sciences, premedicine, physics, fine arts, education, and business. The School of Business has won international business competitions in 2 of the past 3 years. Additional academic offerings include programs in Washington, DC; Cairo, Egypt; Los Angeles, California; San José, Costa Rica; Moscow, Russia; and Oxford, England. Southern Nazarene University helps students prepare for their future and a life of service.

Total Enrollment: 1,731
UG Enrollment: 1,536 (56% W)
Application Deadline: 8/15
Entrance: noncompetitive
Tuition & Fees: $6438
Room & Board: $3716
SAT≥500: N/R   **ACT≥21:** 85%
Denominational Affiliation: Nazarene

GENERAL INFORMATION Independent-religious comprehensive coed institution. Awards associate, bachelor's, master's degrees. Founded 1899. *Setting:* 40-acre suburban campus with easy access to Oklahoma City. *Faculty:* 118 (50 full-time, 68 part-time); student-undergrad faculty ratio is 17:1. *Library Holdings:* 167,145 books, 211,544 microform titles, 626 periodicals, 3,744 records, tapes, and CDs. *Computers:* 75 terminals, PCs for student use in computer center, classrooms, library.

UNDERGRADUATE PROFILE 1,536 students from 38 states and territories, 24 other countries. 56% women, 16% part-time, 63% state residents, 60% live on campus, 8% transferred in, 20% have campus jobs, 2% international, 21% 25 or older, 2% Native American, 3% Hispanic, 4% African American, 2% Asian American. *Retention:* 85% of 1992 freshmen returned.

FRESHMEN 319 total. 538 applied, 100% were accepted, 59% of whom enrolled. 10% from top 10% of their high school class, 30% from top quarter, 60% from top half.

ACADEMIC PROGRAM Core, honor code. Calendar: semesters. Academic remediation for entering students, English as a second language program offered during academic year, advanced placement, accelerated degree program, self-designed majors, summer session for credit, part-time degree program (daytime, evenings), external degree programs, adult/continuing education programs, internships. Off-campus study through Christian College Coalition. ROTC: Army (c).

STUDY-ABROAD SITES Costa Rica, Egypt, England, Russia.

MAJORS Accounting, adult and continuing education, applied mathematics, art education, art/fine arts, aviation administration, behavioral sciences, biblical languages, biblical studies, biology/biological sciences, business administration/commerce/management, business economics, business education, chemistry, child care/child and family studies, child psychology/child development, commercial art, communication, computer information systems, computer programming, computer science, criminal justice, data processing, (pre)dentistry sequence, early childhood education, economics, education, elementary education, engineering (general), English, environmental studies, family and consumer studies, family services, German, gerontology, health education, health science, history, human resources, information science, instrumental music, interior design, international studies, journalism, laboratory technologies, (pre)law sequence, liberal arts/general studies, literature, management information systems, marketing/retailing/merchandising, mathematics, medical laboratory technology, medical technology, (pre)medicine sequence, ministries, modern languages, music, music business, music education, natural sciences, nursing, occupational therapy, pastoral studies, pharmacy/pharmaceutical sciences, philosophy, physical education, physical therapy, physics, piano/organ, political science/government, psychology, reading education, religious education, religious studies, sacred music, science, science education, secondary education, secretarial studies/office management, social science, sociology, Spanish, speech/rhetoric/public address/debate, theater arts/drama, theology, (pre)veterinary medicine sequence, voice, wind and percussion instruments, zoology.

EXPENSES FOR 1994–95 Comprehensive fee of $10,154 includes full-time tuition ($6090), mandatory fees ($348), and college room and board ($3716). College room only: $1876. Part-time tuition: $203 per credit hour.

FINANCIAL AID *College-administered aid for undergraduates 1993–94:* 882 need-based scholarships (average $1250), 1,109 non-need scholarships (average $1824), low-interest long-term loans from college funds (average $1300), loans from external sources (average $3275), FSEOG, Federal Work-Study, part-time jobs. Average total aid for freshmen: $5875, meeting 76% of need (aid provided to 100% of those qualified). *Application forms required:* FFS; required for some: IRS; accepted: FAF, state, FAFSA. *Priority deadline:* 3/1. *Payment plans:* tuition prepayment, installment. *Waivers:* full or partial for employees or children of employees and senior citizens.

COLLEGE LIFE Orientation program (5 days, no cost, parents included). Drama-theater group, choral groups, student-run newspaper. *Most popular organizations:* Business Gaming Team, yearbook, jazz band, international student associations (AMS and AWS), intramural sports societies. *Major annual events:* Youth Extravaganza, Homecoming, Pow-Wow Weekend, Mother/Daughter Weekend. *Student services:* health clinic, personal-psychological counseling. *Safety:* student patrols, late-night transport-escort service, controlled dormitory access.

ATHLETICS Member NAIA. *Intercollegiate:* basketball M(s)/W(s), cross-country running M, soccer M(s)/W(s), softball W(s), tennis M(s)/W(s), track and field M, volleyball W(s). *Intramural:* basketball, football, softball, swimming and diving, table tennis (Ping-Pong), tennis, volleyball, weight lifting. *Contact:* Mr. Bobby Martin, Athletic Director, 405-491-6390.

APPLYING/FRESHMEN Open admission. *Option:* deferred entrance. *Required:* school transcript, SAT I or ACT, TOEFL for international students. *Recommended:* 3 years of high school math and science, 2 years of high school foreign language, recommendations, interview. Test scores used for counseling/placement. *Application deadline:* 8/15. *Notification:* continuous.

APPLYING/TRANSFER *Required:* high school transcript, college transcript. *Recommended:* 3 years of high school math and science, some high school foreign language, recommendations, interview, minimum 2.0 GPA. *Required for some:* standardized test scores. *Entrance level:* minimally difficult. *Application deadline:* 8/15. *Notification:* continuous.

CONTACT Ms. Tollya Stroud, Director of Admissions, Southern Nazarene University, 6729 Northwest 39th Expressway, Bethany, OK 73008; 405-491-6324 or toll-free 800-648-9899.

SPRING ARBOR COLLEGE
Spring Arbor, Michigan

> **SPECIAL NOTE FROM THE COLLEGE** At Spring Arbor College there is a community of learners with 3 essential commitments: the serious study of the liberal arts, Jesus Christ as the community's perspective for learning, and critical participation in the affairs of the contemporary world. Everything that is done at Spring Arbor is based on these ideas, from an interest in fostering lifelong learning and developing thinking skills with many different applications to chapel programming, ministry opportunities, and the recognition of the lordship of Christ over the environment and all of life to the College's cross-cultural study requirement and belief that students need to be informed world citizens with a global perspective.

Total Enrollment: 919 (all UG)

Women: 61%

Application Deadline: rolling

Entrance: moderately difficult

Tuition & Fees: $9556

Room & Board: $3750

SAT≥500: N/R   **ACT≥21:** 51%

Denominational Affiliation: Free Methodist

GENERAL INFORMATION Independent-religious 4-year coed institution. Awards associate, bachelor's degrees. Founded 1873. *Setting:* 70-acre rural campus. *Faculty:* 95 (65 full-time, 42% with terminal degrees, 30 part-time). *Library Holdings:* 84,597 books, 280 microform titles, 1,252 periodicals, 1 on-line bibliographic service, 2 CD-ROMs, 3,918 records, tapes, and CDs. *Computers:* 30 terminals, PCs for student use in computer center, student center, learning center. Access to campuswide network from computer center. *Service:* e-mail.

UNDERGRADUATE PROFILE 919 students from 19 states and territories, 8 other countries. 61% women, 20% part-time, 89% state residents, 51% live on campus, 8% transferred in, 4% international, 0% Native American, 0% Hispanic, 4% African American. *Retention:* 77% of 1992 freshmen returned. *Graduation:* 29% graduate in 4 years.

FRESHMEN 181 total; 164 from public schools. 401 applied, 90% were accepted, 50% of whom enrolled. 15% from top 10% of their high school class, 32% from top quarter, 70% from top half. 5 National Merit Scholarship Finalists, 2 National Merit Scholars, 8 valedictorians.

ACADEMIC PROGRAM Core, Christian liberal arts education curriculum, honor code. Calendar: 4-1-4. Academic remediation for entering students, services for LD students, advanced placement, self-designed majors, honors program, summer session for credit, part-time degree program (daytime, evenings), external degree programs, adult/continuing education programs, internships. Off-campus study at Christian College Consortium.

MAJORS Accounting, art/fine arts, biology/biological sciences, business administration/commerce/management, business economics, chemistry, communication, computer science, early childhood education, elementary education, English, French, history, liberal arts/general studies, mathematics, ministries, music, philosophy, physical education, physics, psychology, religious studies, secondary education, social science, social work, sociology, Spanish, speech/rhetoric/public address/debate.

EXPENSES FOR 1994–95 *Application fee:* $15. Comprehensive fee of $13,306 includes full-time tuition ($9450), mandatory fees ($106), and college room and board ($3750). Part-time mandatory fees: $25 per term. Part-time tuition per credit: $175 for the first 7 credits, $285 for the next 4 credits.

FINANCIAL AID *College-administered aid for undergraduates 1993–94:* need-based scholarships, 1,016 non-need scholarships (average $1050), low-interest long-term loans from external sources (average $3600), FSEOG, Federal Work-Study, 280 part-time jobs. *Application forms required:* FAFSA; required for some: IRS, institutional. *Priority deadline:* 2/15. *Payment plans:* installment, deferred payment. *Waivers:* full or partial for employees or children of employees and senior citizens.

COLLEGE LIFE Orientation program (2 days, no cost, parents included). Choral group, student-run newspaper, radio station. *Most popular organizations:* Action Jackson, Cougarettes, Multicultural Organization. *Major annual events:* Arbor Games, Homecoming, Ormston Porchfest. *Student services:* health clinic, personal-psychological counseling. *Safety:* late-night transport-escort service.

ATHLETICS Member NAIA. *Intercollegiate:* baseball M(s), basketball M(s)/W(s), cross-country running M(s)/W(s), golf M(s), soccer M(s)/W(s), softball W(s), tennis M(s)/W(s), track and field M(s)/W(s), volleyball W(s). *Intramural:* basketball, football, softball, volleyball, water polo. *Contact:* Mr. Henry Burbridge, Director of Athletics, 517-750-1200 Ext. 1503.

APPLYING/FRESHMEN *Options:* early entrance, deferred entrance, midyear entrance. *Required:* school transcript, SAT I or ACT, TOEFL for international students. *Recommended:* essay, 2 years of high school foreign language, interview, guidance counselor's evaluation form. Test scores used for admission. *Application deadline:* rolling. *Notification:* continuous.

APPLYING/TRANSFER *Required:* high school transcript, college transcript, minimum 2.0 GPA, guidance counselor's evaluation form. *Recommended:* essay, interview. *Required for some:* standardized test scores. *Application deadline:* rolling. *Notification:* continuous.

CONTACT Mr. Steve Schippers, Director of Admissions, Spring Arbor College, 106 Main Street, Spring Arbor, MI 49283; 517-750-1200 Ext. 1470 or toll-free 800-968-0011.

STERLING COLLEGE
Sterling, Kansas

Total Enrollment: 519 (all UG)

Women: 47%

Application Deadline: rolling

Entrance: minimally difficult

Tuition & Fees: $8380

Room & Board: $3260

SAT≥500: N/R   **ACT≥21:** 60%

Denominational Affiliation: Presbyterian

GENERAL INFORMATION Independent-religious 4-year coed institution. Awards associate, bachelor's degrees. Founded 1887. *Setting:* 46-acre small-town campus. *Faculty:* 83 (31 full-time, 52% with terminal degrees, 52 part-time); student-undergrad faculty ratio is 14:1. *Library Holdings:* 84,000 books, 1,200 microform titles, 450 periodicals, 1,000 records, tapes, and CDs. *Computers:* 27 terminals, PCs for student use in computer center.

UNDERGRADUATE PROFILE 519 students from 26 states and territories, 5 other countries. 47% women, 9% part-time, 85% state residents, 12% transferred in, 1% international, 15% 25 or older, 1% Native American, 3% Hispanic, 9% African American, 1% Asian American. *Retention:* 64% of 1992 freshmen returned.

FRESHMEN 150 total. 479 applied, 78% were accepted, 34% of whom enrolled. 17% from top 10% of their high school class, 36% from top quarter, 68% from top half.

ACADEMIC PROGRAM Core. Calendar: 4-1-4. Advanced placement, honors program, summer session for credit, part-time degree program (daytime), internships. Off-campus study at 6 members of the Associated Colleges of Central Kansas. Unusual degree programs: 3-2 agronomy with Kansas State University.

MAJORS Accounting, art education, art/fine arts, behavioral sciences, biology/biological sciences, business administration/commerce/management, business education, chemistry, child care/child and family studies, communication, computer science, criminal justice, (pre)dentistry sequence, education, elementary education, English, history, home economics, home economics education, (pre)law sequence, liberal arts/general studies, mathematics, (pre)medicine sequence, music, music business, music education, natural sciences, nutrition, philosophy, physical education, piano/organ, political science/government, psychology, religious education, religious studies, secondary education, sociology, special education, speech/rhetoric/public address/debate, theater arts/drama, (pre)veterinary medicine sequence, voice.

EXPENSES FOR 1994–95 Comprehensive fee of $11,640 includes full-time tuition ($8280), mandatory fees ($100), and college room and board ($3260). Part-time tuition per credit hour: $190 for the first 6 credit hours, $265 for the next 5 credit hours.

FINANCIAL AID *College-administered aid for undergraduates 1993–94:* need-based scholarships, non-need scholarships (average $750), low-interest long-term loans from external sources (average $2000), FSEOG, Federal Work-Study, part-time jobs. Average total aid for freshmen: $8890, meeting 98% of need. *Application forms required:* FFS, IRS, FAFSA; accepted: FAF. *Priority deadline:* 4/21.

COLLEGE LIFE Orientation program (2 days, no cost, parents included). Drama-theater group, student-run newspaper. *Student services:* health clinic, personal-psychological counseling.

ATHLETICS Member NAIA. *Intercollegiate:* baseball M, basketball M(s)/W(s), cross-country running M(s)/W(s), football M(s), soccer M(s)/W(s), softball W, tennis M(s)/W(s), track and field M(s)/W(s), volleyball W(s). *Intramural:* basketball, soccer, table tennis (Ping-Pong), tennis, track and field, volleyball.

APPLYING/FRESHMEN *Options:* early entrance, deferred entrance. *Required:* school transcript, SAT I or ACT, TOEFL for international students. *Recommended:* 3 years of high school math and science, some high school foreign language. Test scores used for admission and counseling/placement. *Application deadline:* rolling. *Notification:* continuous.

APPLYING/TRANSFER *Required:* college transcript, minimum 2.2 GPA. *Entrance level:* minimally difficult. *Application deadline:* rolling. *Notification:* continuous.

CONTACT Mr. Dennis W. Dutton, Director of Admissions, Sterling College, Sterling, KS 67579; 800-346-1017 (toll-free).

Tabor College
Hillsboro, Kansas

SPECIAL NOTE FROM THE COLLEGE Tabor's religious heritage places utmost importance on a voluntary, adult commitment to follow Christ. This includes a life of personal devotion and outer witness, serious corporate biblical study, and service to others, which is the foundation of Tabor's mission statement. The academic program, therefore, is designed to develop servants of Christ for all walks of life. This occurs in a Christian learning community, which emphasizes fellowship and mutual accountability. Themes of stewardship and service infuse the College's majors. The student development program stresses personal growth, self-discipline, acceptance of responsibility, and the development of decision-making skills. Tabor provides global travel/service experiences each Interterm and structured opportunities to serve others for Christ through a variety of local ministries.

Total Enrollment: 434 (all UG)

Women: 44%

Application Deadline: rolling

Entrance: moderately difficult

Tuition & Fees: $8680

Room & Board: $3520

SAT≥500: N/R   **ACT≥21:** 67%

Denominational Affiliation: Mennonite Brethren

GENERAL INFORMATION Independent-religious 4-year coed institution. Awards associate, bachelor's degrees. Founded 1908. *Setting:* 26-acre small-town campus with easy access to Wichita. *Faculty:* 50 (32 full-time, 18 part-time); student-undergrad faculty ratio is 16:1. *Library Holdings:* 70,000 books, 450 periodicals, 2,000 records, tapes, and CDs. *Computers:* 45 terminals, PCs for student use in computer center, administration/business building.

UNDERGRADUATE PROFILE 434 students from 25 states and territories, 7 other countries. 44% women, 8% part-time, 51% state residents, 75% live on campus, 22% transferred in, 3% international, 9% 25 or older, 1% Native American, 3% Hispanic, 4% African American, 1% Asian American. *Retention:* 66% of 1992 freshmen returned.

FRESHMEN 113 total. 19% from top 10% of their high school class, 20% from top quarter, 77% from top half. 3 National Merit Scholarship Finalists, 3 National Merit Scholars.

ACADEMIC PROGRAM Core. Calendar: 4-1-4. Average class size 20 in required courses. Academic remediation for entering students, English as a second language program offered during academic year and summer, advanced placement, self-designed majors, tutorials, summer session for credit, part-time degree program (daytime, evenings), external degree programs, adult/continuing education programs, internships. Off-campus study at Associated Colleges of Central Kansas.

MAJORS Accounting, actuarial science, applied mathematics, biblical studies, biology/biological sciences, business administration/commerce/management, business education, chemistry, computer science, (pre)dentistry sequence, education, elementary education, (pre)engineering sequence, English, environmental biology, health education, history, humanities, international studies, journalism, (pre)law sequence, legal secretarial studies, mathematics, medical secretarial studies, medical technology, (pre)medicine sequence, ministries, music, music education, natural sciences, philosophy, physical education, piano/organ, psychology, religious studies, science, science education, secondary education, secretarial studies/office management, social science, social work, sociology, special education, voice.

EXPENSES FOR 1994–95 *Application fee:* $10. Comprehensive fee of $12,200 includes full-time tuition ($8480), mandatory fees ($200), and college room and board ($3520). Part-time tuition per term ranges from $176 to $3883. Part-time mandatory fees: $200 per year. Part-time mandatory fees per semester (8-11 credit hours): $100.

FINANCIAL AID *College-administered aid for undergraduates 1993–94:* 100 need-based scholarships (average $620), 420 non-need scholarships (average $1730), low-interest long-term loans from external sources (average $2000), FSEOG, Federal Work-Study, 65 part-time jobs. Average total aid for freshmen: $4552, meeting 40% of need (aid provided to 100% of those qualified). *Application forms required:* FAFSA. *Priority deadline:* 3/1. *Payment plan:* installment. *Waivers:* full or partial for employees or children of employees, adult students, and senior citizens.

COLLEGE LIFE Orientation program (2½ days, no cost, parents included). Drama-theater group, choral group, student-run newspaper. *Most popular organizations:* Student Activities Board, Stuco, Campus Ministries Council. *Major annual events:* Homecoming, Missions/Services Emphasis Week, Opening Bible Conference. *Student services:* personal-psychological counseling.

ATHLETICS Member NAIA. *Intercollegiate:* baseball M(s), basketball M(s)/W(s), cross-country running M(s)/W(s), football M(s), soccer M(s), softball W(s), tennis M(s)/W(s), track and field M(s)/W(s), volleyball W(s). *Intramural:* basketball, football, golf, racquetball, soccer, table tennis (Ping-Pong), tennis, track and field, volleyball, weight lifting. *Contact:* Mr. Gary Myers, Athletic Director, 316-947-3121.

APPLYING/FRESHMEN *Required:* essay, school transcript, 2 recommendations, SAT I or ACT, TOEFL for international students. *Recommended:* interview. Test scores used for admission and counseling/placement. *Application deadline:* rolling. *Notification:* continuous.

APPLYING/TRANSFER *Required:* essay, standardized test scores, high school transcript, 2 recommendations, college transcript, minimum 2.0 GPA. *Recommended:* interview, minimum 3.0 GPA. *Application deadline:* rolling. *Notification:* continuous.

CONTACT Mr. Glenn Lygrisse, Director of Enrollment Management, Tabor College, Hillsboro, KS 67063; 316-947-3121.

TAYLOR UNIVERSITY
Upland, Indiana

SPECIAL NOTE FROM THE UNIVERSITY Taylor University seeks Christian scholars who wish to experience thoughtful and rigorous academic studies thoroughly integrated with biblical Christianity. It seeks students who will respond to a supportive campus community that expects responsible decision making in the context of Christian freedom. It seeks students who will endeavor to translate their 4-year experience into lifelong learning and ministering the redemptive love of Jesus Christ to a world in need. Taylor's President, Dr. Jay Kesler, and outstanding Christian faculty invite students to consider the call to become a part of Taylor's exceptional student body and begin their own Taylor Tradition.

Total Enrollment: 1,849 (all UG)
Women: 51%
Application Deadline: rolling
Entrance: very difficult
Tuition & Fees: $11,175
Room & Board: $4000
SAT≥500: 73% V, 72% M   **ACT≥21:** N/R
Denominational Affiliation: interdenominational

GENERAL INFORMATION Independent 4-year coed institution. Awards associate, bachelor's degrees. Founded 1846. *Setting:* 250-acre rural campus with easy access to Indianapolis. *Faculty:* 131 (99 full-time, 61% with terminal degrees, 32 part-time); student-undergrad faculty ratio is 18:1. *Library Holdings:* 165,000 books, 8,200 microform titles, 720 periodicals, 3,829 records, tapes, and CDs. *Computers:* 237 terminals, PCs for student use in computer labs, library, dorms. Student computer-purchase plan available. Access to campuswide network, Internet from computer labs, library, dorms. *Services:* e-mail, mainframe access, library catalog search and reservation, VAX notes, conferencing bulletin boards.

UNDERGRADUATE PROFILE 1,849 students from 49 states and territories, 12 other countries. 51% women, 5% part-time, 33% state residents, 85% live on campus, 11% transferred in, 60% have need-based financial aid, 15% have non-need-based financial aid, 2% international, 1% Hispanic, 2% African American, 2% Asian American. *Retention:* 97% of 1992 freshmen returned.

FRESHMEN 433 total. 1,769 applied, 62% were accepted, 40% of whom enrolled. 48% from top 10% of their high school class, 84% from top quarter, 96% from top half. 37 valedictorians.

ACADEMIC PROGRAM Core, honor code. Calendar: 4-1-4. 701 courses offered in 1993–94; average class size 30 in required courses. Academic remediation for entering students, English as a second language program, advanced placement, accelerated degree program, self-designed majors, tutorials, honors program, summer session for credit, part-time degree program (daytime, summer), adult/continuing education programs, internships. Off-campus study at members of the Christian College Coalition and the Christian College Consortium. Unusual degree programs: 3-2 engineering with Washington University, medical technology.

STUDY-ABROAD SITES Australia, China, Costa Rica, England, France, Israel, New Zealand, Russia, Singapore, Spain.

MAJORS Accounting, art education, art/fine arts, art/graphic arts, artificial intelligence, athletic training, biblical languages, biblical studies, biology/biological sciences, broadcasting, business administration/commerce/management, chemistry, communication, computer information systems, computer programming, computer science, creative writing, criminal justice, (pre)dentistry sequence, early childhood education, economics, education, elementary education, English, environmental biology, environmental sciences, environmental studies, French, history, international business, international economics, international studies, journalism, (pre)law sequence, liberal arts/general studies, literature, management information systems, mathematics, medical laboratory technology, medical technology, (pre)medicine sequence, middle school education, ministries, modern languages, music, music education, natural sciences, philosophy, physical education, physics, political science/government, psychology, public relations, recreation and leisure services, religious education, religious studies, sacred music, science education, secondary education, social science, social work, sociology, Spanish, speech/rhetoric/public address/debate, systems science, theater arts/drama, theology, (pre)veterinary medicine sequence, voice.

EXPENSES FOR 1994–95 *Application fee:* $20. Comprehensive fee of $15,175 includes full-time tuition ($10,965), mandatory fees ($210), and college room and board ($4000). College room only: $1900. Part-time tuition per credit hour ranges from $315 to $395 according to course load.

FINANCIAL AID *College-administered aid for undergraduates 1993–94:* 1,784 need-based scholarships (average $1885), non-need scholarships (average $845), short-term loans, low-interest long-term loans from college funds (average $1350), loans from external sources (average $2770), FSEOG, Federal Work-Study, 75 part-time jobs. Average total aid for freshmen: $8779, meeting 85% of need (aid provided to 99% of those qualified). *Application forms required:* institutional, FAFSA; required for some: IRS. *Application deadline:* continuous to 3/1. *Payment plan:* installment. *Waivers:* full or partial for employees or children of employees. Must reapply each year. *Average indebtedness of graduates:* $6500.

COLLEGE LIFE Orientation program (3 days, parents included). Drama-theater group, choral group, student-run newspaper, radio station. *Social organizations:* 30 open to all. *Most popular organizations:* Student Activities Council, Taylor World Outreach, Taylor Student Organization. *Major annual events:* Homecoming, Taylathon, Spiritual Renewal Week. *Student services:* health clinic, personal-psychological counseling. *Safety:* late-night transport-escort service.

ATHLETICS Member NAIA. *Intercollegiate:* baseball M, basketball M/W, cross-country running M/W, equestrian sports M(c)/W(c), football M, golf M, soccer M/W(c), softball W, tennis M/W, track and field M/W, volleyball M(c)/W. *Intramural:* badminton, basketball, cross-country running, football, golf, racquetball, soccer, softball, table tennis (Ping-Pong), tennis, track and field, volleyball. *Contact:* Dr. Joe Romine, Athletic Director, 317-998-5311.

APPLYING/FRESHMEN Preference given to Evangelical Christians. *Options:* early entrance, deferred entrance, midyear entrance. *Required:* essay, school transcript, 3 years of high school math and science, 2 recommendations, SAT I or ACT, TOEFL for international students. *Recommended:* minimum 3.0 GPA, 2 years of high school foreign language, interview. Test scores used for admission. *Application deadline:* rolling. *Notification:* continuous.

APPLYING/TRANSFER *Required:* essay, high school transcript, recommendations, college transcript, minimum 2.5 GPA. *Recommended:* standardized test scores, 3 years of high school math and science, some high school foreign language, interview. *Application deadline:* rolling. *Notification:* continuous.

CONTACT Mr. Stephen Mortland, Director of Admissions, Taylor University, 500 West Reade Avenue, Upland, IN 46989-1001; 317-998-5134 or toll-free 800-882-3456.

TAYLOR UNIVERSITY, FORT WAYNE CAMPUS

Fort Wayne, Indiana

> **SPECIAL NOTE FROM THE UNIVERSITY** Students describe Taylor Fort Wayne as a place where "someone new is instantly recognized as a visitor" but where "no one remains a stranger for long." Because of its small student body, Taylor Fort Wayne offers students a unique opportunity for impact and significance. On a campus of Taylor Fort Wayne's size, there can be no insignificant individuals. Each student, whether a freshman or a senior, has meaningful opportunities to move into significant leadership roles. Students at Taylor Fort Wayne can truly mold the character of the campus, while at the same time developing their own character.

Total Enrollment: 388 (all UG)

Women: 60%

Application Deadline: rolling

Entrance: moderately difficult

Tuition & Fees: $9000

Room & Board: $3600

Denominational Affiliation: interdenominational

GENERAL INFORMATION Independent-religious 4-year coed institution. Part of Taylor University. Awards associate, bachelor's degrees. Founded 1992. *Setting:* 32-acre suburban campus. *Faculty:* 34 (21 full-time, 62% with terminal degrees, 13 part-time); student-undergrad faculty ratio is 13:1. *Library Holdings:* 61,523 books, 68 microform titles, 378 periodicals, 1 on-line bibliographic service, 5 CD-ROMs, 4,510 records, tapes, and CDs. *Computers:* 33 terminals, PCs for student use in computer labs, learning resource center, library. Student computer-purchase plan available. Access to campuswide network, Internet from computer labs, learning resource center, library, student rooms; on-line documentation available. *Services:* e-mail, file transfer, mainframe access, library catalog search and reservation.

UNDERGRADUATE PROFILE 388 students from 24 states and territories, 4 other countries. 60% women, 26% part-time, 68% state residents, 39% live on campus, 8% transferred in, 85% have need-based financial aid, 16% have non-need-based financial aid, 43% have campus jobs, 1% international, 28% 25 or older, 1% Native American, 1% Hispanic, 5% African American, 1% Asian American. *Retention:* 61% of 1992 freshmen returned.

FRESHMEN 116 total. 528 applied, 95% were accepted, 23% of whom enrolled. 21% from top 10% of their high school class, 45% from top quarter, 82% from top half.

ACADEMIC PROGRAM Core, liberal arts curriculum, honor code. Calendar: 4-1-4. 203 courses offered in 1993–94; average class size 25 in required courses. Academic remediation for entering students, services for LD students, advanced placement, self-designed majors, tutorials, summer session for credit, part-time degree program (daytime, evenings, summer), co-op programs and internships. Off-campus study at Christian College Coalition, Christian College Consortium, Wesleyan Urban Coalition.

STUDY-ABROAD SITES England, Israel.

MAJORS Biblical studies, business administration/commerce/management, criminal justice, early childhood education, elementary education, liberal arts/general studies, ministries, music, pastoral studies, psychology, public relations, religious education.

EXPENSES FOR 1994–95 *Application fee:* $20. Comprehensive fee of $12,600 includes full-time tuition ($8914), mandatory fees ($86), and college room and board ($3600). Part-time tuition per semester hour ranges from $125 to $318.

FINANCIAL AID *College-administered aid for undergraduates 1993–94:* 491 need-based scholarships (average $830), 24 non-need scholarships (average $860), low-interest long-term loans from college funds (average $540), FSEOG, Federal Work-Study, part-time jobs. *Application forms required:* institutional, FAFSA; required for some: IRS. *Priority deadline:* 3/1. *Payment plan:* installment. *Waivers:* full or partial for employees or children of employees and senior citizens. *Notification:* continuous. Must reapply each year.

COLLEGE LIFE Orientation program (2½ days, parents included). Drama-theater group, choral group. *Social organizations:* 10 open to all. *Most popular organizations:* Delta Pi Sigma, Married Student Fellowship. *Major annual events:* Christmas Banquet, Annual Talent Show, Homecoming/Parents' Weekend. *Student services:* health clinic, personal-psychological counseling. *Safety:* late-night transport-escort service, controlled dormitory access, 12-hour night patrols by trained personnel.

ATHLETICS *Intercollegiate:* basketball M/W, soccer M, volleyball W. *Intramural:* basketball, cross-country running, fencing, football, softball, table tennis (Ping-Pong), tennis. *Contact:* Mr. Bud Hamilton, Athletic Director, 219-456-2111 Ext. 2230.

APPLYING/FRESHMEN *Options:* deferred entrance, midyear entrance. *Required:* essay, school transcript, minimum 2.0 GPA, 3 years of high school math and science, 2 recommendations, SAT I or ACT, TOEFL for international students. *Recommended:* minimum 3.0 GPA, some high school foreign language, interview. Test scores used for admission. *Application deadline:* rolling.

APPLYING/TRANSFER *Required:* essay, high school transcript, 3 years of high school math and science, 1 recommendation, college transcript, minimum 2.5 GPA. *Recommended:* interview. *Required for some:* standardized test scores. *Entrance level:* moderately difficult. *Application deadline:* rolling.

CONTACT Mr. D. Nathan Phinney, Director of Admissions, Taylor University, 1025 West Rudisill Boulevard, Fort Wayne, IN 46807-2197; 219-456-2111 or toll-free 800-233-3922; fax: 219-456-2119.

TREVECCA NAZARENE COLLEGE
Nashville, Tennessee

Total Enrollment: 1,357

UG Enrollment: 983 (56% W)

Application Deadline: rolling

Entrance: noncompetitive

Tuition & Fees: $6656

Room & Board: $3345

Denominational Affiliation: Nazarene

GENERAL INFORMATION Independent-religious comprehensive coed institution. Awards associate, bachelor's, master's degrees. Founded 1901. *Setting:* 55-acre urban campus. *Undergraduate faculty:* 123 (61 full-time, 62 part-time); student-undergrad faculty ratio is 16:1. *Library Holdings:* 103,315 books, 191,685 microform titles, 1,069 periodicals, 4,099 records, tapes, and CDs, catalogue file automated, 13 library terminals. *Computers:* 3 computer labs with MACs and IBM compatible PCs; all computers connected to VAX/VMS Cluster; 24-hour student access to campus network from room connections.

UNDERGRADUATE PROFILE 983 students from 33 states and territories, 8 other countries. 56% women, 22% part-time, 62% state residents, 12% transferred in, 2% international, 0% Native American, 2% Hispanic, 8% African American, 1% Asian American. *Retention:* 63% of 1992 freshmen returned. *Graduation:* 25% graduate in 4 years.

FRESHMEN 156 total. 235 applied, 100% were accepted, 66% of whom enrolled.

ACADEMIC PROGRAM Core, honor code. Calendar: semesters. Academic remediation for entering students, advanced placement, accelerated degree program, summer session for credit, part-time degree program (daytime, summer), adult/continuing education programs, internships. Off-campus study at Vanderbilt University, Tennessee State University, Belmont University, David Lipscomb University. ROTC: Army (c), Naval (c), Air Force (c).

MAJORS Accounting, behavioral sciences, biology/biological sciences, broadcasting, business administration/commerce/management, business education, chemistry, child care/child and family studies, communication, computer information systems, computer science, early childhood education, education, elementary education, (pre)engineering sequence, English, health education, history, humanities, human resources, (pre)law sequence, liberal arts/general studies, mathematics, medical assistant technologies, medical secretarial studies, medical technology, (pre)medicine sequence, ministries, music, music business, music education, natural sciences, pastoral studies, philosophy, physical education, physical fitness/exercise science, physical therapy, physician's assistant studies, psychology, radio and television studies, religious education, religious studies, sacred music, science education, secondary education, secretarial studies/office management, social science, social work, special education, speech/rhetoric/public address/debate, theater arts/drama, theology.

EXPENSES FOR 1994–95 Comprehensive fee of $10,381 includes full-time tuition ($6656), mandatory fees ($780), and college room and board ($3345). College room only: $1420. Part-time tuition: $208 per semester hour. Part-time mandatory fees per semester range from $60 to $110.

FINANCIAL AID *College-administered aid for undergraduates 1993–94:* 50 need-based scholarships, 450 non-need scholarships (average $3000), short-term loans, low-interest long-term loans from external sources (average $2000), FSEOG, Federal Work-Study, 221 part-time jobs. *Application forms required:* FAFSA; accepted: FAF. *Priority deadline:* 4/15. *Payment plan:* installment. *Waivers:* full or partial for employees or children of employees and senior citizens.

COLLEGE LIFE Orientation program (3 days, no cost, parents included). Choral group. *Student services:* health clinic, personal-psychological counseling. *Safety:* 24-hour patrols, student patrols, room security.

ATHLETICS Member NAIA. *Intercollegiate:* baseball M(s), basketball M(s), softball W(s), volleyball W(s). *Intramural:* badminton, basketball, bowling, football, gymnastics, racquetball, soccer, softball, swimming and diving, tennis, volleyball, weight lifting, wrestling. *Contact:* Dr. David Altopp, Athletic Director, 615-248-1271.

APPLYING/FRESHMEN Open admission. *Options:* early entrance, deferred entrance. *Required:* school transcript, medical history, ACT, TOEFL for international students. *Required for some:* recommendations. Test scores used for counseling/placement. *Application deadline:* rolling.

APPLYING/TRANSFER *Required:* college transcript, medical history. *Required for some:* recommendations. *Entrance level:* noncompetitive. *Application deadline:* rolling; PA deadline 1/1.

CONTACT Mr. Jan R. Forman, Dean of Enrollment Services, Trevecca Nazarene College, 333 Murfreesboro Road, Nashville, TN 37210; 615-248-1782.

TRINITY CHRISTIAN COLLEGE
Palos Heights, Illinois

SPECIAL NOTE FROM THE COLLEGE Trinity Christian College is located in Palos Heights, a suburb southwest of Chicago. Its proximity to the city offers students access to cultural, educational, and employment opportunities through the College-wide internship program and the Chicago Metropolitan Studies Program. Trinity offers majors in 21 areas of study; in addition, there are 25 minor programs available. The nursing program is fully accredited by the National League for Nursing. Trinity graduates enjoy the benefits of a solid, Christian, liberal arts education. They have an excellent acceptance rate into graduate programs in business, education, science, and medicine as well as great success in career placement.

Total Enrollment: 608 (all UG)

Women: 60%

Application Deadline: 8/15

Entrance: moderately difficult

Tuition & Fees: $10,200

Room & Board: $3990

SAT≥500: N/R   **ACT≥21:** 85%

Denominational Affiliation: interdenominational

GENERAL INFORMATION Independent-religious 4-year coed institution. Awards bachelor's degrees. Founded 1959. *Setting:* 53-acre suburban campus with easy access to Chicago. *Faculty:* 67 (40 full-time, 58% with terminal degrees, 27 part-time); student-undergrad faculty ratio is 12:1. *Library Holdings:* 55,000 books, 30,000 microform titles, 325 periodicals, 10 CD-ROMs, 600 records, tapes, and CDs. *Computers:* 60 terminals, PCs for student use in computer center, library.

UNDERGRADUATE PROFILE 608 students from 19 states and territories, 5 other countries. 60% women, 8% part-time, 62% state residents, 72% live on campus, 23% transferred in, 54% have need-based financial aid, 83% have non-need-based financial aid, 43% have campus jobs, 1% international, 9% 25 or older, 1% Native American, 1% Hispanic, 4% African American, 1% Asian American. *Retention:* 73% of 1992 freshmen returned.

FRESHMEN 166 total; 62 from public schools. 597 applied, 99% were accepted, 28% of whom enrolled. 5% from top 10% of their high school class, 27% from top quarter, 63% from top half. 15 student government officers, 4 yearbook editors, 2 high school newspaper editors.

ACADEMIC PROGRAM Core. Calendar: semesters. Average class size 20 in required courses. Academic remediation for entering students, advanced placement, accelerated degree program, tutorials, part-time degree program (daytime, evenings), adult/continuing education programs, co-op programs and internships. Off-campus study at Chicago State University, Saint Xavier College, Moraine Valley Community College.

STUDY-ABROAD SITES the Netherlands, Spain.

MAJORS Accounting, art/fine arts, biology/biological sciences, business administration/commerce/management, business education, chemistry, communication, computer science, (pre)dentistry sequence, education, elementary education, English, history, mathematics, medical technology, (pre)medicine sequence, music, music education, nursing, painting/drawing, philosophy, physical education, piano/organ, psychology, religious education, religious studies, science education, secondary education, sociology, theology, (pre)veterinary medicine sequence, Western civilization and culture.

EXPENSES FOR 1994–95 *Application fee:* $20. Comprehensive fee of $14,190 includes full-time tuition ($10,200) and college room and board ($3990). College room only: $2050.

FINANCIAL AID *College-administered aid for undergraduates 1993–94:* 210 need-based scholarships (average $1881), 417 non-need scholarships (average $1955), low-interest long-term loans from external sources (average $2895), FSEOG, Federal Work-Study, 247 part-time jobs. *Application forms required:* FAF; required for some: IRS, state; accepted: FFS, FAFSA. *Priority deadline:* 2/15. *Payment plan:* installment. *Waivers:* full or partial for employees or children of employees and senior citizens. *Notification:* 4/1. *Average indebtedness of graduates:* $11,000.

COLLEGE LIFE Orientation program (4 days, no cost, parents included). Drama-theater group, choral group, student-run newspaper. *Most popular organizations:* Student Association, Student Ministries, student-run campus newspaper. *Major annual event:* Homecoming. *Student services:* personal-psychological counseling, shuttle bus. *Safety:* late-night transport-escort service.

ATHLETICS *Intercollegiate:* baseball M(s), basketball M(s)/W(s), golf M(s)/W, soccer M(s), softball W(s), volleyball M/W(s). *Intramural:* badminton, basketball, cross-country running, field hockey, football, racquetball, soccer, table tennis (Ping-Pong), tennis, track and field, volleyball, weight lifting. *Contact:* Mr. Dave Ribbens, Athletic Director, 708-597-3000.

APPLYING/FRESHMEN *Options:* early entrance, deferred entrance, midyear entrance. *Required:* school transcript, minimum 2.2 GPA, ACT, TOEFL for international students. *Recommended:* 3 years of high school math and science, some high school foreign language. *Required for some:* essay, recommendations, interview. Test scores used for admission. *Application deadline:* 8/15. *Notification:* continuous until 8/15.

APPLYING/TRANSFER *Required:* college transcript, minimum 2.2 GPA. *Recommended:* standardized test scores, 3 years of high school math and science, some high school foreign language. *Required for some:* essay, high school transcript, recommendations, interview. *Entrance level:* moderately difficult. *Application deadline:* 8/15.

CONTACT Mr. David Lageveen, Director of Admissions, Trinity Christian College, 6601 West College Drive, Palos Heights, IL 60463; 708-597-3000 Ext. 307 or toll-free 800-748-0085.

TRINITY COLLEGE
Deerfield, Illinois

> **SPECIAL NOTE FROM THE COLLEGE** Trinity College, committed to a Christian liberal arts education, is located on Chicago's North Shore. Students are trained to make their profession of choice their mission field. They are challenged to honestly examine their faith and to discover personal answers to the "whys" and "hows" of believing and how their commitment to Christ relates to their academics, lifestyle, and professional goals. Students acquire book knowledge but also have opportunities to gain practical experience. Activities and internship programs provide chances for students to develop leadership, organizational, and communication skills, as well as gain valuable experience in their major. Trinity students discover challenging academics, an enlightening spiritual life, and lots of fun. They enjoy Chicago, a city with continuous energy, and, most important, build lifelong friendships with Christians from all over the country.

Total Enrollment: 872 (all UG)
Women: 49%
Application Deadline: rolling
Entrance: moderately difficult
Tuition & Fees: $10,420
Room & Board: $4300
SAT≥500: N/R   **ACT≥21:** 67%
Denominational Affiliation: Evangelical Free Church of America

GENERAL INFORMATION Independent-religious 4-year coed institution. Awards bachelor's degrees. Founded 1897. *Setting:* 120-acre suburban campus with easy access to Chicago. *Faculty:* 70 (41 full-time, 29 part-time); student-undergrad faculty ratio is 16:1. *Library Holdings:* 115,000 books, 32,000 microform titles, 508 periodicals, 929 records, tapes, and CDs. *Computers:* 25 terminals, PCs for student use in computer center, library.

UNDERGRADUATE PROFILE 872 students from 28 states and territories, 3 other countries. 49% women, 14% part-time, 48% state residents, 85% live on campus, 32% transferred in, 3% international, 13% 25 or older, 1% Native American, 3% Hispanic, 14% African American, 5% Asian American. *Retention:* 78% of 1992 freshmen returned.

FRESHMEN 213 total. Of the students who applied, 78% were accepted. 17% from top 10% of their high school class, 39% from top quarter, 70% from top half. 1 National Merit Scholarship Finalist.

ACADEMIC PROGRAM Core. Calendar: semesters. Academic remediation for entering students, advanced placement, self-designed majors, honors program, summer session for credit, part-time degree program (daytime), adult/continuing education programs, co-op programs and internships. Off-campus study at 13 members of the Christian College Consortium.

MAJORS Biblical studies, biology, biology/(pre)medicine, biology/secondary education, business management and economics (accounting, human resources, management, marketing), chemistry, chemistry/(pre)medicine, computer information systems, elementary education, English, English/communications, English/secondary education, general studies, history, history/secondary education, humanities, mathematics, mathematics/secondary education, music (advanced theory, music pedagogy, performance), church music, music/K-12, philosophy, physical education/K-12, psychology, social science, sociology, sport and wellness management, sports medicine/athletic training, youth ministry.

EXPENSES FOR 1994–95 *Application fee:* $20. Comprehensive fee of $14,720 includes full-time tuition ($10,270), mandatory fees ($150), and college room and board ($4300). College room only: $2190. Part-time tuition: $425 per hour.

FINANCIAL AID *College-administered aid for undergraduates 1993–94:* need-based scholarships (average $300), non-need scholarships (average $750), low-interest long-term loans from college funds (average $900), loans from external sources (average $2000), FSEOG, Federal Work-Study, part-time jobs. *Application forms required:* FAF, FAFSA; accepted: FFS. *Priority deadline:* 4/1.

COLLEGE LIFE Orientation program (4 days, no cost). Music groups, drama group,student-run newspaper. *Most popular organizations:* Student Senate, College Union, Trinity Summer Mission. *Major annual events:* Homecoming, Santa Lucia. *Student services:* personal-psychological counseling.

ATHLETICS Member NAIA. *Intercollegiate:* basketball M(s)/W(s), cross-country running M/W, football M(s), golf M(s), soccer M(s)/W, tennis M(s)/W(s), track and field M/W, volleyball M/W(s), wrestling M. *Intramural:* basketball, football, soccer, swimming, tennis, volleyball. *Contact:* Mr. Dave Seils, Athletic Director, 708-317-7095.

APPLYING/FRESHMEN *Required:* essay, school transcript, 1 recommendation, SAT I or ACT, TOEFL for international students. *Recommended:* 3 years of high school math and science. Test scores used for admission. *Application deadline:* rolling.

APPLYING/TRANSFER *Required:* essay, high school transcript, 1 recommendation, college transcript, minimum 2.0 GPA. *Recommended:* 3 years of high school math and science. *Entrance level:* moderately difficult. *Application deadline:* rolling.

CONTACT Mr. Gary Larson, Director of Admissions, Trinity College, 2077 Half Day Road, Deerfield, IL 60015; 708-317-7000 or toll-free 800-4-TCD-NOW.

TRINITY WESTERN UNIVERSITY
Langley, British Columbia, Canada

SPECIAL NOTE FROM THE UNIVERSITY Trinity Western is set on a wooded 100-acre campus. Its students enjoy the solitude of a rural environment and have easy access to the beautiful urban center of Vancouver, just 20 miles away. Trinity is committed to the development of godly Christian leaders—men and women who will take their education and skills into the marketplace and work for the cause of Christ. The whole-student approach to education provides an environment that challenges students to develop intellectually, socially, physically, and spiritually.

Total Enrollment: 2,005
UG Enrollment: 1,858 (54% W)
Application Deadline: rolling
Entrance: moderately difficult
Tuition & Fees: $7024 (Can.)
Room & Board: $4484 (Can.)
Denominational Affiliation: Evangelical Free Church of America

GENERAL INFORMATION Independent-religious comprehensive coed institution. Awards bachelor's, master's degrees. Founded 1962. *Setting:* 100-acre small-town campus with easy access to Vancouver. *Faculty:* 109 (61 full-time, 80% with terminal degrees, 48 part-time); student-undergrad faculty ratio is 18:1. *Library Holdings:* 91,924 books, 175,273 microform titles, 654 periodicals, 2,140 records, tapes, and CDs. *Computers:* 36 terminals, PCs for student use in computer center, library.

UNDERGRADUATE PROFILE 1,858 students from 10 provinces and territories, 30 other countries. 54% women, 32% part-time, 68% province residents, 37% live on campus, 10% transferred in, 8% international, 18% 25 or older, 1% Native American, 1% black. *Retention:* 65% of 1992 freshmen returned.

FRESHMEN 578 total. 1,167 applied, 70% were accepted, 70% of whom enrolled.

ACADEMIC PROGRAM Core, honor code. Calendar: semesters. Academic remediation for entering students, English as a second language program offered during academic year, advanced placement, tutorials, honors program, summer session for credit, part-time degree program (daytime, evenings, summer), adult/continuing education programs, co-op programs and internships. Off-campus study at Simon Fraser University in education.

STUDY-ABROAD SITES Costa Rica, England.

MAJORS Applied mathematics, art/fine arts, biblical studies, biology/biological sciences, business administration/commerce/management, chemistry, communication, computer science, (pre)dentistry sequence, education, elementary education, English, geography, history, humanities, human services, (pre)law sequence, liberal arts/general studies, linguistics, mathematics, (pre)medicine sequence, music, natural sciences, nursing, philosophy, physical education, psychology, religious studies, science, secondary education, social science, theater arts/drama, (pre)veterinary medicine sequence.

EXPENSES FOR 1994–95 *Application fee:* $35. Comprehensive fee of $11,508 includes full-time tuition ($6730), mandatory fees ($294), and college room and board ($4484). Part-time tuition: $229 per semester hour. (All figures are in Canadian dollars.)

FINANCIAL AID *College-administered aid for undergraduates 1993–94:* 431 need-based scholarships (average $906), 209 non-need scholarships (average $723), low-interest long-term loans from external sources (average $5224), 337 part-time jobs. *Application forms required:* institutional; required for some: FAF, government; accepted: FFS, IRS, FAFSA. *Priority deadline:* 4/1. *Payment plan:* installment. *Waivers:* full or partial for employees or children of employees and senior citizens. Must reapply each year.

COLLEGE LIFE Orientation program (4 days, no cost, parents included). Drama-theater group, choral group, student-run newspaper. *Social organizations:* social clubs. *Student services:* health clinic, personal-psychological counseling. *Safety:* 24-hour emergency response devices and patrols, student patrols, late-night transport-escort service.

ATHLETICS *Intercollegiate:* basketball M/W, rugby M, soccer M, volleyball M/W. *Intramural:* badminton, basketball, football, ice hockey, racquetball, soccer, table tennis (Ping-Pong), tennis, volleyball. *Contact:* Mr. Murray Hall, Director of Athletics, 604-888-7511 Ext. 2701.

APPLYING/FRESHMEN *Options:* early entrance, deferred entrance. *Required:* essay, school transcript, minimum 2.0 GPA, 2 recommendations, TOEFL for international students. *Recommended:* 3 years of high school math and science, some high school foreign language. *Required for some:* interview, SAT I or ACT. Test scores used for admission. *Application deadline:* rolling. *Notification:* continuous.

APPLYING/TRANSFER *Required:* essay, high school transcript, 2 recommendations, college transcript. *Recommended:* 3 years of high school math and science, some high school foreign language, minimum 2.0 GPA. *Required for some:* standardized test scores, interview. *Entrance level:* moderately difficult. *Application deadline:* rolling. *Notification:* continuous.

CONTACT Mr. Kirk Kauffeldt, Director of Admissions, Trinity Western University, 7600 Glover Road, Langley, BC V3A 6H4, Canada; 604-888-7008.

UNION UNIVERSITY
Jackson, Tennessee

SPECIAL NOTE FROM THE UNIVERSITY Union University distinctively blends faith and learning in a caring, supportive environment. Faculty members challenge students to critically evaluate the world around them and to study many academic disciplines. Graduates are encouraged to apply Christian principles to all aspects of life. The entire campus community is committed to serving God. Since 1990, students have raised $250,000 for mission projects including Backyard Bible Clubs, summer missionaries, and Habitat for Humanity houses. Students, faculty members, and alumni volunteer annually for a medical mission to Central America. Union is an excellent choice for students desiring to share Christ on campus, in their community, and throughout the world.

Total Enrollment: 2,005
UG Enrollment: 1,914 (65% W)
Application Deadline: rolling
Entrance: moderately difficult
Tuition & Fees: $5780
Room & Board: $2530
SAT≥500: N/R   **ACT≥21:** 72%
Denominational Affiliation: Southern Baptist

GENERAL INFORMATION Independent-religious comprehensive coed institution. Awards associate, bachelor's, master's degrees. Founded 1823. *Setting:* 230-acre small-town campus with easy access to Memphis. *Faculty:* 166 (123 full-time, 42% with terminal degrees, 43 part-time); student-undergrad faculty ratio is 12:1. *Library Holdings:* 177,642 books, 273,921 microform titles, 1,200 periodicals, 21,040 records, tapes, and CDs. *Computers:* 120 terminals, PCs for student use in computer center, computer labs, classrooms, library. Student computer-purchase plan available. Access to campuswide network, BITNET, Internet from computer center, computer labs, classrooms, library, student rooms. *Services:* e-mail, database computer-search services, library catalog search and reservation.

UNDERGRADUATE PROFILE 1,914 students from 32 states and territories, 9 other countries. 65% women, 19% part-time, 78% state residents, 50% live on campus, 14% transferred in, 1% international, 0% Native American, 0% Hispanic, 6% African American, 0% Asian American. *Retention:* 85% of 1993 freshmen returned.

FRESHMEN 406 total. 846 applied, 89% were accepted, 54% of whom enrolled.

ACADEMIC PROGRAM Core, honor code. Calendar: 4-1-4. Advanced placement, accelerated degree program, self-designed majors, honors program, summer session for credit, part-time degree program (daytime, evenings), adult/continuing education programs, internships. A few graduate courses open to undergraduate students. Off-campus study at Lambuth University, Freed-Hardeman University. Unusual degree programs: 3-2 engineering with Tennessee Technological University, University of Memphis, University of Tennessee, Knoxville, medical technology with University of Tennessee, Memphis.

MAJORS Accounting, art education, art/fine arts, biology/biological sciences, business administration/commerce/management, business economics, business education, chemistry, communication, computer information systems, computer science, data processing, dental services, (pre)dentistry sequence, early childhood educa-tion, economics, education, elementary education, English, finance/banking, French, Greek, health education, history, interdisciplinary studies, journalism, (pre)law sequence, marine biology, marketing/retailing/merchandising, mathematics, (pre)medicine sequence, music, music education, nursing, philosophy, physical education, psychology, radio and television studies, religious studies, sacred music, science, science education, secondary education, social work, sociology, Spanish, telecommunications, theology, (pre)veterinary medicine sequence, voice.

EXPENSES FOR 1994–95 *Application fee:* $10. Comprehensive fee of $8310 includes full-time tuition ($5780) and college room and board ($2530). Part-time tuition: $240 per semester hour.

FINANCIAL AID *College-administered aid for undergraduates 1993–94:* 510 need-based scholarships, non-need scholarships, short-term loans (average $300), low-interest long-term loans from college funds (average $1000), loans from external sources (average $1400), FSEOG, 200 part-time jobs. Average total aid for freshmen: $3302, meeting 80% of need (aid provided to 92% of those qualified). *Application forms required:* FAFSA, IRS, institutional. *Priority deadline:* 5/15. *Payment plans:* installment, deferred payment. *Waivers:* full or partial for employees or children of employees.

COLLEGE LIFE Orientation program (4 days, $50). Drama-theater group, choral group, student-run newspaper, radio station. *Social organizations:* 3 national fraternities, 3 national sororities; 26% of eligible men and 27% of eligible women are members. *Most popular organizations:* Baptist Student Union, Fellowship of Christian Athletes, Student Activities Council. *Major annual events:* Campus Day, Miss Union Pageant, Homecoming. *Student services:* health clinic, personal-psychological counseling. *Safety:* 24-hour patrols, room security.

ATHLETICS Member NAIA. *Intercollegiate:* baseball M(s), basketball M(s)/W(s), golf M(s), softball W, tennis M(s)/W(s). *Intramural:* baseball, basketball, bowling, cross-country running, football, golf, racquetball, soccer, softball, swimming and diving, table tennis (Ping-Pong), tennis, track and field, volleyball. *Contact:* Dr. David Blackstock, Director of Athletics, 901-668-1818.

APPLYING/FRESHMEN *Option:* early entrance. *Required:* school transcript, minimum 2.0 GPA, SAT I or ACT, TOEFL for international students. *Required for some:* essay, 3 years of high school math and science, some high school foreign language, recommendations, interview. Test scores used for admission. *Application deadline:* rolling.

APPLYING/TRANSFER *Required:* college transcript, minimum 2.0 GPA, good standing at previous institution. *Required for some:* standardized test scores, high school transcript, 3 years of high school math, recommendations, interview. *Entrance level:* minimally difficult. *Application deadline:* rolling.

CONTACT Mr. Carroll Griffin, Director of Admissions, Union University, 2447 Highway 45 Bypass, Jackson, TN 38305; 901-661-5000.

WARNER PACIFIC COLLEGE
Portland, Oregon

SPECIAL NOTE FROM THE COLLEGE Warner Pacific College is shaped by an assumption that there must be a strong and reinforcing relationship among faith, learning, and life. Faculty members are selected for their ability to teach; for evidence of thoughtful personal, spiritual, and professional growth; and for being experts in their subject areas. There is a conviction that students are expected to develop servant leadership and a global perspective by staffing and managing the Bethlehem Inn, an overnight shelter for homeless families, and through international experiences such as the mission service program in Mexico. Well-trained residence and counseling staffs help students resolve normal difficulties. All students benefit from the Academic Support Center. Warner Pacific is located 15 minutes from downtown Portland, Oregon, and is less than 2 hours by car from Mt. Hood ski slopes and Pacific Ocean beaches.

Total Enrollment: 651
UG Enrollment: 640 (61% W)
Application Deadline: rolling
Entrance: moderately difficult
Tuition & Fees: $8142
Room & Board: $4032
SAT≥500: 14% V, 43% M   **ACT≥21:** 50%
Denominational Affiliation: Church of God

GENERAL INFORMATION Independent-religious comprehensive coed institution. Awards associate, bachelor's, master's degrees. Founded 1937. *Setting:* 15-acre urban campus. *Faculty:* 57 (33 full-time, 39% with terminal degrees, 24 part-time); student-undergrad faculty ratio is 15:1. *Library Holdings:* 42,210 books, 1,155 microform titles, 233 periodicals, 1,100 records, tapes, and CDs. *Computers:* 8 terminals, PCs for student use in computer center, library.

UNDERGRADUATE PROFILE 640 students from 18 states and territories, 12 other countries. 61% women, 19% part-time, 74% state residents, 67% transferred in, 56% have need-based financial aid, 15% have non-need-based financial aid, 24% have campus jobs, 7% international, 40% 25 or older, 1% Native American, 1% Hispanic, 3% African American, 3% Asian American. *Retention:* 84% of 1992 freshmen returned. *Graduation:* 17% graduate in 4 years.

FRESHMEN 53 total. 112 applied, 78% were accepted, 61% of whom enrolled.

ACADEMIC PROGRAM Core. Calendar: semesters. 361 courses offered in 1993–94. Academic remediation for entering students, English as a second language program offered during academic year and summer, services for LD students, advanced placement, self-designed majors, honors program, summer session for credit, part-time degree program (daytime, evenings, summer), external degree programs, adult/continuing education programs, co-op programs and internships. Off-campus study at Mt. Hood Community College, Concordia College (OR), Oregon Independent Colleges Association. ROTC: Army (c), Air Force (c).

STUDY-ABROAD SITES Guatemala, Honduras, Russia.

MAJORS American studies, biblical studies, biology/biological sciences, business administration/commerce/management, educa-tion, elementary education, English, health science, history, human development, liberal arts/general studies, mathematics, ministries, music, music education, pastoral studies, physical education, psychology, religious education, religious studies, science, science education, secondary education, social science, social work, sociology, theology.

ESTIMATED EXPENSES FOR 1994–95 *Application fee:* $50. Comprehensive fee of $12,174 includes full-time tuition ($7940), mandatory fees ($202), and college room and board ($4032 minimum). Part-time tuition per semester hour: $75 for the first 5 semester hours, $306 for the next 6 semester hours.

FINANCIAL AID *College-administered aid for undergraduates 1993–94:* 178 need-based scholarships (average $920), 240 non-need scholarships (average $1291), low-interest long-term loans from college funds (average $2428), loans from external sources (average $2748), FSEOG, Federal Work-Study, 32 part-time jobs. *Forms required for some financial aid applicants:* IRS; accepted: FFS, FAF, FAFSA, SINGLEFILE Form of United Student Aid Funds. *Priority deadline:* 5/1. *Payment plan:* installment. *Waivers:* full or partial for children of alumni and employees or children of employees.

COLLEGE LIFE Orientation program (5 days, no cost, parents included). Drama-theater group, choral group, student-run newspaper. *Major annual events:* Homecoming, Spring Banquet, Knight Fest. *Student services:* legal services, health clinic, personal-psychological counseling. *Safety:* late-night transport-escort service.

ATHLETICS *Intramural:* badminton, basketball, bowling, cross-country running, field hockey, football, golf, racquetball, skiing (cross-country), skiing (downhill), soccer, softball, table tennis (Ping-Pong), tennis, track and field, volleyball, weight lifting.

APPLYING/FRESHMEN *Options:* early entrance, early action, deferred entrance. *Required:* school transcript, 2 recommendations, SAT I or ACT, TOEFL for international students. *Required for some:* interview. Test scores used for admission and counseling/placement. *Application deadlines:* rolling, 12/15 for early action. *Notification:* continuous, 1/30 for early action.

APPLYING/TRANSFER *Required:* standardized test scores, 2 recommendations, college transcript, minimum 2.0 GPA. *Required for some:* high school transcript, interview. *Application deadline:* rolling. *Notification:* continuous.

CONTACT Mr. Bill Stenberg, Dean of Admissions, Warner Pacific College, 2219 Southeast 68th Avenue, Portland, OR 97215; 503-775-4366 Ext. 510.

WARNER SOUTHERN COLLEGE
Lake Wales, Florida

SPECIAL NOTE FROM THE COLLEGE Warner Southern College is located in beautiful central Florida, just a few miles south of Walt Disney World, on Lake Caloosa. Warner Southern offers a rich atmosphere of concern for each student and is committed to serving students in every area of their lives. It is an accredited 4-year Christian college in the liberal arts tradition, offering a broad scope of majors in which students are able to excel. Students develop a close bond with their professors because of the low student-faculty ratio and with fellow students because of the friendly atmosphere. Students often remark that they enjoy the size of the classes and the spiritual atmosphere that exists on the campus.

Total Enrollment: 518 (all UG)
Women: 56%
Application Deadline: rolling
Entrance: minimally difficult
Tuition & Fees: $6750
Room & Board: $3270
SAT≥500: 13% V, 29% M **ACT≥21:** 16%
Denominational Affiliation: Church of God

GENERAL INFORMATION Independent-religious 4-year coed institution. Awards associate, bachelor's degrees. Founded 1968. *Setting:* 350-acre rural campus with easy access to Tampa and Orlando. *Faculty:* 50 (26 full-time, 24 part-time); student-undergrad faculty ratio is 11:1. *Library Holdings:* 66,000 books, 6,200 microform titles, 5,500 periodicals, 3,320 records, tapes, and CDs. *Computers:* 21 terminals, PCs for student use in computer center, library.

UNDERGRADUATE PROFILE 518 students from 32 states and territories, 6 other countries. 56% women, 8% part-time, 76% state residents, 49% transferred in, 3% international, 54% 25 or older, 0% Native American, 1% Hispanic, 8% African American, 1% Asian American. *Retention:* 40% of 1992 freshmen returned.

FRESHMEN 72 total. 249 applied, 77% were accepted, 38% of whom enrolled. 12% from top 10% of their high school class, 41% from top quarter, 86% from top half.

ACADEMIC PROGRAM Core. Calendar: semesters. Academic remediation for entering students, English as a second language program offered during academic year, advanced placement, accelerated degree program, tutorials, summer session for credit, part-time degree program (daytime, evenings), adult/continuing education programs, internships. ROTC: Army (c).

MAJORS Accounting, adult and continuing education, biblical studies, biology/biological sciences, business administration/commerce/management, communication, elementary education, English, liberal arts/general studies, ministries, music, music education, pastoral studies, physical education, psychology, religious studies, science education, secondary education, theology.

EXPENSES FOR 1993–94 *Application fee:* $20. Comprehensive fee of $10,020 includes full-time tuition ($6100), mandatory fees ($650), and college room and board ($3270 minimum). College room only: $1500 (minimum). Part-time tuition per credit hour ranges from $120 to $175. Part-time mandatory fees per credit hour range from $45 to $65.

FINANCIAL AID *College-administered aid for undergraduates 1993–94:* 50 need-based scholarships (average $725), 124 non-need scholarships (average $613), low-interest long-term loans from external sources (average $2800), FSEOG, Federal Work-Study, 58 part-time jobs. Average total aid for freshmen: $10,116, meeting 99% of need. *Forms required for some financial aid applicants:* FFS, IRS, FAFSA; accepted: FAF. *Priority deadline:* 4/1. *Payment plan:* installment. *Waivers:* full or partial for employees or children of employees.

COLLEGE LIFE Orientation program (2 days, parents included). Drama-theater group, choral group, student-run newspaper, radio station. *Social organizations:* 4 open to all. *Most popular organizations:* Drama Club, Young Americans, Concert Choir, Fellowship of Christian Athletes. *Student services:* health clinic, personal-psychological counseling, shuttle bus. *Safety:* 24-hour emergency response devices and patrols, late-night transport-escort service, controlled dormitory access.

ATHLETICS Member NAIA. *Intercollegiate:* baseball M(s), basketball M(s)/W(s), cross-country running M(s)/W(s), volleyball W(s). *Intramural:* basketball, football, racquetball, table tennis (Ping-Pong), tennis, volleyball. *Contact:* Mr. Rick Chesterman, Athletic Director, 813-638-1426 Ext. 257.

APPLYING/FRESHMEN Preference given to Christians. *Options:* early entrance, early decision, deferred entrance, midyear entrance. *Required:* essay, school transcript, minimum 2.0 GPA, 1 recommendation, SAT I or ACT, TOEFL for international students. *Required for some:* interview. Test scores used for admission and counseling/placement. *Application deadlines:* rolling, 10/15 for early decision. *Notification:* continuous, 12/1 for early decision.

APPLYING/TRANSFER *Required:* essay, standardized test scores, 1 recommendation, college transcript, minimum 2.0 GPA. *Required for some:* interview. *Entrance level:* minimally difficult. *Application deadline:* rolling. *Notification:* continuous.

CONTACT Mrs. Valerie Rutland, Director of Admissions, Warner Southern College, U.S. Highway 27 South, Lake Wales, FL 33853; 813-638-1426 Ext. 208 or toll-free 800-949-7248.

WESTERN BAPTIST COLLEGE
Salem, Oregon

> **SPECIAL NOTE FROM THE COLLEGE** A Christian college with a difference! As soon as students step onto the beautiful 100-acre campus in Salem, Oregon, they discover the family atmosphere and caring community of professing Christians that make Western Baptist College so special. They also discover a high-quality Bible-centered education coupled with a strong liberal arts program. Each freshman joins a core group of students from the same geographical area and together bond into a "new student experience." This initial experience is enhanced by Western Baptist's fellowship system—permanent groups designed to involve all students both spiritually and socially. Yes, Western is a college with a difference. (A new residence hall with a student activity area will be completed in December of 1994.)

Total Enrollment: 536 (all UG)

Women: 55%

Application Deadline: rolling

Entrance: minimally difficult

Tuition & Fees: $9400

Room & Board: $4000

SAT≥500: 22% V, 38% M   **ACT≥21:** N/R

Denominational Affiliation: Baptist

GENERAL INFORMATION Independent-religious 4-year coed institution. Awards associate, bachelor's degrees. Founded 1935. *Setting:* 100-acre urban campus with easy access to Portland. *Faculty:* 45 (22 full-time, 23% with terminal degrees, 23 part-time); student-undergrad faculty ratio is 19:1. *Library Holdings:* 63,014 books, 1,347 microform titles, 385 periodicals, 2,818 records, tapes, and CDs. *Computers:* 9 terminals, PCs for student use in computer center.

UNDERGRADUATE PROFILE 536 students from 25 states and territories, 5 other countries. 55% women, 4% part-time, 58% state residents, 51% live on campus, 17% transferred in, 1% international, 22% 25 or older, 2% Native American, 2% Hispanic, 1% African American, 2% Asian American. *Retention:* 83% of 1992 freshmen returned. *Graduation:* 34% graduate in 4 years.

FRESHMEN 118 total. 259 applied, 85% were accepted, 54% of whom enrolled.

ACADEMIC PROGRAM Core, interdisciplinary curriculum. Calendar: semesters. Average class size 50 in required courses. Advanced placement, honors program, summer session for credit, adult/continuing education programs, internships. ROTC: Army (c), Air Force (c).

MAJORS Accounting, biblical studies, business, community services, elementary education, English, family studies, finance, humani-ties, interdisciplinary studies, (pre)law sequence, liberal arts/general studies, management and communications, mathematics, ministries, music, music education, pastoral studies, physical education, psychology, recreation and leisure services, secondary education, social science, theology.

EXPENSES FOR 1994–95 *Application fee:* $25. Comprehensive fee of $13,400 includes full-time tuition ($9200), mandatory fees ($200), and college room and board ($4000). Part-time tuition: $383 per credit hour.

FINANCIAL AID *College-administered aid for undergraduates 1993–94:* 286 need-based scholarships (average $889), 658 non-need scholarships (average $1191), loans from external sources (average $3349), FSEOG, Federal Work-Study, 150 part-time jobs. Average total aid for freshmen: $4940, meeting 35% of need (aid provided to 100% of those qualified). *Forms required for some financial aid applicants:* IRS, FAFSA. *Priority deadline:* 2/15. *Payment plan:* installment. *Waivers:* full or partial for employees or children of employees. *Notification:* 4/1. *Average indebtedness of graduates:* $11,000.

COLLEGE LIFE Orientation program (5 days, no cost, parents included). Drama-theater group, choral group. *Major annual events:* Homecoming, Christmas Alive, College Daze. *Student services:* health clinic. *Safety:* 24-hour emergency response devices, student patrols, late-night transport-escort service, room security.

ATHLETICS Member NAIA. *Intercollegiate:* baseball M, basketball M(s)/W(s), soccer M(s)/W, volleyball W(s). *Intramural:* basketball, football, soccer, volleyball. *Contact:* Mr. Timothy Hills, Athletic Director, 503-581-8600 Ext. 7021.

APPLYING/FRESHMEN *Option:* midyear entrance. *Required:* essay, school transcript, 3 recommendations, minimum 2.5 high school GPA, SAT I or ACT, TOEFL for international students. Test scores used for admission. *Application deadline:* rolling.

APPLYING/TRANSFER *Required:* essay, 3 recommendations, college transcript, minimum 2.0 GPA.

CONTACT Admissions Offi. Western Baptist College, 5000 Deer Park Drive, SE, Salem, OR 97301-9392; 800-845-3005 (toll-free).

WESTMONT COLLEGE
Santa Barbara, California

SPECIAL NOTE FROM THE COLLEGE Westmont's distinctive is an unusually high-quality liberal arts program combined with enthusiastic, evangelical Christian faith. Close interaction among students and faculty members is a Westmont hallmark. Student life is characterized by freedom to make choices, but there is an expectation of responsibility towards the community and its minimal regulations. Opportunities beyond the classroom include cross-cultural studies in Western and Eastern Europe, Africa, Costa Rica, and the Holy Land. Semester study programs are available in San Francisco and Washington, DC.

Total Enrollment: 1,285 (all UG)
Women: 61%
Application Deadline: 2/15
Entrance: moderately difficult
Tuition & Fees: $15,186
Room & Board: $5304
SAT≥500: 56% V, 72% M   **ACT≥21:** 90%
Denominational Affiliation: interdenominational

GENERAL INFORMATION Independent-religious 4-year coed institution. Awards bachelor's degrees. Founded 1940. *Setting:* 133-acre suburban campus. *Faculty:* 115 (79 full-time, 81% with terminal degrees, 36 part-time); student-undergrad faculty ratio is 15:1. *Library Holdings:* 150,000 books, 20,687 microform titles, 710 periodicals, 3 on-line bibliographic services, 14 CD-ROMs, 4,553 records, tapes, and CDs. *Computers:* 19 terminals, PCs for student use in library, academic buildings.

UNDERGRADUATE PROFILE 1,285 students from 37 states and territories, 11 other countries. 61% women, 1% part-time, 75% state residents, 82% live on campus, 15% transferred in, 59% have need-based financial aid, 21% have non-need-based financial aid, 60% have campus jobs, 2% international, 1% 25 or older, 1% Native American, 4% Hispanic, 1% African American, 4% Asian American. *Retention:* 91% of 1993 freshmen returned. *Graduation:* 70% graduate in 4 years.

FRESHMEN 351 total; 274 from public schools. 950 applied, 75% were accepted, 49% of whom enrolled. 42% from top 10% of their high school class, 70% from top quarter, 91% from top half. 5 National Merit Scholarship Finalists, 2 National Merit Scholars.

ACADEMIC PROGRAM Core, challenging humanities and sciences curriculum, honor code. Calendar: semesters. 673 courses offered in 1993–94; average class size 23 in required courses. Academic remediation for entering students, services for LD students, advanced placement, accelerated degree program, self-designed majors, Freshman Honors College, tutorials, honors program, summer session for credit, co-op programs and internships. Off-campus study at 12 members of the Christian College Consortium, 88 members of the Christian College Coalition. ROTC: Army (c). Unusual degree programs: 3-2 engineering with Stanford University, Washington University, 9 campuses of the University of California, California Polytechnic State University, San Luis Obispo.

STUDY-ABROAD SITES Austria, Belgium, Canada, Costa Rica, England, France, Germany, Greece, Hong Kong, Israel, Italy, Kenya, Russia, Switzerland, Turkey, Uganda.

MAJORS Anthropology, art/fine arts, behavioral sciences, biology/biological sciences, business economics, chemistry, communication, computer science, (pre)dentistry sequence, economics, education, elementary education, engineering (general), engineering physics, English, French, history, international studies, (pre)law sequence, liberal arts/general studies, literature, mathematics, (pre)medicine sequence, ministries, modern languages, music, natural sciences, philosophy, physical education, physical fitness/exercise science, physical sciences, physics, political science/government, psychology, religious studies, secondary education, social science, sociology, Spanish, theater arts/drama, (pre)veterinary medicine sequence.

EXPENSES FOR 1994–95 *Application fee:* $30. Comprehensive fee of $20,490 includes full-time tuition ($14,320), mandatory fees ($866), and college room and board ($5304). College room only: $3080. Part-time tuition: $760 per unit.

FINANCIAL AID *College-administered aid for undergraduates 1993–94:* 987 need-based scholarships (average $5500), non-need scholarships, short-term loans (average $100), low-interest long-term loans from college funds (average $3000), loans from external sources (average $4000), FSEOG, Federal Work-Study, 250 part-time jobs. Average total aid for freshmen: $11,990, meeting 94% of need (aid provided to 100% of those qualified). *Application forms required:* FAF, IRS, FAFSA; required for some: state; accepted: FFS. *Priority deadline:* 3/1. *Payment plans:* installment, deferred payment. *Waivers:* full or partial for employees or children of employees. *Notification:* 4/15. *Average indebtedness of graduates:* $15,000.

COLLEGE LIFE Orientation program (5 days, no cost, parents included). Drama-theater group, choral group, student-run newspaper, radio station. *Social organizations:* 40 open to all. *Most popular organizations:* Christian Concerns, Student Government, Leadership Development, music and theater ensembles. *Major annual events:* Homecoming, Spring Sing, Fall Follies. *Student services:* health clinic, personal-psychological counseling, women's center, shuttle bus. *Safety:* 24-hour emergency response devices and patrols, late-night transport-escort service, controlled dormitory access, room security.

ATHLETICS Member NAIA. *Intercollegiate:* baseball M(s), basketball M(s), cross-country running M(s)/W(s), lacrosse W(c), rugby M(c), soccer M(s)/W(s), tennis M(s)/W(s), track and field M(s)/W(s), volleyball M(c)/W(s). *Intramural:* badminton, basketball, cross-country running, football, golf, racquetball, soccer, softball, swimming and diving, table tennis (Ping-Pong), tennis, volleyball, water polo. *Contact:* Dr. Ron Mulder, Director of Athletics, 805-565-6105.

APPLYING/FRESHMEN *Options:* early entrance, early action, deferred entrance, midyear entrance. *Required:* essay, school transcript, SAT I or ACT, TOEFL for international students. *Recommended:* 3 years of high school math and science, 2 years of high school foreign language, recommendations, interview, SAT II: Writing Test. Test scores used for admission. *Application deadlines:* 2/15, 12/1 for early action. *Notification:* 3/15, 1/15 for early action.

APPLYING/TRANSFER *Required:* essay, high school transcript, college transcript, minimum 2.0 GPA, minimum 2.5 GPA for transfers from 2-year colleges. *Recommended:* 3 years of high school math and science, some high school foreign language, recommendations, interview. *Required for some:* standardized test scores. *Entrance level:* moderately difficult. *Application deadline:* 3/15. *Notification:* 4/1.

CONTACT Mr. David Morley, Director of Admissions, Westmont College, 955 La Paz Road, Santa Barbara, CA 93108; 805-565-6200.

WHEATON COLLEGE
Wheaton, Illinois

Total Enrollment: 2,575
UG Enrollment: 2,256 (53% W)
Application Deadline: 2/1
Entrance: very difficult
Tuition & Fees: $11,480
Room & Board: $4200
SAT≥500: 79% V, 95% M   **ACT≥21:** 99%
Denominational Affiliation: nondenominational

GENERAL INFORMATION Independent-religious comprehensive coed institution. Awards bachelor's, master's, doctorate degrees. Founded 1860. *Setting:* 80-acre suburban campus with easy access to Chicago. *Faculty:* 261 (155 full-time, 85% with terminal degrees, 106 part-time); student-undergrad faculty ratio is 15:1. *Library Holdings:* 375,828 books, 310,672 microform titles, 2,209 periodicals, 3 on-line bibliographic services, 25 CD-ROMs, 25,917 records, tapes, and CDs. *Computers:* 70 terminals, PCs for student use in computer labs.

UNDERGRADUATE PROFILE 2,256 students from 51 states and territories, 8 other countries. 53% women, 2% part-time, 22% state residents, 89% live on campus, 4% transferred in, 45% have need-based financial aid, 16% have non-need-based financial aid, 43% have campus jobs, 1% international, 2% 25 or older, 1% Native American, 2% Hispanic, 2% African American, 6% Asian American. *Retention:* 92% of 1992 freshmen returned. *Graduation:* 70% graduate in 4 years.

FRESHMEN 547 total. 1,432 applied, 64% were accepted, 59% of whom enrolled. 56% from top 10% of their high school class, 86% from top quarter, 97% from top half. 34 National Merit Scholarship Finalists, 34 National Merit Scholars.

ACADEMIC PROGRAM Core, liberal arts curriculum. Calendar: semesters. Average class size 28 in required courses. Services for LD students, advanced placement, self-designed majors, summer session for credit, internships. More than half of graduate courses open to undergraduate students. Off-campus study at members of the Christian College Consortium. ROTC: Army. Unusual degree programs: 3-2 engineering with University of Illinois, Case Western Reserve University, Washington University, Illinois Institute of Technology, nursing with Rush University, Emory University, Goshen College, University of Rochester, Vanderbilt University.

STUDY-ABROAD SITES England, France, Germany, Israel, the Netherlands, Russia, Spain.

MAJORS Archaeology, art education, art/fine arts, art history, biblical languages, biblical studies, biology/biological sciences, business economics, chemistry, communication, computer science, economics, elementary education, engineering (general), environmental sciences, French, geology, German, history, interdisciplinary studies, journalism, literature, mathematics, modern languages, music, music business, music education, music history, nursing, philosophy, physical education, physics, piano/organ, politi-

cal science/government, psychology, religious education, religious studies, science education, secondary education, sociology, Spanish, speech/rhetoric/public address/debate, stringed instruments, studio art, theater arts/drama, voice, wind and percussion instruments.

EXPENSES FOR 1994–95 *Application fee:* $30. Comprehensive fee of $15,680 includes full-time tuition ($11,480) and college room and board ($4200). College room only: $2440. Part-time tuition: $480 per hour.

FINANCIAL AID *College-administered aid for undergraduates 1993–94:* 1,011 need-based scholarships (average $4755), 362 non-need scholarships (average $812), low-interest long-term loans from college funds (average $1371), loans from external sources (average $3834), FSEOG, Federal Work-Study, 970 part-time jobs. Average total aid for freshmen: $9583, meeting 80% of need (aid provided to 100% of those qualified). *Application forms required:* institutional, FAFSA; required for some: IRS. *Priority deadline:* 3/15. *Payment plan:* installment. *Waivers:* full or partial for employees or children of employees. *Average indebtedness of graduates:* $6388.

COLLEGE LIFE Orientation program (3 days, no cost, parents included). Drama-theater group, choral group, student-run newspaper, radio station. *Social organizations:* 41 open to all. *Most popular organizations:* Christian Service Council, College Union, choral groups, College Republicans. *Major annual events:* Homecoming, Air Jam, class films. *Student services:* health clinic, personal-psychological counseling. *Safety:* 24-hour patrols, late-night transport-escort service.

ATHLETICS Member NCAA. All Division III. *Intercollegiate:* baseball M, basketball M/W, crew M(c)/W(c), cross-country running M/W, equestrian sports W(c), football M, golf M, ice hockey M(c), lacrosse M(c)/W(c), soccer M/W, softball W, swimming and diving M/W, tennis M/W, track and field M/W, volleyball M(c)/W, wrestling M. *Intramural:* badminton, basketball, football, golf, racquetball, skiing (cross-country), soccer, softball, table tennis (Ping-Pong), tennis, volleyball, water polo, weight lifting. *Contact:* Mr. Tony Ladd, Chair of Physical Education and Athletics, 708-752-5125.

APPLYING/FRESHMEN Preference given to Christians. *Options:* early action, deferred entrance, midyear entrance. *Required:* essay, school transcript, 2 recommendations, interview, SAT I or ACT, TOEFL for international students. *Recommended:* 3 years of high school math and science, 2 years of high school foreign language, SAT II: Subject Tests, SAT II: Writing Test. Test scores used for admission. *Application deadlines:* 2/1, 12/1 for early action. *Notification:* 4/10, 2/10 for early action.

APPLYING/TRANSFER *Required:* essay, high school transcript, 2 recommendations, interview, college transcript. *Recommended:* 3 years of high school math and science, 2 years of high school foreign language, minimum 3.0 GPA. *Required for some:* standardized test scores. *Entrance level:* moderately difficult. *Application deadline:* 3/1. *Notification:* 4/15.

CONTACT Mr. Dan Crabtree, Director of Admissions, Wheaton College, 501 East College Avenue, Wheaton, IL 60187; 708-752-5005 or toll-free 800-222-2419 (out-of-state).

WHITWORTH COLLEGE
Spokane, Washington

> **SPECIAL NOTE FROM THE COLLEGE** For over a century, Whitworth has dedicated itself to a blend of educational components: an integration of faith and learning in the classroom featuring rigorous academics taught by Christian scholars, active residential life, and a commitment to fostering an understanding of other cultures within the nation and the world. Study tours and exchanges provide opportunities for students to experience countries throughout Europe, Asia, and Central America. Cooperative education experiences and internships, which allow students to gain experience and build contacts in the professional community, are encouraged. Whitworth's stated mission is to equip its graduates to honor God, follow Christ, and serve humanity.

Total Enrollment: 1,839
UG Enrollment: 1,430 (59% W)
Application Deadline: 3/1
Entrance: moderately difficult
Tuition & Fees: $11,965
Room & Board: $4300
SAT≥500: 47% V, 69% M   **ACT≥21:** N/R
Denominational Affiliation: Presbyterian

GENERAL INFORMATION Independent-religious comprehensive coed institution. Awards bachelor's, master's degrees. Founded 1890. *Setting:* 200-acre suburban campus. *Undergraduate faculty:* 95 (80 full-time, 80% with terminal degrees, 15 part-time); student-undergrad faculty ratio is 15:1. *Library Holdings:* 135,373 books, 58,000 microform titles, 725 periodicals, 4 CD-ROMs, 2,476 records, tapes, and CDs. *Computers:* 90 terminals, PCs for student use in computer center, library, labs. Students must have own computer. Access to campuswide network from computer center, library.

UNDERGRADUATE PROFILE 1,430 students from 27 states and territories, 26 other countries. 59% women, 11% part-time, 60% state residents, 65% live on campus, 31% transferred in, 7% international, 17% 25 or older, 1% Native American, 2% Hispanic, 1% African American, 3% Asian American. *Retention:* 73% of 1992 freshmen returned.

FRESHMEN 363 total. 1,132 applied, 83% were accepted, 39% of whom enrolled. 27% from top 10% of their high school class, 62% from top quarter, 93% from top half.

ACADEMIC PROGRAM Core, honor code. Calendar: 4-1-4. Academic remediation for entering students, English as a second language program offered during academic year, advanced placement, self-designed majors, tutorials, summer session for credit, part-time degree program (daytime, evenings, summer), adult/continuing education programs, co-op programs and internships. Off-campus study at 3 members of the Intercollegiate Center for Nursing, 2 members of the Intercollegiate Language Study Consortium. ROTC: Army (c). Unusual degree programs: 3-2 engineering with University of Southern California, Washington University.

STUDY-ABROAD SITES China, Costa Rica, England, France, Germany, Guatemala, Honduras, Hong Kong, Israel, Korea, Mexico, Nicaragua.

MAJORS Accounting, American studies, art education, art/fine arts, art history, arts administration, biology/biological sciences, business administration/commerce/management, chemistry, communication, computer science, (pre)dentistry sequence, economics, elementary education, English, French, history, international business, international studies, journalism, (pre)law sequence, mathematics, (pre)medicine sequence, music, music education, nursing, peace studies, philosophy, physical education, physics, piano/organ, political science/government, psychology, religious studies, secondary education, sociology, Spanish, special education, speech/rhetoric/public address/debate, sports medicine, studio art, theater arts/drama, (pre)veterinary medicine sequence, voice.

EXPENSES FOR 1993–94 Comprehensive fee of $16,265 includes full-time tuition ($11,840), mandatory fees ($125), and college room and board ($4300). Part-time tuition and fees per credit: $230 for the first 4 credits, $460 for the next 7 credits.

FINANCIAL AID *College-administered aid for undergraduates 1993–94:* 843 need-based scholarships (average $4396), 148 non-need scholarships (average $3950), low-interest long-term loans from college funds (average $1443), loans from external sources (average $2408), FSEOG, Federal Work-Study, 340 part-time jobs. Average total aid for freshmen: $14,424, meeting 84% of need (aid provided to 100% of those qualified). *Application forms required:* FAF; required for some: IRS; accepted: FFS, FAFSA. *Priority deadline:* 3/1. *Payment plans:* tuition prepayment, installment. *Waivers:* full or partial for children of alumni and employees or children of employees.

COLLEGE LIFE Orientation program (4 days, no cost, parents included). Drama-theater group, choral group, student-run newspaper, radio station. *Most popular organizations:* International Club, Habitat for Humanity, En Christo. *Major annual events:* Homecoming, Community Building Day, Spring Fest. *Student services:* health clinic, personal-psychological counseling. *Safety:* 24-hour emergency response devices and patrols, late-night transport-escort service, room security.

ATHLETICS Member NAIA. *Intercollegiate:* baseball M, basketball M(s)/W(s), cross-country running M(s)/W(s), football M(s), soccer M(s)/W(s), swimming and diving M(s)/W(s), tennis M(s)/W(s), track and field M(s)/W(s), volleyball W(s). *Intramural:* basketball, football, rugby, skiing (cross-country), skiing (downhill), softball, table tennis (Ping-Pong), volleyball, water polo. *Contact:* Mr. Kevin Bryant, Athletic Director, 509-466-3211.

APPLYING/FRESHMEN *Options:* early decision, deferred entrance. *Required:* essay, school transcript, recommendations, SAT I or ACT, TOEFL for international students. *Recommended:* 3 years of high school math and science, some high school foreign language. *Required for some:* interview. Test scores used for admission. *Application deadlines:* 3/1, 11/30 for early decision. *Notification:* 12/15 for early decision.

APPLYING/TRANSFER *Required:* essay, recommendations, college transcript, minimum 2.5 GPA. *Recommended:* 3 years of high school math and science, some high school foreign language. *Required for some:* standardized test scores, high school transcript, interview. *Entrance level:* moderately difficult. *Application deadline:* 7/1.

CONTACT Mr. Ken Moyer, Director of Admissions, Whitworth College, Spokane, WA 99251; 509-466-3212 or toll-free 800-533-4668.

Special Programs

This section contains descriptions of special study programs available to students at member schools of the Christian College Coalition. The Coalition sponsors six study programs: the American Studies Program, the Latin American Studies Program, the Los Angeles Film Studies Center, the Middle East Studies Program, the Oxford Summer School Program, and the Russian Studies Program. Other opportunities are also available, including the Au Sable Institute of Environmental Studies, the Institute for Family Studies, the Institute of Holy Land Studies and the Wesleyan Urban Coalition. While these four programs are not directly sponsored by the Coalition, oversight for each is guided by at least ten "participating colleges" within the Coalition membership.

American Studies Program

Students in today's complex, competitive world face many challenges: to expand their world, to gain the education and experience they need, to get perspective, and to put their beliefs into practice.

For nearly two decades, the Coalition's American Studies Program (ASP) has challenged students to integrate their faith with the realities of the marketplace and public life through a semester of experiential learning in Washington, D.C. In the ASP, students can gain the experience they need to live and work in a biblically faithful way in society and in their chosen field.

Students enrolled at any of the colleges listed in this guide are invited to participate in this unique work-study program. ASP students earn academic credit by working about 25 hours a week as an unpaid intern in their intended vocational field and by participating in interdisciplinary, issue-oriented seminar classes.

Washington, D.C., is a stimulating educational laboratory that offers on-the-job training to help ASP students build a solid foundation for their future. ASP students live and study in the Coalition's Dellenback Center on Capitol Hill, which includes student apartments, a library, dining facilities, and a classroom.

Designed for juniors and seniors with a wide range of academic majors and career interests, the ASP provides many types of internships, including those in executive and congressional offices; business and trade associations; the law and social services; radio, TV, and print media; and think tanks, cultural institutions, and inner-city ministries. The American Studies Program works with students to tailor an internship to fit their unique talents and aspirations.

While participating in the contemporary, issue-oriented seminar program, students and faculty members analyze current topics in domestic and international policy through two public policy units. In addition, each term begins and ends with a two-week unit on the foundation of Christian public involvement.

Over the years, the ASP has provided over 1,500 college students with real-world experiences that have helped them gain the critical knowledge and preparation they need to begin understanding their life's vocation.

Because of its unique location in Washington, D.C., the program has a special way of challenging students to consider the meaning of the Lordship of Christ in all areas of life, including career choices, public policy issues, and personal relationships.

ASP has had life-changing impact on its participants. As one alumnus says:

I loved the program because it challenged me to look deeper into beliefs I already had and to explore beliefs I'd never considered, substantiating them through Scripture and faith. The responsibilities expected of me, combined with the job skills I learned in the internship, provided a smoother transition from college to the workplace.

Additional information on the American Studies Program is available from the academic dean's office at any of the colleges listed in this guide or by contacting:

American Studies Program
Christian College Coalition
327 Eighth Street, NE
Washington, D.C. 20002
Telephone: 202-546-3086

Latin American Studies Center

An opportunity to live and learn in Latin America is available to students in their junior or senior year from Coalition member colleges through the Latin American Studies Program (LASP). Located in San José, Costa Rica, the Program is committed to helping students examine and live out the Lordship of Jesus Christ in an international context.

Each semester a group of 25 to 35 students is selected to participate in this seminar/service experience in Latin America. The academic program, for which credit is awarded by the student's home institution, involves a combination of learning, serving, and observing.

The learning component includes intensive language study at the Spanish Language Institute in San José, where class assignment is based on language proficiency. In this program, students study for a period of six weeks and practice their language skills with local Costa Ricans, including the host families that provide a home away from home for each LASP student. These families are chosen for their Christian commitment and their willingness to share their culture and their friendship. At the same time, students take part in seminars coordinated by the LASP staff that deal with such issues as Third World development, Latin American history and culture, and the role of the church. Conducted in English and in Spanish, these seminar sessions enable students to interact with outside speakers who bring a rich variety of perspectives to current issues.

The serving component involves hands-on experience working in a "servant role" in the Third World through participation in a service "opportunity." In order to get a better understanding of the complexities of Latin society, students are placed in a variety of service activities such as working in orphanages or with abused children or in such fields as agriculture, economic development, education, environmental stewardship, and health.

In addition to living with Costa Rican families, the observing component of the program gives students the opportunity to travel to at least two other Central American countries. By visiting Latin American countries outside Costa Rica, including Guatemala, Honduras, and Nicaragua, students enjoy a rich diversity of cultures in the cities, villages, and countryside of those areas.

After participating in the Coalition's Latin American Studies Program, one student had this to say of his experience:

I feel this semester has been one of the hardest, most fun, most worthwhile experiences of my whole life, and I know that what I have learned will affect me always.

Applicants are required to have a minimum 2.75 GPA and the equivalent of one year of college-level Spanish. Additional information on the Latin American Studies Program is available from the academic dean's office at any of the colleges listed in this guide or by contacting:

Latin American Studies Program
Christian College Coalition
329 Eighth Street, NE
Washington, D.C. 20002
Telephone: 202-546-8713

Los Angeles Film Studies Center

In January 1991, the Christian College Coalition inaugurated the Los Angeles Film Studies Center (LAFSC). This unique program serves as an introduction to the work and workings of the mainstream Hollywood film industry.

The LAFSC is conveniently located in Los Angeles near several of the major film and television studios. Accommodations are provided across the street from the center in a corporate apartment complex featuring exceptional recreational facilities and comfortable furnished units.

The curriculum is designed to allow students exposure to the industry, to the many academic disciplines that might be appropriate to it, and to critical thinking and reflection on what it means to be a Christian in the film world. As such, the curriculum is balanced between courses of a theoretical nature and courses that offer students an applied introduction to the world of film.

LAFSC students participate in three seminar courses and an internship in the film or television industry, described below:

- Inside Hollywood: The Work and Workings of the Film Industry. This seminar examines the creative and operational aspects of the film business, taking full advantage of studio tours, location filming, and a variety of guest lecturers from a cross-section of the industry. Class discussion will provide a Christian perspective on issues raised by guest presenters and will probe the common personal, professional, and public ethical issues of the entertainment business.
- Introduction to Filmmaking. Students receive an introduction to the theory and practice of motion picture filmmaking. Topics include the filmmaking process and equipment, converting ideas to images, and the use of lighting, editing, and sound in film. Students make several short Super 8 mm films.
- Film in Culture: Exploring a Christian Perspective on the Nature and Influence of Film. This seminar course provides a survey of film and the film industry, highlighting film's influence on, and reflection of, American culture during the late nineteenth and twentieth centuries. Particular emphasis will be placed on Christian perspectives on culture. The course will include a survey of the presentation of religious subject matter in film.
- Internships: All LAFSC students are assigned a non-paid internship in some aspect of the Hollywood film or television industry as arranged by the LAFSC staff. These internships are primarily in an office setting such as development companies, agencies, personal management companies, production offices, etc. Students are expected to work 20–24 hours a week throughout the entire semester. The internship serves as a laboratory to provide students with real-life exposure to the industry and as a basis for discussion and reflection in the other courses.

Students interested in the Los Angeles Film Studies Center are invited to request additional information from the academic dean's office at any of the colleges listed in this guide or to contact the LAFSC directly:

Los Angeles Film Studies Center
3800 Barham Boulevard, Suite 202
Los Angeles, CA 90068
Telephone: 213-882-6224

Middle East Studies Program

———— ॐ ————

The Middle East, often called "the cradle of civilization," has always been a fascinating and complex region. The Christian College Coalition's Middle East Studies Program (MESP), based in Cairo, Egypt, exists to help college students understand the history, peoples, and cultures of the Middle East. Juniors and seniors enrolled at any of the colleges listed in this guide are eligible to apply for this unique learning experience.

While living in Cairo, students study spoken Arabic and participate in three interdisciplinary seminar courses designed to provide insights into the historical, religious, political, and economic dimensions of life in the Middle East. Academic credit for participation in the Middle East Studies Program is awarded by the student's home institution.

- The first course, "Peoples and Cultures of the Middle East," introduces students to the many different societies and ways of life in the region.
- The course "Islam in the Modern World" explains the basic tenets of the Islamic faith and seeks to give students an understanding of how Christians relate to Muslim countries and individuals.
- "Conflict and Change in the Middle East Today" addresses the ongoing quest for peace in this region, identifying the obstacles and the triumphs.

In all three seminar classes, personal interaction with resident scholars, local business people, religious leaders, and government officials enhances the education experience and provides perspectives no textbook can equal.

MESP students also study the spoken Arabic language with a certified language instructor for thirteen weeks. Ample opportunities exist to practice conversational skills with Egyptian students, other teachers, business people, and friends of the MESP.

Each week, students participate in a service opportunity in cooperation with one of the many organizations in Cairo, gaining valuable hands-on work experience and interaction with local Egyptians.

Safe and comfortable housing is provided in the international dormitory of the American University in Cairo. The MESP headquarters and classroom is a 5-minute walk from the dormitory. Students have access to the American University's library and computer facilities.

During the semester, MESP students travel by bus to Israel and the Territories to see the historic land of the Bible and to explore the many dimensions of the ongoing efforts for peace between Arabs and Israelis. On free weekends, students are able to travel within Egypt to Sinai, Alexandria, and Giza as well as to other locations.

Participants in the Middle East Studies Program have the opportunity to gather a wide array of experiences. Says one student, "The MESP has, above all else, exposed me to a culture whose basis is not in Christianity. I now have a good Muslim friend whose faith is as strong as mine. It's an interesting situation for me to be in, because whenever I've been with people of deep faith before, they've been Christian."

Additional information about the Middle East Studies Program is available from the academic dean's office at any of the colleges listed in this guide or by contacting:

Middle East Studies Program
Christian College Coalition
329 Eighth Street, NE
Washington, D.C. 20002
Telephone: 202-546-8713

Oxford Summer School Program

Students at the colleges and universities listed in this guide are eligible to apply for admission to the Oxford Summer School Program, a multidisciplinary program of study of the events of the Renaissance and Reformation. Located in Oxford, England, the program is cosponsored by the Christian College Coalition and the Centre for Medieval and Renaissance Studies, which is affiliated with Oxford's Keble College.

Inaugurated in 1991, the six-week program explores the Renaissance and Reformation through the study of the philosophy, art, literature, science, music, politics, and religion of this era. Many classes are conducted by Oxford dons, who also meet with students in seminars and in one-on-one tutorials that are typical of the Oxford method of education.

Lectures, classes, meals, and social activities are held in St. Michael's Hall, which also houses faculty offices and the Centre's library. Students take residence at St. Michael's or at Wycliffe Hall, located next to the University's beautiful park.

Weekly field trips to places of importance outside Oxford introduce students to the great cathedrals, castles, and historic towns nearby. Special activities include chapel, a garden party and formal dinner at Keble College, the annual Carl F. H. Henry Lecture, a weekly colloquium on faith and learning, and an evening at Shakespeare's Stratford-upon-Avon. The resources of Oxford, such as the world-famous Bodleian Library, are available to students.

The Program has positively influenced the students who have participated:

I would definitely suggest this program for all students, regardless of one's major.

The Oxford summer program is an excellent opportunity for students to grow intellectually, but more importantly, to grow in their personal faith.

Further information is available from the academic dean's office at any of the colleges listed in this guide or by contacting:

Oxford Summer School
Program
Christian College
Coalition
329 Eighth Street, NE
Washington, D.C. 20002
Telephone: 202-546-8713

Russian Studies Program

Juniors and seniors enrolled at one of the colleges listed in this guide have the opportunity to discover firsthand the richness of the Russian language, culture, and history through the Russian Studies Program (RSP).

The RSP is unique in the fact that it makes use of the rich resources found in three distinct locations: Moscow, Nizhni Novgorod, and St. Petersburg. The first two weeks of the semester are spent in Moscow, where students receive an orientation to life in Russia and take in the city's extraordinary museums, galleries, landmarks, and historical resources.

Following a trip through the cities of the "Golden Ring," Nizhni Novgorod, formerly Gorky, becomes home for the next eleven weeks. As the "test site" for President Yeltsin's economic reform, the city is an ideal learning environment. Two seminar classes explore the challenges facing Russians today. "Russian History and Culture" introduces students to nineteenth- and twentieth-century Russia, combining lectures during afternoon sessions with sightseeing and excursions to significant sites. Guest speakers offer a diversity of perspectives on the issues at hand. The second seminar, "Post-Communist Russia in Transition," focuses on contemporary Russia and her struggle to rebuild society following the collapse of Communism. Briefings by business leaders and public policy representatives add to the breadth of the course. Students are introduced to the complexities of economic transition from a centrally planned to a free-market economy. They also study efforts to build democratic institutions in Russia and analyze the debate over religious freedom and the role of Russian churches.

In addition to seminar classes, RSP students receive daily Russian language instruction by qualified native Russian language teachers. The course is designed for beginning and intermediate levels. Prior knowledge of the Russian language is not required. Contacts with Russian students, particularly in Nizhni Novgorod, facilitate language acquisition.

During the last three weeks of the program, St. Petersburg provides the setting for students to work in service projects with various local community and church organizations, business enterprises, and schools. Known for its rich cultural and historical resources and outstanding architecture, St. Petersburg tells the story of Russian life under both the tsars and the Communists. Living with a Russian family in the city gives RSP students exceptional insights into the realities of Russian life.

One RSP student observed, "The thing that surprised me most about Russian culture is the existence of religious history. I had thought of Russia as an antireligious country, but not even seventy years of communism could break the power of their religious past."

Said another student, "What really amazed me was the genuine sense of caring radiating from the Russians. . . . It felt like home there."

Additional information about the Russian Studies Program is available from the academic dean's office at any of the colleges listed in this guide or by contacting:

Russian Studies Program
Christian College Coalition
329 Eighth Street, NE
Washington, D.C. 20002
Telephone: 202-546-8713

Au Sable Institute of Environmental Studies

Students at the colleges listed in this guide are eligible for course work at Au Sable Institute of Environmental Studies, an institute for Christian environmental stewardship located in the north woods near the tip of Michigan's Lower Peninsula.

Au Sable courses usually can be applied toward course requirements at the student's home college or university. Eighteen courses are offered in a three-week January term, a three-week May term, and two five-week summer sessions and include courses in environmental studies, natural history, field biology, environmental ethics, restoration ecology, groundwater stewardship, and global development and ecological sustainability. Vocational certification also is granted to students who complete a program of study for which they receive certification upon graduation from their home institution.

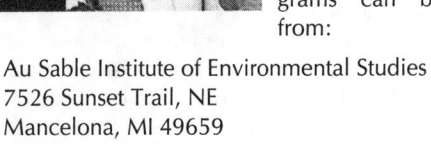

Some students select a Christian college so that they can take course work at Au Sable—an institute known worldwide for its leadership in Christian environmental stewardship. The Au Sable Outreach Office also provides bibliographies and reprints for faculty members and students of all the colleges listed in this guide via phone (602-255-0950) or fax (608-255-4228) as a free service to those doing projects and papers on Christian environmental stewardship.

Scholarships and fellowships up to $1200 per session are available to students attending the Institute from member institutions of the Christian College Coalition.

Information on Au Sable is available from the academic dean's office at any of the colleges listed in this guide. An official bulletin describing courses and programs can be obtained from:

Au Sable Institute of Environmental Studies
7526 Sunset Trail, NE
Mancelona, MI 49659
Telephone: 616-587-8686

Institute for Family Studies

Students at the colleges listed in this guide are invited to participate in the Institute for Family Studies in Colorado Springs, Colorado, which opens in the fall of 1995.

Developed by Focus on the Family, the Institute offers a specialized one-semester program for selected students from various academic disciplines at accredited colleges and universities. The goal is to produce future leaders who can intelligently confront societal assumptions about the family from diverse vantage points.

Focus on the Family began in 1977 in response to Dr. James C. Dobson's increasing concern for the American family and has grown into an international organization with more than fifty ministries, including a daily broadcast and a publishing division. Focus on the Family developed the Institute for Family Studies with the guidance of several presidents, deans, and faculty members at Coalition member colleges.

At the Institute's headquarters located on the front range of the majestic Rocky Mountains, students attend an

on-site program for fifteen weeks offered in the spring and fall semesters. Priority is given to applicants whose major and career interests point toward future service to families.

Institute students also serve in an internship in the Focus on the Family community. Further involvement in the community is encouraged through such programs as prison and community literacy and church-based systems for single-parent families, unwed mothers, and latch-key children.

The Institute wants each student to return to his or her own area of the country equipped to set up caring systems to help turn around the societal trends responsible for the present social upheaval.

Juniors and seniors attending Coalition member colleges and universities are eligible to apply. Additional information is available by contacting:

Institute for Family Studies
Focus on the Family
8606 Explorer Drive
Colorado Springs, CO 80920

Institute of Holy Land Studies

Students at the colleges and universities listed in this guide are eligible to apply for admission to the programs offered by the Institute of Holy Land Studies in Jerusalem, Israel. The Institute serves as an extension campus for thirty-seven Coalition schools and approximately seventy other colleges, universities, and seminaries around the world.

The Institute's historic campus is located on Mount Zion adjacent to the southwest corner of the Old City wall. Jerusalem itself offers a remarkable mixture of religious and secular cultures. The Institute is international in character, with graduate and undergraduate students from many continents.

Students in the Institute's semester and full-year programs enhance their understanding of Scripture and of the cultures of the Middle East through rigorous study of the history, archaeology, geography, language, and literature of the region. They also obtain an understanding of the cultural, philosophical, and religious expressions of the ancient and modern peoples, including the relationship of Israel with other Middle East nations. Students are also encouraged to make use of the unique academic and cultural resources available to them in the classroom and in their fieldwork throughout the region. Several graduate and undergraduate short-term programs focusing on historical geography are also available.

Students from those Coalition schools that are part of the Consortium of Associated Schools of the Institute of Holy Land Studies should apply for study through their home institution. Institute course credit is transferable to those schools by prior agreement. Other students should apply directly through the Institute. All students should coordinate their program selection with their academic adviser to be sure the courses selected are appropriate for their program of study.

Additional information is available by contacting:

Institute of Holy Land Studies
4249 East State Street, Suite 203
Rockford, IL 61108
(815) 229-5900

Wesleyan Urban Coalition

The Wesleyan Urban Coalition (WUC) was formed in 1980 in Chicago to link the needs and opportunities of the city with the faith and gifts of today's college and seminary students. As a cooperative venture of Christian colleges, the WUC prepares students for America's multicultural and urban future.

Chicago serves as an ideal laboratory for ministry and career preparation. WUC programs prepare students to serve full-time in urban or cross-cultural settings, identify career paths in the urban environment, and understand social justice and cultural issues. "Urban Semesters" provide a foundation for understanding urban cultures, systems, and poverty through an individually tailored internship and course of study. Miniterms provide a three-week introduction to cultural perspectives and interpretation. Interning for 10–20 hours per week gives students the opportunity to gain practical experience in a variety of fields. WUC has more than 100 potential placement sites in Chicago.

WUC members include many of the colleges listed in this guide. Students enrolled at Coalition member colleges that are not yet members of the Wesleyan Urban Coalition may also enroll in WUC programs for credit. College sophomores, juniors, or seniors in good standing are eligible to apply. Individual study programs are approved in advance by academic advisers and academic deans of the student's home institution as part of the application process.

Many students find their time at WUC to be life-changing. One student observed, "I had the time of my life and would have loved to stay for three months. I learned more about myself than I expected to learn in a lifetime. I wish everyone had the opportunity to go through WUC!"

Additional information on the Wesleyan Urban Coalition is available by contacting:

Wesleyan Urban Coalition
Olive Branch Mission
1043 West Madison
Chicago, IL 60187
Telephone: 312-243-3373
800-986-5483 (toll-free)

Indexes

Majors Index

ACCOUNTING
Anderson University, IN
Asbury College, KY
Azusa Pacific University, CA
Bartlesville Wesleyan College, OK
Belhaven College, MS
Bethel College, IN
Bethel College, KS
Bethel College, MN
Biola University, CA
Bluffton College, OH
Bryan College, TN
Calvin College, MI
Campbellsville College, KY
Campbell University, NC
Cedarville College, OH
Central Wesleyan College, SC
Colorado Christian University, CO
Cornerstone College, MI
Dallas Baptist University, TX
Dordt College, IA
Eastern Mennonite University, VA
Erskine College, SC
Evangel College, MO
Fresno Pacific College, CA
Geneva College, PA
Gordon College, MA
Goshen College, IN
Grace College, IN
Grand Canyon University, AZ
Greenville College, IL
Houghton College, NY
Huntington College, IN
Indiana Wesleyan University, IN
John Brown University, AR
Judson College, IL
King College, TN
The King's College, NY
Lee College, TN
LeTourneau University, TX
Malone College, OH
Master's College and Seminary, CA
Messiah College, PA
MidAmerica Nazarene College, KS
Milligan College, TN
Mississippi College, MS
Montreat-Anderson College, NC
Mount Vernon Nazarene College, OH
North Park College, IL
Northwestern College, IA
Northwestern College, MN
Northwest Nazarene College, ID
Oklahoma Baptist University, OK
Olivet Nazarene University, IL
Palm Beach Atlantic College, FL
Point Loma Nazarene College, CA
Redeemer College, ON
Roberts Wesleyan College, NY
Seattle Pacific University, WA
Simpson College, CA
Sioux Falls College, SD
Southern California College, CA
Southern Nazarene University, OK
Spring Arbor College, MI
Sterling College, KS
Tabor College, KS
Taylor University, IN
Trevecca Nazarene College, TN
Trinity Christian College, IL
Trinity College, IL
Union University, TN
Warner Southern College, FL
Western Baptist College, OR
Whitworth College, WA

ACTUARIAL SCIENCE
Tabor College, KS

ADULT AND CONTINUING EDUCATION
Bethel College, MN
Biola University, CA
Colorado Christian University, CO
Milligan College, TN
Northwest Christian College, OR
Northwestern College, MN
Nyack College, NY
Olivet Nazarene University, IL
Southern Nazarene University, OK
Warner Southern College, FL

ADVERTISING
Campbell University, NC
Milligan College, TN

AEROSPACE ENGINEERING
Bethel College, IN
Eastern Nazarene College, MA

AGRICULTURAL BUSINESS
Dordt College, IA
MidAmerica Nazarene College, KS
Northwestern College, MN

AGRICULTURAL SCIENCES
Dordt College, IA

AIRCRAFT MAINTENANCE
LeTourneau University, TX

AMERICAN STUDIES
Cedarville College, OH
Montreat-Anderson College, NC
Oklahoma Baptist University, OK
Warner Pacific College, OR
Whitworth College, WA

ANIMAL SCIENCES
Dordt College, IA

ANTHROPOLOGY
Biola University, CA
Judson College, IL
North Park College, IL
Olivet Nazarene University, IL

Southern California College, CA
Westmont College, CA

APPLIED ART
Azusa Pacific University, CA
Biola University, CA
Mississippi College, MS
Mount Vernon Nazarene College, OH
Northwest Nazarene College, ID
Oklahoma Baptist University, OK
Sioux Falls College, SD

APPLIED MATHEMATICS
Asbury College, KY
Biola University, CA
Campbell University, NC
Geneva College, PA
Sioux Falls College, SD
Southern Nazarene University, OK
Tabor College, KS
Trinity Western University, BC

ARCHAEOLOGY
Wheaton College, IL

ART EDUCATION
Anderson University, IN
Asbury College, KY
Bethel College, KS
Bethel College, MN
Biola University, CA
Bluffton College, OH
Calvin College, MI
Campbellsville College, KY
Evangel College, MO
Goshen College, IN
Grace College, IN
Grand Canyon University, AZ
Greenville College, IL
Houghton College, NY
Indiana Wesleyan University, IN
Malone College, OH
Mississippi College, MS
Mount Vernon Nazarene College, OH
North Park College, IL
Northwestern College, MN
Northwest Nazarene College, ID
Oklahoma Baptist University, OK
Olivet Nazarene University, IL
Palm Beach Atlantic College, FL
Point Loma Nazarene College, CA
Roberts Wesleyan College, NY
Sioux Falls College, SD
Southern Nazarene University, OK
Sterling College, KS
Taylor University, IN
Union University, TN
Wheaton College, IL
Whitworth College, WA

ART/FINE ARTS
Anderson University, IN
Asbury College, KY

ART/FINE ARTS (continued)

Azusa Pacific University, CA
Belhaven College, MS
Bethel College, IN
Bethel College, KS
Bethel College, MN
Biola University, CA
Bluffton College, OH
California Baptist College, CA
Calvin College, MI
Campbellsville College, KY
Campbell University, NC
Dallas Baptist University, TX
Dordt College, IA
Eastern Mennonite University, VA
Evangel College, MO
Gordon College, MA
Goshen College, IN
Grace College, IN
Grand Canyon University, AZ
Greenville College, IL
Houghton College, NY
Huntington College, IN
Indiana Wesleyan University, IN
John Brown University, AR
Judson College, IL
King College, TN
Malone College, OH
Messiah College, PA
Milligan College, TN
Mississippi College, MS
Mount Vernon Nazarene College, OH
North Park College, IL
Northwestern College, IA
Northwestern College, MN
Northwest Nazarene College, ID
Oklahoma Baptist University, OK
Olivet Nazarene University, IL
Pacific Christian College, CA
Palm Beach Atlantic College, FL
Point Loma Nazarene College, CA
Redeemer College, ON
Roberts Wesleyan College, NY
Seattle Pacific University, WA
Southern Nazarene University, OK
Spring Arbor College, MI
Sterling College, KS
Taylor University, IN
Trinity Christian College, IL
Trinity Western University, BC
Union University, TN
Westmont College, CA
Wheaton College, IL
Whitworth College, WA

ART HISTORY

Bethel College, MN
Calvin College, MI
Eastern College, PA
Messiah College, PA
Wheaton College, IL
Whitworth College, WA

ARTIFICIAL INTELLIGENCE

Taylor University, IN

ARTS ADMINISTRATION

Whitworth College, WA

ART THERAPY

Biola University, CA
Goshen College, IN

ASTRONOMY

Eastern College, PA

ATHLETIC TRAINING

Anderson University, IN
Azusa Pacific University, CA
Cedarville College, OH
Eastern Nazarene College, MA
Erskine College, SC
Fresno Pacific College, CA
Grand Canyon University, AZ
John Brown University, AR
MidAmerica Nazarene College, KS
Olivet Nazarene University, IL
Point Loma Nazarene College, CA
Taylor University, IN
Trinity College, IL

AUTOMOTIVE TECHNOLOGIES

LeTourneau University, TX

AVIATION ADMINISTRATION

Geneva College, PA
Southern Nazarene University, OK

AVIATION TECHNOLOGY

LeTourneau University, TX

BEHAVIORAL SCIENCES

Bartlesville Wesleyan College, OK
California Baptist College, CA
Cedarville College, OH
Erskine College, SC
Evangel College, MO
Grace College, IN
Messiah College, PA
Northwest College of the Assemblies of
    God, WA
Redeemer College, ON
Sioux Falls College, SD
Southern Nazarene University, OK
Sterling College, KS
Trevecca Nazarene College, TN
Westmont College, CA

BIBLICAL LANGUAGES

Asbury College, KY
Bethel College, IN
Cornerstone College, MI
Grace College, IN
Master's College and Seminary, CA
Southern Nazarene University, OK
Taylor University, IN
Wheaton College, IL

BIBLICAL STUDIES

Anderson University, IN
Asbury College, KY
Atlantic Baptist College, NB
Azusa Pacific University, CA
Belhaven College, MS
Bethel College, IN
Bethel College, KS
Bethel College, MN
Biola University, CA
Bryan College, TN
Calvin College, MI
Campbellsville College, KY
Campbell University, NC
Cedarville College, OH
Central Wesleyan College, SC
Colorado Christian University, CO
Cornerstone College, MI

Covenant College, GA
Dallas Baptist University, TX
Eastern College, PA
Eastern Mennonite University, VA
Eastern Nazarene College, MA
Erskine College, SC
Evangel College, MO
Fresno Pacific College, CA
Geneva College, PA
George Fox College, OR
Gordon College, MA
Goshen College, IN
Grace College, IN
Grand Canyon University, AZ
Greenville College, IL
Houghton College, NY
Huntington College, IN
Indiana Wesleyan University, IN
John Brown University, AR
Judson College, IL
King College, TN
The King's College, NY
Lee College, TN
LeTourneau University, TX
Malone College, OH
Master's College and Seminary, CA
Messiah College, PA
Milligan College, TN
Mississippi College, MS
Montreat-Anderson College, NC
Mount Vernon Nazarene College, OH
North Park College, IL
Northwest Christian College, OR
Northwest College of the Assemblies of
    God, WA
Northwestern College, MN
Northwest Nazarene College, ID
Nyack College, NY
Oklahoma Baptist University, OK
Olivet Nazarene University, IL
Pacific Christian College, CA
Point Loma Nazarene College, CA
Redeemer College, ON
Seattle Pacific University, WA
Simpson College, CA
Southern California College, CA
Southern Nazarene University, OK
Tabor College, KS
Taylor University, IN
Taylor University, Fort Wayne Campus, IN
Trinity College, IL
Trinity Western University, BC
Warner Pacific College, OR
Warner Southern College, FL
Western Baptist College, OR
Wheaton College, IL

BILINGUAL/BICULTURAL EDUCATION

Biola University, CA
Calvin College, MI
Fresno Pacific College, CA
Goshen College, IN

BIOCHEMISTRY

Azusa Pacific University, CA
Biola University, CA
Calvin College, MI
Eastern Mennonite University, VA
John Brown University, AR
Mount Vernon Nazarene College, OH
Olivet Nazarene University, IL
Point Loma Nazarene College, CA

BIOLOGY/BIOLOGICAL SCIENCES

Anderson University, IN
Asbury College, KY
Azusa Pacific University, CA
Bartlesville Wesleyan College, OK
Belhaven College, MS
Bethel College, IN
Bethel College, KS
Bethel College, MN
Biola University, CA
Bluffton College, OH
Bryan College, TN
California Baptist College, CA
Calvin College, MI
Campbellsville College, KY
Campbell University, NC
Cedarville College, OH
Central Wesleyan College, SC
Colorado Christian University, CO
Cornerstone College, MI
Covenant College, GA
Dallas Baptist University, TX
Dordt College, IA
Eastern College, PA
Eastern Mennonite University, VA
Eastern Nazarene College, MA
Erskine College, SC
Evangel College, MO
Fresno Pacific College, CA
Geneva College, PA
George Fox College, OR
Gordon College, MA
Goshen College, IN
Grace College, IN
Grand Canyon University, AZ
Greenville College, IL
Houghton College, NY
Huntington College, IN
Indiana Wesleyan University, IN
John Brown University, AR
Judson College, IL
King College, TN
The King's College, NY
The King's University College, AB
Lee College, TN
LeTourneau University, TX
Malone College, OH
Master's College and Seminary, CA
MidAmerica Nazarene College, KS
Milligan College, TN
Mississippi College, MS
Mount Vernon Nazarene College, OH
North Park College, IL
Northwestern College, IA
Northwest Nazarene College, ID
Oklahoma Baptist University, OK
Olivet Nazarene University, IL
Palm Beach Atlantic College, FL
Point Loma Nazarene College, CA
Redeemer College, ON
Roberts Wesleyan College, NY
Seattle Pacific University, WA
Sioux Falls College, SD
Southern California College, CA
Southern Nazarene University, OK
Spring Arbor College, MI
Sterling College, KS
Tabor College, KS
Taylor University, IN
Trevecca Nazarene College, TN
Trinity Christian College, IL
Trinity College, IL
Trinity Western University, BC

Union University, TN
Warner Pacific College, OR
Warner Southern College, FL
Westmont College, CA
Wheaton College, IL
Whitworth College, WA

BIOMEDICAL ENGINEERING

Eastern Nazarene College, MA

BIOMEDICAL TECHNOLOGIES

Campbell University, NC

BIOPHYSICS

Olivet Nazarene University, IL

BOTANY/PLANT SCIENCES

Redeemer College, ON

BROADCASTING

Asbury College, KY
Biola University, CA
Campbell University, NC
Cedarville College, OH
Cornerstone College, MI
Evangel College, MO
Geneva College, PA
Goshen College, IN
Huntington College, IN
John Brown University, AR
Malone College, OH
Milligan College, TN
Mount Vernon Nazarene College, OH
Northwestern College, MN
Northwest Nazarene College, ID
Oklahoma Baptist University, OK
Olivet Nazarene University, IL
Southern California College, CA
Taylor University, IN
Trevecca Nazarene College, TN

BUSINESS ADMINISTRATION/ COMMERCE/MANAGEMENT

Anderson University, IN
Asbury College, KY
Azusa Pacific University, CA
Bartlesville Wesleyan College, OK
Belhaven College, MS
Bethel College, IN
Bethel College, KS
Bethel College, MN
Biola University, CA
Bluffton College, OH
Bryan College, TN
California Baptist College, CA
Calvin College, MI
Campbellsville College, KY
Campbell University, NC
Cedarville College, OH
Central Wesleyan College, SC
Colorado Christian University, CO
Cornerstone College, MI
Covenant College, GA
Dallas Baptist University, TX
Dordt College, IA
Eastern College, PA
Eastern Mennonite University, VA
Eastern Nazarene College, MA
Erskine College, SC
Evangel College, MO
Fresno Pacific College, CA
Geneva College, PA
George Fox College, OR

Gordon College, MA
Goshen College, IN
Grace College, IN
Grand Canyon University, AZ
Greenville College, IL
Houghton College, NY
Huntington College, IN
Indiana Wesleyan University, IN
John Brown University, AR
Judson College, IL
King College, TN
The King's College, NY
Lee College, TN
LeTourneau University, TX
Malone College, OH
Master's College and Seminary, CA
Messiah College, PA
MidAmerica Nazarene College, KS
Milligan College, TN
Mississippi College, MS
Montreat-Anderson College, NC
Mount Vernon Nazarene College, OH
North Park College, IL
Northwest Christian College, OR
Northwest College of the Assemblies of
   God, WA
Northwestern College, IA
Northwestern College, MN
Northwest Nazarene College, ID
Nyack College, NY
Oklahoma Baptist University, OK
Olivet Nazarene University, IL
Pacific Christian College, CA
Palm Beach Atlantic College, FL
Point Loma Nazarene College, CA
Redeemer College, ON
Roberts Wesleyan College, NY
Seattle Pacific University, WA
Simpson College, CA
Sioux Falls College, SD
Southern California College, CA
Southern Nazarene University, OK
Spring Arbor College, MI
Sterling College, KS
Tabor College, KS
Taylor University, IN
Taylor University, Fort Wayne Campus, IN
Trevecca Nazarene College, TN
Trinity Christian College, IL
Trinity College, IL
Trinity Western University, BC
Union University, TN
Warner Pacific College, OR
Warner Southern College, FL
Western Baptist College, OR
Whitworth College, WA

BUSINESS ECONOMICS

Biola University, CA
Bluffton College, OH
Calvin College, MI
Campbellsville College, KY
Campbell University, NC
Cedarville College, OH
Dallas Baptist University, TX
George Fox College, OR
Grand Canyon University, AZ
Huntington College, IN
King College, TN
Milligan College, TN
Montreat-Anderson College, NC
Olivet Nazarene University, IL
Southern Nazarene University, OK
Spring Arbor College, MI
Union University, TN

BUSINESS ECONOMICS *(continued)*
Westmont College, CA
Wheaton College, IL

BUSINESS EDUCATION
Bartlesville Wesleyan College, OK
Bethel College, IN
Biola University, CA
Bluffton College, OH
Campbellsville College, KY
Cedarville College, OH
Cornerstone College, MI
Dallas Baptist University, TX
Dordt College, IA
Evangel College, MO
Fresno Pacific College, CA
Geneva College, PA
Goshen College, IN
Grand Canyon University, AZ
Greenville College, IL
Huntington College, IN
John Brown University, AR
Lee College, TN
Malone College, OH
MidAmerica Nazarene College, KS
Mount Vernon Nazarene College, OH
Northwestern College, IA
Northwest Nazarene College, ID
Oklahoma Baptist University, OK
Point Loma Nazarene College, CA
Southern Nazarene University, OK
Sterling College, KS
Tabor College, KS
Trevecca Nazarene College, TN
Trinity Christian College, IL
Union University, TN

CHEMICAL ENGINEERING
Bethel College, IN
Geneva College, PA

CHEMICAL ENGINEERING TECHNOLOGY
Northwest Nazarene College, ID

CHEMISTRY
Anderson University, IN
Asbury College, KY
Azusa Pacific University, CA
Bartlesville Wesleyan College, OK
Belhaven College, MS
Bethel College, IN
Bethel College, KS
Bethel College, MN
Biola University, CA
Bluffton College, OH
Calvin College, MI
Campbellsville College, KY
Campbell University, NC
Cedarville College, OH
Central Wesleyan College, SC
Covenant College, GA
Dordt College, IA
Eastern College, PA
Eastern Mennonite University, VA
Eastern Nazarene College, MA
Erskine College, SC
Evangel College, MO
Geneva College, PA
George Fox College, OR
Gordon College, MA
Goshen College, IN
Grand Canyon University, AZ

Greenville College, IL
Houghton College, NY
Huntington College, IN
Indiana Wesleyan University, IN
John Brown University, AR
Judson College, IL
King College, TN
The King's College, NY
The King's University College, AB
Lee College, TN
LeTourneau University, TX
Malone College, OH
Messiah College, PA
MidAmerica Nazarene College, KS
Milligan College, TN
Mississippi College, MS
Mount Vernon Nazarene College, OH
North Park College, IL
Northwestern College, IA
Northwest Nazarene College, ID
Oklahoma Baptist University, OK
Olivet Nazarene University, IL
Point Loma Nazarene College, CA
Roberts Wesleyan College, NY
Seattle Pacific University, WA
Sioux Falls College, SD
Southern California College, CA
Southern Nazarene University, OK
Spring Arbor College, MI
Sterling College, KS
Tabor College, KS
Taylor University, IN
Trevecca Nazarene College, TN
Trinity Christian College, IL
Trinity College, IL
Trinity Western University, BC
Union University, TN
Westmont College, CA
Wheaton College, IL
Whitworth College, WA

CHILD CARE/CHILD AND FAMILY STUDIES
Bethel College, MN
Bluffton College, OH
Campbell University, NC
Evangel College, MO
Goshen College, IN
Oklahoma Baptist University, OK
Olivet Nazarene University, IL
Southern Nazarene University, OK
Sterling College, KS
Trevecca Nazarene College, TN

CHILD PSYCHOLOGY/CHILD DEVELOPMENT
Bluffton College, OH
Fresno Pacific College, CA
Oklahoma Baptist University, OK
Olivet Nazarene University, IL
Pacific Christian College, CA
Point Loma Nazarene College, CA
Sioux Falls College, SD
Southern Nazarene University, OK

CHILDREN'S MINISTRY
Pacific Christian College, CA

CHORAL MUSIC
Northwest College, WA

CHRISTIAN EDUCATION
Northwestern College, IA

CIVIL ENGINEERING
Bethel College, IN
Calvin College, MI
Geneva College, PA
George Fox College, OR

CIVIL ENGINEERING TECHNOLOGY
Messiah College, PA

CLASSICS
Calvin College, MI

CLINICAL PSYCHOLOGY
Messiah College, PA
Redeemer College, ON

COMMERCIAL ART
Bethel College, IN
Biola University, CA
Bluffton College, OH
Campbell University, NC
Grace College, IN
John Brown University, AR
Sioux Falls College, SD
Southern Nazarene University, OK

COMMUNICATION
Anderson University, IN
Azusa Pacific University, CA
Bartlesville Wesleyan College, OK
Bethel College, IN
Bethel College, KS
Bethel College, MN
Biola University, CA
Bluffton College, OH
Bryan College, TN
California Baptist College, CA
Calvin College, MI
Campbellsville College, KY
Campbell University, NC
Cedarville College, OH
Colorado Christian University, CO
Cornerstone College, MI
Dordt College, IA
Eastern College, PA
Eastern Nazarene College, MA
Evangel College, MO
Fresno Pacific College, CA
Geneva College, PA
George Fox College, OR
Goshen College, IN
Grace College, IN
Grand Canyon University, AZ
Greenville College, IL
Houghton College, NY
Huntington College, IN
Indiana Wesleyan University, IN
John Brown University, AR
Judson College, IL
Lee College, TN
Malone College, OH
Master's College and Seminary, CA
Messiah College, PA
MidAmerica Nazarene College, KS
Milligan College, TN
Mississippi College, MS
Montreat-Anderson College, NC
Mount Vernon Nazarene College, OH
North Park College, IL
Northwest Christian College, OR
Northwestern College, IA
Northwestern College, MN

Nyack College, NY
Oklahoma Baptist University, OK
Olivet Nazarene University, IL
Pacific Christian College, CA
Palm Beach Atlantic College, FL
Point Loma Nazarene College, CA
Roberts Wesleyan College, NY
Seattle Pacific University, WA
Sioux Falls College, SD
Southern California College, CA
Southern Nazarene University, OK
Spring Arbor College, MI
Sterling College, KS
Taylor University, IN
Trevecca Nazarene College, TN
Trinity Christian College, IL
Trinity College, IL
Trinity Western University, BC
Union University, TN
Warner Southern College, FL
Westmont College, CA
Wheaton College, IL
Whitworth College, WA

COMMUNITY SERVICES
Eastern Mennonite University, VA
Western Baptist College, OR

COMPUTER ENGINEERING
Eastern Nazarene College, MA
George Fox College, OR
LeTourneau University, TX

COMPUTER INFORMATION SYSTEMS
Bartlesville Wesleyan College, OK
Biola University, CA
Campbellsville College, KY
Campbell University, NC
Cedarville College, OH
Colorado Christian University, CO
Cornerstone College, MI
Eastern Mennonite University, VA
Eastern Nazarene College, MA
George Fox College, OR
Goshen College, IN
Indiana Wesleyan University, IN
Judson College, IL
Lee College, TN
Messiah College, PA
Northwestern College, MN
Northwest Nazarene College, ID
Oklahoma Baptist University, OK
Olivet Nazarene University, IL
Palm Beach Atlantic College, FL
Sioux Falls College, SD
Southern Nazarene University, OK
Taylor University, IN
Trevecca Nazarene College, TN
Trinity College, IL
Union University, TN

COMPUTER MANAGEMENT
Dallas Baptist University, TX
Oklahoma Baptist University, OK

COMPUTER PROGRAMMING
Biola University, CA
Eastern Mennonite University, VA
Northwest Nazarene College, ID
Southern Nazarene University, OK
Taylor University, IN

COMPUTER SCIENCE
Anderson University, IN
Asbury College, KY
Azusa Pacific University, CA
Belhaven College, MS
Bethel College, IN
Bethel College, MN
Biola University, CA
Bluffton College, OH
Bryan College, TN
Calvin College, MI
Campbell University, NC
Covenant College, GA
Dallas Baptist University, TX
Dordt College, IA
Eastern Mennonite University, VA
Eastern Nazarene College, MA
Evangel College, MO
Fresno Pacific College, CA
Geneva College, PA
George Fox College, OR
Gordon College, MA
Goshen College, IN
Grand Canyon University, AZ
Greenville College, IL
Huntington College, IN
Judson College, IL
The King's College, NY
LeTourneau University, TX
Malone College, OH
Messiah College, PA
MidAmerica Nazarene College, KS
Milligan College, TN
Mississippi College, MS
Mount Vernon Nazarene College, OH
Northwestern College, IA
Northwest Nazarene College, ID
Oklahoma Baptist University, OK
Olivet Nazarene University, IL
Point Loma Nazarene College, CA
Roberts Wesleyan College, NY
Seattle Pacific University, WA
Sioux Falls College, SD
Southern Nazarene University, OK
Spring Arbor College, MI
Sterling College, KS
Tabor College, KS
Taylor University, IN
Trevecca Nazarene College, TN
Trinity Christian College, IL
Trinity Western University, BC
Union University, TN
Westmont College, CA
Wheaton College, IL
Whitworth College, WA

COMPUTER TECHNOLOGIES
LeTourneau University, TX
Mount Vernon Nazarene College, OH

CONSTRUCTION ENGINEERING
John Brown University, AR

CONSTRUCTION MANAGEMENT
John Brown University, AR

CORRECTIONS
Oklahoma Baptist University, OK

CREATIVE WRITING
Bethel College, MN
Eastern College, PA

Houghton College, NY
Indiana Wesleyan University, IN
Taylor University, IN

CRIMINAL JUSTICE
Anderson University, IN
Bluffton College, OH
Calvin College, MI
Campbellsville College, KY
Cedarville College, OH
Central Wesleyan College, SC
Dallas Baptist University, TX
Evangel College, MO
Grace College, IN
Grand Canyon University, AZ
Indiana Wesleyan University, IN
Mississippi College, MS
Mount Vernon Nazarene College, OH
Oklahoma Baptist University, OK
Olivet Nazarene University, IL
Roberts Wesleyan College, NY
Southern Nazarene University, OK
Sterling College, KS
Taylor University, IN
Taylor University, Fort Wayne Campus, IN

DATA PROCESSING
Campbellsville College, KY
Campbell University, NC
Eastern Mennonite University, VA
Mount Vernon Nazarene College, OH
Northwest Nazarene College, ID
Southern Nazarene University, OK
Union University, TN

DENTAL SERVICES
Union University, TN

(PRE)DENTISTRY SEQUENCE
Anderson University, IN
Belhaven College, MS
Bethel College, IN
Bethel College, KS
Bethel College, MN
Calvin College, MI
Campbellsville College, KY
Campbell University, NC
Cedarville College, OH
Dallas Baptist University, TX
Dordt College, IA
Eastern Mennonite University, VA
Eastern Nazarene College, MA
Evangel College, MO
George Fox College, OR
Goshen College, IN
Grand Canyon University, AZ
Greenville College, IL
Houghton College, NY
Huntington College, IN
Indiana Wesleyan University, IN
King College, TN
LeTourneau University, TX
Malone College, OH
Milligan College, TN
Mississippi College, MS
Mount Vernon Nazarene College, OH
North Park College, IL
Northwestern College, IA
Northwest Nazarene College, ID
Oklahoma Baptist University, OK
Olivet Nazarene University, IL
Palm Beach Atlantic College, FL
Point Loma Nazarene College, CA
Redeemer College, ON

(PRE)DENTISTRY SEQUENCE (continued)

Roberts Wesleyan College, NY
Sioux Falls College, SD
Southern Nazarene University, OK
Sterling College, KS
Tabor College, KS
Taylor University, IN
Trinity Christian College, IL
Trinity Western University, BC
Union University, TN
Westmont College, CA
Whitworth College, WA

DIETETICS

Bluffton College, OH
Goshen College, IN
Messiah College, PA
Northwest Nazarene College, ID
Olivet Nazarene University, IL
Point Loma Nazarene College, CA
Seattle Pacific University, WA

DRAFTING AND DESIGN

LeTourneau University, TX

DRAMA THERAPY

Northwest Nazarene College, ID

EARLY CHILDHOOD EDUCATION

Anderson University, IN
Bethel College, IN
Bethel College, KS
Bethel College, MN
Bluffton College, OH
Calvin College, MI
Campbell University, NC
Cedarville College, OH
Central Wesleyan College, SC
Dallas Baptist University, TX
Eastern Mennonite University, VA
Eastern Nazarene College, MA
Erskine College, SC
Evangel College, MO
Gordon College, MA
Goshen College, IN
Greenville College, IL
Houghton College, NY
John Brown University, AR
The King's College, NY
Malone College, OH
Messiah College, PA
MidAmerica Nazarene College, KS
Milligan College, TN
Mount Vernon Nazarene College, OH
North Park College, IL
Nyack College, NY
Olivet Nazarene University, IL
Pacific Christian College, CA
Palm Beach Atlantic College, FL
Sioux Falls College, SD
Southern Nazarene University, OK
Spring Arbor College, MI
Taylor University, IN
Taylor University, Fort Wayne Campus, IN
Trevecca Nazarene College, TN
Union University, TN

EARTH SCIENCE

Campbell University, NC
Olivet Nazarene University, IL

ECONOMICS

Anderson University, IN
Bethel College, IN
Bethel College, KS
Bethel College, MN
Biola University, CA
Bluffton College, OH
Calvin College, MI
Campbellsville College, KY
Campbell University, NC
Cedarville College, OH
Dallas Baptist University, TX
George Fox College, OR
Gordon College, MA
Goshen College, IN
Grand Canyon University, AZ
Greenville College, IL
Huntington College, IN
Indiana Wesleyan University, IN
King College, TN
Mississippi College, MS
Montreat-Anderson College, NC
North Park College, IL
Northwestern College, IA
Oklahoma Baptist University, OK
Olivet Nazarene University, IL
Palm Beach Atlantic College, FL
Point Loma Nazarene College, CA
Seattle Pacific University, WA
Sioux Falls College, SD
Southern Nazarene University, OK
Taylor University, IN
Trinity College, IL
Union University, TN
Westmont College, CA
Wheaton College, IL
Whitworth College, WA

EDUCATION

Anderson University, IN
Asbury College, KY
Azusa Pacific University, CA
Bartlesville Wesleyan College, OK
Bethel College, IN
Bethel College, MN
Biola University, CA
Bluffton College, OH
California Baptist College, CA
Calvin College, MI
Campbell University, NC
Cedarville College, OH
Central Wesleyan College, SC
Cornerstone College, MI
Dallas Baptist University, TX
Dordt College, IA
Eastern Mennonite University, VA
Eastern Nazarene College, MA
Evangel College, MO
Fresno Pacific College, CA
Geneva College, PA
George Fox College, OR
Goshen College, IN
Greenville College, IL
Houghton College, NY
Huntington College, IN
Indiana Wesleyan University, IN
John Brown University, AR
Judson College, IL
King College, TN
The King's College, NY
Lee College, TN
Malone College, OH
Master's College and Seminary, CA
Messiah College, PA

Milligan College, TN
Mississippi College, MS
Montreat-Anderson College, NC
Mount Vernon Nazarene College, OH
North Park College, IL
Northwestern College, MN
Northwest Nazarene College, ID
Nyack College, NY
Oklahoma Baptist University, OK
Olivet Nazarene University, IL
Palm Beach Atlantic College, FL
Redeemer College, ON
Roberts Wesleyan College, NY
Seattle Pacific University, WA
Simpson College, CA
Sioux Falls College, SD
Southern California College, CA
Southern Nazarene University, OK
Sterling College, KS
Tabor College, KS
Taylor University, IN
Trevecca Nazarene College, TN
Trinity Christian College, IL
Trinity College, IL
Trinity Western University, BC
Union University, TN
Warner Pacific College, OR
Westmont College, CA

EDUCATIONAL ADMINISTRATION

Campbell University, NC

ELECTRICAL ENGINEERING

Bethel College, IN
Calvin College, MI
Cedarville College, OH
Eastern Nazarene College, MA
Geneva College, PA
George Fox College, OR
John Brown University, AR
LeTourneau University, TX
Seattle Pacific University, WA

ELECTRICAL ENGINEERING TECHNOLOGY

LeTourneau University, TX

ELEMENTARY EDUCATION

Anderson University, IN
Asbury College, KY
Bartlesville Wesleyan College, OK
Belhaven College, MS
Bethel College, IN
Bethel College, KS
Bethel College, MN
Biola University, CA
Bluffton College, OH
Bryan College, TN
California Baptist College, CA
Calvin College, MI
Campbellsville College, KY
Campbell University, NC
Cedarville College, OH
Central Wesleyan College, SC
Colorado Christian University, CO
Cornerstone College, MI
Covenant College, GA
Dallas Baptist University, TX
Dordt College, IA
Eastern College, PA
Eastern Mennonite University, VA
Eastern Nazarene College, MA

Erskine College, SC
Evangel College, MO
Fresno Pacific College, CA
Geneva College, PA
George Fox College, OR
Gordon College, MA
Goshen College, IN
Grace College, IN
Grand Canyon University, AZ
Greenville College, IL
Houghton College, NY
Huntington College, IN
Indiana Wesleyan University, IN
John Brown University, AR
Judson College, IL
King College, TN
The King's College, NY
Lee College, TN
Malone College, OH
Master's College and Seminary, CA
Messiah College, PA
MidAmerica Nazarene College, KS
Milligan College, TN
Mississippi College, MS
Mount Vernon Nazarene College, OH
North Park College, IL
Northwest College of the Assemblies of
   God, WA
Northwestern College, IA
Northwestern College, MN
Northwest Nazarene College, ID
Nyack College, NY
Oklahoma Baptist University, OK
Olivet Nazarene University, IL
Pacific Christian College, CA
Palm Beach Atlantic College, FL
Redeemer College, ON
Roberts Wesleyan College, NY
Seattle Pacific University, WA
Simpson College, CA
Sioux Falls College, SD
Southern California College, CA
Southern Nazarene University, OK
Spring Arbor College, MI
Sterling College, KS
Tabor College, KS
Taylor University, IN
Taylor University, Fort Wayne Campus, IN
Trevecca Nazarene College, TN
Trinity Christian College, IL
Trinity College, IL
Trinity Western University, BC
Union University, TN
Warner Pacific College, OR
Warner Southern College, FL
Western Baptist College, OR
Westmont College, CA
Wheaton College, IL
Whitworth College, WA

ENGINEERING (GENERAL)
Calvin College, MI
Dordt College, IA
Geneva College, PA
George Fox College, OR
John Brown University, AR
LeTourneau University, TX
Milligan College, TN
Olivet Nazarene University, IL
Southern Nazarene University, OK
Westmont College, CA
Wheaton College, IL

ENGINEERING AND APPLIED SCIENCES
George Fox College, OR
Seattle Pacific University, WA

ENGINEERING DESIGN
LeTourneau University, TX

ENGINEERING MANAGEMENT
John Brown University, AR

ENGINEERING MECHANICS
Cedarville College, OH

ENGINEERING PHYSICS
Eastern Nazarene College, MA
Northwest Nazarene College, ID
Olivet Nazarene University, IL
Point Loma Nazarene College, CA
Westmont College, CA

ENGINEERING SCIENCES
Bethel College, IN
Dordt College, IA
George Fox College, OR
Olivet Nazarene University, IL

(PRE)ENGINEERING SEQUENCE
Anderson University, IN
Belhaven College, MS
Bethel College, MN
Campbellsville College, KY
Campbell University, NC
Covenant College, GA
Eastern Mennonite University, VA
Houghton College, NY
Huntington College, IN
Indiana Wesleyan University, IN
Malone College, OH
Mount Vernon Nazarene College, OH
Northwestern College, MN
Northwest Nazarene College, ID
Sioux Falls College, SD
Tabor College, KS
Trevecca Nazarene College, TN

ENGINEERING TECHNOLOGY
John Brown University, AR
LeTourneau University, TX

ENGLISH
Anderson University, IN
Asbury College, KY
Atlantic Baptist College, NB
Azusa Pacific University, CA
Bartlesville Wesleyan College, OK
Belhaven College, MS
Bethel College, IN
Bethel College, KS
Bethel College, MN
Biola University, CA
Bluffton College, OH
Bryan College, TN
California Baptist College, CA
Calvin College, MI
Campbellsville College, KY
Campbell University, NC
Cedarville College, OH
Central Wesleyan College, SC
Colorado Christian University, CO
Cornerstone College, MI
Covenant College, GA

Dallas Baptist University, TX
Dordt College, IA
Eastern Mennonite University, VA
Eastern Nazarene College, MA
Erskine College, SC
Evangel College, MO
Fresno Pacific College, CA
Geneva College, PA
George Fox College, OR
Gordon College, MA
Goshen College, IN
Grace College, IN
Grand Canyon University, AZ
Greenville College, IL
Houghton College, NY
Huntington College, IN
Indiana Wesleyan University, IN
John Brown University, AR
Judson College, IL
King College, TN
The King's College, NY
The King's University College, AB
Lee College, TN
LeTourneau University, TX
Malone College, OH
Master's College and Seminary, CA
Messiah College, PA
MidAmerica Nazarene College, KS
Milligan College, TN
Mississippi College, MS
Montreat-Anderson College, NC
Mount Vernon Nazarene College, OH
North Park College, IL
Northwest College, WA
Northwestern College, IA
Northwestern College, MN
Northwest Nazarene College, ID
Nyack College, NY
Oklahoma Baptist University, OK
Olivet Nazarene University, IL
Pacific Christian College, CA
Palm Beach Atlantic College, FL
Redeemer College, ON
Roberts Wesleyan College, NY
Seattle Pacific University, WA
Simpson College, CA
Sioux Falls College, SD
Southern California College, CA
Southern Nazarene University, OK
Spring Arbor College, MI
Sterling College, KS
Tabor College, KS
Taylor University, IN
Trevecca Nazarene College, TN
Trinity Christian College, IL
Trinity College, IL
Trinity Western University, BC
Union University, TN
Warner Pacific College, OR
Warner Southern College, FL
Western Baptist College, OR
Westmont College, CA
Whitworth College, WA

ENVIRONMENTAL BIOLOGY
Cedarville College, OH
Grand Canyon University, AZ
Greenville College, IL
Tabor College, KS
Taylor University, IN

ENVIRONMENTAL SCIENCES
Bethel College, KS
Calvin College, MI

ENVIRONMENTAL SCIENCES (continued)
Dordt College, IA
Northwestern College, IA
Olivet Nazarene University, IL
Taylor University, IN
Wheaton College, IL

ENVIRONMENTAL STUDIES
Montreat-Anderson College, NC
Southern Nazarene University, OK
Taylor University, IN

EUROPEAN STUDIES
Biola University, CA
Calvin College, MI
Seattle Pacific University, WA

EXPERIMENTAL PSYCHOLOGY
Messiah College, PA
Redeemer College, ON

FAMILY AND CONSUMER STUDIES
Anderson University, IN
Northwest Nazarene College, ID
Seattle Pacific University, WA
Southern Nazarene University, OK
Western Baptist College, OR

FAMILY SERVICES
Goshen College, IN
Messiah College, PA
Northwest Nazarene College, ID
Olivet Nazarene University, IL
Point Loma Nazarene College, CA
Southern Nazarene University, OK

FASHION DESIGN AND TECHNOLOGY
Bluffton College, OH
Campbell University, NC

FASHION MERCHANDISING
Bluffton College, OH
Campbell University, NC
George Fox College, OR
Northwest Nazarene College, ID
Olivet Nazarene University, IL

FILM STUDIES
Biola University, CA
Calvin College, MI
Olivet Nazarene University, IL

FINANCE/BANKING
Anderson University, IN
Bethel College, MN
Campbell University, NC
Cedarville College, OH
Dallas Baptist University, TX
Grand Canyon University, AZ
Indiana Wesleyan University, IN
Master's College and Seminary, CA
North Park College, IL
Northwestern College, MN
Oklahoma Baptist University, OK
Olivet Nazarene University, IL
Palm Beach Atlantic College, FL
Southern California College, CA
Union University, TN
Western Baptist College, OR

FLIGHT TRAINING
LeTourneau University, TX

FOOD SCIENCES
Olivet Nazarene University, IL
Seattle Pacific University, WA

FOOD SERVICES MANAGEMENT
Campbell University, NC
Olivet Nazarene University, IL

FRENCH
Anderson University, IN
Asbury College, KY
Bethel College, IN
Calvin College, MI
Campbell University, NC
Eastern College, PA
Eastern Mennonite University, VA
Eastern Nazarene College, MA
Erskine College, SC
Gordon College, MA
Grace College, IN
Greenville College, IL
Houghton College, NY
King College, TN
The King's College, NY
Messiah College, PA
North Park College, IL
Northwestern College, IA
Oklahoma Baptist University, OK
Redeemer College, ON
Spring Arbor College, MI
Taylor University, IN
Union University, TN
Westmont College, CA
Wheaton College, IL
Whitworth College, WA

FUNERAL SERVICE
Milligan College, TN

GEOCHEMISTRY
Olivet Nazarene University, IL

GEOGRAPHY
Calvin College, MI
Messiah College, PA
Trinity Western University, BC

GEOLOGY
Calvin College, MI
Olivet Nazarene University, IL
Wheaton College, IL

GEOPHYSICS
Olivet Nazarene University, IL

GERMAN
Anderson University, IN
Bethel College, KS
Calvin College, MI
Dordt College, IA
Eastern Mennonite University, VA
Goshen College, IN
Grace College, IN
Messiah College, PA
North Park College, IL
Oklahoma Baptist University, OK
Southern Nazarene University, OK
Wheaton College, IL

GERMANIC LANGUAGES AND LITERATURE
Calvin College, MI

GERONTOLOGY
Bethel College, IN
Greenville College, IL
Roberts Wesleyan College, NY
Southern Nazarene University, OK

GRAPHIC ARTS
Anderson University, IN
Campbell University, NC
Grace College, IN
Grand Canyon University, AZ
Huntington College, IN
John Brown University, AR
Northwestern College, MN
Northwest Nazarene College, ID
Olivet Nazarene University, IL
Point Loma Nazarene College, CA
Roberts Wesleyan College, NY
Taylor University, IN

GREEK
Biola University, CA
Calvin College, MI
Central Wesleyan College, SC
Grace College, IN
Union University, TN

GUIDANCE AND COUNSELING
Geneva College, PA

HEALTH EDUCATION
Anderson University, IN
Bethel College, IN
Bethel College, KS
Bethel College, MN
Bluffton College, OH
Campbellsville College, KY
Campbell University, NC
Cedarville College, OH
Eastern College, PA
Eastern Mennonite University, VA
John Brown University, AR
Lee College, TN
Malone College, OH
MidAmerica Nazarene College, KS
Milligan College, TN
Northwest Nazarene College, ID
Sioux Falls College, SD
Southern Nazarene University, OK
Tabor College, KS
Trevecca Nazarene College, TN
Union University, TN

HEALTH SCIENCE
Asbury College, KY
Campbell University, NC
Covenant College, GA
Mount Vernon Nazarene College, OH
Northwest College of the Assemblies of God, WA
Northwestern College, IA
Northwest Nazarene College, ID
Southern Nazarene University, OK
Warner Pacific College, OR

HEALTH SERVICES ADMINISTRATION
Eastern College, PA

John Brown University, AR
Oklahoma Baptist University, OK

HISPANIC STUDIES
Goshen College, IN

HISTORY
Anderson University, IN
Asbury College, KY
Atlantic Baptist College, NB
Azusa Pacific University, CA
Bartlesville Wesleyan College, OK
Belhaven College, MS
Bethel College, IN
Bethel College, KS
Bethel College, MN
Biola University, CA
Bluffton College, OH
Bryan College, TN
California Baptist College, CA
Calvin College, MI
Campbellsville College, KY
Campbell University, NC
Cedarville College, OH
Central Wesleyan College, SC
Colorado Christian University, CO
Cornerstone College, MI
Covenant College, GA
Dallas Baptist University, TX
Dordt College, IA
Eastern College, PA
Eastern Mennonite University, VA
Eastern Nazarene College, MA
Erskine College, SC
Evangel College, MO
Fresno Pacific College, CA
Geneva College, PA
George Fox College, OR
Gordon College, MA
Goshen College, IN
Grand Canyon University, AZ
Greenville College, IL
Houghton College, NY
Huntington College, IN
Indiana Wesleyan University, IN
John Brown University, AR
Judson College, IL
King College, TN
The King's College, NY
The King's University College, AB
Lee College, TN
LeTourneau University, TX
Malone College, OH
Master's College and Seminary, CA
Messiah College, PA
MidAmerica Nazarene College, KS
Milligan College, TN
Mississippi College, MS
Montreat-Anderson College, NC
Mount Vernon Nazarene College, OH
North Park College, IL
Northwest College, WA
Northwestern College, IA
Northwest Nazarene College, ID
Nyack College, NY
Oklahoma Baptist University, OK
Olivet Nazarene University, IL
Palm Beach Atlantic College, FL
Point Loma Nazarene College, CA
Redeemer College, ON
Roberts Wesleyan College, NY
Seattle Pacific University, WA
Simpson College, CA
Sioux Falls College, SD

Southern California College, CA
Southern Nazarene University, OK
Spring Arbor College, MI
Sterling College, KS
Tabor College, KS
Taylor University, IN
Trevecca Nazarene College, TN
Trinity Christian College, IL
Trinity College, IL
Trinity Western University, BC
Union University, TN
Warner Pacific College, OR
Westmont College, CA
Wheaton College, IL
Whitworth College, WA

HOME ECONOMICS
Bluffton College, OH
Campbell University, NC
George Fox College, OR
Master's College and Seminary, CA
Messiah College, PA
Mississippi College, MS
Mount Vernon Nazarene College, OH
Northwest Nazarene College, ID
Olivet Nazarene University, IL
Point Loma Nazarene College, CA
Sterling College, KS

HOME ECONOMICS EDUCATION
Bluffton College, OH
Campbell University, NC
George Fox College, OR
Mississippi College, MS
Mount Vernon Nazarene College, OH
Northwest Nazarene College, ID
Olivet Nazarene University, IL
Point Loma Nazarene College, CA
Sterling College, KS

HUMAN DEVELOPMENT
Lee College, TN
Warner Pacific College, OR

HUMAN ECOLOGY
Bethel College, KS

HUMANITIES
Belhaven College, MS
Biola University, CA
Bluffton College, OH
Calvin College, MI
Colorado Christian University, CO
Fresno Pacific College, CA
Houghton College, NY
Messiah College, PA
Milligan College, TN
Northwestern College, IA
Oklahoma Baptist University, OK
Redeemer College, ON
Roberts Wesleyan College, NY
Sioux Falls College, SD
Southern California College, CA
Tabor College, KS
Trevecca Nazarene College, TN
Trinity College, IL
Trinity Western University, BC
Western Baptist College, OR

HUMAN RESOURCES
Bethel College, IN
Geneva College, PA

George Fox College, OR
Grand Canyon University, AZ
Messiah College, PA
MidAmerica Nazarene College, KS
Northwestern College, MN
Olivet Nazarene University, IL
Point Loma Nazarene College, CA
Roberts Wesleyan College, NY
Simpson College, CA
Southern Nazarene University, OK
Trevecca Nazarene College, TN
Trinity College, IL

HUMAN SERVICES
Milligan College, TN
Montreat-Anderson College, NC
Mount Vernon Nazarene College, OH
Northwest Nazarene College, ID
Trinity Western University, BC

INDUSTRIAL ADMINISTRATION
LeTourneau University, TX

INDUSTRIAL ENGINEERING
Geneva College, PA

INFORMATION SCIENCE
Biola University, CA
Oklahoma Baptist University, OK
Southern Nazarene University, OK

INSTRUMENTAL MUSIC
Southern Nazarene University, OK

INTERDISCIPLINARY STUDIES
Calvin College, MI
Cornerstone College, MI
Covenant College, GA
Dallas Baptist University, TX
John Brown University, AR
Northwest Christian College, OR
Northwest College of the Assemblies of
    God, WA
Northwest Nazarene College, ID
Nyack College, NY
Oklahoma Baptist University, OK
Olivet Nazarene University, IL
Seattle Pacific University, WA
Sioux Falls College, SD
Union University, TN
Western Baptist College, OR
Wheaton College, IL

INTERIOR DESIGN
Campbell University, NC
George Fox College, OR
Mississippi College, MS
Northwest Nazarene College, ID
Southern Nazarene University, OK

INTERNATIONAL BUSINESS
Campbell University, NC
Cedarville College, OH
Eastern Mennonite University, VA
Grand Canyon University, AZ
King College, TN
MidAmerica Nazarene College, KS
North Park College, IL
Northwestern College, MN
Palm Beach Atlantic College, FL
Taylor University, IN
Whitworth College, WA

INTERNATIONAL ECONOMICS
Cedarville College, OH
Taylor University, IN

INTERNATIONAL RELATIONS
Bethel College, MN
Gordon College, MA

INTERNATIONAL STUDIES
Azusa Pacific University, CA
Bethel College, KS
Bethel College, MN
Biola University, CA
Campbell University, NC
Cedarville College, OH
George Fox College, OR
Houghton College, NY
John Brown University, AR
Lee College, TN
North Park College, IL
Northwest Nazarene College, ID
Southern Nazarene University, OK
Tabor College, KS
Taylor University, IN
Westmont College, CA
Whitworth College, WA

INTERIOR DESIGN
George Fox College, OR

JAPANESE
Calvin College, MI

JOURNALISM
Asbury College, KY
Bethel College, IN
Biola University, CA
Calvin College, MI
Campbell University, NC
Dordt College, IA
Evangel College, MO
Geneva College, PA
Goshen College, IN
John Brown University, AR
Malone College, OH
Messiah College, PA
Mississippi College, MS
Northwestern College, MN
Oklahoma Baptist University, OK
Olivet Nazarene University, IL
Point Loma Nazarene College, CA
Southern California College, CA
Southern Nazarene University, OK
Tabor College, KS
Taylor University, IN
Union University, TN
Wheaton College, IL
Whitworth College, WA

LABORATORY TECHNOLOGIES
Evangel College, MO
Southern Nazarene University, OK

LATIN
Calvin College, MI

LATIN AMERICAN STUDIES
Geneva College, PA

LAW ENFORCEMENT/POLICE SCIENCES
Indiana Wesleyan University, IN
Mississippi College, MS

(PRE)LAW SEQUENCE
Anderson University, IN
Bartlesville Wesleyan College, OK
Belhaven College, MS
Bethel College, KS
Bethel College, MN
Biola University, CA
Bluffton College, OH
Calvin College, MI
Campbellsville College, KY
Campbell University, NC
Cedarville College, OH
Cornerstone College, MI
Covenant College, GA
Dallas Baptist University, TX
Eastern Mennonite University, VA
Eastern Nazarene College, MA
Evangel College, MO
Fresno Pacific College, CA
Geneva College, PA
George Fox College, OR
Goshen College, IN
Grace College, IN
Grand Canyon University, AZ
Greenville College, IL
Houghton College, NY
Huntington College, IN
Indiana Wesleyan University, IN
John Brown University, AR
Judson College, IL
King College, TN
LeTourneau University, TX
Malone College, OH
Messiah College, PA
Mississippi College, MS
Mount Vernon Nazarene College, OH
North Park College, IL
Northwestern College, IA
Northwest Nazarene College, ID
Oklahoma Baptist University, OK
Olivet Nazarene University, IL
Palm Beach Atlantic College, FL
Point Loma Nazarene College, CA
Redeemer College, ON
Sioux Falls College, SD
Southern California College, CA
Southern Nazarene University, OK
Sterling College, KS
Tabor College, KS
Taylor University, IN
Trevecca Nazarene College, TN
Trinity Western University, BC
Union University, TN
Western Baptist College, OR
Westmont College, CA
Whitworth College, WA

LEGAL SECRETARIAL STUDIES
Northwestern College, MN
Tabor College, KS

LIBERAL ARTS/GENERAL STUDIES
Anderson University, IN
Atlantic Baptist College, NB
Azusa Pacific University, CA
Bartlesville Wesleyan College, OK
Bethel College, IN

Bethel College, MN
Biola University, CA
Bluffton College, OH
Bryan College, TN
California Baptist College, CA
Calvin College, MI
Campbell University, NC
Central Wesleyan College, SC
Colorado Christian University, CO
Dallas Baptist University, TX
Eastern College, PA
Eastern Mennonite University, VA
Eastern Nazarene College, MA
Fresno Pacific College, CA
George Fox College, OR
Goshen College, IN
Grand Canyon University, AZ
Greenville College, IL
Indiana Wesleyan University, IN
John Brown University, AR
The King's College, NY
Malone College, OH
Master's College and Seminary, CA
Messiah College, PA
MidAmerica Nazarene College, KS
Milligan College, TN
Montreat-Anderson College, NC
Mount Vernon Nazarene College, OH
Northwest Christian College, OR
Northwest College of the Assemblies of God, WA
Northwestern College, MN
Northwest Nazarene College, ID
Nyack College, NY
Olivet Nazarene University, IL
Pacific Christian College, CA
Point Loma Nazarene College, CA
Redeemer College, ON
Seattle Pacific University, WA
Simpson College, CA
Sioux Falls College, SD
Southern Nazarene University, OK
Spring Arbor College, MI
Sterling College, KS
Taylor University, IN
Taylor University, Fort Wayne Campus, IN
Trevecca Nazarene College, TN
Trinity College, IL
Trinity Western University, BC
Warner Pacific College, OR
Warner Southern College, FL
Western Baptist College, OR
Westmont College, CA

LINGUISTICS
Bartlesville Wesleyan College, OK
Calvin College, MI
Judson College, IL
Trinity Western University, BC

LITERATURE
Bethel College, MN
Biola University, CA
Calvin College, MI
Eastern College, PA
Fresno Pacific College, CA
George Fox College, OR
Grand Canyon University, AZ
Houghton College, NY
Judson College, IL
Montreat-Anderson College, NC
Mount Vernon Nazarene College, OH
North Park College, IL
Northwestern College, MN

Olivet Nazarene University, IL
Point Loma Nazarene College, CA
Redeemer College, ON
Southern Nazarene University, OK
Taylor University, IN
Westmont College, CA
Wheaton College, IL

MANAGEMENT INFORMATION SYSTEMS

Azusa Pacific University, CA
Bethel College, MN
Biola University, CA
Dallas Baptist University, TX
Dordt College, IA
Fresno Pacific College, CA
Grace College, IN
Greenville College, IL
Oklahoma Baptist University, OK
Point Loma Nazarene College, CA
Sioux Falls College, SD
Southern Nazarene University, OK
Taylor University, IN

MANUFACTURING ENGINEERING

Eastern Nazarene College, MA

MARINE BIOLOGY

Union University, TN

MARKETING/RETAILING/ MERCHANDISING

Anderson University, IN
Azusa Pacific University, CA
Biola University, CA
Cedarville College, OH
Cornerstone College, MI
Dallas Baptist University, TX
Evangel College, MO
Grand Canyon University, AZ
Greenville College, IL
LeTourneau University, TX
Messiah College, PA
Montreat-Anderson College, NC
Mount Vernon Nazarene College, OH
North Park College, IL
Northwestern College, MN
Oklahoma Baptist University, OK
Olivet Nazarene University, IL
Palm Beach Atlantic College, FL
Sioux Falls College, SD
Southern California College, CA
Southern Nazarene University, OK
Trinity College, IL
Union University, TN

MARRIAGE AND FAMILY COUNSELING

Oklahoma Baptist University, OK

MATHEMATICS

Anderson University, IN
Asbury College, KY
Azusa Pacific University, CA
Bartlesville Wesleyan College, OK
Belhaven College, MS
Bethel College, IN
Bethel College, KS
Bethel College, MN
Biola University, CA
Bluffton College, OH

Bryan College, TN
Calvin College, MI
Campbellsville College, KY
Campbell University, NC
Cedarville College, OH
Central Wesleyan College, SC
Colorado Christian University, CO
Dallas Baptist University, TX
Dordt College, IA
Eastern College, PA
Eastern Mennonite University, VA
Eastern Nazarene College, MA
Erskine College, SC
Evangel College, MO
Fresno Pacific College, CA
Geneva College, PA
George Fox College, OR
Gordon College, MA
Goshen College, IN
Grace College, IN
Grand Canyon University, AZ
Greenville College, IL
Houghton College, NY
Huntington College, IN
Indiana Wesleyan University, IN
John Brown University, AR
Judson College, IL
King College, TN
The King's College, NY
Lee College, TN
LeTourneau University, TX
Malone College, OH
Master's College and Seminary, CA
Messiah College, PA
MidAmerica Nazarene College, KS
Milligan College, TN
Mississippi College, MS
Montreat-Anderson College, NC
Mount Vernon Nazarene College, OH
North Park College, IL
Northwestern College, IA
Northwestern College, MN
Northwest Nazarene College, ID
Oklahoma Baptist University, OK
Olivet Nazarene University, IL
Palm Beach Atlantic College, FL
Point Loma Nazarene College, CA
Redeemer College, ON
Roberts Wesleyan College, NY
Seattle Pacific University, WA
Sioux Falls College, SD
Southern California College, CA
Southern Nazarene University, OK
Spring Arbor College, MI
Sterling College, KS
Tabor College, KS
Taylor University, IN
Trevecca Nazarene College, TN
Trinity Christian College, IL
Trinity College, IL
Trinity Western University, BC
Union University, TN
Warner Pacific College, OR
Western Baptist College, OR
Westmont College, CA
Wheaton College, IL
Whitworth College, WA

MECHANICAL DESIGN TECHNOLOGY

LeTourneau University, TX

MECHANICAL ENGINEERING

Bethel College, IN
Calvin College, MI
Cedarville College, OH
Eastern Nazarene College, MA
Geneva College, PA
John Brown University, AR
LeTourneau University, TX

MECHANICAL ENGINEERING TECHNOLOGY

LeTourneau University, TX

MEDICAL ASSISTANT TECHNOLOGIES

Trevecca Nazarene College, TN

MEDICAL LABORATORY TECHNOLOGY

Houghton College, NY
Indiana Wesleyan University, IN
Oklahoma Baptist University, OK
Southern Nazarene University, OK
Taylor University, IN

MEDICAL SECRETARIAL STUDIES

Tabor College, KS
Trevecca Nazarene College, TN

MEDICAL TECHNOLOGY

Anderson University, IN
Asbury College, KY
Bluffton College, OH
Calvin College, MI
Campbellsville College, KY
Campbell University, NC
Cedarville College, OH
Central Wesleyan College, SC
Dordt College, IA
Eastern College, PA
Eastern Mennonite University, VA
Evangel College, MO
Geneva College, PA
Greenville College, IL
Houghton College, NY
Huntington College, IN
Indiana Wesleyan University, IN
John Brown University, AR
King College, TN
The King's College, NY
Lee College, TN
Malone College, OH
Messiah College, PA
Mississippi College, MS
Mount Vernon Nazarene College, OH
North Park College, IL
Northwestern College, IA
Northwest Nazarene College, ID
Olivet Nazarene University, IL
Roberts Wesleyan College, NY
Sioux Falls College, SD
Southern Nazarene University, OK
Tabor College, KS
Taylor University, IN
Trevecca Nazarene College, TN
Trinity Christian College, IL

(PRE)MEDICINE SEQUENCE

Anderson University, IN
Asbury College, KY
Bartlesville Wesleyan College, OK

(PRE)MEDICINE SEQUENCE (continued)

Belhaven College, MS
Bethel College, IN
Bethel College, KS
Bethel College, MN
Biola University, CA
Bluffton College, OH
Calvin College, MI
Campbellsville College, KY
Campbell University, NC
Cedarville College, OH
Covenant College, GA
Dallas Baptist University, TX
Dordt College, IA
Eastern Mennonite University, VA
Eastern Nazarene College, MA
Evangel College, MO
Fresno Pacific College, CA
Geneva College, PA
George Fox College, OR
Goshen College, IN
Grace College, IN
Grand Canyon University, AZ
Greenville College, IL
Houghton College, NY
Huntington College, IN
Indiana Wesleyan University, IN
John Brown University, AR
Judson College, IL
King College, TN
LeTourneau University, TX
Malone College, OH
Messiah College, PA
Milligan College, TN
Mississippi College, MS
Mount Vernon Nazarene College, OH
North Park College, IL
Northwestern College, IA
Northwest Nazarene College, ID
Oklahoma Baptist University, OK
Olivet Nazarene University, IL
Palm Beach Atlantic College, FL
Point Loma Nazarene College, CA
Redeemer College, ON
Sioux Falls College, SD
Southern California College, CA
Southern Nazarene University, OK
Sterling College, KS
Tabor College, KS
Taylor University, IN
Trevecca Nazarene College, TN
Trinity Christian College, IL
Trinity College, IL
Trinity Western University, BC
Union University, TN
Westmont College, CA
Whitworth College, WA

MENTAL HEALTH/ REHABILITATION COUNSELING

Evangel College, MO
Indiana Wesleyan University, IN

METALLURGICAL ENGINEERING

Bethel College, IN

MIDDLE SCHOOL EDUCATION

Biola University, CA
Campbell University, NC
Eastern Mennonite University, VA
Gordon College, MA
John Brown University, AR

Northwest College of the Assemblies of
God, WA
Seattle Pacific University, WA
Sioux Falls College, SD
Taylor University, IN

MILITARY SCIENCE

Campbell University, NC

MINISTRIES

Anderson University, IN
Asbury College, KY
Azusa Pacific University, CA
Bartlesville Wesleyan College, OK
Belhaven College, MS
Bethel College, IN
Bethel College, MN
Biola University, CA
Bluffton College, OH
Campbellsville College, KY
Central Wesleyan College, SC
Colorado Christian University, CO
Dallas Baptist University, TX
Eastern College, PA
Eastern Mennonite University, VA
Eastern Nazarene College, MA
Fresno Pacific College, CA
Geneva College, PA
George Fox College, OR
Gordon College, MA
Grace College, IN
Grand Canyon University, AZ
Greenville College, IL
Houghton College, NY
Huntington College, IN
Indiana Wesleyan University, IN
John Brown University, AR
LeTourneau University, TX
Malone College, OH
Master's College and Seminary, CA
MidAmerica Nazarene College, KS
Milligan College, TN
Northwest Christian College, OR
Northwest College of the Assemblies of
God, WA
Northwestern College, MN
Northwest Nazarene College, ID
Nyack College, NY
Oklahoma Baptist University, OK
Pacific Christian College, CA
Roberts Wesleyan College, NY
Simpson College, CA
Southern California College, CA
Southern Nazarene University, OK
Spring Arbor College, MI
Tabor College, KS
Taylor University, IN
Taylor University, Fort Wayne Campus, IN
Trevecca Nazarene College, TN
Warner Pacific College, OR
Warner Southern College, FL
Western Baptist College, OR
Westmont College, CA

MISSIONS

Huntingdon College, IN
Northwest Christian College, OR

MODERN LANGUAGES

Biola University, CA
Gordon College, MA
Greenville College, IL
The King's College, NY
Lee College, TN

Messiah College, PA
MidAmerica Nazarene College, KS
Mississippi College, MS
Mount Vernon Nazarene College, OH
North Park College, IL
Oklahoma Baptist University, OK
Olivet Nazarene University, IL
Redeemer College, ON
Southern Nazarene University, OK
Taylor University, IN
Westmont College, CA
Wheaton College, IL

MOLECULAR BIOLOGY

Bethel College, MN

MUSIC

Anderson University, IN
Asbury College, KY
Azusa Pacific University, CA
Belhaven College, MS
Bethel College, IN
Bethel College, KS
Bethel College, MN
Biola University, CA
Bluffton College, OH
Bryan College, TN
California Baptist College, CA
Calvin College, MI
Campbellsville College, KY
Campbell University, NC
Cedarville College, OH
Central Wesleyan College, SC
Colorado Christian University, CO
Cornerstone College, MI
Covenant College, GA
Dallas Baptist University, TX
Dordt College, IA
Eastern College, PA
Eastern Mennonite University, VA
Eastern Nazarene College, MA
Erskine College, SC
Evangel College, MO
Fresno Pacific College, CA
Geneva College, PA
George Fox College, OR
Gordon College, MA
Goshen College, IN
Grace College, IN
Grand Canyon University, AZ
Greenville College, IL
Houghton College, NY
Huntington College, IN
Indiana Wesleyan University, IN
John Brown University, AR
Judson College, IL
King College, TN
The King's College, NY
The King's University College, AB
Lee College, TN
Malone College, OH
Master's College and Seminary, CA
Messiah College, PA
MidAmerica Nazarene College, KS
Milligan College, TN
Mississippi College, MS
Mount Vernon Nazarene College, OH
North Park College, IL
Northwestern College, IA
Northwestern College, MN
Northwest Nazarene College, ID
Nyack College, NY
Oklahoma Baptist University, OK
Olivet Nazarene University, IL

Pacific Christian College, CA
Palm Beach Atlantic College, FL
Point Loma Nazarene College, CA
Redeemer College, ON
Roberts Wesleyan College, NY
Seattle Pacific University, WA
Simpson College, CA
Sioux Falls College, SD
Southern California College, CA
Southern Nazarene University, OK
Spring Arbor College, MI
Sterling College, KS
Tabor College, KS
Taylor University, IN
Taylor University, Fort Wayne Campus, IN
Trevecca Nazarene College, TN
Trinity Christian College, IL
Trinity College, IL
Trinity Western University, BC
Union University, TN
Warner Pacific College, OR
Warner Southern College, FL
Western Baptist College, OR
Westmont College, CA
Wheaton College, IL
Whitworth College, WA

MUSICAL INSTRUMENT TECHNOLOGY
Calvin College, MI

MUSIC BUSINESS
Anderson University, IN
Bryan College, TN
Geneva College, PA
Grand Canyon University, AZ
Indiana Wesleyan University, IN
Point Loma Nazarene College, CA
Sioux Falls College, SD
Southern Nazarene University, OK
Sterling College, KS
Trevecca Nazarene College, TN
Wheaton College, IL

MUSIC EDUCATION
Anderson University, IN
Asbury College, KY
Bethel College, IN
Bethel College, KS
Bethel College, MN
Biola University, CA
Bluffton College, OH
Bryan College, TN
Calvin College, MI
Campbellsville College, KY
Campbell University, NC
Cedarville College, OH
Central Wesleyan College, SC
Colorado Christian University, CO
Cornerstone College, MI
Covenant College, GA
Dallas Baptist University, TX
Dordt College, IA
Eastern Mennonite University, VA
Eastern Nazarene College, MA
Erskine College, SC
Evangel College, MO
Fresno Pacific College, CA
Geneva College, PA
George Fox College, OR
Gordon College, MA
Goshen College, IN
Grace College, IN
Grand Canyon University, AZ

Greenville College, IL
Houghton College, NY
Huntington College, IN
Indiana Wesleyan University, IN
John Brown University, AR
The King's College, NY
Lee College, TN
Malone College, OH
Master's College and Seminary, CA
Messiah College, PA
MidAmerica Nazarene College, KS
Milligan College, TN
Mississippi College, MS
Mount Vernon Nazarene College, OH
North Park College, IL
Northwestern College, IA
Northwestern College, MN
Northwest Nazarene College, ID
Nyack College, NY
Oklahoma Baptist University, OK
Olivet Nazarene University, IL
Palm Beach Atlantic College, FL
Point Loma Nazarene College, CA
Roberts Wesleyan College, NY
Seattle Pacific University, WA
Simpson College, CA
Sioux Falls College, SD
Southern California College, CA
Southern Nazarene University, OK
Sterling College, KS
Tabor College, KS
Taylor University, IN
Trevecca Nazarene College, TN
Trinity Christian College, IL
Trinity College, IL
Union University, TN
Warner Pacific College, OR
Warner Southern College, FL
Western Baptist College, OR
Wheaton College, IL
Whitworth College, WA

MUSIC HISTORY
Calvin College, MI
Wheaton College, IL

MUSIC THERAPY
Calvin College, MI

NATURAL RESOURCE MANAGEMENT
Huntington College, IN
Mount Vernon Nazarene College, OH

NATURAL SCIENCES
Bartlesville Wesleyan College, OK
Bethel College, KS
Calvin College, MI
Campbell University, NC
Covenant College, GA
Dordt College, IA
Erskine College, SC
Fresno Pacific College, CA
Goshen College, IN
Houghton College, NY
Lee College, TN
LeTourneau University, TX
Master's College and Seminary, CA
Messiah College, PA
Oklahoma Baptist University, OK
Olivet Nazarene University, IL
Redeemer College, ON
Roberts Wesleyan College, NY

Southern Nazarene University, OK
Sterling College, KS
Tabor College, KS
Taylor University, IN
Trevecca Nazarene College, TN
Trinity Western University, BC
Westmont College, CA

NURSING
Anderson University, IN
Asbury College, KY
Azusa Pacific University, CA
Bartlesville Wesleyan College, OK
Bethel College, IN
Bethel College, KS
Bethel College, MN
Biola University, CA
Calvin College, MI
Cedarville College, OH
Central Wesleyan College, SC
Covenant College, GA
Eastern College, PA
Eastern Mennonite University, VA
Goshen College, IN
Grand Canyon University, AZ
Indiana Wesleyan University, IN
Judson College, IL
The King's College, NY
Malone College, OH
Messiah College, PA
MidAmerica Nazarene College, KS
Milligan College, TN
Mississippi College, MS
Mount Vernon Nazarene College, OH
North Park College, IL
Nyack College, NY
Oklahoma Baptist University, OK
Olivet Nazarene University, IL
Point Loma Nazarene College, CA
Roberts Wesleyan College, NY
Seattle Pacific University, WA
Southern Nazarene University, OK
Trinity Christian College, IL
Trinity Western University, BC
Union University, TN
Wheaton College, IL
Whitworth College, WA

(PRE)NURSING SEQUENCE
Belhaven College, MS
Campbellsville College, KY

NUTRITION
Bluffton College, OH
Goshen College, IN
Seattle Pacific University, WA
Sterling College, KS

OCCUPATIONAL THERAPY
Calvin College, MI
Southern Nazarene University, OK

(PRE)OPTOMETRY SEQUENCE
Campbellsville College, KY

PAINTING/DRAWING
Biola University, CA
Judson College, IL
Northwest Nazarene College, ID
Trinity Christian College, IL

PARALEGAL STUDIES
Milligan College, TN
Mississippi College, MS

PASTORAL STUDIES
Anderson University, IN
Bethel College, IN
Biola University, CA
Campbellsville College, KY
Campbell University, NC
Cedarville College, OH
Central Wesleyan College, SC
Colorado Christian University, CO
Cornerstone College, MI
Dallas Baptist University, TX
Eastern Nazarene College, MA
Geneva College, PA
Greenville College, IL
Houghton College, NY
Indiana Wesleyan University, IN
John Brown University, AR
Lee College, TN
Messiah College, PA
Milligan College, TN
Northwest Christian College, OR
Northwest College of the Assemblies of
     God, WA
Northwestern College, MN
Northwest Nazarene College, ID
Nyack College, NY
Oklahoma Baptist University, OK
Olivet Nazarene University, IL
Pacific Christian College, CA
Point Loma Nazarene College, CA
Simpson College, CA
Sioux Falls College, SD
Southern California College, CA
Southern Nazarene University, OK
Taylor University, Fort Wayne Campus, IN
Trevecca Nazarene College, TN
Warner Pacific College, OR
Warner Southern College, FL
Western Baptist College, OR

PEACE STUDIES
Bethel College, KS
Bluffton College, OH
Whitworth College, WA

PHARMACY/PHARMACEUTICAL SCIENCES
Southern Nazarene University, OK

(PRE)PHARMACY SEQUENCE
Campbellsville College, KY

PHILOSOPHY
Anderson University, IN
Asbury College, KY
Azusa Pacific University, CA
Belhaven College, MS
Bethel College, IN
Bethel College, MN
Biola University, CA
Bluffton College, OH
Calvin College, MI
Campbell University, NC
Dallas Baptist University, TX
Dordt College, IA
Eastern College, PA
Geneva College, PA
Gordon College, MA
Greenville College, IL

Houghton College, NY
Huntington College, IN
Indiana Wesleyan University, IN
Judson College, IL
The King's University College, AB
Mount Vernon Nazarene College, OH
North Park College, IL
Northwest College of the Assemblies of
     God, WA
Northwestern College, IA
Northwest Nazarene College, ID
Nyack College, NY
Oklahoma Baptist University, OK
Olivet Nazarene University, IL
Point Loma Nazarene College, CA
Redeemer College, ON
Seattle Pacific University, WA
Sioux Falls College, SD
Southern Nazarene University, OK
Spring Arbor College, MI
Sterling College, KS
Tabor College, KS
Taylor University, IN
Trevecca Nazarene College, TN
Trinity Christian College, IL
Trinity College, IL
Trinity Western University, BC
Union University, TN
Westmont College, CA
Wheaton College, IL
Whitworth College, WA

PHYSICAL EDUCATION
Anderson University, IN
Asbury College, KY
Azusa Pacific University, CA
Bartlesville Wesleyan College, OK
Bethel College, IN
Bethel College, KS
Bethel College, MN
Biola University, CA
Bluffton College, OH
California Baptist College, CA
Calvin College, MI
Campbellsville College, KY
Campbell University, NC
Cedarville College, OH
Central Wesleyan College, SC
Cornerstone College, MI
Dallas Baptist University, TX
Dordt College, IA
Eastern College, PA
Eastern Mennonite University, VA
Eastern Nazarene College, MA
Erskine College, SC
Evangel College, MO
Fresno Pacific College, CA
George Fox College, OR
Goshen College, IN
Grace College, IN
Grand Canyon University, AZ
Greenville College, IL
Houghton College, NY
Huntington College, IN
Indiana Wesleyan University, IN
John Brown University, AR
Judson College, IL
The King's College, NY
Lee College, TN
LeTourneau University, TX
Malone College, OH
Master's College and Seminary, CA
Messiah College, PA
MidAmerica Nazarene College, KS
Milligan College, TN

Mount Vernon Nazarene College, OH
North Park College, IL
Northwestern College, IA
Northwestern College, MN
Northwest Nazarene College, ID
Oklahoma Baptist University, OK
Olivet Nazarene University, IL
Pacific Christian College, CA
Palm Beach Atlantic College, FL
Point Loma Nazarene College, CA
Redeemer College, ON
Seattle Pacific University, WA
Sioux Falls College, SD
Southern California College, CA
Southern Nazarene University, OK
Spring Arbor College, MI
Sterling College, KS
Tabor College, KS
Taylor University, IN
Trevecca Nazarene College, TN
Trinity Christian College, IL
Trinity College, IL
Trinity Western University, BC
Union University, TN
Warner Pacific College, OR
Warner Southern College, FL
Western Baptist College, OR
Westmont College, CA
Wheaton College, IL
Whitworth College, WA

PHYSICAL FITNESS/EXERCISE SCIENCE
Bluffton College, OH
Campbell University, NC
Cedarville College, OH
Dordt College, IA
Gordon College, MA
Grand Canyon University, AZ
Huntington College, IN
John Brown University, AR
North Park College, IL
Oklahoma Baptist University, OK
Seattle Pacific University, WA
Sioux Falls College, SD
Trevecca Nazarene College, TN
Westmont College, CA

PHYSICAL SCIENCES
Asbury College, KY
Biola University, CA
California Baptist College, CA
Calvin College, MI
Goshen College, IN
Houghton College, NY
Indiana Wesleyan University, IN
Judson College, IL
Oklahoma Baptist University, OK
Olivet Nazarene University, IL
Roberts Wesleyan College, NY
Westmont College, CA

PHYSICAL THERAPY
Campbell University, NC
Eastern Nazarene College, MA
Olivet Nazarene University, IL
Southern Nazarene University, OK
Trevecca Nazarene College, TN

(PRE)PHYSICAL THERAPY SEQUENCE
Campbellsville College, KY

PHYSICIAN'S ASSISTANT STUDIES

Campbell University, NC
Trevecca Nazarene College, TN

PHYSICS

Anderson University, IN
Azusa Pacific University, CA
Bethel College, KS
Bethel College, MN
Biola University, CA
Bluffton College, OH
Calvin College, MI
Dordt College, IA
Eastern Nazarene College, MA
Erskine College, SC
Geneva College, PA
Gordon College, MA
Goshen College, IN
Greenville College, IL
Houghton College, NY
King College, TN
Messiah College, PA
MidAmerica Nazarene College, KS
Mississippi College, MS
North Park College, IL
Northwest Nazarene College, ID
Oklahoma Baptist University, OK
Point Loma Nazarene College, CA
Roberts Wesleyan College, NY
Seattle Pacific University, WA
Southern Nazarene University, OK
Spring Arbor College, MI
Taylor University, IN
Westmont College, CA
Wheaton College, IL
Whitworth College, WA

PIANO/ORGAN

Belhaven College, MS
Bethel College, IN
Biola University, CA
Campbellsville College, KY
Campbell University, NC
Covenant College, GA
Dallas Baptist University, TX
Erskine College, SC
Grace College, IN
Grand Canyon University, AZ
Houghton College, NY
Huntington College, IN
Indiana Wesleyan University, IN
John Brown University, AR
Lee College, TN
Milligan College, TN
Mississippi College, MS
Mount Vernon Nazarene College, OH
Northwest College of the Assemblies of God, WA
Nyack College, NY
Oklahoma Baptist University, OK
Olivet Nazarene University, IL
Roberts Wesleyan College, NY
Sioux Falls College, SD
Southern Nazarene University, OK
Sterling College, KS
Tabor College, KS
Trinity Christian College, IL
Wheaton College, IL
Whitworth College, WA

POLITICAL SCIENCE/ GOVERNMENT

Anderson University, IN
Azusa Pacific University, CA
Bartlesville Wesleyan College, OK
Bethel College, KS
Bethel College, MN
Bluffton College, OH
California Baptist College, CA
Calvin College, MI
Campbellsville College, KY
Campbell University, NC
Cedarville College, OH
Colorado Christian University, CO
Dordt College, IA
Eastern College, PA
Evangel College, MO
Fresno Pacific College, CA
Geneva College, PA
Gordon College, MA
Goshen College, IN
Greenville College, IL
Houghton College, NY
Indiana Wesleyan University, IN
King College, TN
Master's College and Seminary, CA
Mississippi College, MS
North Park College, IL
Northwestern College, IA
Northwest Nazarene College, ID
Oklahoma Baptist University, OK
Palm Beach Atlantic College, FL
Point Loma Nazarene College, CA
Redeemer College, ON
Seattle Pacific University, WA
Sioux Falls College, SD
Southern California College, CA
Southern Nazarene University, OK
Sterling College, KS
Taylor University, IN
Westmont College, CA
Wheaton College, IL
Whitworth College, WA

PSYCHOLOGY

Anderson University, IN
Asbury College, KY
Azusa Pacific University, CA
Belhaven College, MS
Bethel College, IN
Bethel College, KS
Bethel College, MN
Biola University, CA
Bluffton College, OH
Bryan College, TN
California Baptist College, CA
Calvin College, MI
Campbellsville College, KY
Campbell University, NC
Cedarville College, OH
Central Wesleyan College, SC
Colorado Christian University, CO
Cornerstone College, MI
Covenant College, GA
Dallas Baptist University, TX
Dordt College, IA
Eastern College, PA
Eastern Mennonite University, VA
Eastern Nazarene College, MA
Erskine College, SC
Evangel College, MO
Fresno Pacific College, CA
Geneva College, PA
George Fox College, OR

Gordon College, MA
Goshen College, IN
Grace College, IN
Grand Canyon University, AZ
Greenville College, IL
Houghton College, NY
Huntington College, IN
Indiana Wesleyan University, IN
John Brown University, AR
Judson College, IL
King College, TN
The King's College, NY
The King's University College, AB
Lee College, TN
LeTourneau University, TX
Malone College, OH
Messiah College, PA
MidAmerica Nazarene College, KS
Milligan College, TN
Mississippi College, MS
Mount Vernon Nazarene College, OH
North Park College, IL
Northwest Christian College, OR
Northwest College, WA
Northwestern College, IA
Northwestern College, MN
Northwest Nazarene College, ID
Nyack College, NY
Oklahoma Baptist University, OK
Olivet Nazarene University, IL
Pacific Christian College, CA
Palm Beach Atlantic College, FL
Point Loma Nazarene College, CA
Redeemer College, ON
Roberts Wesleyan College, NY
Seattle Pacific University, WA
Simpson College, CA
Sioux Falls College, SD
Southern California College, CA
Southern Nazarene University, OK
Spring Arbor College, MI
Sterling College, KS
Tabor College, KS
Taylor University, IN
Taylor University, Fort Wayne Campus, IN
Trevecca Nazarene College, TN
Trinity Christian College, IL
Trinity College, IL
Trinity Western University, BC
Union University, TN
Warner Pacific College, OR
Warner Southern College, FL
Western Baptist College, OR
Westmont College, CA
Wheaton College, IL
Whitworth College, WA

PUBLIC ADMINISTRATION

California Baptist College, CA
Campbell University, NC
Cedarville College, OH
Evangel College, MO

PUBLIC AFFAIRS AND POLICY STUDIES

Oklahoma Baptist University, OK

PUBLIC RELATIONS

Biola University, CA
Campbell University, NC
John Brown University, AR
Master's College and Seminary, CA
MidAmerica Nazarene College, KS
Oklahoma Baptist University, OK

PUBLIC RELATIONS (continued)

Sioux Falls College, SD
Taylor University, IN
Taylor University, Fort Wayne Campus, IN

RADIO AND TELEVISION STUDIES

Biola University, CA
Campbell University, NC
Cedarville College, OH
Evangel College, MO
Geneva College, PA
John Brown University, AR
Malone College, OH
Master's College and Seminary, CA
Messiah College, PA
Milligan College, TN
Oklahoma Baptist University, OK
Olivet Nazarene University, IL
Sioux Falls College, SD
Southern California College, CA
Trevecca Nazarene College, TN
Union University, TN

RADIOLOGICAL SCIENCES

Malone College, OH

RADIOLOGICAL TECHNOLOGY

Sioux Falls College, SD

READING EDUCATION

Seattle Pacific University, WA
Southern Nazarene University, OK

RECREATIONAL FACILITIES MANAGEMENT

Indiana Wesleyan University, IN
John Brown University, AR

RECREATION AND LEISURE SERVICES

Asbury College, KY
Bethel College, IN
Bluffton College, OH
California Baptist College, CA
Calvin College, MI
Campbellsville College, KY
Evangel College, MO
Gordon College, MA
Greenville College, IL
Houghton College, NY
Huntington College, IN
Indiana Wesleyan University, IN
Messiah College, PA
Montreat-Anderson College, NC
Northwestern College, IA
Northwest Nazarene College, ID
Oklahoma Baptist University, OK
Seattle Pacific University, WA
Taylor University, IN
Western Baptist College, OR

RECREATION THERAPY

Eastern Mennonite University, VA

RELIGIOUS EDUCATION

Asbury College, KY
Biola University, CA
Bryan College, TN
Calvin College, MI

Campbellsville College, KY
Campbell University, NC
Cedarville College, OH
Cornerstone College, MI
Dallas Baptist University, TX
Eastern Nazarene College, MA
Erskine College, SC
Houghton College, NY
Indiana Wesleyan University, IN
John Brown University, AR
The King's College, NY
Lee College, TN
Malone College, OH
Messiah College, PA
MidAmerica Nazarene College, KS
Milligan College, TN
Mississippi College, MS
Mount Vernon Nazarene College, OH
Northwest College of the Assemblies of God, WA
Northwestern College, MN
Northwest Nazarene College, ID
Nyack College, NY
Oklahoma Baptist University, OK
Olivet Nazarene University, IL
Pacific Christian College, CA
Point Loma Nazarene College, CA
Seattle Pacific University, WA
Simpson College, CA
Southern California College, CA
Southern Nazarene University, OK
Sterling College, KS
Taylor University, IN
Taylor University, Fort Wayne Campus, IN
Trevecca Nazarene College, TN
Trinity Christian College, IL
Warner Pacific College, OR
Wheaton College, IL

RELIGIOUS STUDIES

Anderson University, IN
Atlantic Baptist College, NB
Azusa Pacific University, CA
Bartlesville Wesleyan College, OK
Bethel College, IN
Bethel College, KS
Biola University, CA
Bluffton College, OH
California Baptist College, CA
Calvin College, MI
Campbellsville College, KY
Central Wesleyan College, SC
Cornerstone College, MI
Dallas Baptist University, TX
Eastern College, PA
Eastern Mennonite University, VA
Eastern Nazarene College, MA
Fresno Pacific College, CA
George Fox College, OR
Goshen College, IN
Grand Canyon University, AZ
Greenville College, IL
Houghton College, NY
Huntington College, IN
Indiana Wesleyan University, IN
John Brown University, AR
Judson College, IL
King College, TN
The King's College, NY
LeTourneau University, TX
Messiah College, PA
MidAmerica Nazarene College, KS
Milligan College, TN
Mississippi College, MS

Montreat-Anderson College, NC
Mount Vernon Nazarene College, OH
North Park College, IL
Northwest Christian College, OR
Northwest College of the Assemblies of God, WA
Northwestern College, IA
Northwest Nazarene College, ID
Nyack College, NY
Oklahoma Baptist University, OK
Olivet Nazarene University, IL
Palm Beach Atlantic College, FL
Point Loma Nazarene College, CA
Redeemer College, ON
Roberts Wesleyan College, NY
Seattle Pacific University, WA
Sioux Falls College, SD
Southern California College, CA
Southern Nazarene University, OK
Spring Arbor College, MI
Sterling College, KS
Tabor College, KS
Taylor University, IN
Trevecca Nazarene College, TN
Trinity Christian College, IL
Trinity Western University, BC
Union University, TN
Warner Pacific College, OR
Warner Southern College, FL
Westmont College, CA
Wheaton College, IL
Whitworth College, WA

RESPIRATORY THERAPY

Lee College, TN

RETAIL MANAGEMENT

Bluffton College, OH

ROMANCE LANGUAGES

Olivet Nazarene University, IL
Redeemer College, ON

SACRED MUSIC

Anderson University, IN
Belhaven College, MS
Bethel College, IN
Bethel College, MN
Calvin College, MI
Campbellsville College, KY
Cedarville College, OH
Central Wesleyan College, SC
Colorado Christian University, CO
Dallas Baptist University, TX
Erskine College, SC
Evangel College, MO
Grace College, IN
Grand Canyon University, AZ
Greenville College, IL
Houghton College, NY
Indiana Wesleyan University, IN
Malone College, OH
MidAmerica Nazarene College, KS
Milligan College, TN
Mount Vernon Nazarene College, OH
Northwest Christian College, OR
Northwest College of the Assemblies of God, WA
Northwest Nazarene College, ID
Nyack College, NY
Oklahoma Baptist University, OK
Olivet Nazarene University, IL
Point Loma Nazarene College, CA

Simpson College, CA
Southern Nazarene University, OK
Taylor University, IN
Trevecca Nazarene College, TN
Trinity College, IL
Union University, TN

SCANDINAVIAN LANGUAGES/ STUDIES
North Park College, IL

SCIENCE
Bartlesville Wesleyan College, OK
Belhaven College, MS
Bethel College, IN
Bethel College, KS
Calvin College, MI
Cedarville College, OH
Eastern Nazarene College, MA
Geneva College, PA
George Fox College, OR
Houghton College, NY
Huntington College, IN
Indiana Wesleyan University, IN
Judson College, IL
King College, TN
Lee College, TN
Malone College, OH
Milligan College, TN
Mount Vernon Nazarene College, OH
Northwestern College, MN
Northwest Nazarene College, ID
Oklahoma Baptist University, OK
Olivet Nazarene University, IL
Palm Beach Atlantic College, FL
Redeemer College, ON
Roberts Wesleyan College, NY
Seattle Pacific University, WA
Southern California College, CA
Southern Nazarene University, OK
Tabor College, KS
Trinity Western University, BC
Union University, TN
Warner Pacific College, OR

SCIENCE EDUCATION
Anderson University, IN
Asbury College, KY
Bartlesville Wesleyan College, OK
Bethel College, IN
Bethel College, KS
Bethel College, MN
Biola University, CA
Bryan College, TN
Calvin College, MI
Campbellsville College, KY
Campbell University, NC
Cedarville College, OH
Cornerstone College, MI
Dallas Baptist University, TX
Eastern Mennonite University, VA
Evangel College, MO
Fresno Pacific College, CA
George Fox College, OR
Goshen College, IN
Grace College, IN
Grand Canyon University, AZ
Houghton College, NY
Huntington College, IN
Indiana Wesleyan University, IN
Malone College, OH
Milligan College, TN
Mississippi College, MS

Mount Vernon Nazarene College, OH
Northwest Nazarene College, ID
Oklahoma Baptist University, OK
Olivet Nazarene University, IL
Sioux Falls College, SD
Southern Nazarene University, OK
Tabor College, KS
Taylor University, IN
Trevecca Nazarene College, TN
Trinity Christian College, IL
Union University, TN
Warner Pacific College, OR
Warner Southern College, FL
Wheaton College, IL

SECONDARY EDUCATION
Asbury College, KY
Bartlesville Wesleyan College, OK
Bethel College, IN
Bethel College, MN
Biola University, CA
Bluffton College, OH
California Baptist College, CA
Calvin College, MI
Campbellsville College, KY
Campbell University, NC
Cedarville College, OH
Colorado Christian University, CO
Cornerstone College, MI
Dallas Baptist University, TX
Eastern College, PA
Eastern Mennonite University, VA
Evangel College, MO
Fresno Pacific College, CA
Geneva College, PA
George Fox College, OR
Gordon College, MA
Goshen College, IN
Grand Canyon University, AZ
Greenville College, IL
Houghton College, NY
Huntington College, IN
Indiana Wesleyan University, IN
John Brown University, AR
The King's College, NY
Lee College, TN
Malone College, OH
Master's College and Seminary, CA
Messiah College, PA
MidAmerica Nazarene College, KS
Montreat-Anderson College, NC
Mount Vernon Nazarene College, OH
North Park College, IL
Northwest College of the Assemblies of
    God, WA
Northwestern College, MN
Northwest Nazarene College, ID
Nyack College, NY
Oklahoma Baptist University, OK
Olivet Nazarene University, IL
Pacific Christian College, CA
Palm Beach Atlantic College, FL
Redeemer College, ON
Roberts Wesleyan College, NY
Seattle Pacific University, WA
Simpson College, CA
Sioux Falls College, SD
Southern California College, CA
Southern Nazarene University, OK
Spring Arbor College, MI
Sterling College, KS
Tabor College, KS
Taylor University, IN

Trevecca Nazarene College, TN
Trinity Christian College, IL
Trinity College, IL
Trinity Western University, BC
Union University, TN
Warner Pacific College, OR
Warner Southern College, FL
Western Baptist College, OR
Westmont College, CA
Wheaton College, IL
Whitworth College, WA

SECRETARIAL STUDIES/OFFICE MANAGEMENT
Anderson University, IN
Bartlesville Wesleyan College, OK
Bethel College, IN
Campbellsville College, KY
Cedarville College, OH
Dordt College, IA
Evangel College, MO
Grace College, IN
Huntington College, IN
Indiana Wesleyan University, IN
John Brown University, AR
Lee College, TN
Milligan College, TN
Mount Vernon Nazarene College, OH
Northwestern College, IA
Northwestern College, MN
Northwest Nazarene College, ID
Oklahoma Baptist University, OK
Olivet Nazarene University, IL
Point Loma Nazarene College, CA
Sioux Falls College, SD
Southern Nazarene University, OK
Tabor College, KS
Trevecca Nazarene College, TN

SOCIAL SCIENCE
Azusa Pacific University, CA
Bartlesville Wesleyan College, OK
Bethel College, IN
Bethel College, KS
Biola University, CA
Bluffton College, OH
California Baptist College, CA
Calvin College, MI
Campbell University, NC
Cedarville College, OH
Central Wesleyan College, SC
Dordt College, IA
Eastern Nazarene College, MA
Evangel College, MO
Fresno Pacific College, CA
Grand Canyon University, AZ
Houghton College, NY
Indiana Wesleyan University, IN
John Brown University, AR
Judson College, IL
The King's University College, AB
Lee College, TN
Malone College, OH
Messiah College, PA
Mississippi College, MS
Mount Vernon Nazarene College, OH
North Park College, IL
Northwestern College, MN
Northwest Nazarene College, ID
Nyack College, NY
Oklahoma Baptist University, OK
Olivet Nazarene University, IL
Pacific Christian College, CA

SOCIAL SCIENCE (continued)

Roberts Wesleyan College, NY
Seattle Pacific University, WA
Simpson College, CA
Sioux Falls College, SD
Southern California College, CA
Southern Nazarene University, OK
Spring Arbor College, MI
Tabor College, KS
Taylor University, IN
Trevecca Nazarene College, TN
Trinity College, IL
Trinity Western University, BC
Warner Pacific College, OR
Western Baptist College, OR
Westmont College, CA

SOCIAL WORK

Anderson University, IN
Asbury College, KY
Azusa Pacific University, CA
Bethel College, KS
Bethel College, MN
Bluffton College, OH
Calvin College, MI
Campbellsville College, KY
Campbell University, NC
Cedarville College, OH
Cornerstone College, MI
Dordt College, IA
Eastern College, PA
Eastern Mennonite University, VA
Eastern Nazarene College, MA
Evangel College, MO
Fresno Pacific College, CA
George Fox College, OR
Gordon College, MA
Goshen College, IN
Greenville College, IL
Indiana Wesleyan University, IN
Malone College, OH
Messiah College, PA
Milligan College, TN
Mississippi College, MS
Mount Vernon Nazarene College, OH
Northwestern College, IA
Northwest Nazarene College, ID
Oklahoma Baptist University, OK
Pacific Christian College, CA
Roberts Wesleyan College, NY
Sioux Falls College, SD
Spring Arbor College, MI
Tabor College, KS
Taylor University, IN
Trevecca Nazarene College, TN
Union University, TN
Warner Pacific College, OR

SOCIOLOGY

Anderson University, IN
Asbury College, KY
Atlantic Baptist College, NB
Azusa Pacific University, CA
Bethel College, IN
Bethel College, KS
Biola University, CA
Bluffton College, OH
California Baptist College, CA
Calvin College, MI
Campbellsville College, KY
Cedarville College, OH
Cornerstone College, MI
Covenant College, GA

Dallas Baptist University, TX
Eastern College, PA
Eastern Mennonite University, VA
Eastern Nazarene College, MA
Evangel College, MO
Fresno Pacific College, CA
Geneva College, PA
George Fox College, OR
Gordon College, MA
Goshen College, IN
Grace College, IN
Grand Canyon University, AZ
Greenville College, IL
Houghton College, NY
Huntington College, IN
Indiana Wesleyan University, IN
Judson College, IL
The King's College, NY
Lee College, TN
Messiah College, PA
Milligan College, TN
Mississippi College, MS
Mount Vernon Nazarene College, OH
North Park College, IL
Northwestern College, IA
Northwest Nazarene College, ID
Oklahoma Baptist University, OK
Point Loma Nazarene College, CA
Redeemer College, ON
Roberts Wesleyan College, NY
Seattle Pacific University, WA
Sioux Falls College, SD
Southern California College, CA
Southern Nazarene University, OK
Spring Arbor College, MI
Sterling College, KS
Tabor College, KS
Taylor University, IN
Trinity Christian College, IL
Trinity College, IL
Union University, TN
Warner Pacific College, OR
Westmont College, CA
Wheaton College, IL
Whitworth College, WA

SPANISH

Anderson University, IN
Asbury College, KY
Bethel College, IN
Bethel College, MN
Biola University, CA
Bluffton College, OH
California Baptist College, CA
Calvin College, MI
Campbell University, NC
Cedarville College, OH
Dordt College, IA
Eastern College, PA
Eastern Mennonite University, VA
Eastern Nazarene College, MA
Erskine College, SC
Evangel College, MO
Fresno Pacific College, CA
Geneva College, PA
George Fox College, OR
Gordon College, MA
Goshen College, IN
Grace College, IN
Greenville College, IL
Houghton College, NY
Indiana Wesleyan University, IN
The King's College, NY
Malone College, OH
Messiah College, PA

MidAmerica Nazarene College, KS
Mississippi College, MS
Mount Vernon Nazarene College, OH
North Park College, IL
Northwestern College, IA
Oklahoma Baptist University, OK
Point Loma Nazarene College, CA
Southern Nazarene University, OK
Spring Arbor College, MI
Taylor University, IN
Union University, TN
Westmont College, CA
Wheaton College, IL
Whitworth College, WA

SPECIAL EDUCATION

Bethel College, KS
Bluffton College, OH
Calvin College, MI
Cedarville College, OH
Central Wesleyan College, SC
Eastern Mennonite University, VA
Erskine College, SC
Evangel College, MO
Gordon College, MA
Grand Canyon University, AZ
Greenville College, IL
Huntington College, IN
John Brown University, AR
Malone College, OH
Master's College and Seminary, CA
Milligan College, TN
Mississippi College, MS
Mount Vernon Nazarene College, OH
Northwest Nazarene College, ID
Oklahoma Baptist University, OK
Seattle Pacific University, WA
Sterling College, KS
Tabor College, KS
Trevecca Nazarene College, TN
Whitworth College, WA

SPEECH PATHOLOGY AND AUDIOLOGY

Biola University, CA
Calvin College, MI
Geneva College, PA
Northwest Nazarene College, ID

SPEECH/RHETORIC/PUBLIC ADDRESS/DEBATE

Anderson University, IN
Asbury College, KY
Bethel College, KS
Bethel College, MN
Bluffton College, OH
Calvin College, MI
Cedarville College, OH
Cornerstone College, MI
Evangel College, MO
Geneva College, PA
Grand Canyon University, AZ
Greenville College, IL
Judson College, IL
Master's College and Seminary, CA
Messiah College, PA
Northwestern College, IA
Northwest Nazarene College, ID
Oklahoma Baptist University, OK
Olivet Nazarene University, IL
Sioux Falls College, SD
Southern California College, CA
Southern Nazarene University, OK

Spring Arbor College, MI
Sterling College, KS
Taylor University, IN
Trevecca Nazarene College, TN
Wheaton College, IL
Whitworth College, WA

SPEECH THERAPY
Biola University, CA

SPORTS ADMINISTRATION
Bluffton College, OH
Campbell University, NC
Cedarville College, OH
Erskine College, SC
Fresno Pacific College, CA
LeTourneau University, TX
Mount Vernon Nazarene College, OH

SPORTS MEDICINE
Calvin College, MI
George Fox College, OR
John Brown University, AR
Malone College, OH
Messiah College, PA
Mount Vernon Nazarene College, OH
North Park College, IL
Oklahoma Baptist University, OK
Trinity College, IL
Whitworth College, WA

STRINGED INSTRUMENTS
Covenant College, GA
Houghton College, NY
Messiah College, PA
Oklahoma Baptist University, OK
Olivet Nazarene University, IL
Wheaton College, IL

STUDIO ART
Anderson University, IN
Bethel College, MN
Biola University, CA
Calvin College, MI
Campbell University, NC
Eastern College, PA
Grand Canyon University, AZ
Indiana Wesleyan University, IN
Malone College, OH
North Park College, IL
Northwest Nazarene College, ID
Roberts Wesleyan College, NY
Wheaton College, IL
Whitworth College, WA

SYSTEMS ENGINEERING
Eastern Nazarene College, MA

SYSTEMS SCIENCE
Taylor University, IN

TEACHER AIDE STUDIES
Dordt College, IA
Eastern Mennonite University, VA
Olivet Nazarene University, IL

TEACHING ENGLISH AS A SECOND LANGUAGE
Bartlesville Wesleyan College, OK
Biola University, CA
Goshen College, IN
Northwest College, WA

TECHNICAL WRITING
Cedarville College, OH

TELECOMMUNICATIONS
Calvin College, MI
George Fox College, OR
Oklahoma Baptist University, OK
Union University, TN

TEXTILES AND CLOTHING
Bluffton College, OH
Olivet Nazarene University, IL
Seattle Pacific University, WA

THEATER ARTS/DRAMA
Anderson University, IN
Bethel College, IN
Bethel College, KS
Bethel College, MN
Biola University, CA
California Baptist College, CA
Calvin College, MI
Campbell University, NC
Cedarville College, OH
Colorado Christian University, CO
Dordt College, IA
Goshen College, IN
Grand Canyon University, AZ
Greenville College, IL
Huntington College, IN
Judson College, IL
King College, TN
Malone College, OH
Milligan College, TN
Mount Vernon Nazarene College, OH
North Park College, IL
Northwestern College, IA
Northwestern College, MN
Oklahoma Baptist University, OK
Point Loma Nazarene College, CA
Redeemer College, ON
Seattle Pacific University, WA
Sioux Falls College, SD
Southern California College, CA
Southern Nazarene University, OK
Sterling College, KS
Taylor University, IN
Trevecca Nazarene College, TN
Trinity Western University, BC
Westmont College, CA
Wheaton College, IL
Whitworth College, WA

THEOLOGY
Azusa Pacific University, CA
Bartlesville Wesleyan College, OK
Bethel College, KS
Bethel College, MN
Biola University, CA
Calvin College, MI
Campbell University, NC
Cedarville College, OH
Central Wesleyan College, SC
Colorado Christian University, CO
Dordt College, IA
Eastern Mennonite University, VA
Grand Canyon University, AZ
Greenville College, IL
Huntington College, IN
Indiana Wesleyan University, IN
John Brown University, AR
Lee College, TN
Malone College, OH

Master's College and Seminary, CA
Messiah College, PA
Mount Vernon Nazarene College, OH
North Park College, IL
Northwest Christian College, OR
Northwest College of the Assemblies of God, WA
Northwestern College, MN
Northwest Nazarene College, ID
Oklahoma Baptist University, OK
Olivet Nazarene University, IL
Pacific Christian College, CA
Point Loma Nazarene College, CA
Redeemer College, ON
Seattle Pacific University, WA
Southern Nazarene University, OK
Taylor University, IN
Trevecca Nazarene College, TN
Trinity Christian College, IL
Union University, TN
Warner Pacific College, OR
Warner Southern College, FL
Western Baptist College, OR

(PRE)VETERINARY MEDICINE SEQUENCE
Anderson University, IN
Bartlesville Wesleyan College, OK
Bethel College, MN
Calvin College, MI
Campbellsville College, KY
Campbell University, NC
Cedarville College, OH
Dordt College, IA
Eastern Mennonite University, VA
Eastern Nazarene College, MA
Evangel College, MO
George Fox College, OR
Goshen College, IN
Grand Canyon University, AZ
Greenville College, IL
Houghton College, NY
Huntington College, IN
Indiana Wesleyan University, IN
King College, TN
LeTourneau University, TX
Malone College, OH
Messiah College, PA
Milligan College, TN
Mount Vernon Nazarene College, OH
North Park College, IL
Northwestern College, IA
Northwest Nazarene College, ID
Oklahoma Baptist University, OK
Olivet Nazarene University, IL
Point Loma Nazarene College, CA
Redeemer College, ON
Sioux Falls College, SD
Southern California College, CA
Southern Nazarene University, OK
Sterling College, KS
Taylor University, IN
Trinity Christian College, IL
Trinity Western University, BC
Union University, TN
Westmont College, CA
Whitworth College, WA

VOICE
Belhaven College, MS
Bethel College, IN
Biola University, CA
Calvin College, MI
Campbellsville College, KY

VOICE *(continued)*

Campbell University, NC
Cedarville College, OH
Colorado Christian University, CO
Covenant College, GA
Dallas Baptist University, TX
Erskine College, SC
Grand Canyon University, AZ
Houghton College, NY
Huntington College, IN
Indiana Wesleyan University, IN
John Brown University, AR
Judson College, IL
Lee College, TN
Messiah College, PA
Mount Vernon Nazarene College, OH
North Park College, IL
Northwest College of the Assemblies of
    God, WA
Nyack College, NY
Oklahoma Baptist University, OK

Olivet Nazarene University, IL
Roberts Wesleyan College, NY
Sioux Falls College, SD
Southern Nazarene University, OK
Sterling College, KS
Tabor College, KS
Taylor University, IN
Union University, TN
Wheaton College, IL
Whitworth College, WA

WELDING ENGINEERING

LeTourneau University, TX

WELDING TECHNOLOGY

LeTourneau University, TX

WESTERN CIVILIZATION AND CULTURE

Trinity Christian College, IL

WIND AND PERCUSSION INSTRUMENTS

Covenant College, GA
Grand Canyon University, AZ
Houghton College, NY
Indiana Wesleyan University, IN
Mount Vernon Nazarene College, OH
Olivet Nazarene University, IL
Sioux Falls College, SD
Southern Nazarene University, OK
Wheaton College, IL

YOUTH MINISTRIES

Gordon College, MA
Huntingdon College, IN
Pacific Christian College, CA
Trinity College, IL

ZOOLOGY

Southern Nazarene University, OK

Athletics Index

M—for men; W—for women; (s) scholarships offered

BADMINTON

Redeemer College, ON	M, W

BASEBALL

Anderson University, IN	M
Asbury College, KY	M
Atlantic Baptist College, NB	M, W
Azusa Pacific University, CA	M(s)
Belhaven College, MS	M(s)
Bethel College, IN	M(s)
Bethel College, MN	M
Biola University, CA	M(s)
Bluffton College, OH	M
California Baptist College, CA	M(s)
Calvin College, MI	M
Campbellsville College, KY	M(s)
Campbell University, NC	M(s)
Cedarville College, OH	M(s)
Central Wesleyan College, SC	M
Cornerstone College, MI	M(s)
Dallas Baptist University, TX	M(s)
Eastern College, PA	M
Eastern Mennonite University, VA	M
Eastern Nazarene College, MA	M
Erskine College, SC	M(s)
Evangel College, MO	M
Geneva College, PA	M(s)
George Fox College, OR	M(s)
Gordon College, MA	M
Goshen College, IN	M
Grace College, IN	M(s)
Grand Canyon University, AZ	M
Huntington College, IN	M(s)
Indiana Wesleyan University, IN	M(s)
Judson College, IL	M(s)
King College, TN	M(s)
LeTourneau University, TX	M(s)
Malone College, OH	M(s)
Master's College and Seminary, CA	M(s)
Messiah College, PA	M
MidAmerica Nazarene College, KS	M(s)
Milligan College, TN	M
Montreat-Anderson College, NC	M(s)
Mount Vernon Nazarene College, OH	M(s)
North Park College, IL	M
Northwestern College, IA	M(s)
Northwestern College, MN	M(s)
Nyack College, NY	M
Oklahoma Baptist University, OK	M(s)
Olivet Nazarene University, IL	M(s)
Palm Beach Atlantic College, FL	M(s)
Point Loma Nazarene College, CA	M(s)
Sioux Falls College, SD	M
Southern California College, CA	M(s)
Spring Arbor College, MI	M(s)
Sterling College, KS	M
Tabor College, KS	M(s)
Taylor University, IN	M
Trevecca Nazarene College, TN	M(s)
Trinity Christian College, IL	M(s)
Union University, TN	M(s)
Warner Southern College, FL	M(s)
Western Baptist College, OR	M
Westmont College, CA	M(s)
Wheaton College, IL	M
Whitworth College, WA	M

BASKETBALL

Anderson University, IN	M, W
Asbury College, KY	M, W
Atlantic Baptist College, NB	M, W
Azusa Pacific University, CA	M(s), W(s)
Bartlesville Wesleyan College, OK	M(s), W(s)
Belhaven College, MS	M(s), W(s)
Bethel College, IN	M(s), W(s)
Bethel College, KS	M(s), W(s)
Bethel College, MN	M, W
Biola University, CA	M(s), W(s)
Bluffton College, OH	M, W
Bryan College, TN	M(s), W(s)
California Baptist College, CA	M(s), W(s)
Calvin College, MI	M, W
Campbellsville College, KY	M(s), W(s)
Campbell University, NC	M(s), W(s)
Cedarville College, OH	M(s), W(s)
Central Wesleyan College, SC	M(s), W(s)
Colorado Christian University, CO	M(s), W(s)
Cornerstone College, MI	M(s), W(s)
Covenant College, GA	M(s), W(s)
Dordt College, IA	M, W
Eastern College, PA	M
Eastern Mennonite University, VA	M, W
Eastern Nazarene College, MA	M, W
Erskine College, SC	M(s), W(s)
Evangel College, MO	M(s), W(s)
Fresno Pacific College, CA	M(s), W(s)
Geneva College, PA	M(s), W(s)
George Fox College, OR	M(s), W(s)
Gordon College, MA	M, W
Goshen College, IN	M, W
Grace College, IN	M(s), W(s)
Grand Canyon University, AZ	M(s), W(s)
Greenville College, IL	M, W
Houghton College, NY	M(s), W(s)
Huntington College, IN	M(s), W(s)
Indiana Wesleyan University, IN	M(s), W(s)
John Brown University, AR	M(s), W(s)
Judson College, IL	M(s), W(s)
King College, TN	M(s), W(s)
The King's College, NY	M(s), W(s)
The King's University College, AB	M, W
Lee College, TN	M(s), W(s)

LeTourneau University, TX	M(s), W(s)
Malone College, OH	M(s), W(s)
Master's College and Seminary, CA	M(s), W(s)
Messiah College, PA	M, W
MidAmerica Nazarene College, KS	M(s), W(s)
Milligan College, TN	M(s), W(s)
Mississippi College, MS	M(s), W(s)
Montreat-Anderson College, NC	M(s), W(s)
Mount Vernon Nazarene College, OH	M(s), W(s)
North Park College, IL	M, W
Northwest Christian College, OR	M
Northwest College of the Assemblies of God, WA	M, W
Northwestern College, IA	M(s), W(s)
Northwestern College, MN	M(s), W(s)
Northwest Nazarene College, ID	M(s), W(s)
Nyack College, NY	M(s), W(s)
Oklahoma Baptist University, OK	M(s), W(s)
Olivet Nazarene University, IL	M(s), W(s)
Pacific Christian College, CA	M, W
Palm Beach Atlantic College, FL	M(s)
Point Loma Nazarene College, CA	M(s), W(s)
Redeemer College, ON	M, W
Roberts Wesleyan College, NY	M(s), W(s)
Seattle Pacific University, WA	M(s), W(s)
Simpson College, CA	M, W
Sioux Falls College, SD	M(s), W(s)
Southern California College, CA	M(s), W(s)
Southern Nazarene University, OK	M(s), W(s)
Spring Arbor College, MI	M(s), W(s)
Sterling College, KS	M(s), W(s)
Tabor College, KS	M(s), W(s)
Taylor University, IN	M, W
Taylor University, Fort Wayne Campus, IN	M, W
Trevecca Nazarene College, TN	M(s)
Trinity Christian College, IL	M(s), W(s)
Trinity College, IL	M(s), W(s)
Trinity Western University, BC	M, W
Union University, TN	M(s), W(s)
Warner Southern College, FL	M(s), W(s)
Western Baptist College, OR	M(s), W(s)
Westmont College, CA	M(s)
Wheaton College, IL	M, W
Whitworth College, WA	M(s), W(s)

CREW

Seattle Pacific University, WA	M, W
Wheaton College, IL	M, W

CROSS-COUNTRY RUNNING

Anderson University, IN	M, W

CROSS-COUNTRY RUNNING (continued)

Asbury College, KY	M, W
Azusa Pacific University, CA	M(s), W(s)
Belhaven College, MS	M(s), W(s)
Bethel College, IN	M(s), W(s)
Bethel College, MN	M, W
Biola University, CA	M(s), W(s)
Bluffton College, OH	M, W
Bryan College, TN	M(s), W(s)
Calvin College, MI	M, W
Campbellsville College, KY	M(s), W(s)
Campbell University, NC	M(s), W(s)
Cedarville College, OH	M(s), W(s)
Covenant College, GA	M, W
Dordt College, IA	M, W
Eastern College, PA	M, W
Eastern Mennonite University, VA	M, W
Eastern Nazarene College, MA	M, W
Erskine College, SC	M(s), W(s)
Evangel College, MO	M(s), W(s)
Fresno Pacific College, CA	M(s), W(s)
Geneva College, PA	M(s), W(s)
George Fox College, OR	M(s), W(s)
Gordon College, MA	M, W
Goshen College, IN	M, W
Grand Canyon University, AZ	M(s), W(s)
Greenville College, IL	M, W
Houghton College, NY	M(s), W(s)
Huntington College, IN	M(s), W(s)
Indiana Wesleyan University, IN	M(s), W(s)
Judson College, IL	M(s), W(s)
The King's College, NY	M(s), W(s)
LeTourneau University, TX	M, W
Malone College, OH	M(s), W(s)
Master's College and Seminary, CA	M(s), W(s)
Messiah College, PA	M, W
MidAmerica Nazarene College, KS	M(s), W(s)
Mississippi College, MS	M(s)
North Park College, IL	M, W
Northwest Christian College, OR	W
Northwest College, WA	M, W
Northwestern College, IA	M(s), W(s)
Northwestern College, MN	M(s), W(s)
Oklahoma Baptist University, OK	M(s), W(s)
Olivet Nazarene University, IL	M(s), W(s)
Palm Beach Atlantic College, FL	W(s)
Point Loma Nazarene College, CA	M(s), W(s)
Redeemer College, ON	M, W
Roberts Wesleyan College, NY	M, W
Seattle Pacific University, WA	M(s), W(s)
Sioux Falls College, SD	M(s), W(s)
Southern California College, CA	M(s), W(s)
Southern Nazarene University, OK	M
Spring Arbor College, MI	M(s), W(s)
Sterling College, KS	M(s), W(s)
Tabor College, KS	M(s), W(s)
Taylor University, IN	M, W
Trinity College, IL	M, W
Warner Southern College, FL	M(s), W(s)
Westmont College, CA	M(s), W(s)
Wheaton College, IL	M, W
Whitworth College, WA	M(s), W(s)

EQUESTRIAN SPORTS

Erskine College, SC	W
Taylor University, IN	M, W
Wheaton College, IL	W

FIELD HOCKEY

Eastern College, PA	W
Eastern Mennonite University, VA	W
Gordon College, MA	W
Houghton College, NY	W(s)
Messiah College, PA	W

FOOTBALL

Anderson University, IN	M
Azusa Pacific University, CA	M(s)
Bethel College, KS	M(s)
Bethel College, MN	M
Bluffton College, OH	M
Campbellsville College, KY	M
Evangel College, MO	M(s)
Geneva College, PA	M(s)
Greenville College, IL	M
Malone College, OH	M(s)
MidAmerica Nazarene College, KS	M(s)
Mississippi College, MS	M(s)
North Park College, IL	M
Northwestern College, IA	M(s)
Northwestern College, MN	M(s)
Olivet Nazarene University, IL	M(s)
Sioux Falls College, SD	M(s)
Sterling College, KS	M(s)
Tabor College, KS	M(s)
Taylor University, IN	M
Trinity College, IL	M(s)
Wheaton College, IL	M
Whitworth College, WA	M(s)

GOLF

Anderson University, IN	M
Belhaven College, MS	M(s)
Bethel College, IN	M(s)
Bethel College, MN	M
Bluffton College, OH	M
Calvin College, MI	M, W
Campbellsville College, KY	M(s)
Campbell University, NC	M(s), W(s)
Cedarville College, OH	M(s)
Central Wesleyan College, SC	M(s)
Colorado Christian University, CO	M(s)
Cornerstone College, MI	M(s)
Dordt College, IA	M, W
Eastern Mennonite University, VA	M
Erskine College, SC	M(s)
Goshen College, IN	M
Grace College, IN	M(s)
Grand Canyon University, AZ	M(s)
Greenville College, IL	M
Huntington College, IN	M(s), W(s)
Indiana Wesleyan University, IN	M(s)
King College, TN	M(s), W
Lee College, TN	M(s)
Malone College, OH	M(s)
Messiah College, PA	M
Milligan College, TN	M(s)
Mississippi College, MS	M(s)
Mount Vernon Nazarene College, OH	M(s)
Northwestern College, IA	M(s), W(s)
Northwestern College, MN	M(s)

EQUESTRIAN SPORTS through columns continue:

Olivet Nazarene University, IL	M
Palm Beach Atlantic College, FL	M(s), W(s)
Point Loma Nazarene College, CA	M(s)
Spring Arbor College, MI	M(s)
Taylor University, IN	M
Trinity Christian College, IL	M(s), W
Trinity College, IL	M(s)
Union University, TN	M(s)
Wheaton College, IL	M

GYMNASTICS

Seattle Pacific University, WA	W(s)

ICE HOCKEY

Bethel College, MN	M
Calvin College, MI	M
Dordt College, IA	M
Redeemer College, ON	M, W
Wheaton College, IL	M

LACROSSE

Calvin College, MI	M
Eastern College, PA	W
Gordon College, MA	M
Westmont College, CA	W
Wheaton College, IL	M, W

RUGBY

Trinity Western University, BC	M
Westmont College, CA	M

SOCCER

Anderson University, IN	M, W
Asbury College, KY	M
Atlantic Baptist College, NB	M, W
Azusa Pacific University, CA	M(s), W(s)
Bartlesville Wesleyan College, OK	M(s), W(s)
Belhaven College, MS	M(s), W
Bethel College, IN	M(s)
Bethel College, KS	M(s)
Bethel College, MN	M, W
Biola University, CA	M(s), W(s)
Bluffton College, OH	M, W
Bryan College, TN	M(s)
California Baptist College, CA	M(s), W(s)
Calvin College, MI	M, W
Campbellsville College, KY	M(s)
Campbell University, NC	M(s), W(s)
Cedarville College, OH	M(s)
Central Wesleyan College, SC	M(s)
Colorado Christian University, CO	M(s), W(s)
Cornerstone College, MI	M(s)
Covenant College, GA	M(s)
Dallas Baptist University, TX	M
Dordt College, IA	M
Eastern College, PA	M, W
Eastern Mennonite University, VA	M
Eastern Nazarene College, MA	M
Erskine College, SC	M(s), W(s)
Fresno Pacific College, CA	M(s)
Geneva College, PA	M(s), W(s)
George Fox College, OR	M(s), W(s)
Gordon College, MA	M, W
Goshen College, IN	M, W
Grace College, IN	M(s)
Grand Canyon University, AZ	M(s)
Greenville College, IL	M, W
Houghton College, NY	M(s), W(s)

Huntington College, IN	M(s)
Indiana Wesleyan University, IN	M(s), W(s)
John Brown University, AR	M(s)
Judson College, IL	M(s), W(s)
King College, TN	M(s)
The King's College, NY	M(s), W(s)
Lee College, TN	M(s)
LeTourneau University, TX	M(s)
Malone College, OH	M(s)
Master's College and Seminary, CA	M(s), W(s)
Messiah College, PA	M, W
Milligan College, TN	M(s)
Montreat-Anderson College, NC	M(s)
Mount Vernon Nazarene College, OH	M(s)
North Park College, IL	M, W
Northwest College of the Assemblies of God, WA	M
Northwestern College, IA	M, W
Northwestern College, MN	M(s)
Northwest Nazarene College, ID	M(s)
Nyack College, NY	M(s), W
Olivet Nazarene University, IL	M
Pacific Christian College, CA	M
Palm Beach Atlantic College, FL	M(s), W(s)
Point Loma Nazarene College, CA	M(s)
Redeemer College, ON	M, W
Roberts Wesleyan College, NY	M(s), W(s)
Seattle Pacific University, WA	M(s)
Simpson College, CA	M
Southern California College, CA	M(s), W(s)
Southern Nazarene University, OK	M(s), W(s)
Spring Arbor College, MI	M(s), W(s)
Sterling College, KS	M(s), W(s)
Tabor College, KS	M(s)
Taylor University, IN	M, W
Taylor University, Fort Wayne Campus, IN	M
Trinity Christian College, IL	M(s)
Trinity College, IL	M(s), W
Trinity Western University, BC	M
Western Baptist College, OR	M(s), W
Westmont College, CA	M(s), W(s)
Wheaton College, IL	M, W
Whitworth College, WA	M(s), W(s)

SOFTBALL

Anderson University, IN	W
Asbury College, KY	W
Atlantic Baptist College, NB	M, W
Azusa Pacific University, CA	W(s)
Belhaven College, MS	W
Bethel College, IN	W(s)
Bethel College, MN	W
Biola University, CA	W(s)
Bluffton College, OH	W
California Baptist College, CA	W(s)
Calvin College, MI	W
Campbellsville College, KY	W(s)
Campbell University, NC	W(s)
Cedarville College, OH	W(s)
Central Wesleyan College, SC	W(s)
Cornerstone College, MI	W(s)
Dordt College, IA	W
Eastern College, PA	W
Eastern Mennonite University, VA	W

Eastern Nazarene College, MA	W
Erskine College, SC	W(s)
Evangel College, MO	W(s)
Geneva College, PA	W(s)
George Fox College, OR	W(s)
Gordon College, MA	W
Goshen College, IN	W
Grace College, IN	W(s)
Huntington College, IN	W(s)
Indiana Wesleyan University, IN	W(s)
Judson College, IL	W(s)
King College, TN	W(s)
The King's College, NY	W(s)
Lee College, TN	M, W(s)
Malone College, OH	W(s)
Messiah College, PA	W
MidAmerica Nazarene College, KS	W(s)
Milligan College, TN	W
Mount Vernon Nazarene College, OH	W(s)
North Park College, IL	W
Northwestern College, IA	M(s), W(s)
Northwestern College, MN	W(s)
Nyack College, NY	W
Olivet Nazarene University, IL	W(s)
Pacific Christian College, CA	W
Point Loma Nazarene College, CA	W
Simpson College, CA	W
Southern California College, CA	W(s)
Southern Nazarene University, OK	W(s)
Spring Arbor College, MI	W(s)
Sterling College, KS	W
Tabor College, KS	W(s)
Taylor University, IN	W
Trevecca Nazarene College, TN	W(s)
Trinity Christian College, IL	W(s)
Union University, TN	W
Wheaton College, IL	W

SWIMMING AND DIVING

Asbury College, KY	M, W
Calvin College, MI	M, W
Campbellsville College, KY	M(s), W(s)
John Brown University, AR	M(s), W(s)
Wheaton College, IL	M, W
Whitworth College, WA	M(s), W(s)

TENNIS

Anderson University, IN	M, W
Asbury College, KY	M, W
Azusa Pacific University, CA	M(s)
Belhaven College, MS	M(s), W(s)
Bethel College, IN	M(s), W(s)
Bethel College, KS	M(s), W(s)
Bethel College, MN	M, W
Biola University, CA	M(s), W(s)
Bluffton College, OH	M, W
California Baptist College, CA	M(s), W(s)
Calvin College, MI	M, W
Campbellsville College, KY	M(s), W(s)
Campbell University, NC	M(s), W(s)
Cedarville College, OH	M(s), W(s)
Colorado Christian University, CO	M(s), W(s)
Cornerstone College, MI	M(s)
Dordt College, IA	M, W
Eastern College, PA	M, W
Eastern Mennonite University, VA	M, W

Eastern Nazarene College, MA	M, W
Erskine College, SC	M(s), W(s)
Geneva College, PA	M(s), W(s)
George Fox College, OR	M, W
Gordon College, MA	M, W
Goshen College, IN	M, W
Grace College, IN	M(s), W
Grand Canyon University, AZ	W(s)
Greenville College, IL	M, W
Huntington College, IN	M(s), W(s)
Indiana Wesleyan University, IN	M(s), W(s)
John Brown University, AR	M(s), W(s)
Judson College, IL	M(s), W(s)
King College, TN	M(s), W(s)
Lee College, TN	M(s), W(s)
Malone College, OH	M(s), W(s)
Messiah College, PA	M, W
Milligan College, TN	M(s), W(s)
Mississippi College, MS	M(s), W(s)
North Park College, IL	M, W
Northwestern College, IA	M(s), W(s)
Northwestern College, MN	M(s)
Oklahoma Baptist University, OK	M(s)
Olivet Nazarene University, IL	M, W
Palm Beach Atlantic College, FL	W(s)
Point Loma Nazarene College, CA	M(s), W(s)
Sioux Falls College, SD	M(s), W(s)
Southern California College, CA	M
Southern Nazarene University, OK	M(s), W(s)
Spring Arbor College, MI	M(s), W(s)
Sterling College, KS	M(s), W(s)
Tabor College, KS	M(s), W(s)
Taylor University, IN	M, W
Trinity College, IL	M(s), W(s)
Union University, TN	M(s), W(s)
Westmont College, CA	M(s), W(s)
Wheaton College, IL	M, W
Whitworth College, WA	M(s), W(s)

TRACK AND FIELD

Anderson University, IN	M, W
Azusa Pacific University, CA	M(s), W(s)
Bethel College, IN	M, W
Bethel College, KS	M(s), W(s)
Bethel College, MN	M, W
Biola University, CA	M(s), W(s)
Bluffton College, OH	M, W
Calvin College, MI	M, W
Campbell University, NC	M(s), W(s)
Cedarville College, OH	M(s), W(s)
Dordt College, IA	M, W
Eastern Mennonite University, VA	M, W
Evangel College, MO	M(s), W(s)
Fresno Pacific College, CA	M(s), W(s)
Geneva College, PA	M(s), W(s)
George Fox College, OR	M(s), W(s)
Goshen College, IN	M, W
Grace College, IN	M, W
Greenville College, IL	M, W
Houghton College, NY	M(s), W(s)
Huntington College, IN	M(s), W(s)
Indiana Wesleyan University, IN	M(s), W(s)
LeTourneau University, TX	M, W
Malone College, OH	M(s), W(s)
Messiah College, PA	M, W
MidAmerica Nazarene College, KS	M(s), W(s)

TRACK AND FIELD (continued)

Mississippi College, MS	M(s)
North Park College, IL	M, W
Northwestern College, IA	M(s), W(s)
Northwestern College, MN	M(s), W(s)
Northwest Nazarene College, ID	M(s), W(s)
Oklahoma Baptist University, OK	M(s), W(s)
Point Loma Nazarene College, CA	M(s), W(s)
Roberts Wesleyan College, NY	M(s), W(s)
Seattle Pacific University, WA	M(s), W(s)
Sioux Falls College, SD	M(s), W(s)
Southern California College, CA	M(s), W(s)
Southern Nazarene University, OK	M
Spring Arbor College, MI	M(s), W(s)
Sterling College, KS	M(s), W(s)
Tabor College, KS	M(s), W(s)
Taylor University, IN	M, W
Trinity College, IL	M, W
Westmont College, CA	M(s), W(s)
Wheaton College, IL	M, W
Whitworth College, WA	M(s), W(s)

VOLLEYBALL

Anderson University, IN	W
Asbury College, KY	W
Azusa Pacific University, CA	M, W(s)
Bartlesville Wesleyan College, OK	W(s)
Bethel College, IN	W(s)
Bethel College, KS	W(s)
Bethel College, MN	W
Biola University, CA	W(s)
Bluffton College, OH	W
Bryan College, TN	W(s)
California Baptist College, CA	W(s)
Calvin College, MI	M, W
Campbellsville College, KY	W
Campbell University, NC	W(s)
Cedarville College, OH	W(s)
Central Wesleyan College, SC	W(s)
Colorado Christian University, CO	W(s)
Cornerstone College, MI	W(s)
Covenant College, GA	W
Dallas Baptist University, TX	W(s)
Dordt College, IA	W
Eastern College, PA	M, W
Eastern Mennonite University, VA	M, W
Eastern Nazarene College, MA	M, W
Erskine College, SC	W(s)
Evangel College, MO	W(s)
Fresno Pacific College, CA	W
Geneva College, PA	M, W(s)
George Fox College, OR	W(s)
Gordon College, MA	W
Goshen College, IN	W
Grace College, IN	W(s)
Grand Canyon University, AZ	W(s)
Greenville College, IL	W
Houghton College, NY	W(s)
Huntington College, IN	W(s)
Indiana Wesleyan University, IN	W(s)
John Brown University, AR	W(s)
Judson College, IL	W(s)
King College, TN	W(s)
The King's University College, AB	M, W
Lee College, TN	W(s)
LeTourneau University, TX	W(s)
Malone College, OH	W(s)
Master's College and Seminary, CA	W(s)
Messiah College, PA	W
MidAmerica Nazarene College, KS	W(s)
Milligan College, TN	W(s)
Mississippi College, MS	W(s)
Montreat-Anderson College, NC	W(s)
Mount Vernon Nazarene College, OH	W(s)
North Park College, IL	M, W
Northwest College of the Assemblies of God, WA	W
Northwestern College, IA	W(s)
Northwestern College, MN	W(s)
Northwest Nazarene College, ID	W(s)
Nyack College, NY	M, W(s)
Olivet Nazarene University, IL	M, W
Pacific Christian College, CA	M, W
Palm Beach Atlantic College, FL	W(s)
Point Loma Nazarene College, CA	W(s)
Redeemer College, ON	M, W
Seattle Pacific University, WA	W(s)
Simpson College, CA	M, W
Sioux Falls College, SD	W(s)
Southern California College, CA	W(s)
Southern Nazarene University, OK	W(s)
Spring Arbor College, MI	W(s)
Sterling College, KS	W(s)
Tabor College, KS	W(s)
Taylor University, IN	M, W
Taylor University, Fort Wayne Campus, IN	W
Trevecca Nazarene College, TN	W(s)
Trinity Christian College, IL	M, W(s)
Trinity College, IL	M, W(s)
Trinity Western University, BC	M, W
Warner Southern College, FL	W(s)
Western Baptist College, OR	W(s)
Westmont College, CA	M, W(s)
Wheaton College, IL	M, W
Whitworth College, WA	W(s)

Study Abroad Index

AUSTRALIA
George Fox College, OR
Taylor University, IN

AUSTRIA
Westmont College, CA

BELGIUM
Westmont College, CA

BELIZE
Eastern Nazarene College, MA

BRAZIL
Grand Canyon University, AZ

CANADA
Westmont College, CA

CHINA
Bethel College, KS
California Baptist College, CA
Eastern Mennonite University, VA
Geneva College, PA
Grand Canyon University, AZ
Lee College, TN
Messiah College, PA
Oklahoma Baptist University, OK
Taylor University, IN
Whitworth College, WA

COLOMBIA
Messiah College, PA

COSTA RICA
Azusa Pacific University, CA
Biola University, CA
Bluffton College, OH
California Baptist College, CA
Dordt College, IA
Eastern Mennonite University, GA
Geneva College, PA
George Fox College, OR
Gordon College, MA
Goshen College, IN
Malone College, OH
North Park College, IL
Northwestern College, IA
Northwestern College, MN
Seattle Pacific University, WA
Southern California College, CA
Southern Nazarene University, OK
Taylor University, IN
Trinity Western University, BC
Westmont College, CA
Whitworth College, WA

DOMINICAN REPUBLIC
Goshen College, IN
Roberts Wesleyan College, NY

ECUADOR
Azusa Pacific University, CA
Bethel College, IN

EGYPT
Dordt College, IA
Eastern Mennonite University, VA
George Fox College, OR
Gordon College, MA
North Park College, IL
Northwestern College, IA
Northwestern College, MN
Southern Nazarene University, OK

EL SALVADOR
Eastern Mennonite University, VA

ENGLAND
Bethel College, KS
Bethel College, MN
Biola University, CA
Calvin College, MI
Campbellsville College, KY
Central Wesleyan College, SC
Dallas Baptist University, TX
Eastern Mennonite University, VA
Erskine College, SC
Geneva College, PA
Gordon College, MA
The King's College, NY
Lee College, TN
Messiah College, PA
Mississippi College, MS
North Park College, IL
Olivet Nazarene University, IL
Palm Beach Atlantic College, FL
Roberts Wesleyan College, NY
Southern Nazarene University, OK
Taylor University, IN
Taylor University, Fort Wayne Campus, IN
Trinity Western University, BC
Westmont College, CA
Wheaton College, IL
Whitworth College, WA

FRANCE
Bethel College, KS
Campbellsville College, KY
Campbell University, NC
Eastern Mennonite University, VA
Eastern Nazarene College, MA
Erskine College, SC
Fresno Pacific College, CA

George Fox College, OR
Gordon College, MA
Grace College, IN
King College, TN
The King's College, NY
Messiah College, PA
North Park College, IL
Northwestern College, IA
Northwestern College, MN
Olivet Nazarene University, IL
Redeemer College, ON
Roberts Wesleyan College, NY
Taylor University, IN
Westmont College, CA
Wheaton College, IL
Whitworth College, WA

GERMANY
Bethel College, KS
Bethel College, MN
Calvin College, MI
Dordt College, IA
Eastern Mennonite University, VA
Eastern Nazarene College, MA
Fresno Pacific College, CA
George Fox College, OR
Gordon College, MA
Goshen College, IN
Grace College, IN
Lee College, TN
Messiah College, PA
Mississippi College, MS
North Park College, IL
Westmont College, CA
Wheaton College, IL
Whitworth College, WA

GREAT BRITAIN
Eastern Nazarene College, MA
George Fox College, OR

GREECE
George Fox College, OR
Messiah College, PA
Westmont College, CA

GUATEMALA
Bluffton College, OH
Eastern Mennonite University, VA
George Fox College, OR
Malone College, OH
Warner Pacific College, OR
Whitworth College, WA

HONDURAS
Eastern Mennonite University, VA
Northwestern College, MN

HONDURAS *(continued)*
Warner Pacific College, OR
Whitworth College, WA

HONG KONG
Malone College, OH
Warner Pacific College, OR
Westmont College, CA
Whitworth College, WA

HUNGARY
Grand Canyon University, AZ

INDONESIA
Goshen College, IN

IRELAND
Bluffton College, OH
Eastern Mennonite University, VA
Northeastern College, MN

ISRAEL
Bethel College, MN
Biola University, CA
Campbellsville College, KY
Eastern Mennonite University, VA
Fresno Pacific College, CA
George Fox College, OR
Gordon College, MA
King College, TN
Messiah College, PA
Northwestern College, MN
Southern California College, CA
Taylor University, IN
Taylor University, Fort Wayne Campus, IN
Westmont College, CA
Wheaton College, IL
Whitworth College, WA

ITALY
George Fox College, OR
Westmont College, CA

IVORY COAST
Eastern Mennonite University, VA
Goshen College, IN

JAMAICA
Bethel College, IN
Huntington College, IN

JAPAN
Azusa Pacific University, CA
Bethel College, KS
Biola University, CA
Eastern Mennonite University, VA
Messiah College, PA
North Park College, IL
Northwestern College, MN
Oklahoma Baptist University, OK
Sioux Falls College, SD

JORDAN
Eastern Mennonite University, VA

KENYA
Gordon College, MA
Malone College, OH

Messiah College, PA
Seattle Pacific University, WA
Westmont College, CA

KOREA
Biola University, CA
King College, TN
North Park College, IL
Seattle Pacific University, WA
Whitworth College, WA

MEXICO
Bethel College, KS
Bluffton College, OH
Campbell University, NC
Dordt College, IA
Fresno Pacific College, CA
George Fox College, OR
Grace College, IN
King College, TN
The King's College, NY
North Park College, IL
Northwestern College, IA
Whitworth College, WA

MOROCCO
King College, TN

THE NETHERLANDS
Calvin College, MI
Dordt College, IA
George Fox College, OR
King College, TN
Northwestern College, IA
Redeemer College, ON
Trinity Christian College, IL
Wheaton College, IL

NEW GUINEA
King College, TN

NEW ZEALAND
Taylor University, IN

NICARAGUA
Bluffton College, OH
Whitworth College, WA

NIGERIA
Calvin College, MI

NORWAY
North Park College, IL

POLAND
Bluffton College, OH

RUSSIA
Biola University, CA
Bluffton College, OH
California Baptist College, CA
Dordt College, IA
Eastern Mennonite University, VA
Geneva College, PA
George Fox College, OR
Gordon College, MA
Grace College, IN
Grand Canyon University, AZ

The King's College, NY
Malone College, OH
North Park College, IL
Northwestern College, IA
Roberts Wesleyan College, NY
Seattle Pacific University, WA
Southern Nazarene University, OK
Taylor University, IN
Warner Pacific College, OR
Westmont College, CA
Wheaton College, IL

SCOTLAND
Erskine College, SC

SINGAPORE
Taylor University, IN

SOUTH AFRICA
North Park College, IL

SPAIN
Bethel College, KS
Calvin College, MI
Cedarville College, OH
Dordt College, IA
Eastern Nazarene College, MA
Erskine College, SC
Fresno Pacific College, CA
George Fox College, OR
Grace College, IN
Grand Canyon University, AZ
King College, TN
The King's College, NY
Messiah College, PA
Northwestern College, IA
Olivet Nazarene University, IL
Seattle Pacific University, WA
Taylor University, IN
Trinity Christian College, IL
Wheaton College, IL

SWEDEN
Bethel College, MN
North Park College, IL

SWITZERLAND
Eastern Nazarene College, MA
George Fox College, OR
Westmont College, CA

TAIWAN
Azusa Pacific University, CA
Seattle Pacific University, WA

TURKEY
Westmont College, CA

UGANDA
Westmont College, CA

UKRAINE
Lee College, TN

WALES
Campbell University, NC

Graduate Majors Index

M—Master's degree; D—doctoral degree; P—professional degree; O—other advanced degree

ART EDUCATION
Mississippi College, MS   M

ART/FINE ARTS
Mississippi College, MS   M

BILINGUAL AND BICULTURAL EDUCATION
Eastern College, PA   M
Eastern Nazarene College, MA   M
Fresno Pacific College, CA   M
Point Loma Nazarene College, CA   M

BIOLOGY AND BIOMEDICAL SCIENCES
Mississippi College, MS   M

BUSINESS ADMINISTRATION AND MANAGEMENT
Azusa Pacific University, CA   M
Campbell University, NC   M
Central Wesleyan College, SC   M
Dallas Baptist University, TX   M
Eastern College, PA   M
George Fox College, OR   M
Grand Canyon University, AZ   M
Indiana Wesleyan University, IN   M
LeTourneau University, TX   M
MidAmerica Nazarene College, KS   M
Mississippi College, MS   M
Olivet Nazarene University, IL   M
Palm Beach Atlantic College, FL   M
Seattle Pacific University, WA   M
Southern Nazarene University, OK   M
Trevecca Nazarene College, TN   M
Union University, TN   M

BUSINESS EDUCATION
Indiana Wesleyan University, IN   M
Mississippi College, MS   M

CLINICAL PSYCHOLOGY
George Fox College, OR   M,D
Wheaton College, IL   M,D

COMMUNICATION
Wheaton College, IL   M

COMPUTER EDUCATION
Fresno Pacific College, CA   M
Mississippi College, MS   M

COMPUTER SCIENCE
Azusa Pacific University, CA   M
Mississippi College, MS   M

COUNSELING PSYCHOLOGY
California Baptist College, CA   M
Eastern Nazarene College, MA   M

Mississippi College, MS   M
Southern Nazarene University, OK   M

COUNSELOR EDUCATION
Campbell University, NC   M
Dallas Baptist University, TX   M
Fresno Pacific College, CA   M
Malone College, OH   M
Mississippi College, MS   M,O
Point Loma Nazarene College, CA   M
Trevecca Nazarene College, TN   M
Whitworth College, WA   M

CURRICULUM AND INSTRUCTION
Calvin College, MI   M
Campbell University, NC   M
Fresno Pacific College, CA   M
Malone College, OH   M
MidAmerica Nazarene College, KS   M
Olivet Nazarene University, IL   M
Seattle Pacific University, WA   M
Simpson College, CA   M
Southern Nazarene University, OK   M
Trevecca Nazarene College, TN   M

EARLY CHILDHOOD EDUCATION
Dallas Baptist University, TX   M
Eastern Nazarene College, MA   M
Malone College, OH   M
Southern Nazarene University, OK   M

ECONOMICS
Eastern College, PA   M

EDUCATION
Azusa Pacific University, CA   M
Calvin College, MI   M
Campbell University, NC   M,O
Covenant College, GA   M
Dallas Baptist University, TX   M
Eastern College, PA   M
Eastern Nazarene College, MA   M,O
Fresno Pacific College, CA   M
George Fox College, OR   M
Grand Canyon University, AZ   M
Malone College, OH   M
MidAmerica Nazarene College, KS   M
Milligan College, TN   M
Mississippi College, MS   M,O
Northwestern College, IA
Northwest Nazarene College, ID   M
Olivet Nazarene University, IL   M
Point Loma Nazarene College, CA   M,D,O
Seattle Pacific University, WA   M
Simpson College, CA

Sioux Falls College, SD   M
Southern Nazarene University, OK   M
Trevecca Nazarene College, TN   M
Union University, TN   M
Whitworth College, WA   M

EDUCATIONAL ADMINISTRATION
Azusa Pacific University, CA   M
Calvin College, MI   M
Campbell University, NC   M,O
Dallas Baptist University, TX   M
Eastern Nazarene College, MA   M,O
Fresno Pacific College, CA   M
Malone College, OH   M
Mississippi College, MS   M
Point Loma Nazarene College, CA   M,D,O
Seattle Pacific University, WA   M
Trevecca Nazarene College, TN   M
Whitworth College, WA   M

EDUCATIONAL MEDIA/ INSTRUCTIONAL TECHNOLOGY
Azusa Pacific University, CA   M
Fresno Pacific College, CA   M

EDUCATIONAL PSYCHOLOGY
Fresno Pacific College, CA   M

EDUCATION OF THE GIFTED
Grand Canyon University, AZ   M
Whitworth College, WA   M

EDUCATION OF THE MULTIPLY HANDICAPPED
Fresno Pacific College, CA   M

ELEMENTARY EDUCATION
Campbell University, NC   M
Dallas Baptist University, TX   M
Eastern Nazarene College, MA   M
Grand Canyon University, AZ   M
Mississippi College, MS   M
Northwestern College, IA   M
Olivet Nazarene University, IL   M
Southern Nazarene University, OK   M
Trevecca Nazarene College, TN   M

ENGLISH
Mississippi College, MS   M
Southern Nazarene University, OK   M

ENGLISH EDUCATION
Campbell University, NC   M
Olivet Nazarene University, IL   M

FINANCE AND BANKING
Dallas Baptist University, TX	M
Eastern College, PA	M

HEALTH EDUCATION
Eastern College, PA	M

HEALTH SERVICES MANAGEMENT AND HOSPITAL ADMINISTRATION
Eastern College, PA	M
Mississippi College, MS	M

HIGHER EDUCATION
Azusa Pacific University, CA	M

HISTORY
Mississippi College, MS	M

HUMAN RESOURCES DEVELOPMENT
Azusa Pacific University, CA	M
Eastern College, PA	M

INTERDISCIPLINARY PROGRAMS IN THE HUMANITIES, ARTS, AND SOCIAL SCIENCES
Mississippi College, MS	M
Wheaton College, IL	M

INTERNATIONAL BUSINESS
Azusa Pacific University, CA	M
Dallas Baptist University, TX	M

JOURNALISM
Wheaton College, IL	M

LAW
Campbell University, NC	P
Mississippi College, MS	P

LIBERAL STUDIES
Dallas Baptist University, TX	M

LINGUISTICS
Biola University, CA	M

MANAGEMENT INFORMATION SYSTEMS
Dallas Baptist University, TX	M
Seattle Pacific University, WA	M

MARKETING
Dallas Baptist University, TX	M
Eastern College, PA	M

MARRIAGE AND FAMILY THERAPY
Azusa Pacific University, CA	M
Eastern Nazarene College, MA	M
Mississippi College, MS	M
Northwest Christian College, OR	M
Oklahoma Baptist University, OK	M
Seattle Pacific University, WA	M

MASS AND ORGANIZATIONAL COMMUNICATION
Mississippi College, MS	M

MATHEMATICS EDUCATION
Campbell University, NC	M
Fresno Pacific College, CA	M
Mississippi College, MS	M

MIDDLE SCHOOL EDUCATION
Campbell University, NC	M
Eastern Nazarene College, MA	M
Malone College, OH	M

MISSIONS AND MISSIOLOGY
Cornerstone College, MI	P,M,D
Nyack College, NY	M
Pacific Christian College, CA	M
Simpson College, CA	M
Wheaton College, IL	M,O

MUSIC
Azusa Pacific University, CA	M
Mississippi College, MS	M
Pacific Christian College, CA	M
Seattle Pacific University, WA	M

MUSIC EDUCATION
Eastern Nazarene College, MA	M
Mississippi College, MS	M

NONPROFIT MANAGEMENT
Eastern College, PA	M

NORTH AMERICAN STUDIES
Wheaton College, IL	M

NURSING
Azusa Pacific University, CA	M
Indiana Wesleyan University, IN	M
Seattle Pacific University, WA	

NURSING ADMINISTRATION
Seattle Pacific University, WA	M

NURSING EDUCATION
Indiana Wesleyan University, IN	M

PASTORAL MINISTRY AND COUNSELING
Azusa Pacific University, CA	M
Bethel College, IN	M
Central Wesleyan College, SC	M
Eastern Mennonite University, VA	M
Eastern Nazarene College, MA	M
Cornerstone College, MI	P,M,D
Huntington College, IN	M
Malone College, OH	M
Mount Vernon Nazarene, OH College	M
Olivet Nazarene University, IL	M
Pacific Christian College, CA	M
Trinity Western University, BC	P,M

PHARMACY
Campbell University, NC	P

PHYSICAL EDUCATION AND HUMAN MOVEMENT STUDIES
Azusa Pacific University, CA	M
Campbell University, NC	M
Eastern Nazarene College, MA	M
Malone College, OH	M
Seattle Pacific University, WA	M
Whitworth College, WA	M

PSYCHOLOGY
Biola University, CA	D
Geneva College, PA	M
George Fox College, OR	M
Southern Nazarene University, OK	M
Wheaton College, IL	M,D

PUBLIC HEALTH NURSING
Indiana Wesleyan University, IN	M

RADIO, TELEVISION, AND FILM
Wheaton College, IL	M

READING
Calvin College, MI	M
Dallas Baptist University, TX	M
Eastern Nazarene College, MA	M
Fresno Pacific College, CA	M
Grand Canyon University, AZ	M
Malone College, OH	M
Olivet Nazarene University, IL	M
Seattle Pacific University, WA	M
Sioux Falls College, SD	M
Southern Nazarene University, OK	M
Whitworth College, WA	M

RELIGION
Eastern Mennonite University, VA	M
Cornerstone College, MI	M
Northwest Nazarene College, ID	M
Olivet Nazarene University, IL	M
Point Loma Nazarene College, CA	M
Seattle Pacific University, WA	M
Simpson College, CA	M
Southern California College, CA	M
Southern Nazarene University, OK	M
Trevecca Nazarene College, TN	M
Warner Pacific College, OR	M
Wheaton College, IL	M

RELIGIOUS EDUCATION
Cornerstone College, MI	P,M,D
Indiana Wesleyan University, IN	M
Wheaton College, IL	M
Whitworth College, WA	M

SCIENCE EDUCATION
Fresno Pacific College, CA	M
Mississippi College, MS	M
Olivet Nazarene University, IL	M

SECONDARY EDUCATION
Campbell University, NC	M
Eastern Nazarene College, MA	M
Grand Canyon University, AZ	M
Mississippi College, MS	M
Olivet Nazarene University, IL	M

SOCIAL SCIENCES EDUCATION
Campbell University, NC	M

SOCIOLOGY
Mississippi College, MS	M

SOFTWARE ENGINEERING
Azusa Pacific University, CA	M

SPECIAL EDUCATION
Azusa Pacific University, CA	M

Calvin College, MI	M
Eastern Nazarene College, MA	M,O
Fresno Pacific College, CA	M
Malone College, OH	M
Point Loma Nazarene College, CA	M
Whitworth College, WA	M

SPEECH AND INTERPERSONAL COMMUNICATION

Southern Nazarene University, OK	M

SPORTS ADMINISTRATION

Seattle Pacific University, WA	M

TEACHING ENGLISH AS A SECOND LANGUAGE

Azusa Pacific University, CA	M,O

Biola University, CA	M,O
Eastern Nazarene College. MA	M
Fresno Pacific College, CA	M
Grand Canyon University, AZ	M
Whitworth College, WA	M

TELECOMMUNICATIONS

Azusa Pacific University, CA	M

THEOLOGY

Anderson University, IN	P,M
Azusa Pacific University, CA	P,M
Bethel College, IN	M
Biola University, CA	P,M,D
Dallas Baptist University, TX	M
Eastern Mennonite University, VA	P,M

Cornerstone College, MI	P,M,D
Huntington College, IN	M
Master's College and Seminary, CA	P,M
Mount Vernon Nazarene, OH College	M
Nyack College, NY	P,M
Olivet Nazarene University, IL	M
Simpson College, CA	M
Southern Nazarene University, OK	M
Wheaton College, IL	M,O

URBAN EDUCATION

Grand Canyon University, AZ	M